Literati Identity and Its Fictional Representations
in Late Imperial China

Literati Identity and Its Fictional Representations in Late Imperial China

Stephen J. Roddy

STANFORD UNIVERSITY PRESS

STANFORD, CALIFORNIA 1998

Stanford University Press
Stanford, California
©1998 by the Board of Trustees of the
Leland Stanford Junior University
Printed in the United States of America
CIP data appear at the end of the book

For Bih-hsya, Erika, and Chloe

Acknowledgments

I am deeply indebted to the teachers, colleagues, and friends who persevered with me during the long gestation of this book. Andrew Plaks demonstrated seemingly inexhaustible patience during my years in graduate school, and his lofty standards inspired me to attempt more than I believed myself capable of. Willard Peterson and Yu-kung Kao made incisive comments on the dissertation on which this work is based. I thank David Rolston and Pao-chen Ch'en for their careful readings of various sections of the book. John Ziemer of Stanford University Press went beyond the call of duty in bringing this project to fruition, and I have benefited enormously from his advice. I would also like to acknowledge the anonymous reader for the Press, whose comments enabled me to reconceptualize much of the framework on which the book rests, and Katherine Carlitz, who helped me to put it all together. Jan Spauschus Johnson and Andrew Lewis patiently guided me through the editing process. Needless to say, any errors or infelicities that remain are mine alone.

Takeuchi Minoru, Ono Kazuko, Kominami Ichiro, Terazuka Yoshikazu, Ito Sohei, Zhou Xianshen, Chen Xizhong, Yuan Xingpei, Li Hanqiu, and Chen Meilin were generous with both scholarly guidance and hospitality during my stays in Japan and China. I also wish to express my gratitude to the following organizations for their financial support: the Pacific Cultural Foundation for a semester at National Taiwan University; the Japan Foundation for language study at the Inter-University Center for Japanese Language Studies; the Fulbright Commission for my stint at the Institute for Humanistic Studies, Kyoto University; the Committee on Scholarly Communication with China for a year at Peking University; and the Stanford University Program in East Asian Studies for travel to the Lou Henry Hoover East Asian Library. In addition, the College of Liberal Arts at the University of Nevada, Las Vegas, granted release time from teaching to revise the manuscript.

My colleagues over the past seven years have offered encouragement and spiritual sustenance on many an occasion. Deborah Arteaga, Chris Buck, Barbara Bundy, Sue Fawn Chung, Eva Corredor, Audrey Gaquin, Mayumi Itoh, Anne Kurashige, John Severance, and Gisela Zimmerman have all contributed to this book in more ways than they may realize. Needless to say, my family has borne the brunt of the strains and vicissitudes of my academic career, and it is to them that this book is affectionately dedicated.

S.J.R.

Contents

Introduction	1
Part I: The Image of the Literati in Qing Discourse	9
1. Literati Identity and the Qing Epistemological Crisis	11
2. Discourses of the Literati and the Literati in Discourse	26
3. The Intellectual Milieus of Three Novelists	63
Part II: The Deconstruction of Literati Identity in *Rulin waishi*	85
4. Scholars, Poets, Painters, and Essayists	87
5. The Decline of Literati Mores	109
6. The Use and Abuse of Ritual	130
Part III: Fictional Reconstructions of Literati Identity	147
7. *Yesou puyan*: A Confucian-Feminist Utopia?	149
8. The Philological Musings of *Jinghua yuan*	171
Conclusion	207
Appendix: Editions of the Novels	233
Notes	237
Bibliography	291
Character List	305
Index	309

Literati Identity and Its Fictional Representations
in Late Imperial China

Introduction

IN A POIGNANT scene near the end of the novel *Rulin waishi* (The unofficial history of the forest of scholars), two of its leading characters, Dr. Yu (Yu Yude) and Du Shaoqing, take a final leave of each other.

"When you have gone, uncle," said Du, "I shall have no one to whom to turn."

Dr. Yu could not help being sad. He invited Du into the cabin. "I can speak frankly to you, Shaoqing," he said. "I used to be a poor scholar, but during the six or seven years that I've been in Nanjing I've saved enough to buy a paddy field producing thirty bushels a year. Now I may be appointed to a ministry, or I may be made a prefect or magistrate. I shall stay at my post two years, or three at the most, and save up enough to buy another plot of land worth twenty bushels of rice a year. Then my wife and I needn't starve, and that's good enough for me. I am not concerned for my son and grandchildren, because in addition to teaching my son the classics I have had him study medicine so that he can make his own living. Why should he be an official?"[1]

Dr. Yu is familiar to the readers of this novel as an idealized figure who stands above the petty scheming and follies that preoccupy most of the novel's characters. His words echo those of the great eremite of the Jin dynasty, Tao Yuanming (Tao Qian) (365–427), who said in resigning his official post that "to serve others [as an official] is to let one's mouth and stomach take control."[2] Like the literati of the novel who hold him up as a model of probity and benign government, Yu appears to have little interest in an official career.

Yet Yu seems to be rejecting more than just the onerous duties of government service. Although a frequent companion of the cultivated members of literati society, he does not share their interest in poetry, essay composition, or learned pursuits. Indeed, other than fulfilling his duties as educational intendant at the Imperial Academy in Nanjing, he stands apart from the literati in all other matters. In the scene just quoted, he seeks only the secure livelihood of modest farm properties and advises his son to pursue a non-literati vocation. Insignificant though this fleeting episode may appear, it looms large as the final statement of one of the few untainted figures in the book. Dr. Yu leaves the novel saying in effect that he is renouncing all that identifies him as a member of the literati.[3]

Rulin waishi (ca. 1750), or the "Unofficial history of the forest of scholars," by Wu Jingzi (1701–55), is the preeminent indictment of literati mores of the imperial period. Lu Xun, who lauded it as the definitive example of the satiric novel, described it in the following words: "Holding firmly to fairness, it uncovers the ills of its day; the special object of its barbs is the forest of scholars."[4] From the earliest extant commentaries of the early nineteenth century down to the present day, the novel has been read as a caustic attack on the literati and the institutions and practices by which they maintained their privileged status in traditional society. Yet as the society from which the novel sprang recedes into history, the object and nature of this attack becomes less and less certain. Is *Rulin waishi* a revolutionary work that repudiates the ideological basis of the literati class, as the Chinese Marxist critics of the early communist period would have it? Or as more recent critics have argued, does it instead judge the hypocrisy and follies of the literati by the standards they themselves upheld? Chinese and non-Chinese readers alike continue to debate the meaning of this novel, whose often enigmatic complexity frustrates attempts to assign to its satirical portrait a clear and unambiguous moral.

While the search for such a moral remains elusive, *Rulin waishi* scholarship of the past two decades has amply demonstrated the degree to which this remarkable novel both reflects Confucian notions and standards of literati behavior and probes their relevance in the society of the author's time. I will attempt to build on this scholarship by seeking to clarify the state of thinking about the literati during the mid-Qing period. Namely, I will locate the representation of the literati of *Rulin waishi* within the broad range of intellectual and literary developments of Wu Jingzi's time—that is, what Michel Foucault called the "discursive formation" of the period. Chapter 1 traces certain key issues that have bearing on the self-image of the literati as described by various significant figures of the seventeenth to the early nineteenth centuries. My aim in this is to delineate the contours of a literati identity that emerge through discussions of literati vocations such as scholarship, literature, and art. The majority of these writings do not directly address the literati per se, yet "the preoccupation with their own identity" (in the words of Jean-François Billeter)[5] ensures that such a profile emerges with some clarity.

Second, I turn to *Rulin waishi* itself and its representation of literati concerns. I first examine the various elements of its literati society, namely, its mixture of scholars, poets, *bagu* editors, and others as examples of discrete versions or "creeds" of literati identity. By determining the distinguishing attributes of each of these categories of literati, as well as the contrast and interplay between them, it becomes possible to chart the contours of the literati identity as conceived by *Rulin waishi*. This largely spatial design is set within the dynamic of historical time, namely, the novel's Ming dynasty chronology, as well as the novel's own internally referential temporal dimension. This time frame superimposes the element of diachronic development, and I analyze it in some detail for its clues to the nature and significance of the evolution of literati mores. My discussion of *Rulin waishi* concludes with a consideration of the final stage of this chronology, the decay and corruption of literati mores set in the late Ming period. Demonstrating that this decline follows both structurally and logically from the articulation of the ideal of ritual propriety, I argue that such a conclusion appears to offer a cautionary tale to the eighteenth-century advocates of literati renewal through ritual activism.

Parrt III discusses two works of fiction written during the mid-to-late Qianlong and Jiaqing periods, that is, roughly thirty to seventy years after *Rulin waishi* was probably completed. While betraying no evidence of influence from Wu Jingzi's novel, these works nonetheless exhibit a similar preoccupation with the status and identity of the literati. In contrast to the largely satirical mode of *Rulin waishi*, they construct utopian realms within which their literati achieve a regeneration of sorts. The first of these, *Yesou puyan* (Humble words of a rustic elder) (ca. 1780), by Xia Jingqu, begins where *Rulin waishi* leaves off, in the bankruptcy of the literati, and elaborately chronicles their regeneration, primarily through a renewal of their commitment to scholarly inquiry. The second and better-known of these novels, *Jinghua yuan* (Flowers in the mirror) (1821/1828),[6] by Li Ruzhen, takes the scholarly preoccupation of its predecessor to even greater lengths. Its predominantly female cast of characters engage in a quest for erudition that ultimately assumes the dimensions of an inquiry into the nature and validity of literati knowledge itself.

It is no coincidence that the three novels treated in Chapters 2 and 3 were written roughly at the beginning, middle, and end of the historical period known as the "Qian-Jia (Qianlong-Jiaqing) Age," or the reigns of the Qing emperors Gaozong (1736–95) and Renzong (1796–20). The Qian-Jia Age is generally regarded as the golden age of the movement known as evidential scholarship or philology (*kaozheng*), when both the methodology and productivity of Qing classical studies achieved full fruition and maturity. Since this movement represents the culmination of intellectual trends in evidence at least as early as the mid-seventeenth century, it can be regarded as a definitive stage in the evolution of Qing thought and culture. Each of the three novels treated here gives testimony to the rise and development of evidential studies during this period. Articulating the goals and aspirations as well as the fears and uncertainties of literati life in this last flowering of traditional Chinese culture, they reflect the considerable impact of evidential studies on perceptions of literati identity.

The ultimate aim of this study lies in delineating the image (or self-image) of the literati, or *shi*,[7] during the Qing period. The Ming and Qing dynasties mark the terminus of the lengthy evolution of the literati as a cultural, legal, and ideological category within Chinese society. The Ming experienced a revival of literati power and self-confidence after the depredations and humiliation endured under Mongol domination and, in its last century, a brilliant fluorescence of literature, philosophy, and art led (though far from monopolized) by literati figures. In the Qing period literati culture was disseminated more widely than at any other time in Chinese history, with vast numbers of Chinese men toiling over examination essays, immersed in the classics and philology, or reveling in artistic and literary pursuits. This expansion of opportunities to pursue such fields resulted in corresponding social diversity among their practitioners. As studies by Yu Ying-shih and others have demonstrated, the interdependence of the literati with merchants and other social strata effectively blurred the boundaries between the literati and their social others to an extent unprecedented in Chinese history.[8] By the eighteenth century this diffusion of literati culture had achieved unparalleled dimensions but in turn had given rise to new questions over the nature and value of literati identity itself.

In this study it will be crucial to explore the ramifications of literati identity where it finds its principal raison d'être, namely, in the discourses of Confucianism (*ru*), which through its stress on education and the criterion of merit as the basis for selection of officials provided the ideological foundation for a nonhereditary bureaucracy.[9] From the Han to the Qing periods, with few interruptions Confucianism was harnessed by the state as a powerful tool in effecting government policies. Moreover, institutionally it gained prominence as the principal curriculum in bureaucratic examinations, the existence of which its doctrines justify, if only implicitly.[10] As the prestige of the civil service examination system grew, its participants and aspirants became increasingly identified with the attainment of competence in the Confucian classical texts, particularly the ones used in the examinations. By the Ming and Qing periods, when literati status was most secure when recognized by the state in the form of examination degrees, the scholar of Confucian texts, or *ru*, was considered the paradigmatic (if not necessarily the predominant type of) literatus.[11]

Classical Confucian texts give little hint of how future elites were to be composed or selected. But by urging men of ambition (regardless of birth) to live by moral precepts and to devote themselves to the pursuit of culture and learning, Confucius and his followers established the standards by which future literati would come to be defined. The men who had cultivated themselves in such a manner were lauded as *junzi*, that is, persons of moral authority who commanded the respect of society at large, and were thus fit to rule. The ideal of the *junzi* came to epitomize Confucianism as a whole, but it was appropriated rather early by the literati, for whom it represented the goal of their efforts.[12]

This core ideal toward which the literati were exhorted to strive encompassed both ethical and intellectual elements—the moral values of benevolence, righteousness, and virtue on the one hand, and a stress on textual and ritual competence on the other. Such a duality makes it representative of what Yu Ying-shih has called the Confucian polarity between knowledge and morality. According to Yu, the Neo-Confucian dichotomy of moral knowledge (*dexing zhi zhi*) and intellectual knowledge (*wenjian zhi zhi* or "knowledge obtained through the senses") can be used as a framework for understanding the history of Confucianism after the Song dynasty. While the literati of the Yuan and Ming dynasties defined their vocation largely in terms of ethics and moral concerns and were correspondingly preoccupied with moral philosophy, Qing thinkers and writers turned toward what Yu calls an intellectualism that reduced Neo-Confucian "pan-moralism to a matter strictly of personal ethics."[13]

A somewhat modified version of the polarity between knowledge and morality delineated by Yu serves as a key conceptual framework for this book. In particular, it is invaluable in understanding the dissonance between Neo-Confucian orthodoxy as enunciated primarily in the writings of Zhu Xi and the other major Song thinkers and emerging modes of thought in the late Ming and Qing periods. Throughout the Ming and Qing periods, Song doctrines retained a nearly unchallenged position as the orthodoxy on which the civil service examinations were based. While valued by the state for their ideological consistency, the tenor and concerns of Song thought grew increasingly removed from contemporary scholarly and philosophical developments. The narrative and discursive writings discussed in this book do not necessarily take issue with Neo-Confucian doctrines per se.[14] Yet what Yu refers to as the intellectualism of a wide range of Qing writers seems to have compelled them to challenge, at least implicitly, certain fundamental assumptions of Song Confucian thought.

It is the contention of this book that by undermining Neo-Confucian orthodoxy, Qing writers implicitly altered the tasks and interests by which the literati had defined themselves for at least five centuries. State orthodoxy served to link literati self-cultivation with a cosmic order that universalized their moral values, thereby exalting their moral, intellectual, and social position and conferring on them the status of what might be called the "universal, generic man."[15] Qing reactions against such universalistic and axiological tendencies can be interpreted on one level as a rejection of a simplistic and inflexible definition of the literati's social eminence. Moreover, certain key figures of the eighteenth century such as Dai Zhen and Zheng Xie articulate a perception that Neo-Confucianism had degenerated into an instrument for the abuse of literati power.

Although *Rulin waishi* has long been viewed as the most significant document of literati discontent, even dissent, of its time, there is some danger in reading it too literally.[16] Several critics have argued for interpreting much of the novel as reflecting the concerns of an older established elite anxious over challenges posed by new social forces, nouveaux riches, in effect, of the Qianlong period.[17] Wu Jingzi was descended from a family of eminent officials (five members of one generation achieved *jinshi* status during the late-Ming and early-Qing periods) that had lately fallen on hard times. But whether we choose to read his novel as the call for restoration of an earlier, prelapsarian order or the first salvo in the wholesale destruction of the imperial order, he was not alone among writers of vernacular fiction of his time. The increasing proportion of the fiction of the seventeenth and eighteenth centuries produced by and for literati readers and writers tended toward the problematization of many aspects of literati culture and institutions.[18] Particularly during the eighteenth century, works such as *Xingshi yinyuan zhuan* and *Honglou meng*, as well as the classical tales of *Liaozhai zhiyi* and *Yuewei caotang biji*, in fact nearly all of what are now regarded as the classics of Qing fiction, satirize elite malfeasance and incompetence. To a much greater extent than in earlier fiction, Qing novels and short stories give vent to literati angst over the increasingly tenuous social and economic circumstances in which many lived.[19]

Of the three novels discussed in this book, *Rulin waishi* is paradigmatic of fiction that revolves both structurally and thematically around its representation of literati activities and concerns. It is also the earliest of the three works, composed sometime during the first fifteen years of the Qianlong era (1736–95). Its author, Wu Jingzi, was the scion of one of the most successful clans of its time in attaining examination status and bureaucratic office, and although far from prominent in his own day, he was certainly well connected in the scholarly and literary circles of Nanjing and Yangzhou, where he spent most of his later years.[20] Wu himself dabbled in classical studies, most notably the *Shijing*, but he appears to have been somewhat of a dilettante in such pursuits. *Rulin waishi* alludes only indirectly and quite briefly to the scholarship of its day; but these references, along with surviving records of Wu's social acquaintances, have invited a good deal of speculation concerning the intellectual leanings of its author.[21] As we will see in Part II, *Rulin waishi* indisputably reflects the scholarly and philosophical issues debated by the associates and friends of the author.

Although Wu Jingzi's life is by no means well documented, it is known in far greater detail than that of Xia Jingqu (1701–83), the author of *Yesou puyan*. Based on the few accounts of him scattered in local gazetteers and *biji* writings, he seems to have spent much of his life working as a clerk for hire in northern and western China. He probably returned to his native Jiangyin only in his later years, and there he apparently completed his novel sometime over the years 1750–80. According to accounts of him, he was well versed in a number of fields of classical and historical studies and furthermore seriously pursued both medicine and divination. The wide range of his interests is indeed reflected in this novel, written during the heyday of evidential scholarship, and almost contemporaneously with the massive, imperially sponsored bibliographical project, Siku quanshu (1772). The erudite achievements of its protagonists can perhaps be viewed as compensatory glorification for those men such as the author, who failed to gain entry into official ranks through the "standard route" of civil examinations.

With Li Ruzhen's (1763–1830?) Jinghua yuan (1821/1828), the scholarly novel reaches its zenith of development. Among these three authors, only Li can be identified unambiguously as a scholar of the evidential school, a disciple of the eminent scholar Ling Tingkan (1757–1809).[22] More than either of its predecessors, his novel explores the intellectual dimensions of literati life and interrogates the nature and functions of literati knowledge itself. As such, it can serve as a convenient terminus of this study, from which to reflect back on the trends observed in the discursive and literary writings of the Qianlong and Jiaqing eras. For it represents perhaps the most extreme development of the intellectualization of the literati self-image that emerges as the dominant motif of all the writings treated in this book.

PART I

The Image of the Literati in Qing Discourse

TO SPEAK of an image in the Chinese context immediately brings to mind the Buddhist-inspired metaphor of "flowers in the mirror and moon in the water" (*jinghua shuiyue*), the phrase from which the novel *Jinghua yuan* takes its title. To seek such reflections amounts to the pursuit of the ephemeral and the elusive, or in the case of the literati, both the reified and the contingent on social and discursive contexts that are themselves far from constant. I have nonetheless somewhat recklessly chosen to employ this term perhaps because it evokes the very illusoriness of the subject itself. For "literati," as I have defined it, refers less to an empirically verifiable social group than to a nexus of cultural, ideological, and sociopolitical values and relationships. That the literati existed during this period as a subject of discourse cannot be denied. The question at hand is how this subject—or more accurately, these subjects—of discourse were used in the reconceptualization of the role of the literati in the period in question.

The following three chapters trace the evolution of how the literati perceived their identity, tasks, and interests from the early years of the Qing period to the late eighteenth century. In Chapter 1 I survey the philosophical and scholarly changes that took place from the Kangxi to the Yongzheng and early Qianlong periods and argue that these both reflected and in turn gave further impetus to the reevaluation of literati morality, scholarly methods, and societal roles. In Chapter 2, I apply this framework to the analysis of a group of discursive texts in the areas of scholarship, literary criticism, painting, and examination essays to determine the degree to which each gives voice to literati identities at odds with those enunciated in the discourses of orthodox scholarship and their variants in belles lettres and the arts. Chronologically, Chapter 2 centers on the early-to-mid Qianlong era, that is, roughly the period of overlap between the three novelists Wu Jingzi, Xia Jingqu, and Li Ruzhen. In Chapter 3 I examine the scholarly interests of a few figures who can be linked with some certainty to at least one of these three novelists. Even a relatively cursory study of the works of thinkers such as Yan Yuan and Ling Tingkan can help to elucidate some of the specific concerns and issues to which the three novels in question can be seen as responding.

The purpose of these wide-ranging forays into Qing discursive texts is to suggest both the contours as well as the pervasiveness of literati attempts to redefine their own identity within the sphere of aesthetic and scholarly pursuits. While fictional works provide one valuable lens from which to view the evolution of literati self-perceptions, these were clearly of minor importance in the eyes of Qing scholars and literary figures. Before seeking to interpret the novels themselves, then, it seems advisable to determine the degree to which they repeat or modify the broad range of discursive practices of their time.

CHAPTER ONE

Literati Identity and the Qing Epistemological Crisis

IN AN ESSAY that can perhaps be described as an early precursor to what we might call the school of "close reading," the Qing philologist Jiao Xun (1763–1820) devotes the entirety of his grandly titled "Explication of the *Odes*" to two short passages taken from that classic.[1] These passages depict the "felling and cutting [of] trees" and the "construction of walls."[2] Jiao Xun's essay exhibits most of what might be called the classic features of the philological scholarship of its time: an unflagging fascination with minute detail and its precise description and, of course, a careful attention to questions of etymology. This philological exercise goes beyond the merely technical, however, for Jiao's purpose in offering these explications seems to be to demonstrate the enduring aesthetic integrity of these lines. They manage within the space of a few characters, he notes, to present an extremely vivid and highly realistic description of their subjects. Jiao has confirmed the accuracy of their descriptions, he claims, by observing workmen in his own courtyard pruning trees and repairing garden walls after a heavy rain.

Jiao does not, however, even mention the role these descriptive passages play in the poems where they appear. The first example, which concerns woodcutting, provides a metaphoric counterpoint between the credulity of the person who has rashly believed a slanderous rumor about the poet and the care that even a lowly woodcutter takes in felling a tree and cutting it into lumber. The carelessness of the poet's persecutor is thus, in the standard commentary by the Song Neo-Confucian Zhu Xi (1127–1200), "not even equal to the work of woodcutters and carpenters."[3] Hence, their function in the poem is, according to Zhu, that of a stimulus (*xing*). The second example appears in a poem describing the "civilizing of the country of Bin," which begins with the allocation of lands and concludes in the investiture of the Zhou founder, King Wen. The lines quoted by Jiao portray, according to Zhu, the construction of the palace and its walls, that is, a significant step in the establishment of King Wen's rule.

Jiao's admiration for the painstaking care with which these two passages portray the mundane details of their subjects does not seem to extend to a consideration of their function in the poems in which they appear. Indeed, he concludes the essay with a criticism of the prevailing standards of taste, which, he feels, have led to the slighting of such seemingly minor aspects of poetry: "Commentators on poetry dismiss the late Tang poets Yao He and Jia Dao as mean and trivial and their style as lowly and decadent. The fault of these poets is thought to lie in their attention to embellishment. I have brought up these two examples to question this [opinion]."

Jiao Xun's "Explication" is illustrative of the concerns, as well as the preoccupations and biases, of mid-Qing philological scholarship. Jiao is determined, it appears, to compensate for the neglect lexical concentration and mimetic intensity had allegedly suffered in recent centuries. Perhaps he would not have denied that in the final analysis, a comprehensive understanding of these poems would require levels of interpretation other than those he offers. But his motive here is to reveal the beauty of the classic in these dimensions alone. Zhu Xi, by contrast, expends little time or effort on philological explication in his commentary on these passages, preferring instead to relate them to the overall structural integrity of the poems in which they appear. One senses that as a result, he perhaps overlooks the power of descriptive detail in his anxiousness to give a complete account of the poems and that he is not averse to twisting textual ambiguities to serve his interpretations.

This brief example is meant to suggest some of the contrasts between the work of late-eighteenth- and early-nineteenth-century textual scholars such as Jiao Xun and the orthodox tradition of Neo-Confucian thought as epitomized in the work of Zhu Xi. In the nomenclature of the mid-Qing period, this divergence was known as the dispute between *kaozheng* and *yili*, or in Benjamin Elman's terms, between the methods of philology and the ideals of philosophy.[4] As seen in this particular example, this contrast was manifested not only in what can be broadly subsumed under scholarly method but in the category of aesthetic judgment as well. Jiao's method sets its sights on the careful analysis of formal elements of its subjects to the almost total exclusion of questions of larger significance. Indeed, the glaring omission of any reference to the allegorical associations and context of the two poems cited is made even more conspicuous by the inclusion of Jiao's observations of his garden workmen, a detail which to some may have been tantamount to committing lèse majesté against the Zhou royalty (to whom these poems were claimed by exegetical tradition to allude). Jiao seems to be celebrating the qualities of the *Odes* most directly accessible to unmediated perception, as well as the ability of the ancients to depict the mundane world unencumbered by allegorical or metaphoric baggage.

We might even go so far as to say that the "Explication of the *Odes*" is representative of the desire of many scholars of the time to conspicuously avoid the debates on questions of metaphoric or ethical significance that figure so prominently in classical scholarship since the Song period. In one sense, of course, they could perhaps be seen as simply "filling in" the gaps, adding a philological sophistication, for example, to Zhu Xi's glosses on poetry. And yet, as Jiao Xun's remarks on late Tang poetry betray, by the late Qianlong and Jiaqing eras the tendency among philologically minded scholars was to criticize or even negate many of the premises of post-Song scholarly methods, or in this case, the accepted canons of literary taste. A certain bias against an overly zealous concern with questions of philology or other subjects lacking immediate ethical import widespread among Neo-Confucian scholars had, in the opinion of many Qing scholars, exerted a distorting and often unhealthy influence on learning, which required correction.[5] This questioning and even rejection of Song learning by those who came to be identified with philological studies ultimately reflects changing perceptions of the proper objects and methods of study and of self-cultivation, that is, not only the methodology but the fundamental tenets of the Cheng-Zhu orthodox school.[6]

Briefly, we might characterize the Neo-Confucian orthodoxy as concerned primarily with ethical, perhaps even "religious," questions, revolving around the practice of self-cultivation.[7] All activities of the individual were seen to relate somehow to the achievement of an ethical transcendence of the mundane or pedestrian levels of existence. In learning, men (and only men, at least for the vast majority of Neo-Confucian writers) were exhorted to go beyond the distracting and confusing interplay of form to seek the underlying significance of things and events.[8] The man of learning was not to allow himself to become preoccupied with the study of any subject that did not lead directly to moral truth; to do otherwise would be "squandering one's moral energies on trifles" (*wanwu sangzhi*). This commitment to seeking a transcendent, formless understanding of the Way was the very basis of Neo-Confucian perceptions of self-cultivation; and thus, scholarship, literary production, and service to the state, those vocations conventionally held to be the hallmarks of literati identity, were all implicitly placed in the service of the larger goal of moral cultivation.[9] By freeing himself from mundane affairs and private desires, and by devoting himself to the pursuit of overarching principles, the man of the Way could—at least in theory—achieve the pinnacle of Confucian perfection, namely sagehood.

"Explication of the *Odes*" contains an unequivocal gesture of opposition to the propensity to generalization, abstraction, and universalism characteristic of orthodox Neo-Confucianism. Indeed, I submit that the relevance of Jiao's remarks extends beyond the scholarly questions he poses here to the very nature of the literati vocation. For if philologists and, by extension, all literati, were not to search for the transcendent truths underlying the objects of their study, as Neo-Confucian doctrine exhorted them to do, but instead concentrate on the more accessible world of form, how then was their relation to the Confucian vision of truth—the Way—to be established? Jiao would of course answer this question unequivocally, for to him an understanding of the classics in their original meaning was the primary duty of any individual dedicated to the Way. But as we have seen from this essay, such an understanding rests first and foremost on the clarification of form, both in the sense of verbal art and as the tangible and concrete world of the present. To attempt to go beyond this in search of something inaccessible to the senses or irrelevant to textual analysis was felt by many of Jiao's contemporaries to be fundamentally wrongheaded. In this they posed an indirect but nonetheless profound challenge to the basic premises that had served to define literati identity for nearly a millennium.

Literati Identity and Intellectual Change in the Qing Period

The emergence of Qing philological scholarship from its precursors in the late Ming to its heyday in the eighteenth and early nineteenth centuries has been charted in a number of studies. As a scholarly methodology, High Qing philology built on the work of many Neo-

Confucian writers of the Song and Ming dynasties, including Zhu Xi himself.[10] Moreover, according to Kai-wing Chow, the preference for Han exegetes over Song scholarship emerged relatively late in the development of Qing scholarship, in the 1730s, and was preceded by nearly a century of relative catholicity toward the entire legacy of classical exegesis.[11] Even in the heyday of philology, noted philologists such as Cheng Yaotian and Shen Tong remained faithful adherents of Cheng-Zhu doctrines. It thus appears that we must avoid simplistically interpreting the rise of philology in terms of an antagonistic stance toward Song Neo-Confucian scholarly practices.

By contrast, recent research by Benjamin Elman, Yu Ying-shih, Frederick Mote, and Kai-wing Chow has helped to clarify the role of social, political, and economic factors in the development of eighteenth-century scholarship. It now seems irrefutable that the unprecedented expansion of the population of literati lacking advanced examination degrees, the political disengagement from and lingering resentment toward Qing "barbarian" rule, and the significant expansion of economic resources available for the support of scholarship stimulated the emergence of philological scholarship during this period. In Elman's analysis, intellectual developments must be seen as integral to the development of a class of professional scholars whose allegiance to their intellectual vocation came to overshadow commitment to the hallowed career paths of bureaucratic service or moral inculcation.[12] In the context of this social transformation, then, dissatisfaction toward Neo-Confucian orthodox doctrines can be interpreted as reflecting not only the internal dynamic of intellectual change but also an awareness of the increasingly anachronistic character of orthodoxy vis-à-vis the daily concerns of much of the elite. Such change thus entailed the reconsideration of literati aims and responsibilities; while this was often merely implicit, some thinkers, among them Yan Yuan and Li Gong, challenged literati roles as defined by Song orthodoxy explicitly.

It would of course be a gross oversimplification to equate the Neo-Confucian legacy (by which I mean both the orthodoxy formulated by Zhu Xi and the broad range of philosophers and literary men of the Song) with the interests of the literati alone. But as John Dardess has demonstrated, the Yuan and early Ming political activists and thinkers who participated in the upheavals of the mid-to-late fourteenth century, and who helped to establish Song learning as the state orthodoxy, were with a high degree of consensus determined to reassert the influence of the literati as a moral and political force.[13] Neo-Confucianism

16 / *The Image of the Literati in Qing Discourse*

provided an important tool in this endeavor. Through succeeding centuries, the orthodoxy as it came to be codified in the mid-to-late Yuan treated the literati as a homogeneous group, unified by their commitment to Confucian cultural and moral tenets. From the point of view of the state's interests, the orthodoxy played an invaluable role. By defining the literati as bound together essentially by a common concern for the public good and a commitment to cultivating their moral and intellectual capacities in preparation for government service, the state subordinated their priorities largely (though certainly not entirely) to its needs. What has been called "imperial Confucianism" lionized the literati as the leaders of society, responsible for most aspects of social life, both in and outside government.

In practice, the unquestioned social eminence of the literati found in orthodox doctrine guaranteed neither their security nor even their survival. In the early Qing, for example, the literati of Jiangnan, the cultural and economic center of the country, were forced by the central government to surrender many of the economic and political privileges they had amassed during the final century of Ming rule.[14] Moreover, competition with bannermen (both Han and Manchu) for bureaucratic appointment restricted the number of positions open to Chinese, thereby reducing opportunities for government service to levels below those of most of the Ming period. Within society itself, rivalry between literati and other occupational groups intensified over the course of Qing rule. Merchants gained unprecedented social prominence through their participation in liturgical activities of the Jiangnan delta and other urban centers and often formed close alliances with literati lineages.[15] In the words of Alexander Woodside, "There was an unprecedented spread of wealth outside the scholar class in the Ch'ing period. This wealth meant that there was growing differentiation in the sources of status legitimization and its rewards. To the educated literati ... the preeminence of the claim of education through schooling and examinations, the preeminence of the claim of educational achievement as the criterion for earning higher status ... appeared to be gravely jeopardized by such differentiation."[16]

Even by the late Ming period the literati hardly constituted a monolithic block.[17] Indeed, the sheer numbers of men possessing literacy sufficient to compete in the examination system ensured that the vast majority never rose beyond the first rank of *tongsheng* (Confucian apprentice). With unprecedented growth in the numbers of educated men, innumerable scholars of high qualifications began to seek employment outside the "standard route" of examination success. Some engaged in scholarly compilations under private as well as public sponsorship; many also served in the large corps of *muliao* or informal advisers in bureaucratic offices throughout the country. Such men no longer faced a straightforward choice between service and retirement, or commitment and eremitism, choices that Neo-Confucian doctrine posed in moralistic rather than economic terms. These men can be thought of as a deracinated elite with little access to the privileges that orthodoxy promised them.[18]

In the first decades of the Qing, Cheng-Zhu doctrines enjoyed something of a revival, largely in reaction to the excesses of the school of the Mind. This initial burst of creativity seems to have ensured the continuing patronage of Song orthodox doctrines by the state. But although subject to occasional modification they quickly ossified into a particularly rigid, codified orthodoxy, defined largely by its role as the curriculum of examination studies. As Qing institutions matured, some adjustments were made to the social conditions of the era. But an official culture that remained inapplicable to the vast majority of literate men began to be perceived as an annoying if not downright harmful anachronism. Zhang Xuecheng (1738–1801), for example, decried the inadequacies of categories that relegated scholars outside officialdom to inaction and political insignificance:

> The scholar is a perspicacious man who, when he does not live under an enlightened and virtuous ruler and is denied a role in government, cannot put his beliefs into effect. He must therefore content himself with preserving the way of the ancient kings to transmit to future generations of men. When such conditions arise, they are the result of historical forces and cannot be helped. But the way of man is broad and great. Should an individual who does not meet with recognition confine himself to preserving the past and awaiting the future, never venturing into the affairs of men?[19]

Zhang is taking issue with the notion that any one ideology can subsume the aspirations of literati of diverse backgrounds and interests beneath its demands for piety, self-cultivation, and political participation.[20] This is not to say that participation in examinations and official life had lost its attraction for men of his generation; but among those for whom scholarship had become a principal vocation, especially in the Jiangnan region, orthodox criteria for the determination of literati identity were irrelevant at best.[21] By the early decades of the eighteenth century, thinkers of various persuasions had put forth persuasive arguments for rethinking social and political categories in order to accommodate the increasing diversity and heterogeneity of literati pursuits and interests, and to justify the pluralization and even a certain professionalization already evident within the elite.[22]

Immanent Principle and Epistemological Doubt

Thus far I have argued that Qing reactions against Song orthodoxy reflected questions over its tenability as an ideology of literati identity. To many it seemed that the categories of Song orthodoxy had little relevance to the daily lives and aspirations of an increasingly heterogeneous elite. While more often than not the contesting of Cheng-Zhu thought took the form of philosophical argument, it is important to realize that the debates over these philosophical issues were inextricably linked to perceptions of literati identity. In essence, mid-Qing criticisms of orthodox Song thought largely concur that however nobly intentioned, the abstract idealism of Song Neo-Confucianism had proved deleterious to the literati in numerous ways. These thinkers generally revived cosmological views based on *qi*, or material ether, and rejected the Neo-Confucian elevation of *li*, or immanent moral principle. They heaped scorn on the universalism of Song Neo-Confucianism, and most pointedly the doctrine of *li*, which in Song orthodoxy was honored as the basis for, and the cardinal means of apprehending, the moral intelligibility of the universe.

The centrality of principle to Song Neo-Confucianism stemmed from the all-inclusive definition it was accorded by Zhu Xi and his successors in the late Song and Yuan periods. Under the educational program formulated by Zhu (and adopted practically in toto by four dynasties), the traditional pursuits of the literatus—namely, mastery of the classics, literary composition, and moral edification—were subsumed under the category of the "investigation of things and the extension of knowledge" (*gewu zhizhi*) given in *The Great Learning* (*Daxue*). This, in turn, was generally glossed as the "exhaustion of principle" (*qiongli*).[23] Hence, all the manifold aspects of literati cultivation were ultimately reducible to the single, unifying vision of principle.[24]

This conception of all-embracing principle came under all-out attack by Qing philologists such as Dai Zhen (1724–77), Ling Tingkan (1757–1809), and Wang Zhong (1745–94). Such men stressed both the diversity of phenomena and the need to seek their meaning within, rather than beyond, their tangible forms. Needless to say, the empirical methodologies that informed the scholarship of these men served as the practical equivalent to their distaste for abstract speculation over principle. Yet even before the full flowering of evidential scholarship, the speculative nature of Song metaphysical thought had become a curious anachronism as early as the seventeenth century. Wei Xi (1624–81) expressed the general frustration with idle speculation very succinctly when he said that "to speak of *li* is like discussing heaven. If someone holds that there is another heaven beyond this one, how can I refute him? And if another holds that no heaven exists outside this one, how can I disprove it? Thus, arguing over *li* is like grasping at empty air. How can one do anything about it?"[25]

More broadly, this distaste for principle resonates with what John Henderson has described as the breakup of the correlative mode of thought, which had served as the metaphysical underpinnings of Neo-Confucian ideology. The Song and Ming propensity to force all worldly phenomena, both human and natural, into symmetrical, a priori correlative relations became the focus of criticism for a number of Qing thinkers. In astronomical and mathematical theory, for example, seventeenth- and eighteenth-century figures increasingly felt the world of natural phenomena to be beyond the capacity of mortal minds to comprehend in its entirety. To them, its many anomalies and exceptions resisted attempts at generalization. They were particularly critical of the works of Song naturalist thinkers such as Shao Yong, whose numerological schemes were seen as oversimplifying and distorting the complexity of nature. It was asserted that the interpretation and observation of natural phenomena required much more than the inductive association of logically parallel but empirically unverifiable correlatives.[26]

From many quarters, in fact, it was said that no principles could be applicable to all circumstances. This heightened awareness of the diversity and complexity of the phenomenal world contributed to a growing appreciation of the difficulty of any full exercise of critical thought. The loss of confidence in the absolute validity of principle, or at the very least, in its accessibility to human comprehension, seems to have gone hand in hand with a recognition of the limits of any individual human mind. Again quoting Wei Xi,

> People only appreciate the things which are close and familiar to them. They have likes and dislikes toward what they know, and cannot extrapolate beyond them to what they don't know, judging others according to their own narrow prejudices.... Any biased statement must have an area

toward which it is blind. Those who see the front walkway are ignorant of the courtyard. Those who see from the inner chambers know not of the hearth. They stick to what they know, and disguise their shortcomings. Hence they are bound to be ignorant of many things.[27]

Increasingly, Zhu Xi's dictum that the individual should reach a stage in his studies at which principle suddenly becomes "clear" (*guantong*)[28] came to seem simplistic and impractical. Even Qing exponents of Neo-Confucian orthodoxy no longer shared with Song scholars a confidence that a stage of completion could be reached, or indeed that knowledge was even potentially finite and hence subject to mastery by an individual.[29] Hence, while insisting on the preeminent role of the rational mind in literati endeavor, many thinkers became acutely conscious of the almost insurmountable obstacles in the way of an attainment of a Neo-Confucian unifying vision.[30] Correspondingly, the concern for some underlying, all-pervasive thread of transcendent value came not only to be questioned but actually blamed as the source of confusion and obfuscation.

Compared to the confidence that Song thought manifests in the power of humans to comprehend cosmic truths, then, a very profound sense of epistemological uncertainty pervades the literature and thought of the eighteenth century. No longer was a knowledge of ethical principle believed to provide a constant and secure touchstone for the multifarious occupations in which the literati engaged. The complexity of the phenomenal world, whether that be the textual legacy of the ancient past or the political, historical, and natural conditions of the present, required that men devote their efforts to the study of form itself. For while phenomena were not devoid of intelligible patterns, a knowledge of theoretical or abstract principles was no longer viewed as wholly applicable to any discipline. Hence, the unity and synthetic homogeneity of the Song view of humanity gave way to views that acknowledged the plurality and diversity of all-under-heaven, both human and natural, and indeed manifested an acute awareness of anomaly, division, and limits.[31]

Reevaluations of Literati Moral and Intellectual Identity

In terms of its role in determining the nature of literati views of their own vocation, the Neo-Confucian doctrine of immanent principle offered to its dedicated adherents the promise of moral intelligibility in a world filled with contradictions and uncertainty. It held that human nature was essentially perfectible, and that the attainment of a state of moral certainty and intellectual completeness was a viable goal for individuals who aspired to literati status. As an ideology of the literati this and similar doctrines reinforced a common identity by giving them a unity in the purposes and forms of intellectual, social, and political behavior, as well as a certain uniformity in the methods and results of moral cultivation. This combined emphasis on social cohesion and intellectual coherence is what William T. de Bary summarizes as the Neo-Confucian search for a "common thread":

> Reality for the Neo-Confucian was to be attained through an integrative process of self-realization based on a synthesis of humanistic (especially philosophical) studies, social action, and personal praxis. To find the unifying thread, the balancing mean, the underlying value or the all-embracing conception remained the fundamental aim of Neo-Confucian teaching. Here the prime symbols are the sage, as microcosm, model of human integrity, and exemplar of self-fulfillment in action, and the Way, as macrocosm, overarching unity, and ultimate process. As the separate values in the Neo-Confucian synthesis underwent their own development in constantly changing and ever more complex historical and cultural circumstances, their meaning and validity were tested in relation to such unifying conceptions.[32]

Ultimately, then, the goal of Neo-Confucian efforts was the attainment of a state of ethical perfection—sagehood—that encompassed the multifarious dimensions of social and intellectual life. As Peter Bol has argued, the Song thinkers who formulated what became the Daoxue movement were responding to the loss of cohesiveness, and a corresponding laxity in ethical standards, among the many literati families no longer able to gain appointment to the civil bureaucracy in the eleventh and twelfth centuries.[33] While Qing literati faced similar circumstances—i.e., an increasingly difficult and crowded path to examination success—the reconceptualization of the literati role by eighteenth-century thinkers turned away from rather than embraced the strongly ethical tenor of Song thought.[34] In repudiating the Neo-Confucian program of self-cultivation, Qing evidential scholars implicitly undermined both its moral absolutism and its idealization of a literati communitas bound together by the Way. For them, universalizing conceptions were no longer adequate for ordering literati life. Even the hitherto sacrosanct Confucian ideal of individual sagehood came to be regarded as smacking of an overweening will to omniscience.[35]

Criticism of the Neo-Confucian stress on moral piety can be traced back to the Song itself, of course, when the appellation "Daoxue" (Learning of the Way) was coined by their opponents to deride rather than compliment the followers of Zhu Xi. Li Zhi in the late Ming period is perhaps the most eloquent adversary of Cheng-Zhu moral rigorism, castigating it for having created a sanctimonious, arrogant, and ineffectual elite. By the eighteenth century many thinkers were agreed that Cheng-Zhu teachings were responsible for an unhealthy preoccupation with moral cultivation, which had in effect brought the literati to a state of incompetence and neglect of their practical needs and duties. Under the pervasive influence of a desire for restoring the literati to social utility, the demands placed on the literatus for the achievement of a moral self-realization were judged to be both misguided and unrealistic. As Jiao Xun put it, while Zhu Xi's doctrines were suited to gentlemen of the very highest caliber, they were less effective in guiding the average literati aspirant, to say nothing of the common man.[36]

This development had important implications for the emerging reformulation of the social and intellectual concerns of the literati. The reaction against Wang Yangming's doctrines had perhaps more than any other factor contributed to a loss of interest in the ideal of individual sagehood. But whatever reasons we may adduce to explain this change, it seems to parallel a growing doubt over the moral sagacity of the literati and their leadership over the populace at large. A number of writers of the seventeenth and eighteenth centuries agree that differences in moral qualities are not what divide literati from the rest of society. Rather, their competence as cognoscenti to become conscious of that which commoners practice unknowingly, and to use their intellectual capacities (for better or worse) in the pursuit of knowledge, was recognized to distinguish them from their social others. Hence, more than ever before, knowledge and practical achievements were seen to be the primary criteria for evaluation of literati attainments.[37]

While notions of a transcendent moral intelligibility were not entirely abandoned, totalizing abstractions came to be regarded with skepticism, even scorn, by many scholars. In fact, abstract thought divorced from objective manifestation was widely blamed as the root of many ills, scholarly, social, and political. In this new climate, scholars were more reluctant to regard ultimate truth or the Way as readily accessible to discovery, and Song thinkers were lambasted for presumptuously regarding scholarship and thought as a direct means to such ends. That scholars of the Qing for the most part engaged in the "investigation of things" without reference to their moral or subjective worth suggests that thought had lost its axiological underpinnings to a degree perhaps unprecedented in Chinese history.[38]

The Arts

Interest in the classics and other textual studies, natural science, history, and government blossomed in the last years of the Ming. After the fall of the dynasty, these fields gained even greater acceptance as men sought to explain the circumstances that had led to the disasters of their era. Many blamed the vacuity of Ming thought, in particular its lack of "concreteness," for the ills afflicting the literati. To correct this, men such as Fang Yizhi (1600–1671) urged study of the empirical objective world through the arts (*daoyi*), a term he used to indicate any field that takes objective reality as its subject. In his *Dongxi Jun* he states: "The mind can wander in the heavens, [but] one must provide an object on which it can ride in order to cultivate the mind. One sets one's sights on the Dao, but continues throughout to cultivate the arts. [This is like] heaven carried by earth, and fire fed on firewood. To view things by using other things, is to see the Dao by means of the Dao."[39]

In recent times, however, people had, under the influence of Neo-Confucianism, given up the study of the arts to search for something beyond them and had come to despise any trivial concern with form. This had left the literati with no way at all to distinguish themselves from anyone else:

> The arts are referred to as the "arts of the Way," and it is thought that this is because people are ashamed to practice them. But do such people realize that men of both past and present who have practiced them feel hesitant to invoke the name of the Way, and thus borrow the term "art"? ... Now people all think that the sweeping away [of all worldly concerns] is the Way. But as a result, glib-tongued vulgar men are able to despise men who honor the classics, and who delight in propriety and righteousness.[40]

It was essential that literati achieve proficiency in some field of inquiry both as the only means of approaching ultimate truth—which was not directly accessible to perception—and to assure their own position in society: "The truly enlightened have nothing in particular to do, so they still engage in learning as their occupation. One could say that they use learning to secure their position, or simply in order to eat and drink."[41] Here, Fang seems to be arguing for the reestablishment of some sort of new lines of demarcation between the literati and the rest of society. But the identification of the arts as the proper domain of literati activity was rather problematic in this regard, since their precise content was a source of controversy in the seventeenth century and beyond. As I shall discuss later, the early Qing figure Yan Yuan (1635–1704) revived a pre-Han meaning of the term Six Arts (*liuyi*) that included horsemanship and mathematics. More broadly used, the arts could designate any number of subjects, from the study of the Confucian classics to fine arts, that is, painting or the playing of certain musical instruments, to skilled crafts, games, and even the examination essay or *bagu*.

Fang Yizhi's identification of the arts as the only accessible means of self-cultivation by the literati thus implies at the very least an attenuation of the post-Song view placing moral cultivation at the center of literati endeavors. The study of the world of form through the application of methodological tools came to preoccupy generations of Qing scholars, thereby essentially confirming in practice what Fang had articulated.[42] By Fang's logic, the study of what might once have been considered trivial forms and institutions could no longer be dismissed out of hand, especially if they derived sanction from the Confucian tradition, as in the minutiae of ritual, ancient artifacts, and classical governmental institutions. As Fang Yizhi put it, perhaps somewhat tongue-in-cheek, "The study of books and observation aid the alaya consciousness,"[43] and as long as it contributes to one's store of rational knowledge, then no particular endeavor however seemingly "trivial" could be disregarded out of hand.[44]

Fang Yizhi's ideas were in many ways prophetic of the changes in intellectual life that were to take place during subsequent centuries. As the diversification of and specialization within scholarly disciplines developed apace, Qing classical scholarship came increasingly to take on the character of the "arts" with few if any direct ties to moral cultivation. This change eventually resulted in renewed acrimony between the practitioners of scholarship as an academic discipline, largely identified with the Han Learning or philological school, and those who sought "meaning" along the lines of the Song exegetical traditions. For Fang Yizhi, any theory that claimed to champion "underlying truth," "meaning," or transcendent profundity smacked of a wish to mask the failures of those who lacked both the energy and intelligence for prolonged study. Nonetheless, the debate continued over the nature and value of knowledge of the formal world, divided between those who sought "names, numbers, and institutions" and those who attempted to re-anchor scholarship to moral and even cosmic truths. Ultimately, of course, the antagonists were contesting the proper domain of literati knowledge, namely, of whether proficiency in formal and textual knowledge or an ethical-spiritual understanding of the Confucian tradition constituted the principal ground that defined literati identity.[45]

CHAPTER TWO

Discourses of the Literati and the Literati in Discourse

THE DEVELOPMENTS outlined in Chapter 1 had consequences that extended far beyond the world of scholarship. The literati as a whole were equally if not more concerned with literary composition, that is, belles lettres and, needless to say, examination studies. Moreover, the arts of painting, calligraphy, and epigraphy preoccupied large numbers of educated men in the eighteenth century. Even a casual survey reveals that not only in scholarship but in letters and the arts as well, theorists reacted against the Neo-Confucian belief in transcendent and intuitive understanding, while reaffirming the importance of formal knowledge and intellectual skills to their respective disciplines. Concurrently, they sought new definitions of the individual writer, artist, and thinker that acknowledged their dependence on historical and social forces and recognized that in their becoming, or self-realization, individuals were limited by objective circumstances. As such, the writings of these theorists exhibit clear relevance to the examination of literati identity, by redefining the individual subject as a participant within his or her respective discipline.

In the following sections I will demonstrate parallel developments in discourses on scholarship, literature, art, and the *bagu* essay. I do not pretend to have provided a comprehensive or even representative account of Qing perceptions of literati identity in these selections. But the examples I have chosen for analysis are useful in identifying discourses that may have been influential both broadly among literati of the Qianlong and Jiaqing periods and in the social and intellectual milieus that have bearing upon the three novelists under study.

Scholarship

By the mid-eighteenth century, much of traditional Confucian scholarship—that is, of classical texts—was regularly subsumed under the rubric *kaozheng*, that is, evidential scholarship or philology, by both its adherents and its detractors. This was in large part due to the general perception that its methods and assumptions had achieved an overwhelming dominance among scholars. What came to be called "Song scholarship" in fact seems to have been confined to a polemic directed against philology and was largely the work of literary figures. Evidential scholarship, increasingly identified as Han Learning by the 1770s, attracted the attention of practically all scholars devoted to classical exegesis, philology, and eventually even history, and its methodological rigor and sophistication contributed to a certain intellectual cohesiveness among Jiangnan scholars, which Elman has identified as resembling a modern professional identity. Nevertheless, this need not have necessitated a rejection of orthodox Neo-Confucian doctrines on the part of many such scholars. Hu Shih observes that most eighteenth-century scholars ceded the territory of faith, that is, adherence to Cheng-Zhu moral teachings, to others, preferring instead to devote their efforts to the analysis and manipulation of empirical knowledge in their chosen fields of inquiry.[1]

Yet while this is certainly true in a general sense, the very nature of their scholarship eventually challenged, both implicitly and explicitly, the entire edifice of Song scholarship and, by extension, the doctrines by which it defined literati self-cultivation. For ultimately even staunchly loyal adherents of Cheng-Zhu doctrines such as Jiang Yong (1681–1762) engaged in technical scholarship divorced from the realm of moral value, and thus fundamentally at odds with the Cheng-Zhu temper.

In this light, then, it certainly seems reasonable to follow Yu Ying-shih, Murase Yuya, and others[2] in regarding Dai Zhen's excursions into moral philosophy as representative if not of an ideology, at least of a common set of assumptions implicitly shared by *kaozheng* scholars. Hong Bang's (1745–79) cryptic remark that Dai's greatest work in this vein, *Mengzi ziyi shuzheng*, is simply an exercise in the study of "punishments, names, measurements, and numbers," and therefore without moral or ideological bias or viewpoint—the proper formula for *kaozheng* scholarship—should perhaps be understood in this light.[3] We need not spill any more ink on the question of whether Dai's interpretation of Mencius is indeed as faithful to Mencian thought as it claims to be. But the basic tenets expressed therein establish new boundaries between the pursuit of ethical and subjective truth and intellectual exercise, thereby giving theoretical justification for the pursuit of exegetical scholarship unencumbered by Neo-Confucian values. Hence, an examination of Dai's philosophical works for their treatment of the broad issues outlined above should reveal positions that though unacknowledged or perhaps even denied by some scholars, nevertheless reflect an unwritten code of evidential scholarship during the mid-to-late eighteenth century.

The outstanding achievement of Dai's philosophical writings is their elaboration of a sophisticated epistemology, which explores with unprecedented insight and forcefulness the interrelations between psychological experience and praxis, as epitomized in his most famous epigram, "To kill people under the guise of principle."[4] The doctrines of Yan Yuan, Li Gong, and Cheng Tingzuo—all of whom appear to have influenced Wu Jingzi at least indirectly—already prefigured many of Dai's insights, particularly in formulating ritual as a sort of rational structure of social intelligibility. Perhaps in response to the challenge of Wang Yangming's doctrines, all seem motivated by a need to articulate in a more sophisticated way the complex interdependence between the structures of experience and those of thought through the medium of ritual. Dai establishes the relation between ritual and mind even more explicitly than most, when he asserts the following:

> When discussing principle, [Mencius] refers to ritual propriety and righteousness but does not bring up wisdom. He has not left wisdom out, for the understanding of ritual propriety and righteousness is [identical to] wisdom. When discussing virtue, [he] refers to wisdom but does not touch upon righteousness or ritual propriety. This does not imply that he has forgotten them, for wisdom is the means of comprehending ritual propriety and righteousness.[5]

For Dai praxis and the cognitive functions are inseparable; failure or success in one realm demands the same in the other. As Hashimoto Takakatsu and others have pointed out, the charge of idealism leveled at Dai by Hou Wailu is wholly unwarranted, since Dai's theory of knowledge focuses on the public or objective dimension of knowledge as "experiential cognition" (*keikenteki ninshiki*), and hence is profoundly social and political in its orientation.[6] Like many Qing thinkers, Dai regards cognition as the center of human life, the origin of the Mencian "four virtues" of humanity, righteousness, propriety, and wisdom. These four virtues rely on the workings of the mind to be "extended and filled out" (*kuo er chong zhi*) to reach their full development. In fact, he insists that the Mencian "roots of goodness" are indistinguishable from cognition: "Thus what is called commiseration and humanity are not outside of human intelligence, 'as if they were some other object hidden in he mind.'"[7] And the uniqueness of human beings consists of the power of their rational faculties to reach a pinnacle of acuity and awareness, far outstripping the broader function of "intuitive perception" (*zhijue*) present in all living things.

> People can extend and develop their knowledge to the point of gaining brilliant insight. At this stage, humanity, righteousness, propriety, and wisdom are all complete. Humanity, righteousness, propriety, and wisdom are none other than the final realization of the mind's rationality.[8]

Hence, as Dai's doctrine of the physical nature of knowledge (*xieqi xinzhi*) seems to corroborate, ethical categories are founded not on an inherently moral nature (*xing*) but rather on the more ambiguous, or even ethically neutral, physical desires and their parallel cognitive faculties. This represents a significant reformulation of ethical distinctions, addressing in particular the ethical rigorism of much of Song and Ming Neo-Confucian doctrines. Not only does Dai neutralize the opposition between desire and goodness; he makes the appetites the very foundation of moral instincts. Qian Mu is certainly right in protesting that these ideas are at variance with the classical opposition between the morally virtuous "gentleman" and the "petty man," and thus profoundly at odds with Confucianism.[9] This, however, is precisely the heart of the matter with which Dai's critique of Neo-Confucian ethics deals—namely, the justification for distinguishing between different groups in society according to their interests and desires. For as many have observed, paramount among the ideas expressed in his philosophical works is his dissatisfaction with the effects of Neo-Confucian ethical rigorism on social justice and the maintenance of a hierarchical social order.

Dai's great grievance against the Cheng-Zhu orthodoxy was what he saw as an almost casual use of ethical absolutes in the evaluation of human conduct: "Intelligence and stupidity are simply distinctions in degree, and not in kind. Good and evil, however, designate opposites, and are not relative terms." The tendency to justify literati ideals in terms of absolute ethical distinctions had, he argued, brought about the tyranny of the morally self-righteous minority. For however noble the original intentions of Song and Ming Neo-Confucian thinkers, the promises made for their curricula of moral and intellectual cultivation had, he asserted, given the literati a wholly unjustified belief in their own infallibility.[10]

According to orthodox Neo-Confucian doctrine, the process of self-cultivation was defined as the purification of the physical nature (*qizhi zhi xing*), which was the locus of desire and evil; this would eventually result, theoretically, in the recovery of one's original purity. Hence, whatever emphasis was placed upon learning or education, the final goal of all such activities amounted to the retrieval of an original completeness or innate perfection. While attempting to remain faithful to the Mencian presumption of original goodness, Dai's theories of the moral nature may have been motivated primarily by the dissatisfaction he (and others) felt with the inadequacies and dangers inherent in Song and Ming Neo-Confucian doctrines of the mind, dangers which had manifested themselves over the course of history. For him, as for many Qing thinkers, humanity's distinguishing feature is not its innate qualities so much as a certain malleability and susceptibility to the influence of prevailing social mores. Hence, any theory of self-cultivation that emphasized a "return" to some lost innocence was to him fatally flawed.[11]

He therefore stressed the function of education as the accretion rather than the recovery of knowledge. The means by which the mind accepts and interiorizes knowledge is not, as Zhu Xi implied, a simple process of confirming one's observations of phenomena through the principles contained in the mind itself; instead, he argued, it should be accomplished through verification by observation of a number of analogous phenomena, all exterior to the self. Although Dai does not deny intuitive awareness or a subjective dimension of experience, he accuses past scholars of having focused on them at the expense of the development of discursive, rational thought. The domain of "feeling" or "intuition" (*jue*) is common to all animate beings, he observes, and in human society must therefore take second place to rational knowledge, which is "nourished" by the observation of external phenomena and indeed cannot exist without it. The contrast with Song scholars such as Zhu Xi could not be clearer, since they generally elevate the powers of "enlightened intuition" (*mingjue*) above all forms of knowledge based on experience of the external world (*wenjian zhi zhi*).[12]

Dai intersperses among such observations remarks more directly relevant to the conduct of technical scholarship. He argues above all for the separation of rational secular knowledge from other, more subjective aspects of human experience and decries the inadequacy of any overarching ethico-religious unity, such as immanent principle, to govern the conduct of scholarship or public affairs. Scholarship must, he thought, be founded instead on principles that can be formulated with clarity and exactitude and tested for their suitability in each particular field where they are to be applied. Dai considered any casual, unverified use of inductive principles not only anathema but the source of error and of social injustice. The only true test of any word or deed was thus its ability to fit the circumstances (*zhongjie*) and its freedom from error; and the means to achieve these aims were the elimination of subjective bias and prejudice (*yijian*), which tended to produce delusion and insensitivity toward the fluidity of change in objective reality. The great bane of Song Neo-Confucianism, that is, the deleterious effect it had had on the nation's political, social, and intellectual life, was directly attributable to its vaunting of the ethical superiority of the literati, for this had given the powerful a justification for imposing their own self-serving or erroneous judgments on the citizenry as a whole.

The achievement of objectively accurate knowledge thus becomes a rigorous and ultimately open-ended investigation of facts. For Dai, no point exists at which scholars can complete their knowledge of principle; there is no final certainty that can serve as a grid into which all data could be subsumed. Like Fang Yizhi, Li Zhi, and others before him, Dai attributes the attractiveness of Neo-Confucianism to humanity's natural tendency toward mental sloth and stasis. Qing thinkers tended to agree that immense difficulties lay in the way of a steadfast, unwavering devotion to thought, blocking all but a tiny minority from consistently and relentlessly using their mental endowments to their full capacity. Knowledge is a vast and uncertain terrain, on which mere mortals are prone to be influenced by one-sidedness or material interests. Even the most brilliant cannot be said to differ fundamentally from the common man, for "in this world, the intelligent are few, and the stupid numerous. Because the few are more intelligent than the majority, they are lauded by all as wise. But they are still quite a distance from the sages."[13]

Hence, in spite of his seeming elitism Dai insists on the essential commonality of humankind. The various dualistic ideals that characterize Neo-Confucian ethical theory, namely, the moral versus the physical natures, the public or heavenly principle as opposed to human desires, and so forth, establish a very compelling justification for social inequalities and for an absolute distinction between literati and their social inferiors. Nearly every aspect of Dai's thought in one way or another denies or impugns the validity of these constructions, which he accuses of creating a complacency among an elite accustomed to regarding its prerogatives as fully sanctioned by Confucian doctrine. Dai insists that the sages did not create absolute distinctions between people; thus, hierarchically arranged social categories find their justification not in moral absolutes but quite simply in social convention. The scholar, he implies, cannot gain social prestige through the intuitive understanding of moral principles whose validity can never be tested. Instead, his position as the leader of his community rests on his intellectual mastery of disciplines established by convention or precedent as the criteria for the selection of officials and on his ability to use his rational capacities in socially effective and meaningful ways. Thus categories of ethical intention, though hardly irrelevant to personal morality, must be considered secondary to the acquirement of intellectual skills, since it is the latter that exert the greatest impact on society: "If people with the proper motivation act on it, their actions may be erroneous if they have not studied sufficiently. This is a failure of knowledge. Even if their minds contain nothing but loyalty, trust, and compassion, they will still cause much harm to the Way."[14]

Scholars are thus ultimately defined not by their innate moral qualities but rather by their role as the guardians, preservers, and manipulators of cultural forms: "Ritual is meant to correct parsimony and meanness, to bring about the transformation of life into culture."[15] It can be said of Qing culture in general that it was characterized by an intense interest in the refinement and sophistication of form, in ritual, in letters, and in a broad range of human endeavor. The Confucian dictum "The unadorned word travels not far"[16] was repeated again and again as the justification for an attention to minutiae and to the surface or formal appearance of all things. Hence, for Dai and many others the "substance" (zhi) of culture seemed ultimately irrelevant or even distasteful if it could not be brought to successful, correct, or coherent expression. They looked generally with scorn on what they saw as the rudeness of late Ming philosophy and literature, which they accused of a misguided search for inner spirit and scant regard for detail. Indeed, virtue came to imply not only the motivation or intention of an action but the manner in which it was executed, its style, so to speak.

Dai's intellectual and moral order thus inclined toward the secularization of the scholars' role in society, denying them the absolute moral authority granted them by the state-supported Neo-Confucian orthodoxy. By advocating the exercise of discursive powers of analysis and judgment over empirical disciplines of knowledge, he implies that only through intellectual effort should scholars attain any preeminence among their fellows. As Yu Ying-shih has said, Qing scholars admired the ability both to achieve "wide learning" and to use such learning in original and insightful ways. Among Qing scholars Dai perhaps best exemplified both erudition as well as brilliant originality in the critical study of texts. But he too warns against believing that such knowledge is equivalent to the possession of immutable truth. In *Mengzi ziyi shuzheng* he castigates the folly of believing any single intellectual position to be unassailable as the primary source of error in thought, action, and government. Such intellectual arrogance had plagued many men, he says, by giving them a false sense of omniscience and certitude divorced from the world of concrete reality. Individual scholars can never attain any unifying vision, he warns, beyond the realm of observable phenomena; they must therefore seek from the infinite field of knowledge facts that contribute to their powers of discernment and prevent them at the same time from imposing any preconceived notions on the world.[17]

Dai often reiterated his desire to go beyond the study of phonology, texts, and institutions—the objects of philological research—to find the underlying, immutable Way, and in his statements relating the disciplines of philosophy, philology, and literature he expresses in several places a preference for the first. But in his *Mengzi ziyi shuzheng* he interprets "philosophy" (*yili*) not as the search for immutable truth but rather as the intellectual attainments for which he strove. *Yili* is there defined as the honing of the powers of rational discrimination: *li* "refers to the mind's power to make distinctions"; *yi* "means the mind's power of judgment."[18] Ultimately, then, what he refers to generally as meaning or truth comes to signify, within the human subject, the mental powers that are to be exercised, not on any transcendent reality, but on what he elsewhere terms the bearers (*jiaofu*) of truth, namely, the vessels of philology and literature. "Literature, philology, and philosophy each have their own source," he is quoted as having said near the end of his life.[19] Literary form, names, and institutions were, in the last analysis, independent realms of endeavor, with their own characters and requirements not assimilable to philosophical truth. Hence, they must be dealt with, Dai implies here, as representing different but perhaps essentially equal aspects of the total body of culture, or *wen*.

Letters

In one sense Dai Zhen's elevation of literature (or strictly speaking, literary composition) to a certain parity with scholarship seems out of character for a thinker who places such a high value on the rational aspects of the human mind and who indeed exhibits a certain scorn for literary creation.[20] Yet this sympathy for the perfection of literary form can perhaps be reconciled with his thought as a whole in light of his appreciation for formal coherence and felicity of expression. In Qing writings across the ideological spectrum (to include the so-called Song learning scholars), the Neo-Confucian prejudice against art and literature seemed hopelessly pedantic and a symptom of the lack of attention to formal sophistication which had produced the notorious "recorded sayings" (*yulu*).[21]

This uniformly high estimation of the worth of culture (*wen*) in its broadest sense was to have important repercussions for the status of the literary arts. Most obviously, literature shared with classical texts the medium of language, which Dai Zhen and others had made the focus of their philological studies. We may lack clear and unequivocal evidence that the theoretical status of literature changed in any important sense during the eighteenth century. But the marked contrast in the nature of literary production and in literary theory between the Ming and Qing suggests some fundamental changes in attitudes toward literature. We know, for example, that most poets and essayists of the Qing were very much influenced by the broad trend in scholarship toward increasing erudition and philological exegesis and reacted against the alleged vacuity and carelessness (*kongshu*) of late Ming literature.[22] Late Ming literary movements such as the Fushe in fact came to symbolize the tragic deficiencies of Ming cultural life, and the names of luminaries such as Chen Jiru (1558–1639) became almost synonymous with what was seen as the depraved practice of literary dilettantism. From a modern perspective, Guo Shaoyu agrees with this estimation of the Ming literary scene and identifies the stereotyped *qingke* or literary guest, of whom Chen was perhaps the most notorious, as the representative figure of that era. As Guo Shaoyu puts it, "Literary men of the Ming for the most part reveled in their own elegant and romantic pursuits. They focused their efforts on literary and artistic discussion, not on scholarly research. They generally fit the image of the literary guest, rather than that of the scholar. This is one area where the intellectual climate of the Ming and Qing periods differed radically."[23]

This observation suggests that Qing literary artists, unlike their Ming predecessors, felt a certain affinity with the scholarly world; and certainly Dai Zhen's comments on the place of literary expression confirm such a view. Literary form came, in fact, to be championed by a number of Qing scholars as well as literary figures as a vessel for the expression of the ineffable Way, the vehicle for rather than a hindrance to intellectual or spiritual endeavors.[24] Hence, hedonistic or opportunistic dilettantism among literary men and women was condemned for its abuse of what was once again seen by a wide range of thinkers as more than mere embellishment. This reasserting of the primacy of "culture" in itself was hardly revolutionary, but it certainly reversed the Neo-Confucian trend toward the denigration of cultural sophistication. What set Qing literary discourse apart from that of earlier eras was its recognition that literary form possessed features that could not be subsumed under any transcendent categories, in effect providing theoretical justification for the independent pursuit of literary ends alone.

Yuan Mei (1716–98), for example, perhaps the most successful and widely known of the literary professionals of his time, defended a professionalized practice of literary endeavors as valid in and of itself, contributing in a very tangible sense to the sum total of cultural and political achievement of a given time:

> It is said that meritorious deeds repay [one's debt to] the nation. But letters can also [be the means to] serve the country. Moreover, literary composition is especially difficult.... What I have called serving the nation through literature need not consist in merely faithfully adhering to classical precedent or putting great effort into praise and flattery. Rather, one should give [one's works] expansive beauty and clarity of argument so that they stand out among literature both past and present. Then people will say that the literature of a certain period had a Mr. So-and-so. That will not necessarily detract from the nation's luster.[25]

One might argue of course that Yuan, whose bohemian tastes raised some eyebrows, and elicited not a few condemnations, from his contemporaries, had to come to the defense of literature precisely because it was still suspected of lacking moral seriousness. What is remarkable about this passage, however, is its suggestion that literary production could be engaged in as a career equal in significance to bureaucratic appointment (the career Yuan chose to abandon in his thirties), requiring a steadfast devotion to literary arts divorced from other pursuits. He implies that literary men could be evaluated solely on the basis of their literary attainments.

As Guo Shaoyu's remarks suggest, literary discourse of the seventeenth and eighteenth centuries experienced a transformation exhibiting numerous parallels to developments in scholarship. The advocacy of a return to the study of texts, particularly the classics, as an antidote to the crudity of late Ming literature by Zhu Yizun, Qian Qianyi, and other early and mid-Qing poets, seems to have set the tone for subsequent developments in writings on poetry. Rational powers of discernment, erudition, and aesthetic judgment were widely recommended as the only sure way to find the proper and fitting expression in a literary work. In reaction to late Ming literary theories, the search for a mode or style that brought one's expression into direct contact with a transcendent reality was in many cases repudiated. Instead, aspects of literary creation more directly accessible to description—what might now be subsumed under the rubric of style—were favored as the primary criteria for the judgment of any work, and their refinement was viewed as the vehicle for literary attainment. With regard to the problem under consideration here, namely, the perception of the literary creator, and his (or in this era, increasingly, her) relation to the work, one development is particularly noteworthy. Literary creation came to be regarded as first and foremost the product of an individual and historically particular creator. Hence, the role of the unique personality came to be a major focus of theorists, in both poetry and prose.

The emergence of new definitions of the relationship between artists and their work meant that the literary artist was given new responsibilities by theorists attempting to describe, and prescribe, the means for producing successful literature. In place of vague references to cosmic principles to be incorporated into a literary work, theorists began to identify the literary creator as an autonomous and self-conscious agent, possessing the power to choose freely among existing literary forms, instead of being possessed by transcendental forces. Whether or not a literary critic chose to articulate the role of the creative agent, few seem to have been immune from the tendency toward increasing sophistication in the description of formal and stylistic features, centered on the language and style of the text. This appreciation for problems of style, and the rejection of the Song and Ming theory of enlightenment as irrelevant to poetic theory, seems to have contributed to a certain revaluation of the canons of literary taste championed by Song and Ming literary theorists. Indeed, during much of the Qing, standards of taste experienced a pluralization largely unprecedented in recent literary history. Hence, it hardly seems coincidental that the literary artist was exhorted to perfect his mastery of craftsmanship as a prerequisite to composition.

Literature was celebrated by Yao Nai (1732–1815), for example, as a domain that provided its practitioners with unparalleled opportunities for the achievement of sublime expression, and even a resonance with cosmic rhythms; and yet this same figure emphasized its fundamental properties as those of an art (*yi*) or even a skill (*ji*) exhibiting features subject to description and analysis. As with scholars working on the textual analysis of the classics, meaning was to be inferred through the medium of language and was indistinguishable from its vessel. These ideas can be said to herald the birth of an aesthetic based first and foremost on formal principles, for which literature stands as an independent mode of cultural expression with its own rules and requirements. Theories of literary creation granting an autonomous position for literature as a discrete domain of activity thus tended toward the historicization, and objectification, of the literary act and its executor. It was argued that the writer must choose consciously, and discerningly, between existing possibilities or models. The term inspiration (*shenqi*), for example, important to earlier literary criticism, continues to serve as a key term for Qing theorists. But its meaning is transformed from the sort of transpersonal animating force it seems to mean in earlier writings to the individual's own creative personality mediated, modified, and fashioned by its conscious employment in art. Eighteenth-century criticism and theory in particular placed an unprecedented responsibility on the individual artist.

Though not fully representative of the trends outlined above, Ye Xie's (1639–1707) *Yuan shi* nonetheless articulates a theory of poetry both remarkably comprehensive in scope and logically consistent; and though apparently rather obscure during his own lifetime, Ye undoubtedly gained notoriety through prominent disciples such as the poet and anthologist Shen Deqian (1673–1769).[26] Furthermore, Ye's work is valuable to this investigation for its clear and coherent delineation of the capacities, both innate and acquired, which it deems essential to successful poetic composition. In particular, Ye argues more cogently than perhaps any other theorist of his time that knowledge and learning must be reaffirmed as central to poetic creation.[27]

Thus developments in early Qing literary theory closely mirrored those in scholarship in their reaction to the more extreme tendencies of late Ming literature. There was an almost universal tendency to stress learning, and the study of texts of all kinds, but especially the classics, to counter the deleterious influence of the late Ming doctrine of spontaneity. Ye Xie should certainly be included among the many proponents of book learning; but he takes it further than most in singling out intelligence and discernment as crucial attributes separating the good poet from the common herd:

> These four [talent, daring, knowledge, and strength] cannot be said to have an order of priority, but nevertheless the crux of the problem is to possess knowledge first. Without knowledge, the other three have nothing to rely on.... If knowledge and discrimination are not keen, then one has not the means to wield the pen. People simply rely on the single word "imitation" [*fa*], under which they subsume everything. But these rules are like the laws of the nation, which are [merely intended to] serve as a warning to the ignorant to prevent them from engaging in their follies.[28]

It would perhaps be wrong to equate the knowledge and understanding spoken of by Ye Xie with the more rational powers of cognition lauded in the philosophical works of Dai Zhen, for despite his intellectualist persuasion Ye probably did not wish to completely abolish the affective qualities of poetry. Still, however, it is worth noting that Ye's rationalist, intellectually inclined view of poetry brings him to conclusions strikingly similar to Dai's positions concerning the role of the individual—namely, as a historically delimited and finite being. In spite of their differences, literary creation and scholarly research shared the problem of defining the relation of individuals, as poets or scholars, to their literary or textual traditions.

While generalizations can hardly do justice to the diversity and complexity of Ming literary views, Ming literary theoretists and writers can be broadly distinguished according to whether they advocated an acceptance, or a rejection, of past literary models. From a Qing vantage point, Ming literary theory suffered from an inability to explain satisfactorily the relation of writers to their literary heritage, a dilemma stemming at least in part from the deficiencies in their epistemological views. Ming theorists were accused of laboring under a simplistic conception of enlightenment, one that did not pay adequate attention to the power of the poetic consciousness to ferret out, select, and assimilate past models. Hence, issues of literary evaluation came to be formulated on the basis of a predetermined hierarchy, or canon of taste, which in the view of many Qing theorists was often both narrow and arbitrary.

The explanatory power of Ye Xie's emphasis on the rational faculties lay in its ability to pose more satisfactorily than earlier the question of the poet's relationship to his or her literary heritage, as well as to the technical problems of form and diction. The faculties of judgment and rationality provide the means to confront the past, so to speak, obviating the need either to adopt any particular past models as the object of imitation or to reject them in favor of subjective inspiration. They are what enable poets to exercise discrimination over their literary past, choosing according to their needs, while remaining the masters of formal rules rather than their slaves. As Ye put it, "Men of letters only manipulate the rules by exercising their talent; they should never follow them in such a way that they become slaves of rules, all the while boasting of their talents."

For Ye Xie, the intellect served as a sort of guarantee of the expression of individuality and became the means for the establishment of the poet's unique voice: "Men should not follow in the steps of their contemporaries, nor should they follow behind the ancients. . . . The creation of meaning and choice of words all flow from the intelligence."[29] According to Guo Shaoyu, Qing literary theorists were generally fascinated by the problem of originality, and the problem of how to achieve it through the intelligent use of past models—in other words, of how to establish independence from literary predecessors.[30] It was their concern for the reconciliation between, and transcendence of, the various canons that led many to deny the absolute validity of any hierarchy of poetic styles or periods. Ye's belief that poetic invention derives from the intelligence serves an important function in this regard. For by asserting that the powers of the mind are limitless, he provides theoretical justification for his belief that no one mode or period of poetry can claim superiority over other periods and forms:

> All things follow one upon another, adding to the beauty and glory of predecessors, and evolving gradually to their fullest flower. Human wisdom and intelligence were first tapped by the ancients and gradually revealed but hardly exhausted by them. They received the more refined ef-

forts of later men, who used and revealed them to an increasing degree. As long as heaven and earth do not come to a standstill, then human intelligence and wisdom will never be exhausted.[31]

He implies here that no single period or style can claim to have achieved perfection, a status which many accorded to the High Tang, for example, or to Song poetry. Such standards are mistaken, he says, because poetry is the product of its particular place within the evolutionary process of the unfolding of culture, a process that is in no sense circumscribed. Poetry should not, in fact, be viewed or interpreted outside its own historical context and often cannot be fully appreciated without an understanding of its position in the historical evolution of poetic forms.[32]

Thus the lack of a hierarchy of styles means that imitation cannot be considered essential to the study and mastery of the modes of expression. In poetic composition, the decisive role is played by the creative powers of the individual consciousness, which imbue the work with a clearly recognizable personal imprint, what Ye Xie calls the "face of the poet" (*shiren zhi mianmu*).[33] He draws an analogy to the performance of a popular song, where a perfect mastery of formal requirements may still lack a crucial "substance" (*zhi*) to endow it with lyric expressiveness: "The singer must give it voice in his throat and expel it through his mouth. Only then will its lilting melody echo through the rafters, and its tones halt the clouds with their beauty."[34] Like Dai Zhen's interpretation of the individual's relation to ritual, formal rules (*fa*) should ultimately be wrought into the exteriorization of the poet's luminous intelligence: "Rules are the manifestations of the intelligence, which finds the proper expression in every encounter.... They are the standards of judgment based on conformity with reason, with the facts and with the emotions. They do not come into existence on their own."[35] Rather than incorporate a given set of rules into his or her lyrical consciousness, the poet must assemble his or her own set of rules, according to his or her own personal, even idiosyncratic, needs.

The concerns expressed by Ye Xie about these aspects of poetic creation were all to varying extents echoed by subsequent critics. In particular, the interest shown in the individual poet's presence in the poem, and in originality, seems to have evolved directly into a new trend toward the appreciation of both the distinctively personal, and autobiographical, on the one hand, and the original or innovative use of poetic form, on the other. Some eighteenth-century poets even looked on their work as a form of autobiography, recording the events of their lives in increasingly careful detail.[36] Novelty and originality were also lauded as aims to strive for. Zhao Yi (1727–1814), for example, remarked in old age that the poems of his youth had grown dated, and that even Du Fu and Li Bai could not be read with as much enthusiasm after repeated readings as when they had been fresh to his young mind. He claimed that he sought in his own poetry to convey the spirit of his own era (*shiyun*) in words that would not merely echo the past but would be "something never said before" (*wei jing ren shuo guo*). Generally speaking, then, there was a tendency toward the historicization of poetic theory and criticism in the Qing, of which Ye Xie's work is representative.[37]

Ye Xie's theory of poetry is largely directed against the tradition that began with the *Canglang shihua* and reached its culmination in the late Ming, namely, that an intuitive enlightenment, the so-called *diyi yi zhi wu*, was the source of poetic inspiration. We have seen that though he denigrates the poets who rely excessively on rules or formal imitation, Ye does not deny any function whatsoever to the use of models. Poetry is a complex and difficult art,[38] and its practice demands all of the powers of the imagination (*shenming*) to be produced successfully; the poet cannot hope to produce great poetry either through mere mastery of the tradition, or the creation of novelty alone.[39] But it is precisely this richness of possibilities and capacity for creativity that makes it possible for poetry to be explored anew in each era; it is an eminently unpredictable terrain, where new potentialities come into existence as history unfolds.

This uncertainty and indeterminacy are in striking contrast to poetic theories that attempt to provide a secure framework for the poet, whether in rules or in the exercise of spontaneity. Rules believed to embody the essence of poetic beauty are, Ye says, devoid of the sanctity attributed to them by their adherents. They have been exalted for a transcendent power that exists only in the imagination. For poetic beauty does not lie beyond the realm of the (five) senses: "The singularity and uniqueness of beautiful [poetry]—does this not have rules? This is only the ordinary workings of the ears, eyes, mouth, and nose, which are illuminated [by the intelligence]. Can we speak of an intelligent rule?"[40]

Likewise, in the field of prose as well Qing theorists reacted to some extent against what they saw as an oversimplified adherence to ready-made formal technique. Zhang Xuecheng, for example, criticized the attempts by theorists of archaic prose styles of the Qin and Han, as well as by the essayists of the so-called Tang and Song prose style, to codify any set of rules. Not only did they tend to be arbitrary, he said, but they simply were not as easy to deduce from their sources as commonly believed.[41] Unlike poetic theory, however, which even in the Qing still tended to place inspiration largely outside the sphere of discursive thought, prose in general suffered more directly from the Neo-Confucian disdain for literature. In the oft-quoted words of Liu Zongyuan, prose was held to be the *zhushuzhe liu,* or the genre for the expression of (moral) content, and thus antithetical to belletristic concern for problems of form and style. But as in poetic theory, the particular achievement of eighteenth-century prose critics was to articulate problems of formal technique at new levels of sophistication. Prose came to be regarded as possessing unique aesthetic properties and requirements, which complement, and do not merely serve as the inferior accessories of, their moral import. This was particularly true for the theorists of the so-called Tongcheng school of prose, who (to our eyes somewhat ironically) championed the cause of literature under the banner of a revived Neo-Confucianism.

Liu Dakui (1697–1779), for example, saw the key to prose composition in its "rhythm" (*yinjie*) and the achievement of an almost musical euphony. He relegates the role of "content" (*shi*) in literature to that of mere "bricks and mortar," to be shaped into artistic form by a master craftsman:

> The principles found in writing are the facts of government and other works already in existence, the stuff of writing. As for the act of writing, that is naturally another matter altogether. For example, a great carpenter wielding his ax may possess marvelous skill, but without mud, lumber, and materials, where can he exercise it? There are many people who possess the materials, on the other hand, but lack the facility to use them well. They cannot be said to be great carpenters. Thus the man of letters is a great carpenter. Meaning, other works, and government, these are the materials of the carpenter.[42]

Among the Tongcheng essayists, Yao Nai (1732–1815) most lucidly enunciated the fundamental distinction between art (*ji*) and morality or meaning (*dao*). In fact, he could be considered as one of the few Chinese thinkers whose doctrines approach the formulation of an independent discipline of aesthetics: "The Way has distinctions of right and wrong, while the arts have those of beauty and ugliness. Poetry and prose are both arts. The subtle and finer of the arts approach the Way, and thus beautiful poetry and prose must be virtuous in their conception."[43] Like Ye Xie and other poetry critics, Yao also saw the value of a work less in the expression of any transcendent values, than in the creation of an individual voice through the medium of language:

> Written characters are like the words spoken by men. If they are animated by the spirit [of the author] their beauty can be seen. Even after one hundred generations the reader feels as if he were conversing with the author. Without this spirit, they are merely characters piled up together. The intention and the spirit combine together to form words. Only then does one have differences in tone, and rhythm, and variation through advancing and retreating.[44]

And just as in poetry, Yao and his fellow critics emphasized the writer's reliance on his or her powers of discernment and the ability to choose from the stylistic alternatives available for the composition of great prose.

The effect of these statements was to establish the theoretical justification for the pursuit of literary excellence on its own merit, without relegating it to inferior status beneath some ethico-religious cultivation of the Way. Literature was not divorced from other concerns of the literatus, as the debates on the unity of philosophy, philology, and literature make plain. Yet in their attempts to integrate what had come to be identified as distinct areas of endeavor, theorists in effect were recognizing the autonomy of the literary fact and its reliance on formal, linguistic criteria for evaluation. The slogan "The Way and literary art merge together" (*dao yu yi he*)[45] placed the arts on an equal footing with "truth."

In the light of the theoretical emancipation of literature from the shackles of theory influenced by Neo-Confucianism, then, Yuan Mei's seemingly unorthodox decision to devote himself to literature reflected the degree to which letters, like scholarship, had come to be regarded as an independent vocation no longer scorned for its formal qualities, or for its alleged neglect of moral cultivation. Rather than seek to link up with some extraliterary realm of truth, the artist was instead urged to find the proper expression for his or her own individuality—that is, the forms or words by which to give voice to a uniquely personal experience.

As a consequence, however, artists, like scholars, were perhaps more than at any other time dependent on their own resources, their own special endowments, which they had to foster and develop. No single "enlightenment" or mastery of any specific style can serve the artist indefinitely, these theorists imply, for literature is, like the mind, inexhaustible, and thus demands unending effort and refinement. To believe the contrary is the refuge of the lazy and untalented, who refuse to fully develop their own possibilities and fail to recognize the basis of all literature in the inexhaustible medium of form.[46] Just as Dai Zhen, Yan Yuan, and many others stressed the importance of the gradual accumulation of knowledge, so did poets and essayists place a new emphasis on pedagogical techniques and the gradual acquisition of literary skill. For as Yuan Mei put it,

> Bells and drums are not music, but if one casts them aside what will be used to create sound? Yiya was skilled in the culinary arts, but he had to begin by preparing dainty dishes using the hundred varieties of livestock [rather than beginning with rare and exotic ingredients]. If one does not start with the coarse, how can he come to the refined? I say, "without study," one will never find one's proper voice.[47]

In letters, as in scholarship, no shortcut can bring the practitioner into direct contact with truth; the expression is mediated through the forms of language and depends on the author's thorough mastery of its forms.[48]

Painting

When Yao Nai and others spoke of the arts (*yi*), more often than not they were referring only to the literary ones, that is, to prose and poetry. As we have already seen, however, the term *yi* was a crucial one for Qing thinkers concerned with defining the scope of activities appropriate to literati cultivation. Though it could be narrowly confined to classical exegesis and literary pursuits, art nevertheless implied a certain mundane attention to craft or skill, especially since in general usage it was taken to refer to the arts not generally thought of as possessing any particular pretentions to sublimity—in other words, those beyond the pale of high culture. However, the fact that some of the leading scholars of the Huizhou school of evidential scholarship were former or practicing artisans, whose scholarly treatises on pre-Qing musical instruments, dress, and archaeological finds seem to have been influenced by, and benefited from, their expertise in the arts in which they had received training, suggests that non-literati, commercially based arts had some impact on the interpretations of this term.[49] More typically, however, arts cultivated by literati were confined to the gentle arts of music, painting, calligraphy, and various leisurely games such as chess and *go*. Among these, painting and calligraphy were considered particularly worthy of serious practice, as an integral aspect of the literati's program of self-cultivation. As a result of the interest they generated, as well as their affinities with literary arts, they became the subject of a body of critical and theoretical discourse of significant proportions and sophistication.

Painting presented both special difficulties and special opportunities to its theorists, since as an occupation it was, unlike either scholarship or literature, more or less open to members of society possessing relatively minimal education in literary fields. Where theories of literature or ethical philosophy could avoid confronting social distinctions directly, theoreticians of the arts were faced with the task of establishing the criteria by which literati art could be distinguished from the products of groups clearly outside their domain.[50]

Just as literary theories of the time stressed intuitive mastery or enlightenment and the transcendence of concern with the mundane details of style, late Ming theories of painting advocated penetration to a domain wholly beyond form. Dong Qichang (1555–1636), who along with Chen Jiru and a few other painters articulated the ideals of literati painting most fully, was in fact well acquainted with the leading ideas of late Ming literary circles such as the Gongan school; certainly his own ideas exhibit an abundance of parallels to those of the Yuan brothers. He did not originate the distinction between the literati and the professional arts, which dates from at least the Song. But by broadening what had "originally been a social classification into an identifiable artistic tradition,"[51] with its aesthetics modeled closely on a Neo-Confucian dualistic metaphysics, he and others developed an artistic identity mirroring in aesthetic terms the Neo-Confucian definition of the literatus.

In many ways, this vaunting of the "literati ideal" (*shiqi*) was even more constricting and rigidly prescribed than that of the Neo-Confucian orthodoxy. For it had practical, stylistic, and social dimensions that all found their definition in a contrast with the professionals, namely court painters and plebeian artists. The ideals enunciated by Dong exerted an almost hegemonic influence over his successors, both in the theory and practice of painting, constituting an orthodoxy closely analogous in this respect to the doctrines of Zhu Xi. But in contrast to the philosophical and literary figures who attempted to discredit Song and Ming doctrines, the literati ideal as formulated by Dong seems to have met with few significant challenges. Nevertheless, the sporadic attacks made upon this ideal by eighteenth-century painters probed in what were sometimes revolutionary ways the implications of Neo-Confucian ethical dualism in the aesthetic expression given them by Dong and others.

Zheng Xie (1693–1765), of the "Yangzhou eccentric" school, was such a painter. His critical remarks on poetry, art, and other subjects are of signal importance for their perceptive criticism of the literatus's role as painter, scholar, and bureaucrat. He, perhaps more than any other eighteenth-century artist, gave expression to a wide-ranging repudiation of the literati amateur ideal, which included within its scope the reexamination of a number of beliefs that had justified the privileging of this ideal. On the level of painting style, he and the other eccentrics of Yangzhou can be considered heirs to the literati school of painting as it had evolved in the late Ming and early Qing expressionist works of Shi Tao, Bada Shanren, and others.[52] But in terms of discourse, he unreservedly challenged the aesthetic canon established and defended by the orthodox critics Dong Qichang, the Four Wangs, and their successors.

The orthodoxy as defined by its adherents stressed the transcendence of formal criteria as the goal toward which true, that is to say literati, art should strive. As Dong Qichang put it, "If you can extricate yourself from the constraints of rules, then you are [like a] fish escaped from the net."[53] Any technique that could be explicitly formulated was to be regarded warily, as a trap to be cast off at the earliest possible moment in favor of naturalness. In essence, the only motivation for seriously studying technique was in order to fend off potential criticism from professional painters: "In case those disguising their shortcomings take refuge among [literati painters], literati should bring their proficiency and skill to a high level, and learn from, and befriend, the myriad things. . . . This will be sufficient to silence the professional painters."[54]

Based on these criteria, then, painters could be described using two categories: the vulgar (*su*) and the elegant (*ya*). The former was tied to the mundane world of work and labor, that is, the practice of selling one's paintings to make a living and restricting one's style to representation. The latter, on the other hand, belonged to the realm of "play": "to use painting as a means of enjoyment" (*yi hua wei le*), and was defined by a subtle, spare style reflecting the painter's withdrawal from the world of form. According to Yang Xin, the works of the Yangzhou painters such as Zheng Xie represent a transcendence of this dualistic view of painting. In "the content and form of their works of calligraphy and painting, they broke through the standards of the vulgar and refined, which were the hallmarks of the literati tradition."[55] In particular, the writing of Zheng Xie aimed directly at the various theoretical tenets by which this aesthetic was justified.[56] Perhaps more than any other thinker of the eighteenth century, he comes closest to a complete repudiation of the Neo-Confucian ideological underpinnings of literati social and cultural dominance.

For a literati painting, the true test of its quality was not its formal execution but its unstated meaning, often expressed as *yanwai zhi yi*, or the "meaning beyond words." This highly prized ability to imbue art with an ineffable content eluded mere study or learning. As Wang Yuanqi (1642–1715) put it, "One has no intention at all of striving for skill or novelty; dexterity radiates from beyond the brush and ink."[57] Through an intuitive understanding comparable to the sudden enlightenment of Huineng, the Sixth Patriarch of Zen, Dong Qichang urged painters to go beyond mere technical mastery of brush and ink, to the realm of sublimity. This enlightenment was, nevertheless, embodied in certain styles, namely the "spare" (*gudan*) style of calligraphically oriented brushstrokes, and the use of "scattered ink" or *pomo*. But in order to excel in literati painting one had primarily to forget simple craftsmanship, and to adopt a mode of quietude.

Zheng Xie railed against the literati aesthetic for its inactivity, which he saw as equivalent to condoning indolence, and for its creation of the myth of a superior literatus, who could achieve some totalizing, final artistic vision of infinitude. Such an ideology was, he declared, inimical to true artistic creation. For the intuitive approach to the study of painting had become, Zheng thought, just what Dong Qichang had in a moment of caution warned against, that is, the refuge of the lazy and untalented. It encouraged artists to avoid exerting themselves in the study of technique. As a result, painters had neglected the basics of painting.

> People nowadays paint stones and branches in heavy tones, and make the leaves large, so that there is hardly a break between them. Adding on water, there is as a result no interaction or balance between snow and bamboo. What sort of painting is this? Such matters only require a modicum of skill in technique. If painters are unwilling to exert themselves even here, then how can they expect to reach the subtleties of painting? If you ask them, they will tell you, "We express our ideas, and don't let such things trouble us." I can't believe how much painting has been ruined by the ... words 'expressing one's ideas.' People who deceive both themselves and others, and never seek to improve themselves, all suffer from this fault. One must

master technique before one can express ideas. It's not true that those who have no technique can express their ideas.[58]

Craftsmanship is the basis on which impressionism must be founded, Zheng asserts, and though he does not deny the validity of the genre, he deplores its influence on painting as a whole.

Yi, translated as "mind," or "ideas," meant perhaps to Zheng something very much like Dai Zhen's "preconceived ideas" (*yijian*). In contrast to the famous bamboo painters of the past, Zheng does not form a mental image of bamboo before he paints it: "When Wen Tong (Yuke) painted bamboo, he visualized the painting in his breast beforehand. When Zheng Banqiao paints bamboo, his breast contains no predetermined image. Light and dark, space and painted areas, long and short, fat and thin, I draw as my hand directs me, and let it form its own composition, as if by itself."[59] It is the imposition of preconceived ideas and notions that he seems to be warning against: "When Shi Tao painted bamboo he liked to 'fight in the wilds,' as if without any organization or discipline; but the discipline is contained within."[60] Form and order exist within the painting itself, without the rather self-conscious or even pretentious act of expressing one's mind.

Painting should not simply serve to enshrine the image of the literatus, the gentleman, over lesser men. The neglect of the lower functions had been epitomized by the paintings in which thistles had been placed beneath orchids, to symbolize the greater man's tolerance for the lesser man. Thistles should not be regarded as the dispensable and undesirable elements of life, for, they serve the irreplaceable function of protecting the tender orchid from danger in the form of herbivorous animals. Hence, Zheng includes many thistles, he says, to show the importance of such men.[61]

Throughout his written works Zheng Xie returns again and again to the theme of the injustice of the social hierarchy and the ignominious role the literati play in it. Their cultivation of "uselessness" had brought them to the sorry state of a merely parasitic existence in society, dependent on the productivity of farmers and other laborers. He thus berates the patriarchs of literati painting Wang Wei and Zhao Mengfu for their neglect of social concerns: "People like Wang Mojie and Zhao Zi'ang are no more than a couple of professional artists of the Tang and Song! Looking over their collections of poetry and prose, can we find one word that touched upon the sufferings of the common people?"[62] To Zheng, the literati have been granted a privileged status for the role they play in government. If they do not fulfill this role, but instead merely seek self-indulgent pleasure, then they have lost all claim to the respect of society at large. Idle pursuit of culture is especially despicable, he says, not because culture itself is morally empty, but because its adherents claim an exalted status unjustified by their true value to the physical and intellectual well-being of their society.

In his writings and paintings, then, Zheng Xie was clearly attempting to go beyond an aesthetic that had narrowly defined all artistic possibilities in terms of an opposition of the vulgar and the refined and exalted the literatus as the wellspring of taste. His mocking attitude toward accepted conventions, his unabashed pursuit of material gain,[63] and even the colloquial style of his poetry and prose all bear the imprint of this urge toward the mixing of the high and low and a disregard for elite sensitivies. The attack on the literati seemed perhaps a mark of eccentricity to many of his contemporaries, but as Vicki Weinstein, Yu Jianhua, and others have noted,[64] simplistic formulas of bohemianism in Yangzhou must be qualified by a recognition of the often staid traditionalism and a marked archaism that pervaded the works of painters associated with this school. Zheng Xie's letters to his cousin Mo and his poetry, though often full of a certain bitter derision toward literati foibles, nonetheless give ample testimony to an abiding faith in the adherence to social convention. It is the hypocrisy and fatuity of those who seek to transcend social norms, professing to live under their own idiosyncratic rules, who come under his most virulent attacks.[65]

It seems significant, then, that the famous seventeen letters addressed to Zheng's younger cousin Mo end on the praise of that ambiguous symbol of literati engagement, the examination essay. Zheng argues that the propensity of the literati to disdain and neglect the arts had in fact led them to scorn the very means by which they achieved their coveted aim of prestige in government service. His own appreciation for the value of pure form was perhaps an important element behind his evaluation of the essay as the apex of literary forms in his own time, and his affirmation of its usefulness as a measure by which to choose men through the examination system.

> During the Ming and Qing dynasties, the examination essay has been used to select men for office. You may have unusual abilities or talents, but you must still rise this way, on the standard route. The more its principles are explored, the keener and sharper they become. The harder its rules are sought, the denser and more complex they become. Spurring one's mental powers to their utmost subtlety, talent and learning cannot be relied upon,

for in the snap of a finger one might fumble. Those who lack concentration and discipline place themselves outside the examinations, saying "I am an adherent of ancient learning."[66]

Here, then, the targets of Zheng's barbs are those who cannot or will not master the essay form and disguise their shortcomings through pretentious claims to a higher authority.

Yet although he insists that the literati take their duties seriously, both in essay composition and in more practical endeavors, Zheng does not advocate a return to a Neo-Confucian preoccupation with ethical concerns. In a discussion of the relative merits of the legendary sages Yao and Shun, Zheng attempts to explain why Confucius reserved his greatest praise for the former. It was, he said, for the simple reason that Yao did not try to accomplish everything within his power. His greatness is analogous to that of heaven, which preserves all things regardless of merit. Yao's accomplishments thus overshadow those of Shun, which are in contrast only the work of a great man: "The praise of virtue and censure of evil is the way of man. That which contains good and evil at every point is the way of heaven. Yao, oh Yao, that is why you are the equal of heaven!"[67] From an aesthetic perspective, ethical dualisms that privilege any one aspect over another deny the fullness and rich diversity of life: "[Even] sages can be guilty of trying to accomplish too much. But what matter can be exhausted? If one leaves one part undone, that is one portion saved [for the future]. This is truly the Way of heaven."[68] The fluidity, indeterminacy, and incompleteness of the world, and of human activities within it, should not be loathed but cherished.

This is in striking contrast to the almost obsessive concern of critics representative of orthodox views with the elimination of the vulgar, which was equated with impurity, and the achievement of a singularity and totality of vision. As Yun Shouping (1633–90) put it, "Painters sweep away the traces of mortal dust, leaving only a desolate and austere loneliness."[69] Such subtlety and brevity of expression had erred, Zheng Xie thought, by restricting the scope of aesthetic possibilities. In poetry, the greatness of the poets Du Fu and Li Bai lay in their broad range and inclusiveness. This is, he says, precisely where they excel over the "bare" style of poets such as Wang Wei and Meng Haoran. Hence, he berated the lauding of a literati spirit (*shiqi*) over other styles for its narrow and incomplete view of artistic expression. In denying both the logical and stylistic tenets of orthodox painting theory, he reaches beyond the immediate concerns of painting to deliver a very potent attack on the Neo-Confucian social hierarchy, to which the literati orthodoxy in painting may be said to be an aesthetic counterpart.

The Examination Essay (*bagu wen*)

Zheng Xie's strangely impassioned defense of the examination essay can perhaps be taken as a gauge of the degree to which the *bagu* or eight-legged essay was held in contempt by many, perhaps even the majority, of his era. He alludes to the general attitude when he states that "the examination essay, ancient style prose, poetry, and songs are called literature. But today people despise the examination essay to the point of virtually expelling it from the realm of writing. Isn't [this attitude] too extreme? They shouldn't deface its beauty without first understanding its depth."[70] As we have seen, an appreciation for the essay seems to fit well with Zheng's rejection of the orthodox literati aesthetic of "forgetting the net and trap," that is, its neglect of form. Yet in light of the opposition to the essay voiced periodically but often forcefully and eloquently during the Qing, we might justifiably wonder to what extent his views were shared by others of his time. Unfortunately, little in the way of a systematic attempt at codifying *bagu* theory and practice has survived to the present. Furthermore, occasional and desultory remarks made in defense of the essay are more often than not marred by inconsistency, and even a certain diffidence. Still, I believe that Qing views supporting *bagu* can roughly be divided into three phases, corresponding in time to the early, middle, and late-middle Qing. This is not to insist that the positions here defined are wholly distinct from one another, for a degree of overlapping of these phases occurred. However, to the extent that they seem to have evolved in succession, my arrangement of them into such a chronology seems justified for our purposes. Moreover, changing attitudes toward the essay present a rather revealing counterpart to the various perceptions of literati interests and activities encountered in other areas of discourse. For the arguments by which essay composition was justified constitute a measure of how the character, and tasks, of the literati were defined.

The early Qing was in some ways a low point for the prestige of the essay. It was attacked for, among other things, its vacuity, narrowness, and especially its blindness to the moral and practical suitability of candidates for government office. Huang Zongxi (1610–95), Gu Yanwu (1613–82), and others urged its abandonment in favor of forms of selection reflecting broader, extraliterary criteria. Nevertheless, the revival of classical studies credited to these same men may have received some stimulus from late Ming interest in the examination essay. In the last decade of the Ming, members of the literary society Fushe ("Restoration Society") had declared in their charter to be committed to clarification of the classics through the practice of *bagu*. Among its members was a young native of Zhejiang by the name of Lü Liuliang (1629–83), who was to become renowned in the early eighteenth century as an anti-Manchu nationalist and posthumous victim of the Yongzheng emperor's wrath against such lingering sentiments.

During his own lifetime, however, Lü was known for his annotations of the *Four Books*, which gained wide circulation as a guide to the study of the *bagu* essay. The views he expressed in this and other works are characterized by their intransigent insistence on adherence to the commentaries of Zhu Xi, a position he took to the extreme of refusing to admit even the possibility of error by Zhu. It is as if he took a malicious pleasure in confuting textually minded critics by the sheer vehemence of his argument. For in a tactical concession, he blithely asserts that Zhu's glosses should be followed, regardless of any errors they might contain. This is because Lü believed them to provide a sort of infallible landmark for study; perfect fidelity to the Zhu Xi exegetical tradition was, he emphasized, the most suitable method for investigating things and attaining to knowledge. For justification, he appealed to the venerable Mencian faith in the power of language. Words comprised the basic unit of the essay, and their correct use was the criterion for the awarding of the literatus's social status; but in a more profound sense, they guide the mind to understanding, he asserted. In fact, they were the very voice of the soul: "The [spoken] word is the voice of the mind, and the [written] word the script of the mind. If the mind has some delusions or secret troubles, these will undoubtedly be revealed in speech and writing. Hence, the spoken word, and the written word, are both the mind."[71]

The analogy to classical studies' newfound philological approach is perhaps too facile, but nevertheless it bears pointing out, for Lü was a contemporary of Gu Yanwu and other classicists who first began to approach textual analysis in earnest using philological techniques. Lü saw the words of the essay as invested with extraordinary power, which both molded and reflected the power of its practitioners to discriminate subtle lexical distinctions. Its practice should not remain a merely intellectual exercise, however, but was to serve a pedagogical purpose, namely, as the cornerstone for the inculcation of a morality founded on the ethical absolutes of profit (*li*) and righteousness (*yi*). According to Lü, the confusion between these two lay at the root of the historical disasters that had afflicted China over the past two thousand years and had culminated in the occupation by Qing "barbarian" rulers. The only way to avoid future catastrophes was for the literati to adhere firmly to the principles of self-sacrifice emphasized by Zhu Xi and other Song philosophers: "Sages and worthies were never willing to compromise even one iota in matters of service and retirement, leaving and approaching, or refusing and receiving. This is not because they were unaware of the [need for] adaptability to circumstances. It is simply that the business of regulating and ordering the world is in their hands. They cannot err by even a fraction."[72]

It is difficult to judge whether or not Lü would have championed the practice of *bagu* had it not already been institutionalized in the examination system.[73] But in any event, he seems to regard it as valuable precisely because it was perhaps the only educational program to which all degree candidates, and officeseekers, had to undergo. A faithful assimilation of the Zhu Xi commentaries, and their reflection in the writing of essays, was the means for instilling moral values into the minds of the literati: "How can we discern whether the principles are clear or not? We must decide on the basis of language and diction."[74]

We recognize in Lü Liuliang's rather rigid prescriptions for the education of the literati certain features not without parallels in the thought of his contemporaries. His puritanical interpretation of Song ethics, vehement insistence on total adherence to principle, and rejection of compromise with expediency seem out of keeping with his times. But despite this seeming divergence from his contemporaries, he is perhaps representative of the general tendency to establish an extrinsic, objectively definable standard of morality and pedagogy. The tedious labor required to master the essay should, he thought, be made to serve moral ends, by imparting a precise knowledge of Neo-Confucian principles. In this, it provided a measure of certitude to the student struggling to come to grips with the difficult issues of his day. And its proximity to the rewards of fame and emolument as the instrument of their attainment made it ideally suited to a moral training which forced the banishment of worldly desires from the mind. In terms of the later development of theories of *bagu*, Lü Liuliang's emphasis on the role of the essay in developing the student's power to make subtle distinctions was perhaps his most significant contribution.

This aspect is taken up by two important arbiters of literary taste of later times, the Tongcheng school theorists Fang Bao (1668–1749) and Yao Nai.

An attention to the formal features of prose style, which was a hallmark of Tongcheng poetics, is perhaps what brought its members to include the essay within their prose theory. Their appreciation of its merits was not of itself divorced from the ethical priorities Lü Liuliang claimed were the central purpose of *bagu* practice. But in the evolution of prose theory from Fang Bao through Liu Dakui to Yao Nai, we can detect a definite trend toward the weakening of an ethical linkage between the essay form and the teachings of the classics and Four Books. Fang Bao, for example, uses arguments similar to those of Lü in his discussions of the essay, closely echoing the latter's claim that it teaches the art of "uncompromising integrity" in small matters: "The essay is an especially shallow technique.... But although the studies of the literatus are trivial, we can see that even there they cannot take their responsibilities lightly."[75] For Lü and to some extent for Fang as well, the writing of essays possessed an active function as shaper of moral acuity, that is, the ability of the writer to make fine distinctions on both intellectual and moral questions.[76] But with time, this formulation of the essay as instrument of moral refinement was downplayed in favor of a perhaps more passive role, as simply the gauge of moral qualities, rather than the agent of their perfection. Dai Zhen, for example, thinks that moral cultivation need not precede mastery of the essay: "If one persists in finding the proper verbal expression, then this would be impossible without a thorough knowledge of the classics and cultivation of virtue. Those who possess virtue, and [later] master literary skills proceed away from the source. Those who aspire to literary composition which accords with the right and correct, and then go on to seek virtue, follow the stream to its source."[77] Literary practice and the achievement of a felicity of expression were not divorced from moral cultivation, but neither were they indistinguishable from it, and in the writing of essays, the two were for Dai theoretically distinct.

According to both Liu Dakui and Yao Nai, the dependence of the essay upon its institutional setting and the complex pressures and distractions which examination success and failure brought on the minds of its writers had effectively destroyed the possibilities for the production of good essays. As the means of obtaining personal benefit, it had in effect become tainted with the very desires and ambitions Lü Liuliang wanted its practice to eliminate. The system that had brought the essay into existence in the first place was, they thought, inimical to literary excellence; it had inevitably resulted in its corruption, and thus eventually to the contempt with which the public at large viewed it.[78] Yao Nai and Liu Dakui's views on the essay represent in effect a retreat from any sanguine estimation of its ethical power. They argued for a certain detachment of the practice of the essay from the realm of moral cultivation, to a simpler, less ambitious one of academic and intellectual training. Says Yao, "The nation has established literary examinations as the means of selecting men for government service, in the hope that everyone will be enabled through it to clearly understand the works of the sages, without falling into error. That is the sole reason. If people write without first attaining a mastery of the classics, how can this be considered true writing?"[79]

It appears that Qianlong era writers who defended the essay rarely resorted to the arguments of earlier times and could even be said to have reacted against them. Liu Dakui is particularly tepid in his evaluation of its strengths, choosing to regard it as simply one more stage in the evolution of literary form.

> The subtle words of Confucius and Mencius have, generally speaking, been clarified through the analyses and discussions of previous eras. Later ages added further to these by creating the examination essay. This development is similar to the [history of] poetry, which [developed into] the regulated verse form. The examination essay uses parallel constructions to "speak on behalf of" the sages and worthies. It isn't limited to expounding the meaning [of the sages], but also imitates the spirit of their writings.... It can be considered one more contribution to literary form and does not conflict with the sages.[80]

Bagu had thus become for Liu an intellectual exercise designed to improve the use of "words," that is, literary skills, specifically the mastery of various literary styles: "Those who practice the essay must understand the meaning of all Six Classics, and delve into the prose of the Qin, Han, Tang and Song dynasties. Only then will their expression be profound."[81]

From this point it was only one step further to the views of Jiao Xun. He denied that the form of the essay possessed any inherent connection with the ethical values associated with Confucian teachings and the state orthodoxy. In his "Discussion of the Examination Essay" (*Shiwen shuo*) he identified the essay's defining characteristic as its formal sophistication: "Ancient style prose is based upon meaning. Examination essay prose is distinguished by its attention to form. If meaning is discarded and only form is discussed, then there is no ancient style prose. If form is abandoned to concentrate on meaning, then there is no examination essay. Thus, these two genres are not interchangeable."[82]

It had long been commonplace to argue that the best way to improve the various deficiencies of the essay was to have them written in the ancient style. With the serious intentions and in the authentic voice of the writer of ancient style prose (rather than merely in imitation of the ancient sages), it could gain an elevation of style which it was perceived to lack. Jiao, however, found nothing wrong with the purely formal qualities of the essay, which in fact suggested affinities to the other arts: "I have said that in learning there are three arts which, though despised by most, are actually capable of great subtlety. These are go, *ci* songs, and the examination essay.... Is it suitable to equate the rules and principles of the essay with the sages' principles of self-cultivation, and ruling over the land, of ordering one's house and bringing order to the nation?"[83] The worth of the arts, of which the essay was one, lay not in any exalted moral or political purpose; and moreover, their principles were each unique to their own disciplines and not reducible to any overarching unities.

The many ironies and, indeed, considerable difficulties of *bagu* composition are illustrated by the career of Dai Mingshi (1653–1713), one of the most celebrated of the victims of Qing sensitivities toward anti-Manchu sentiments. For a span of nearly forty years he taught, edited, and wrote examination essays, for which he achieved national renown. Yet if his own writings are to be believed, he despised them from beginning to end, regarding the whole endeavor as trivial and demeaning. Nevertheless, he thought even less of the way the essay was treated by the successful members of the gentry, namely, as a means of personal advancement, to be tossed aside as soon as the desired results were achieved. He says of a contemporary's essays that

> looking over Mr. Song's compositions, I noticed that those written before he succeeded in the examinations are even better. I feel saddened by this. Those who catch their fish forget the net. Those who obtain a rabbit forget the trap. The examination essay is the net and trap for the examination system. How can it be a small matter to leave the net and trap in a state of neglect after obtaining the benefit of fish and rabbit? If one's former studies are abandoned completely, it's no wonder that when suddenly given responsibility for literary work, one performs haphazardly and crudely.[84]

For its avid practitioners, the essay offered opportunities for formal sophistication, subtlety, and lucidity; as a famous Qianlong era essayist Guan Shiming put it: "Men of the past wrote annotations and commentaries on the classics, thereby creating a separate class of writing. Only the examination essay speaks on behalf of the sages and should merge with them. This pushes its writers toward greater subtlety and profundity in their compositions. It is said that before Zhu Xi, there already existed essays. But these did not achieve the felicity and rigor of later essays."[85] As we have noted, scholars, literary men, and even artists all regarded the search for "subtle exactitude," the *mot juste*, and felicitous expression to be of crucial importance to their enterprises. That the essay was in fact practiced in a similar spirit suggests that it was not essentially at odds with the general tenor of intellectual life in the eighteenth century.[86] In their analyses of the distinctive features of Qing essays, both Lu Qian and Shang Yanliu point out the degree to which the essay was influenced by contemporary trends in scholarship and letters.[87] The increasing formalization and secularization of the essay seem to parallel similar tendencies on the part of scholars and artists to regard their disciplines largely as ends in themselves, rather than as mere vessels for the realization of some transcendent reality. Hence, we might see this reorientation of *bagu* theory as implying a fundamental shift in the perception of the literatus's role, from that of an unquestioned guardian of the public good, to a less absolute one, centered on the attainment of secular knowledge, and no longer exalted as the arbiter of ethical issues. Such a literatus no longer lived in a secure world where his authority was sanctioned by a moral order that championed his virtues over those of other members of society. Might this not be reflected in the increasing interest in the attainment of secular knowledge—its sophistication, logical consistency, and proximity to application? Ultimately, such criteria seem to have been relied on more than ever as a measure of a man's fitness to serve as an officer of the state.[88]

Ji Yun (1724–1805), who served as chief examiner at three metropolitan examinations during the late Qianlong and Jiaqing periods, shares this belief that the examination essay was valuable as a tool to judge the examinees' literary skills and powers of reasoning. However, he felt that it could in no way go beyond this.

> The essays which have been selected were on the whole chosen on the basis of their logical clarity and consistency. . . . As for the ethical qualities or mental fitness of the examinees, this will have to be judged by His Majesty based on their future performance in practical affairs; their posts can then

be assigned accordingly. Their future careers cannot be predicted entirely on the basis of their examination essays, and our own ability to recognize talent certainly cannot reach such precision. Hence, we dare not subscribe to the theory that men can be understood on the basis of their writings, and presume to submit our conclusions before His Majesty as if they were the last word on these men.[89]

Zhang Xuecheng and the Criticism of Han Learning

I have argued in the preceding pages that discourse in various areas of literati activity tended in the eighteenth century toward the denial of the literatus's privileged access to the moral or transcendent truth which had been accorded him by the Cheng-Zhu tradition of Neo-Confucianism. In this era, the individual literatus found himself faced with an environment where the attainment of knowledge or skill in specialized disciplines was more important to the maintenance of his status than ever before and could demand life-long, all-consuming devotion. Dai Zhen, Yao Nai, and others attempted to reassert the indissoluble ties between the pursuit of "knowledge of the world" and an underlying search for moral intelligibility. But as I have shown, their doctrines inevitably argued for the primacy of intellectual inquiry as the most basic of literati concerns. The Way did not, and could not, exist outside of form, and thus its pursuit could never be said to go beyond the study of observable phenomena.

In the late eighteenth century, the historian Zhang Xuecheng wrote a number of essays critical of the dominance of evidential scholarship during the previous half century. He may in fact have shared with philologists many if not most of their assumptions about the nature and function of scholarship; but he goes beyond most in his attempt to evaluate the possibilities of a new reintegration between the moral and intellectual, and public and private, spheres of literati life.[90] Since the positions he takes on the issues of the nature and purpose of learning and the status of the literatus within his social matrix seem in many ways to mark the culmination of the processes we have been describing, they are illuminating in their lucid delineation of the issues and dilemmas facing eighteenth-century literati.

Zhang is renowned for his scathing criticism of the excesses of the philological movement, which in his view had simply lost sight of any concern for fundamental issues. In his discussion of the study of ritual, the field of study most crucial to Qing philologists' views of literati identity, he laments that scholars who had accumulated vast stores of erudition on the various aspects of historical rituals no longer understood the basis for its practice.

> Some believe this to be the ultimate principle, and thus cease to seek for a comprehensive understanding of the ancients, by which they could expand their own minds. This is what the Song scholars called "losing one's moral direction by toying with mere things." One cannot say that these words are too harsh.... The *Changes* says, "Knowledge is what stores past [experience]. Insight is the means of knowing the future." Names and institutions, customs and rituals, careful and detailed research, committing a large body of facts to memory—these are the forms of learning known as "storing the past." A love of study and a sensitive curiosity, understanding of deeper meaning, and insight into the ways of change, and the ability to bring forth new dimensions of understanding—these are the learning of "knowing the future." If one can "store the past" but not "know the future," there are five areas [of the rites] accessible to study. If one tries to extend the principles learned in such study to find a compromise with latter-day institutions, judging the results according to the needs of the day, then governmental affairs and human relations can all be known in advance. The contribution of such scholarship is inestimable. Scholars cannot possess all of the requisite talents. But they should seek what is most suited to their endowment, and exert effort there. This will be good as well.[91]

Here, he sets the standard for the very highest attainment of knowledge—the synthesis of all aspects of understanding into a gestalt of cumulative and integrative functions. But he is also acutely aware of the limitations of the average mind, as well as of the uniqueness of each individual's endowment. Hence, he sees the two broad categories of "specialist" and "generalist" as mutually complementary: "The men who wish to address the needs of their times [and leave writings to posterity] need only seek the general meaning in their studies. Those who undertake specialized research must investigate names and forms to an extreme degree of exactitude and refinement. These two [types of men] complement one another in making contributions to the Way."[92] Not everyone need embark on the sort of career in scholarship that enjoyed popularity during his era.

Thus human beings must follow their own instincts and inclinations, rather than the ephemeral and circular trends of scholarship, to find what suits them best. But this is no easy path, for like Dai Zhen, Zhang sees the attainment of true knowledge as fraught with unending difficulties. In fact, Zhang goes to the extreme of denying the possession of real knowledge to all but a chosen few. Dai Zhen may lament the tendency of recent scholars to become prisoners of their subjective ideas, but he still offers the hope of overcoming such natural inclinations through steadfast devotion and effort. Zhang, however, remains pessimistic about the possibilities for finding genuine, self-revelatory knowledge. And as a consequence, he considers communication between people to be an almost chimerical ideal.

> Huizi said: "The one in flight runs east, while his pursuer also runs east. Though both run to the east, the intentions of each differ." Nowadays many people are running together, but are they able to know the intentions of their fellow runners? Sometimes they seem reliable, at other times not; sometimes it seems as if they understood each other, at other times not. This is why it is difficult to speak of understanding one's fellow travelers on the Way.[93]

Human life is beset by epistemological uncertainty, which envelops all, regardless of their intellectual powers. In these rather troubling circumstances, individuals must hold to two principles. First, they should not allow their efforts to stray into useless abstractions, which lead inevitably into erroneous knowledge. Knowledge requires a "vessel," or form, to provide intelligibility to what is otherwise ambiguously amorphous. And since ultimate truth is inaccessible to direct perception, it must be approached through the mediation of language, history, and other forms. Second, the highly idiosyncratic nature of the individual human mind requires that everyone seek a self-referential, self-revelatory understanding based on their own propensities—in other words, knowledge which incorporates the subjectivity of its possessor.

Zhang places the very highest value on such knowledge as the ultimate goal, and the only real criterion, for study and thought. He regards learning that does not bear an intensely personal imprint with unremitting scorn.[94] This desire for an intuitive, individualized knowledge often seems not so far from that of the Song Neo-Confucians, for whom Zhang expressed great admiration. Yet it is perhaps his almost eccentric nonconformity which leads Zhang to a dispute with, and even a certain distancing from, the Confucian tradition, and which allows him to undertake a critical evaluation of the role of the Confucian literati (*ru*) in history. Under Zhang's searching analysis, the "Way of the Confucian" is accused of straying from that of the sages, and even of distorting the doctrines of Confucius and other ancient exponents of the Way. In fact, in a tirade of indignation he derides the literati for having through their own presumptuousness lost the possibility for an illumination of virtue and truth.

In his essay "On the Origin of the Way" (*Yuan Dao*) Zhang traces the beginnings of the Confucian calling to Zhou times, when, he asserts, government (*zheng*) and education (*jiao*) were united. The Six Classics thus represent not the codification of timeless moral doctrines (he even doubts their authenticity as the works of Confucius); instead, they are the legacy of the "old statutes of the offices of the Zhou." Under the rule of the Zhou house, the Way and its forms were indistinguishable, and men acted as they thought and wrote. In such a state, no gap existed between words and their functions. With the inevitable changes brought about through the workings of historical forces (*shi*), however, men came to specialize in the classics or historical records divorced from the realm of practical application, and the literatus as he was currently recognized came into being. This was not of itself wrong; but the Confucians subsequently made the mistake of assuming their classics to be the sole repositories of the Way.

> The reason why the Confucians have continued to be patronized through the ages, is that they have honored the way of the ancient kings. But the Confucians guard their Six Classics jealously, saying that they are the only books which express the Way. How on earth can one speak of the Way apart from its vehicles? Even an object always retains its shadow. They abandon objects and concrete affairs, of which Confucius taught, and the everyday mundane affairs of human relations, and cling to the Six Classics when speaking of the Way. Hence they no longer have a right to speak of the Way.[95]

Confucians tried to possess the Way as their own, a mistake which lost it both for themselves, and for the world as a whole. The ignorant and common folk retain it in their daily activities, without trying to articulate it. But those who identify some incomplete manifestation of it only contribute to its obfuscation: "The failure to understand the Way is not the fault of the dull or ignorant. It was obscured by the many conflicting opinions of the 'worthy and virtuous.'"[96]

Zhang accuses later Confucians of fatuously presuming that the Master established their own "private" path or way. This is gravely mistaken, he says, for Confucius proclaimed a broad truth, meant for humankind as a whole. The Confucians can only be considered one particular group within society, Zhang says with some derision, and a rather ignominious one at that. They play the pathetically narrow role of "preserving and awaiting," with little else to recommend themselves. They do not understand that the classics they take to be their own, such as the *Book of Changes*, are not merely useless texts but guides to the creation and expansion of new and practical domains of knowledge (*kaiwu chengwu*), tasks which the ineffectual Confucian literatus was apparently never terribly interested in.

It was the loss of the concrete and practical uses of the classics originally present in the administrative system of the Zhou which led the literati into their mistaken notions of moral duty: "Now some say that because the system of officials responsible for preserving the Classics has been lost, 'we' must clarify the teachings through virtue. Thus everyone believes himself to be virtuous." This is the primary failing of those who purport to speak from the authority of the Way. Although "scholarship' in itself can approximate truth, individuals rarely grasp more than one particular element of the broad field of intellectual endeavor. Yet they claim the piece of which they have knowledge to be the whole, all-encompassing truth. Unfortunately, this overweening self-confidence gives rise to a desire to dictate their will to all other members of society. Thus have they destroyed their credibility as spokesmen for the Confucian way. In the present age, what is left for the Confucian is simply to pursue his own studies, not as a potential panacea to be proclaimed to the world at large, but as the individual's own pursuit of truth. "Learning is private," Zhang claimed, and thus distinct from the Way, which is beyond the scope of mere individuals.[97] Scholars should above all avoid imposing their own subjectivity over the rest of the society. Instead, the literati's function in the public domain should be limited to concrete involvement in practical affairs. Social order cannot be maintained by an ideal that exalts the intelligent, and their intellectual credentials, at the expense of the rest of society.

We know that Zhang was generally not, however, as critical of Confucian doctrines as the essay "Yuan Dao" leads us to believe. He professed admiration, in fact, for both Song, and Ming Neo-Confucians in no uncertain terms and considered himself to be the spiritual heir to the so-called Zhedong school of thought, by which he traced his intellectual ancestry to Wang Yangming. Like a number of eighteenth-century figures, Zhang recognized the stabilizing influences that doctrines such as those of the Song Neo-Confucians exerted on society.[98] Even while criticizing the weaknesses of the official orthodoxy, he and a number of other scholars felt a deep reluctance to dismantle it entirely.[99] In so doing, they were in effect recognizing the relevance of Neo-Confucian doctrine within a very important, but also circumscribed, domain, namely, that of the state's interests and needs.

CHAPTER THREE

The Intellectual Milieus of Three Novelists

THE THREE novelists whose works will be examined in Parts II and III of this book were far from prominent in the philosophical, scholarly, or literary movements discussed in Chapter 2. Yet the proximity of these men to the leading intellectual currents of the Jiangnan region begs for readings of their works in the light of the ideas of their associates and contemporaries. In this chapter I examine the works of a few figures for whom the evidence suggests close ties to Wu Jingzi, Xia Jingqu, and Li Ruzhen.

Wu Jingzi

Ever since Hu Shih published *Rulin waishi kaozheng* in 1923, scholars have taken note of several links between Wu Jingzi and the philosophical school of Yan Yuan and Li Gong (1659–1733), known as the Yan-Li school. Although no direct evidence exists of Wu's interest in the doctrines of these two men, these links suggest that he was at least partially acquainted with their doctrines. Wu's great-grandfather Wu Guodui served as the chief examiner at the county examination in 1677 at which Li Gong gained licentiate status. Wu Guodui was so impressed with Li, who took first place, that he sponsored a printing of his works.[1] Several decades later in the 1730s, Wu Jingzi's son Wu Lang studied mathematics with Liu Zhu, who was a disciple of Li Gong. This family connection spanning several generations suggests that Wu possessed at least a passing acquaintance with Yan-Li doctrines. Moreover, one of Wu Jingzi's closest associates in Nanjing, the classical scholar Cheng Tingzuo (1691–1767), was known as Yan Yuan and Li Gong's most influential supporter in the Jiangnan region. Given that the writings of these two figures may have contributed to Wu Jingzi's intellectual development, and that their ideas on ritual in particular are of relevance to his novel, I would like to discuss their thought in some detail.

As I have already noted, the decades following the fall of the Ming can be characterized as a time when thinkers of nearly all persuasions shifted toward empirical, practical, and socially relevant disciplines of inquiry. Within this context, Yan Yuan and his disciple Li Gong clearly represent one of the most radical of the intellectual possibilities of their time. Yet in spite of their relative isolation from the scholarly mainstream (they both lived in North China, far from the center of scholarly life in Jiangnan), Yan-Li thought can be seen as in some sense representative of the prevailing trends.[2] By offering what was up to his time the most thorough, far-reaching, and internally consistent critique of Neo-Confucian thought, Yan Yuan's program was a compelling, if radical, alternative to self-cultivation as it was understood by most of his contemporaries. In particular, their criticisms of Cheng-Zhu philosophy explore the societal and intellectual dimensions of Neo-Confucian thought, and first and foremost its deleterious effects on literati mores.

It should be observed, however, that the cornerstone of the educational program of literati rejuvenation, that is, the identification of ritual as the fundamental fabric uniting the individual to his society, came to be accepted as the ideological basis for eighteenth-century philological scholarship by almost every serious thinker of the period. Benjamin Elman notes that "agreement on the centrality of rituals became the cardinal point that united Han-Learning scholars throughout the Ch'ing dynasty. Their emphasis on decorum and institutions was a direct reaction against what they considered the Neo-Confucian misuse of principle (*li*) for abstract and speculative studies."[3] The fact that Yan and Li were probably the most vocal proponents of the study and practice of ritual and disseminated their ideas over much of the nation through teaching, travel, and correspondence seems to suggest that the obscurity into which their teachings fell in later times belies their importance to the emergence of ritualism among evidential scholars. Hu Shih and more recently Kai-wing Chow have noted the similarity between Yan-Li thought and that of Dai Zhen; as will become clear from the subsequent discussion, Yan and Li anticipated a number of Dai's ideas.

The crux of Yan Yuan's condemnation of Song and later Neo-Confucian thought lay in his opposition both to the reliance on the written word and to the passivity and complacency he accused the orthodox teachings of encouraging. He was not dogmatically opposed to all scholarly activity; instead, he deplored the reliance on literary education largely for its lack of praxis (*xi*), which he saw as fundamental to the learning process. The pedagogical program he adopted to reverse this (that is, the Six Arts of Ritual, Music, Poetry, Calligraphy, Charioteering, and Archery) represented a return to the educational curriculum of pre-Qin China, when the ruling classes required substantial martial skills. On the one hand, it eliminated the most basic of all divisions within the elite, that between its military and civil wings. But on the other hand, it also created new lines of division, for although he stipulated that youth be trained in all six of the arts, any individual should specialize in only one or in the case of ritual, in only one of the five branches of ritual. The purpose of all study was the attainment of proficiency alone, not the pursuit of knowledge as a means to grasp some underlying principle. This proficiency could then be applied in appropriate circumstances for the benefit of society.

Here, Yan was challenging Cheng-Zhu doctrine in two key areas. First he was attacking the notion that any single domain of knowledge or activity could adequately serve the needs of all, or even of a majority. "There are thirty-two different kinds of temperament," he said, and each one must find the route appropriate to his particular endowment.[4] Though he did not directly challenge the doctrine of immanent principle, he in effect denied the basis for an educational program assuming uniformity of purpose or result. In Yan's utopian vision of a society governed according to the ancient rites, no individual literatus could gain a totality of skill sufficient to place him in a position of omnipotence in the exercise of political power. Instead, the literati acted as a corporate body whose various attainments in the arts harmonized in a concert of purposeful activism. The illusion that any individual could attain to complete mastery of all knowledge had, he thought, brought about the decline of the literati into impotence.[5] Hence, Yan emphasized the importance of the collective effort for social efficacy both within the clan or family unit and in society at large.

Second, he not only removed the object of study from the sphere of texts (either in terms of study or production), he divorced it entirely from any search for subjective meaning. As Yan well knew, Zhu Xi condemned any study of forms and institutions on their own merit, as an unhealthy preoccupation with the inessential (*moshi*) at the expense of the moral root (*ben*). Yan alluded in fact to Xie Liangzuo's disparaging remarks about the followers of Zhang Zai, whom Xie had accused of falling into a meaningless pursuit of ritual for its own sake: "[Zhang] Hengqu's followers may have taken names and institutions as the truth, but even if they did so, what harm is there in that?"[6] The quotation he used to defend an interest in the minutiae of ritual, "reaching the heights never abandons the study of the mundane," was repeated by subsequent generations of scholars in defense of their own studies against charges of dissipating energies in insignificant pedantry. One of Yan's most pointed attacks on Neo-Confucian ethics was in fact its fixation with what was termed the root, that is, an abstract knowledge of principle divorced from its manifestations in the everyday world: "The establishment of the root in order to move to the less essential things, or even the belief that the inessential follows naturally from such an act, are both mistaken."[7]

Yan Yuan gained a great deal of notoriety for his attack on Zhu Xi's work on household ritual, *Zhuzi jiali*.[8] This polemic should be seen perhaps as directed not only against Zhu's specific formulation of family rites but also more broadly at all who view ritual as a static, unchanging form, valuable only as a vehicle in the attainment of some inner, higher truth. Precisely because the essence of the rites lay in their materiality, they were not immune to historical forces. Hence, though valuable as points of reference, the ancient rites possessed no inherent superiority in the present day and had to be evaluated on the basis of their practicability. Zhu Xi and Wang Yangming had, as Yan Yuan and Li Gong were fond of pointing out, placed the ancients and their institutions outside the pale of historical time, in a domain of purity and perfection insulated from all later developments. The corruption and decline into which present-day ritual had fallen had paradoxically become ossified by the errors of later generations, who adhered rigidly to Zhu Xi's formulations, believing them to be the unassailable means of transcendence into a world beyond form.[9] As a result, they neglected the study of the forms themselves, in their anxiety to get beyond them, and hence in the opinion of Yan neither examined the ancient rites in detail nor adjusted latter-day forms to bring them into accordance with the needs of their own day.[10]

The fervor with which Yan Yuan proclaimed ritual as a panacea for all contemporary problems, both individual and societal, may have struck his contemporaries as that of a fanatic. Yet his prescription for their application was, on the whole, both rational, and secular in its concern for the adaptation of ancient forms to modern circumstances.

Similarly, although neither he nor Li Gong actually denied the existence of an omnipotent Way, they were adamant in asserting that its realization lay entirely within the scope of ordinary human activity. Ritual was, moreover, the most felicitous expression of the Way in human life.[11] Most importantly, ritual as the expression of a social, rather than individual, ideal of cultivation, justified an essentially corporate view of the literati. The individual participants in this body were thereby freed from the need to search for an all-embracing core of moral truth, instead finding their fulfillment in the mastery of the particular discipline or art with which they were concerned. Concrete learning and achievement were not the means or vehicle for the penetration to a deeper meaning, so to speak, but the goal itself, and progress toward that goal was to be measured in terms of skill and efficacy. Hence, largely doing away with the role of intuitive powers in the learning process, Yan and Li ascribed the uniqueness of human beings to their powers of ratiocination.

The social order Yan envisioned apparently had little to do with any immanent principle informing all aspects of human activity and was thus inevitably more complex than one based on Neo-Confucian dualisms, requiring as it did the sophisticated exercise of rational judgment. It should hardly surprise us, then, that along with the reaffirmation of the centrality of ritual, Yan revived a number of concepts from Xunzi (whose doctrines had been largely neglected if not rejected by all major Neo-Confucian thinkers). Examples include the notion of *bi* or the obscuring of mental powers, and the importance of *wu*, or "error," in moral fallibility. The foregrounding of such notions tended to reduce the relative importance of the integrity of the will (*chengyi*), which figures prominently in Song and Ming Neo-Confucian precepts. Indeed, the Zhu Xi gloss on this term was ridiculed by Yan as simple-minded: "'Sincere and without error,' this is the sincerity of uncouth folk, and not that of Confucians."[12]

Here, then, we might attempt a summary of the attributes and attainments that for Yan Yuan and Li Gong were the measure by which the literatus should be judged. Above all, he was to seek social harmony and efficacy through the acquisition of skill in one of the arts, and through facility in the exercise of ritual as befitted his station. He need not seek for some transcendent truth beyond his daily life, for the rites encompassed all his needs, combining "good method and deep meaning" (*liangfa aoyi*).[13] They deplored the Neo-Confucian preoccupation with pious devotion to reverence (*jing*), which they saw as the raw substance of moral virtue, uncultivated, and thus unexpressed. Affirming physical nature and a certain concern for one's self-interest as the basis, rather than the antithesis, of morality, their prescription for the avoidance of selfishness, the cardinal evil according to Neo-Confucian thinkers, was Confucius's simple dictum: "'Do not do unto others what you would not desire yourself'; this is the means of devoting oneself to the common good, and triumphing over selfishness."[14] And above all, action had to be governed by the assiduous exercise of cognitive powers, choosing the appropriate path in a complex world where simple moral imperatives were inadequate to serve as one's sole guide.[15]

Yan Yuan has gained some attention in the twentieth century for his innovative and sophisticated educational philosophy.[16] His view of individual development as a process of accretion, rather than the tapping of innate potentialities, provided a theoretical basis for his pedagogical emphases. Though he steadfastly insisted on his adherence to the Mencian belief in the goodness of human nature and actually derided Cheng Yi and Zhu Xi for subverting this through their theory of physical nature (*qizhi zhi xing*), he nevertheless came perilously close to a position of neutrality on this issue. Like a number of later Qing thinkers, he seems to have regarded intelligence, rather than a will toward good or compassion, as the distinguishing faculty of human beings. The self gains fulfillment through engagement with the world, for which the exercise of cognitive functions is of central importance. Mental functions exercised on the world beyond the self engage and develop the individual's numinous qualities, which are the essence of one's humanity: "Knowledge has no essence, but takes [external] objects as its essence. It is like people's eyes which, lacking their own essence, take shapes and colors as their essence.... [Hence] although the mind of man is numinous, it must react and engage with the world around it. Otherwise, its numinous qualities have no means to express themselves."[17]

Yan Yuan and Li Gong cannot be said to have proposed an elimination of the hierarchy that exalted the literatus. Rather, the general thrust of their works is to articulate the means by which the literati can define their role as a social and intellectual elite. However, the implications of their educational and moral program in effect undermined the absolute distinction between literatus and commoner and furthermore weakened the position of the individual as the possessor of a moral right to govern. Instead of manifesting in his moral qualities the requisites of political power, the literatus was identified primarily by his mastery of a single skill among the Six Arts and was judged by his proficiency in it. Obviously, the Six Arts as promulgated by Yan and Li were never seriously considered as an alternative to the examination system based on literary composition. Nevertheless, on his visits to the capital Li Gong seems to have won praise from a number of high officials, and the introduction of some works at court gained him favor.[18] Mei Wending, Yan Xishan, and other mathematicians and men with interests in scientific knowledge were contemporaries of Yan, and in his travels in the south Li Gong sought them out, even traveling to Mei's home in Xuancheng. It appears that Yan and Li felt affinities with the increasing number of literati who pursued vocations and knowledge outside the more traditional spheres of literati knowledge. In this context, the Six Arts were not necessarily rejected outright by leading intellectuals; but his proposals may have stimulated discussion over the suitability of the arts as a subject worthy of serious attention.

Furthermore, the privileged status of the rites as the single most important element of the Confucian tradition among Qing thinkers appears to have received some stimulus from Yan-Li doctrines. In addition to its canonical position in the Confucian classics, the formal intricacy of ritual appealed greatly to eighteenth-century scholars. Yan Yuan's valorization of ritual over the substance of morality (*zhongxin*, that is, loyalty and trust) seems to betray a preference for formal learning, a preference that was shared by subsequent generations looking for realms of investigation free from ethical concerns yet still sanctioned by tradition as contributing to Confucian civilization. As we have seen, men such as Dai Zhen, Yao Nai, and other representatives of eighteenth-century thought felt the need to articulate a relationship between the form of ritual and certain underlying, motivating forces, that is, their ultimate moral import. But the exploration of the theoretical dimension in ritual, popular in the mid-to-late eighteenth century, itself represents a rejection of Neo-Confucian ethical dualisms.

As with Dai Zhen, the pretense to an omniscience that could in fact never be achieved was felt by many Qing thinkers to be a fundamental weakness of Neo-Confucian doctrines. Yan Yuan's program effectively dissolved the rationale for the individual attainment of all-encompassing knowledge in favor of the achievement of proficiency in the Six Arts. In fact, he is representative of the turn toward the investigation of empirical fact, either textual or in the natural world, evident among many of his contemporaries. Such thinkers rejected a naive faith in the attainment of the Neo-Confucian promise of all-encompassing knowledge, thereby implicitly excluding the application of intuitive or spiritual understanding from the realm of cognitive or logical thought.

As mentioned above, in addition to his family connections with Li Gong, after moving to Nanjing, Wu Jingzi was on fairly intimate terms with Cheng Tingzuo, an admirer of Yan-Li thought. Cheng appears to have played an important role in the dissemination of Yan-Li thought to other eighteenth-century thinkers. In particular, Dai Zhen's repudiation of many Neo-Confucian ideas is foreshadowed by Yan Yuan and Li Gong in a number of ways, and as Hu Shih has suggested, Cheng Tingzuo may have served as a conduit for the transmission of Yan-Li ideas to Dai.[19] Although Cheng's writings do not attain the depth or sophistication of the major figures of eighteenth-century thought, he is significant to this study by virtue of his relationship to Wu Jingzi. As I will discuss in Part II below, the importance of Cheng's ideas to Wu Jingzi is underscored by the fact that he served as the model for the character Zhuang Shaoguang in *Rulin waishi*. Although Cheng became known to posterity as an advocate of Yan-Li thought, an examination of his writings reveals less than complete adherence to them. The nineteenth-century historian of the Yan-Li school, Dai Wang, noted that Cheng followed Gu Yanwu, Hui Dong (1697–1758), and Huang Zongxi as much as he did Yan Yuan and Li Gong.[20] This is especially significant in light of what appears to be a certain ambivalence to, if not downright skepticism toward, the principal tenets of Yan-Li thought found in *Rulin waishi*, which I will discuss in Chapter 6.

Cheng Tingzuo expressed the fascination with cognitive powers of the human mind that is shared by Yan-Li and Dai Zhen, as well as a broad range of Qing thinkers.[21] In an essay on the origin of humankind, he wrote

> Heaven and earth gave birth to man, and endowed him with a mind. This is the reason why man is inferior to [the creative power of] heaven and earth. But born from heaven and earth, he can possess all of their intelligence. This is where heaven and earth are not the equals of man. Since man possesses this knowledge, he studies heaven and reaches it; he studies earth and reaches earth. All things which heaven can neither know nor accomplish, he can know and do. How could it be that heaven simply let him free to do as he wished?[22]

It is perhaps for comments such as these that Hu Shih labeled Cheng an "anthropocentric" thinker. Singling out the human mind rather than a superhuman, cosmic consciousness, Cheng placed the onus on humans to foster and develop this endowment. For it is cognitive ability rather than ethical or spiritual knowledge that makes humankind unique: "When I observe small children who are learning to speak, and ignorant, uncouth people, I have noticed that if they are completely cut off from exposure to the world, then perhaps [they feel no urge to know]. But once they see or hear something, they are bound to seek to understand its cause."[23]

As with Dai Zhen, identifying the cognitive powers as the primary attribute of human nature seems to have led Cheng to a certain reordering of the ethical priorities of Confucianism. In his surviving works he does not elaborate the substance of his views on this subject clearly (nor does he advocate them consistently), but in any event his description is notable for several distinctive features. Cognition, he implies, is blind to ethically hierarchical distinctions and exists at all levels of society. Moreover, the quest for knowledge is a basic human impulse and seems even to overshadow the "commiserating heart" (*buren zhi xin*), the centerpiece of Mencian Confucianism. Cheng saw the roots of goodness in morally neutral instincts or appetites, including eating and drinking, sexual lust, and fear of death, all of which must be channeled into their proper expression. For him, moral intention took second place to the forces of education, social practice, and the cultivation of ritual propriety as the determinants of morality. As with many representatives of evidential scholarship, Cheng also exhibited tendencies toward the exteriorization of the standards by which behavior is to be judged and even a certain denial of innate moral goodness reminiscent of Xunzi's doctrines.[24]

Although Cheng did not refute Song-Ming Neo-Confucianism with the thoroughness of Dai Zhen, he also waxed eloquent over the problems of the doctrine of principle as manifested in the slogan "preserve heavenly principle, and eliminate human desire."[25] The dualism expressed in this phrase reflects the essence of Zhu Xi's view of human nature, in fact serving as a theoretical basis for much of his moral and intellectual program.[26] According to Cheng, the inculcation of moral goodness could not be reduced to such a simple formula, for principle, he thought, cannot encompass the specificity, and complexity, of moral teachings.

> Song scholars felt [the discovery of] principle to be their duty. Hence, they based their theories on the phrase from the "Chapter on Music" [from *Liji*], "heavenly principle and human desires." ... Confucius instructed Yan

Yuan on how to distinguish between propriety and impropriety. This was the established method of teaching from the time of Tang and Yu, and was composed of a specific program. It is quite different from the teachings of a "single, undifferentiated principle," and the *Collected Annotations* [of Zhu Xi] should not have confused them with the doctrines recorded in the Chapter on Music. Can gentlemen not but doubt the reason why Confucius spoke of ritual, but not principle?[27]

Nor could the blame for all mortal folly and delusion be laid exclusively at the feet of "desire" (as Song Confucians tended to do). He quoted approvingly from Li Gong that "Excessive rigidity or pliancy of character and the superficiality or muddled confusion of knowledge are all able to bring about harm. [Confucius'] words ascribing this to impropriety implicitly recognizes all of these factors. The theory of selfish desires cannot account for all [instances of evil]."[28]

As noted in the discussion of Yan Yuan, ritual as a standard of ethical conduct is not amenable to reduction to the dualisms of Neo-Confucianism (as indeed Cheng himself observes: "How can ritual be compared to signs or numbers?"). It can be thought of as possessing complementary aspects of form (*shu*) and significance (*yi*),[29] Cheng says, but instead of reinforcing the Neo-Confucian hierarchy of mind over body, the physical elements of ritual actually subvert this dualism: "The ears, eyes, nose, mouth, intelligence and other corporeal functions are all brought into accord with the proper, and put the meaning [of ritual] into practice. Their [outward] forms are brilliantly complete, while their significance radiates within the mind of men."[30] The ultimate goal of ritual practice, then, is a sort of luminous awareness that extends beyond the narrowly individual to the social body, creating conditions of ethical and intellectual fulfillment on a communal basis.

As the foregoing remarks demonstrate, Cheng Tingzuo shared a number of beliefs with the Yan-Li school regarding proper literati education and also prefigured Dai Zhen's criticisms of Neo-Confucianism. Yet unlike Li Gong, who in later life turned to mathematics, geography, and other sciences outside the traditional literati curriculum, Cheng appears to have confined himself largely to classical exegesis.[31] Cheng's fictional representation in *Rulin waishi*, Zhuang Shaoguang, is a scholar of *Yijing* (The book of changes), ritual, and other classical texts. Little is said in the novel about the substance of Zhuang's and other scholars' views, and although his life appears to conform in several details to that of Cheng Tingzuo, there is no direct evidence of

Cheng's opinions on contemporary scholarship or philosophy. Instead, by making Cheng's fictional alter ego the embodiment of scholarly attainment (the novel calls him the "most learned man in the empire"), Wu Jingzi appears to single out his views in particular, and more broadly, those of the Yan-Li school regarding literati cultivation, in his treatment of literati mores.

The fact that specialized scholarship such as that practiced by Cheng Tingzuo and his contemporaries is not treated in any detail by *Rulin waishi* perhaps should not surprise us. Although Wu dabbled in classical exegesis, he appears not to have engaged in it as a profession. Moreover, most of Wu's closest associates were known as poets, such as Cheng Jinfang, Yan Changming, and Jin Zhaoyan; he was also acquainted with a few painters, calligraphers, and men of scientific interests.[32] Although he also knew scholars such as Cheng Tingzuo and Jiang Yu, it seems unlikely that Wu himself, who achieved fame for his skill in poetry and parallel prose, had any significant expertise in scholarly exegesis. Moreover, what little evidence remains of a treatise he wrote on the *Odes*, as well as a surviving preface to a work on *Shangshu* by Jiang Yu, suggests that Wu did not fully accept the findings of pioneering evidential scholars such as Yan Ruoju and Gu Yanwu and may not even have been fully aware of them.[33] But as a member of Jiangnan elite circles it appears that he was casually acquainted with quite a few local scholars of some note, particularly those in the Nanjing and Yangzhou areas.

It is intriguing that while their interests may have diverged in other areas, Wu's friends Cheng Tingzuo, Jin Zhaoyan, and Yan Changming all shared a fascination with the theater. Both Cheng and Jin authored southern operas (*chuanqi*), while Yan became famous for an account of Peking Opera actors popular during the mid-to-late Qianlong period. The status of actors and other popular entertainers emerges as a significant issue in the writings of Jin Zhaoyan and Yan Changming. Jin, for example, praised two storytellers Dinglang, and Liu Mizi, for their virtuosity, personal probity, and extraordinary tenacity. Such men have mastered arts that are equal to having "read ten thousand books," Jin wrote.[34] As we shall discuss in Part II, *Rulin waishi* foregrounds several Nanjing actors who consort with the literati there. The novel exploits the dichotomy between these two extremes of the social spectrum, alternately employing actors as foils and alter-egos of their social betters.

Xia Jingqu

Unlike Wu Jingzi, Xia Jingqu, the author of *Yesou puyan*, remains a shadowy figure. Other than brief biographical entries in the gazetteer of Jiangyin County and a surviving collection of poetry, almost no other records of him are known. If the dates currently accepted for him are correct, he was a contemporary of Wu Jingzi. It is thought that he composed his novel over the last decades of his life, probably during the 1760s and 1770s, or twenty to thirty years after Wu Jingzi wrote *Rulin waishi*. Although such dating still remains somewhat speculative, this would make it a product of the mid-Qianlong period, that is, just before and perhaps during the flurry of scholarly activity accompanying the compilation of the imperial catalog known as the Siku quanshu.

Considering that *Yesou puyan* was written by a native of the Jiangnan region during the heyday of Han Learning, it is perhaps surprising that the novel champions Cheng-Zhu orthodoxy with a stridency without parallel in any other work of Qing fiction. As I will discuss in greater detail in Chapter 8, a principal theme of Xia's novel is the eradication of rivals, both real and imagined, to Cheng-Zhu Neo-Confucianism, including not only Lu Xiangshan's (and by inference, Wang Yangming's) school of the Mind but also Buddhism, Taoism, and even Islam, Christianity, Hinduism, and other exotic creeds. Set during the mid-Ming period, the novel makes no reference to anything that could be construed as Han Learning; its bogeymen are defined by ideology rather than scholarly method. Nonetheless, the novel's brand of Neo-Confucianism exudes a distinctly philological flavor, its heroes and heroines propounding a rigorous curriculum of classical exegesis and practical studies as the panacea for the ills of their day.

Such conservative attachment to Cheng-Zhu teachings was by no means uncommon during the eighteenth century. By the mid-to-late Qianlong period resistance to evidential studies had coalesced around the so-called Song Learning school and in particular writers of Tongcheng Prefecture of Anhui. As Kai-wing Chow has observed, such resistance can be seen as venting the frustration of scholars from areas outside the leading cities of Jiangnan and who were excluded from the inner circles of political power centered on Zhu Yun, Ji Yun, and their coterie of Han Learning scholars.[35] In addition, a number of practitioners of philological methodology remained faithful to Cheng-Zhu doctrines, notably Jiang Yong (Dai Zhen's teacher), Cheng Yaotian, and other Huizhou scholars.

Moreover, in Changzhou Prefecture, in which Xia's home Jiangyin was located, Song scholarship maintained its prestige into the mid-to-late eighteenth century. The revival of Cheng-Zhu philosophy in the late Ming had in fact begun in Wuxi (southern Changzhou Prefecture) among the Donglin partisans. Benjamin Elman notes that although "by the mid-eighteenth century academies in Ch'ang-chou were no longer preoccupied with the Neo-Confucian philosophic and political issues that had energized them in the seventeenth century," Song learning was still valued by the local elite as the "ticket" to examination success.[36] This seems also to have been true to some extent of neighboring Suzhou Prefecture, where intellectuals "tended to be from families of older wealth, and were often most interested in book collecting, bibliography, and participation in the state examination process" than in challenging the state orthodoxy on matters of philosophical doctrine.[37] Xia Jingqu's patron and mentor, the staunchly orthodox scholar and official Yang Mingshi (1661–1736), took disciples both in his own home prefecture of Jiangyin, as well as in Wujiang County, located in Suzhou Prefecture.[38]

Yet another factor to consider is the character of the Cheng-Zhu school during the seventeenth and eighteenth centuries. Although some of its adherents were undoubtedly motivated by partisan political concerns, generally speaking the orthodox tradition came to be viewed in large part through the lens of contemporary interests. In Wing-tsit Chan's view, "[It] is too much to claim that the seventeenth century Ch'eng-Chu school created the empirical atmosphere, but certainly it shared in and contributed to it."[39] As I alluded to in my discussion of trends in literary criticism and theory, their advocacy of Cheng-Zhu learning did not prevent writers of the Tongcheng School from jettisoning the Neo-Confucian prejudice against the study of literary form. Eighteenth-century scholarly proponents of Song learning tended to stress its scholarship and statecraft (*jingshi*) and to minimize philosophical speculation. This was particularly true in Changzhou and neighboring regions. As Elman recounts, in a tradition going back to Tang Shunzhi of the mid-Ming period, local scholars held "a commitment not only to a world-ordering theory to which all Confucians adhered but also to technical expertise. The latter often included astronomy for calendar reform, hydraulics for flood control, and cartography for military purposes. Technical competence was an important part of the statecraft issues for Ch'ang-chou literati."[40]

That the titles of works attributed to Xia Jingqu allude to calendrical studies, mathematics, water conservancy, and other technical subjects, and that his novel includes numerous and lengthy debates on these subjects, suggests that Xia belonged squarely to the tradition of Changzhou scholarship. Another disciple of Yang Mingshi, Shen Tong (1688–1752), offers a better-documented example of a scholar of similar background and interests. Shen was active in the same fields Xia appears to have been interested in, namely, ritual texts, medicine, mathematics, calendrical studies, harmonics, water conservancy, and geography. Indeed, Shen's career as a scholar closely mirrored that of Xia. He failed to progress beyond the licentiate degree and spent much of his life working as a tutor for Manchu nobility in Peking and in the compilation of numerous local gazetteers and other scholarly projects. He achieved some renown in part perhaps through his connections with powerful officials such as Fang Bao, Zhang Boxing (1652–1725), and others. Moreover, he was famed for his virtuous conduct (he engaged in numerous austerities during the periods of mourning for his parents). Indeed, the fact that Shen and other reclusive scholars of similar interests, such as Pan Lei (1646–1708) (a disciple of Gu Yanwu) and Wang Xishan (1628–1682) (whose fame as a mathematician equaled that of Mei Wending), hailed from Wujiang suggests that these figures inspired Xia Jingqu in the creation of his protagonist, the polymath Wen Suchen. Wen is a native of Wujiang, and many of his townsmen and relations share a predisposition toward scientific and practical knowledge.

It is in the light of such concerns, then, that the examination of literati identity in *Yesou puyan* can be reconciled with its highly conservative nature on matters of ideology. As Catherine Jami has observed in the case of the mathematical sciences, the eighteenth-century restoration of the Chinese scientific tradition, particularly in mathematics and astronomy, was regarded as highly significant by the scholarly world. But while both innovation and priority in such studies clearly were valued among scholars as a whole, achievement of technical competence never brought its possessor the recognition and rewards that were bestowed through the examination system. As Jami puts it, "Despite an unprecedented revaluation of their status, mathematical sciences did not stand as an alternative, much less a rival, to classical learning."[41] For Changzhou literati, local notables such as Zhuang Cunyu (1719–1788) and his clansmen who achieved both bureaucratic status as well as technical expertise served as the ideals for emulation. But the reality was such that the vast majority of aspirants to office remained in the increasingly overcrowded ranks of low-ranking degree candidates, forced by economic necessity to sell their skills for the financial rewards that they could not achieve through the examination system. It is the resulting "ressentiment" over such conditions that seems to find expression in Xia's novel.

The animosity toward the school of the Mind found in the novel is logically consistent with Xia's loyalty to Song learning, but it may also have been motivated at least in part by more personal reasons. According to his biographical entry in the Jiangyin County gazetteer, Xia was recommended by his patron Yang Mingshi to join in the compilation of the *Baqi tongzhi*, a compendium on the history and institutional features of the eight Manchu banners. But in the end this did not come to pass, and out of financial necessity Xia spent the next several decades working as a clerk and minor functionary in various provincial offices in the north and west of the country. It is impossible to ascertain why Xia failed to gain the post to which he was recommended, but the fact that this project was conducted under the auspices of Li Fu (1675–1750), a staunch defender of the school of the Mind, may have had some impact on Xia. Criticism of Wang Yangming was common in the early Qing, and in the light of the Kangxi emperor's partiality toward Zhu Xi, it often carried political implications, as Wu Jingzi's friend Cheng Jinfang lamented during the mid-Qianlong period.[42] Moreover, the province of Jiangxi—Lu Xiangshan's home—figures prominently in *Yesou puyan* as a center of heterodox activities. Li Fu, who was also a native of that province, defended Lu Xiangshan in part out of regional loyalties. Indeed, in the Qing the disputes between Cheng-Zhu and Lu-Wang adherents were colored by regional loyalties, just as they had been in previous dynasties.

Li Ruzhen

Unlike both Wu Jingzi and Xia Jingqu, the author of *Jinghua yuan*, Li Ruzhen (1763–1830?), was not a native of the Jiangnan region or its vicinity. Like Cao Xueqin, the celebrated author of *Honglou meng* whose life was divided between Nanjing and Peking, Li's regional identification is ambiguous. A native of Daxing, near the capital, Li left his home at the age of nineteen for Haizhou, a salt-producing area in northern Jiangsu province where a brother held a post as a minor functionary. Except for a six-year stint as a prefectural magistrate in Henan, he apparently remained in Haizhou for the rest of his life, eventually marrying the sister of two local scholars with whom he became intimate. Li's identity as a northerner living in the south seems to have colored his surviving writings. First, his novel consciously alternates between northern and southern colloquial language, which also suggests the influence of *Honglou meng*, a work that relies heavily on northern speech while still showing traces of its author's southern upbringing. Second, in his treatise on phonology, *Yinjian* (Mirror of pronunciation), Li draws extensively on both contemporary northern and southern dialects and introduces a number of innovations of classical phonology based on them. Li apparently also pursued his interest in dialects in his now-lost *Guang fangyan*, which was modeled on the Han dynasty work on dialects by Yang Xiong (53 B.C.–A.D. 18).

Li is said to have settled in Haizhou for economic reasons, but it is unclear whether or not he turned to trade, for his career there seems to have been largely scholarly in nature. The city was located in the northern area of Yangzhou Prefecture, the headquarters of the salt gabelle during the Ming and Qing periods, and during the Qianlong period probably the wealthiest region of the empire. Yangzhou salt merchants were famed for their patronage of artists, writers, and most notably, scholars of the classics, history, and other fields of evidential scholarship. Since most of the merchant houses as well as many scholars resident in Yangzhou traced their lineages to Huizhou County, Anhui, the scholarship of both regions is usually referred to together as the "Yangzhou-Huizhou school." Many of the great figures of evidential studies were natives of one or the other of these two areas—men like Jiang Yong, Dai Zhen, Jiao Xun, Ruan Yuan (1764–1849), and Ling Tingkan. As R. Kent Guy notes, Yangzhou scholars "led the way in the development of new philological techniques in the eighteenth century."[43]

Of particular importance to understanding of Li Ruzhen's place within this great intellectual ferment is Ling Tingkan. A highly influential figure in scholarly circles from the 1780s until his death, Ling became Li's teacher when both were resident in Haizhou during the 1780s. As many of Ling's ideas appear to have direct relevance to Li's novel, it will be useful to examine some of Ling's voluminous writings here. I will confine myself to an examination of Ling's principal ideas regarding the nature of ritual, the methods of evidential scholarship, language, and scientific knowledge both Chinese and Western, topics that bear upon the interpretation of *Jinghua yuan*.

Although Ling did not study directly under Dai Zhen, he saw himself as the intellectual heir both to Dai's philological methods and to his ideals regarding the nature of scholarship and the role of the scholar. For Ling and many scholars of his generation Dai's legacy loomed large, yet although they regarded him with awe, Ling and others determined that certain aspects of Dai Zhen's scholarship required some revision. In its general features Ling's thought echoes Dai's quite closely. He emphasized that study without a concrete object results in false knowledge and that ritual provided an ideal antidote to the "empty" principles of Song scholarship. Song scholars were led astray by their confidence in the seemingly universal applicability of principle, which, Ling charged, is rooted in Buddhist and Taoist doctrines. Hence the recovery of ancient meanings required an almost Foucaultian excavation through the accretions of centuries of misunderstanding.

Where Ling Tingkan can be said to contrast with Dai Zhen is in his sensitivity to the opponents of philology. Living in the late-Qianlong and early-Jiaqing eras, Ling witnessed the beginnings of a reaction against philological scholarship, as well as attempts to resolve the increasingly partisan disputes between the advocates of Han and Song Learning. Although squarely within the Han Learning camp, he addressed some of the criticisms leveled against the abuses of some of its practitioners. Taking note of the charge that the immersion in scholarly minutiae failed to address questions of meaning (*yili*), Ling cites Dai Zhen's defense of philology:

> Meaning is none other than that which is found in statutes and regulations. They [its detractors] divide philology and meaning into two things. But if philology is not for the purpose of illuminating meaning, then what is it for? [On the other hand] if meaning does not reside in statutes and regulations, then it will inevitably result in heterodox studies and distorted theories, without one's even being aware of it.[44]

Some philologists could indeed be faulted with failing to seek the Way, Ling admitted. But as with Dai Zhen, the study of phonology, etymology, and textual transmission were central to the task of recovering the meanings of the ancients, which he saw as the prerequisite to finding the Way. As R. Kent Guy observes, "Textual scholarship had replaced, for Ling at least, self-cultivation as the center of the intellectual's life."[45]

Essentially, then, Ling took philology's textual emphasis to its logical conclusion. Dai and others had sought to achieve a balance between the search for larger significance and adherence to rigorous standards of scholarly inquiry. But Ling complained that this had encouraged the rather facile solution that Han philology could be reconciled with Song philosophy, thereby perpetuating the errors of the latter. Even Dai himself had failed to completely free himself from Neo-Confucian paradigms:

> Mr. Dai of my home prefecture rebuked Luo [the Cheng brothers] and Min [Zhu Xi], but upon opening a book, he still tried to explain principles and used the [Neo-Confucian] terms "essence" and "use" in discussing textual studies. He was still only half-enlightened, stuck in a trap from which he could not escape. Other scholars wax enthusiastic about Han learning or Song learning. Some even go so far as to say that study of names and things is best with Han learning, while philosophy is best with Song learning.[46]

He expressed great disdain for such compromises, which are "neither ancient nor modern, neither fox nor badger."[47] Instead of seeking some middle ground between the two schools of thought, then, Ling argued for a renewed commitment to the aim of purging the filter of Neo-Confucian language through which the ancient past had come to be understood. Nonetheless, merely discarding one exegetical tradition or era for another cannot accomplish the ultimate aim of clarifying the classics. The advocates of Han Learning who dogmatically favored earlier exegetical traditions were repeating the mistakes of the past. "To adhere to Cheng-Zhu [exegesis] as scholars since the Yuan and Ming have done is just like the way scholars before the Sui and Tang slavishly followed Zheng [Xuan] and Fu [Qian] [of the Han]," he lamented.[48]

By embracing textual and formal analysis of "names and things" as the only valid means of pursuing ultimate meaning, then, Ling advocated a materialist formula for scholarly investigation even more thoroughgoing than Dai Zhen. One senses that if he were alive today he would choose to pursue a career in archaeology, for he insisted on the importance of even minute and seemingly trivial evidence as clues to the nature of the past. Otherwise devoted Han Learning scholars often failed to pay attention to the all-important details of research. In epigraphy, for example, "even those scholars who keenly pursue evidential research regard [inscriptions] as [curios] similar to tea bowls or incense burners. How frivolous this is!"[49] It is such material evidence that unfiltered through the textual transmissions and exegeses of later eras, provided the most accurate and unadulterated view of the ancients.

Ling's intellectual temperament appears to be fully representative of what I have described as the broad tendencies of Qing evidential scholarship toward the investigation of the concrete and particular, including seemingly trivial subjects, devoid of ethico-religious or metaphysical significance.[50] He himself attributes this in part to his own humble beginnings, for like Dai Zhen and a number of other Huizhou and Yangzhou scholars, he began his career as a merchant.[51] Such men were temperamentally predisposed to the study of "names and objects, measurements and numbers"; and the plethora of material objects that came to Yangzhou, whether ancient texts or the arts and inventions of their own times, possessed an immediacy that seems to have held great appeal for them.

Like Dai Zhen, Ling also pursued interests in mathematics, astronomy, and natural science, which as I discussed above attracted strong followings in Changzhou, Suzhou, and elsewhere during the Qing period. In fact, Ling Tingkan's scholarly output appears to be divided roughly equally between works on the ritual classics and classical phonology, on the one hand, and scientific studies, particularly mathematics, on the other. Although such interests were common among Yangzhou scholars, Ling's mathematical studies may have been reinforced by a ten-year-long stint as an educational official in Tiancheng County, the home of the great mathematician Mei Wending and still a center of mathematical studies in the late eighteenth century.

In addition to lamenting the vestigial effects of Song idealism on Dai Zhen's thought, Ling also criticized Dai for his nativist tendencies in the area of science, and in particular with Dai's attempt to accord priority to Chinese texts over European mathematics. In a letter to Jiao Xun on spherical trigonometry, Ling says, "To say that there were certain names in ancient times, and that now [such things] are called something else—this is fine. But the names that Mr. Dai has proposed are all later than Western [mathematical] methods. This means that Western methods are ancient, and Mr. Dai's names are new. Why then does he insist that Western methods are newer?"[52] Ling lamented that the attacks on Western learning that had continued off and on since the Kangxi period had obscured its value. Even otherwise open-minded advocates of Han Learning such as Dai had failed to appreciate the similarity between their methodologies and those of the West:[53] "Western learning is deep and subtle. Without immersing oneself in it, one cannot understand it. One can gain insight by valuing the past over the present.... Nonetheless, one cannot completely reject [Western explanations] merely because Han scholars had not yet spoken of [such things]. . . . Western learning is like the classical exegesis of Han scholars. Both are based on observation and confirmation. If one abandons concrete verification, then it is meaningless."[54]

Ling's appreciation for Western science and technology thus appears to have allowed for a certain openness toward the outside world, even perhaps a cosmopolitan outlook that recognized the significance of events in the world beyond China's own cultural sphere. Predictably, he laid responsibility for the failure to gain such knowledge at the feet of Song cultural chauvinism. For example, he noted that if the Song scholar Wang Tiaowen had "investigated facts" he would have realized the significance of the solstices and placed China's geographical position north of the equator rather than at the center of the world, as he did.[55] Men of the Song dwelt on empty theories such as the "orthodox transmission" (zhengtong), so that "they exalted one country based on their own narrow opinions and arrogantly disregarded the others as unworthy of recognition as a sovereign state."[56] And he expresses enthusiasm for the recent foreign inventions, particularly those of England, that had made their way to Yangzhou. Within China as well, the past decades had been a time of numerous inventions of practical value, in Yangzhou especially, comparable to and in many cases inspired by those of the West.[57] Literati should be aware of and if possible, knowledgeable about, such technological progress.

The thought of Ling Tingkan brings many of the developments summarized in this chapter to their logical conclusion. While responding to criticisms of philological scholarship from various quarters, he essentially dismissed its opponents as stuck in the outmoded paradigms of Song thought. The evidential scholar must embody the unflagging devotion to "seeking truth from concrete events," devoid of metaphysical speculation or even of an insistence on the priority of ethical truths.[58] Material facts possess a logic of their own that must be carefully researched and documented, not distorted by the imposition of vague a priori abstractions. Perhaps most interesting among his ideas, and of particular relevance to Li Ruzhen, is the implication that material or technological developments in the world at large have the effect of de-sanctifying the myth of Chinese cultural centrality.

As we shall see in Chapter 8, many of the themes of *Jinghua yuan* resonate with Ling Tingkan's thought. Hsin-sheng Kao has noted that Li's novel can be seen as an attempt at "nothing less than uniting two cultural experiences," whether those of Han and Song learning, of northern and southern speech and manners, or of the native and foreign customs of his protagonists.[59] In essence, the novel transposes the intellectual divide discussed in Ling Tingkan's writings to a fictional setting that incorporates issues of gender and culture as well as scholarship. The implications for literati identity are both reassuring and disturbing. For while compromises between these divergent modes of thought or experience were temporarily effective, in the long run they did not resolve the crucial dilemma of how to preserve literati identity as it had come to be constituted. Like Ling Tingkan, who essentially urged his fellow intellectuals to be vigilant against the smug self-satisfaction characteristic of orthodox thought, Li Ruzhen's novel describes the liberation of intellectual endeavors from the fetters of moral self-righteousness and provincialism that plagued the literati of the last years of the Qing dynasty.

PART II

The Deconstruction of Literati Identity in *Rulin waishi*

MOST WESTERN translations of *Rulin waishi* have rendered the term *rulin* as "scholars," "mandarins," "literati," or some related term.[1] To pre-twentieth-century readers of the novel, at least those steeped in classical literature, the word *rulin* (literally "the forest of scholars") probably conveyed something more specific than any of these renderings. Almost all dynastic histories contain *rulin zhuan*, collections of biographies, which usually included entries for men noted for their scholarship in the Confucian classics. The author may have intended *rulin* to be read ironically, since few of the characters in the novel show much talent in that field. Whatever the author may have meant by it, the term *rulin* in the novel's title rather incongruously highlights the scholarly dimensions of literati identity, dimensions that are accorded little if any prominence in the body of the work.[2]

Yet for readers searching for the relevance of this novel to the intellectual life of its author and his contemporaries, and in particular to the intellectualization of literati self-identity discussed in Part I, this title offers a tantalizing hint. Within the novel itself, these issues are epitomized by the motif most clearly relevant to the scholarly world of the author's time, namely the advocacy of Confucian ritual or ritual propriety (*li*).

Needless to say, the inclusion of ritual in the novel in its various forms as the enactment of ritual, ritual propriety, and the revival of ancient rites clearly resonates with the preeminence of these concerns among Qing scholars. What is particularly intriguing about both the rituals and the espousal of ritual revival in *Rulin waishi* are the underlying suggestions of ironic intent. For ritual ultimately proves incapable of inspiring any long-term changes even among its adherents, who treat it largely as an academic exercise, even as a sort of grandiose spectacle. In fact, by the conclusion of the novel the reader is left to wonder whether the advocacy of this seemingly sacrosanct cultural ideal leads in fact to its opposite, namely impropriety, contentiousness, and ineptitude.

In Chapters 4, 5, and 6 I seek to elucidate *Rulin waishi*'s chronicle of the failure of the literati, both individually and as a class, to reclaim or revive any of the ideals of literati public life, whether through ritual or any other exercise in the literary or scholarly arenas. To accomplish this, in Chapter 4 I first examine how *Rulin waishi* creates the setting for its enunciation of a ritualist agenda of literati reform. First in importance is what I have already called the biographical dimension, by which I mean how the novel constructs its composite view of the various components of literati intellectuality. This is best understood, I believe, in terms of the literati vocations of scholarship, arts, literature, and examination studies or *bagu*. Particularly in the first half of the novel, each vocation is explored in some detail through a number of individual or composite biographical sections, which give voice to the worldviews of these various literati vocations or "careers." The polyphony of competing discourses that emerges serves both to define the intellectual dimensions of literati identity and to demonstrate their centrality to the literati malaise to which its satire is directed.[3]

This essentially spatial pattern of competing discourses constitutes an important organizing principle of the novel's portrait of literati mores, but it is not the only one. In Chapter 5 I turn to an analysis of the historical frame of the novel, that is, the references in it to events and figures of the Ming dynasty, to show how these support its theme of decline and corruption. These references place the fictional account of literati maturation in the context of the historical circumstances cited by Qing intellectuals as crucial to the development, and decline, of the literati in the Ming dynasty.

This discussion of history in turn brings us back in Chapter 6 to the question of how the novel accounts for the loss of unifying ideals and the corresponding inability to reconstitute some commonly accepted standards of literati action. None among its various literati identities can encompass the full range and diversity of its constituent members, and indeed each one founders on the attempt to "speak for all," as Zhang Xuecheng would have put it. I contend that ritual as a hegemonizing ideology of literati renewal is paradigmatic of the failure of all literati discourses to take account of the realities of literati society. Hence, in the third and last section of Chapter 6, I will describe the significance of the novel's articulation of ritual discourse to the decline traced in its final sections.

CHAPTER FOUR
Scholars, Poets, Painters, and Essayists

THE PLOT STRUCTURE of *Rulin waishi* is highly episodic or discontinuous, even for a vernacular novel. It has few characters, plot lines, or other easily identifiable features linking its narrative units into a single unified whole. Although in many respects inspired by the model of *Shuihu zhuan*, to which it is structurally similar, *Rulin waishi* nonetheless accentuates the discontinuities of plot inherent in the *Shuihu zhuan*–type structure of linked biographies. No single character or group of characters dominates the novel for more than a few chapters at most, and although more than one critic has likened it to "a string of pearls" with subtle links reinforcing thematic coherence, it can be read quite comfortably as a series of short stories. Moreover, although the city of Nanjing serves as a geographical "center of gravity," so to speak, throughout the novel, this spatial centrality is not complemented by other devices that anchor its disparate units into a coherent whole. Instead, the narrative flows from one discrete episode to the next with only the most tenuous of connections and little semblance of causality. The transitions, such as they are, actually accentuate the discontinuity between the narrative units.[1]

Moreover, devices of repetition or recurrence that might counteract this discontinuity are relatively unpronounced. There is very little cyclical or repetitive patterning through the use of recurrent textual or structural motifs, what Andrew Plaks calls "figural recurrence," characteristic of Chinese literati fiction.[2] Its series of stories lack clear beginnings or endings. Its protagonists are glimpsed at various stages and for varying lengths of time. Although a few of these portraits actually include meaningful changes such as the transition from youth to adulthood or sudden reversals of fortune, only two characters (Wang Mian and Yu Yude) are presented in anything resembling biographical accounts. The great majority of its literati are not accorded similar treatment, but are picked up, and eventually left off, in a desultory and often seemingly almost random fashion.

This episodicity is of course highly suited to the novel's treatment of its subjects. Satire in Western literature tends toward often radical narrative discontinuity, as classic examples such as *Candide* and *Gulliver's Travels* attest. Such formal features are suited to satire because, as Gilbert Highet suggests, the nature of the medium works against narrative continuity.[3] They are particularly important in *Rulin waishi* because much of the novel is devoted to demonstrating the limited nature of literati identities and ideologies. In the main body of the novel (chapters 2–36), groups of characters successively engage in examination studies (by which I mean the curricula of the Four Books and their orthodox commentaries, and the study and practice of *bagu* in preparation for the civil service examinations), poetry and prose, the arts, and scholarship. In a pattern of oscillation between these vocations, each social and geograhical milieu introduces new versions of and arguments for literati identities, as well as denunciations of their perceived rivals, that ultimately expose the inconsistencies or shallowness of these various adherents. The discontinuous narrative structure thus fully complements this subject matter.

Scholarship

Although the title *Rulin waishi* implies a certain prominence for intellectual pursuits, specifically Confucian scholarship, we find precious few examples of men of learning among the novel's characters. Classical Confucian scholarship as practiced by members of *rulin* appears irrelevant to the great majority of the novel's literati, most of whom regard learning as only a means to other ends rather than a vocation justified on its own merits. Nevertheless, the relatively small number of men who engage in classical scholarship (and thereby can justifiably be considered *ru*) occupy a place of strategic importance to the work as a whole. Scholarly concerns assume prominence during the events leading up to the establishment and dedication of the Taibo Temple in chapter 37, the novel's structural center and climax. As its title implies, for the novel the *ru* identity seems to represent the paradigmatic vocation of the literati.

Given the prominence of its scholars, and of their intellectual interests, it will be useful to examine them in some detail. The few men noted for their scholarly interests and attainments belong to the group of men who gather in Nanjing in the middle of the novel, or roughly in chapters 31–36. Although some minor characters possess an interest in learning, only Du Shaoqing, Chi Hengshan, and Zhuang Shaoguang are portrayed as actively engaged in scholarly work. Moreover, these three characters are introduced in an order that suggests a deepening of interests and attainments in classical learning. Du Shaoqing, the least bookish of the three, appears first, in his ancestral home in Tianchang County.[4] Though his days are occupied by merrymaking with a number of dilettantes and rogues who congregate around him, he nonetheless finds some time for the study of classical texts. Chi Hengshan, Du's friend and mentor, is the chief spokesman for the novel's ritualist program of social reform. And Zhuang Shaoguang, the last of the three to appear, is said to be "the most learned man of the empire" and gives evidence of great erudition as well as personal cultivation. Du, Chi, and Zhuang often appear together in later sections of the novel, suggesting their collective identification as the scholarly elite, so to speak, of the work. Moreover, each man is said to have dedicated himself to a single classic—Du, to the *Shijing*, the Classic of Poetry; Chi, to ancient ritual as codified in *Liji*; and Zhuang, to *Yijing*, the Book of Changes.

Du Shaoqing is praised by many characters of the novel as a "hero" (*haojie*), and descriptions of him tend to dwell on his acts of generosity (*haoju*) and unconventional behavior. He indeed earns regional notoriety for giving away or squandering much of his patrimony, and for acts such as strolling about arm-in-arm with his wife in a semipublic garden.[5] It is thus rather incongruous that Du serves as the vehicle for the novel's sole discussion of textual interpretation, expounding his views on two poems of *Shi jing* during a gathering at his Nanjing lodgings (*RWHH*, chap. 34, pp. 468–69; *TS*, pp. 377–79). Asked about his work on this classic, he launches into a spirited discussion of several poems from *Shijing* notorious for their sexually redolent subject matter. The first, "Kai Feng" (South wind), laments a mother's hardships in raising seven sons. Song commentators, having largely repudiated their Han exegetical forebears, fretted over the apparent "licentiousness" (*yin*) of this and other poems. In this particular example, Zhu Xi condemns the mother for harboring illicit desires to remarry but gets around the problem by finding filial sentiment in her children, whom he praises for blaming themselves for their mother's lapse of propriety.[6] Ridiculing this view as baseless, Du argues that a woman with seven sons would hardly be at an age to remarry and that her complaints merely give vent to a perfectly reasonable dissatisfaction with her onerous household duties.

The other poems Du cites, "Nü yue ji ming" (The girl says the cock has crowed) and "Qin Hui" (The Qin and Hui Rivers), belong to the Airs of Zheng, the sexually suggestive passages of which were particularly problematic for Neo-Confucian commentators. Zhu Xi's annotations find moral suasion in the dialogue between a man and woman awaking at dawn found in the first poem: "This poet relates the words of admonishment exchanged between a perspicacious husband and wife.... She tells her husband to rise [early] and go to hunt for fowl. From these words of admonishment, we can see that their feelings are not merely those of a private intimacy."[7] Again, Du rejects the imputation of such pious sentiments, pointedly praising the poem's celebration of marital bliss unsullied by the careerism of officialdom, whose preoccupation with worldly gain he charges with corrupting relations between the sexes.

Even worse than Zhu Xi's narrow and moralistic readings themselves is the slavish adherence to them among contemporary scholars, Du argues. "'When [Zhu Xi] annotated the classics,' said [Du], 'he set forth his views, expecting posterity to compare them to the commentaries of other scholars. Nowadays, however, all the other commentators have been dropped, and [Zhu Xi] is the sole authority. But he can't be blamed for the narrow-mindedness of later scholars.'" Later in the novel, Du's commentary on the classic is said to refer to Han dynasty annotations, paralleling the practices of the so-called Han Learning school just coming into vogue in the early Qianlong period. His interest in reviving earlier exegetical traditions and his repudiation of the general preference for Song exegetes that persisted into the Kangxi and Yongzheng reigns appear to voice what became the prevailing sentiment among Qianlong-era evidential scholars, giving Du's scholarship a certain au courant air.[8]

In spite of the apparent judiciousness of his scholarly pronouncements, however, the context of Du's remarks suggests something more than merely disinterested academic discourse. As his interlocutors remark half in jest, these opinions sound more like a justification for his distaste for officialdom and corresponding delight in unconventional behavior, than a purely neutral analysis of his sources. Here and elsewhere in the novel, Du Shaoqing's opinions are colored by his bohemian rejection of conventional wisdom. Whether discoursing on *Shijing* or the evils of concubinage or geomancy (*RWHH*, chap. 34, pp. 469–70; *TS*, p. 479; *RWHH*, chap. 44, p. 603; *TS*, pp. 492–93), he invariably launches into a tirade against the careerism of his day. This tendency to interpret a classic in terms of his own experiences and preferences suggests the sort of intellectual subjectivity that Qing literati such as Dai Zhen decried as the bane of literati life.

Du Shaoqing's subjectivity is characteristic, even emblematic, of nearly all literati in *Rulin waishi* and manifests itself both in his scholarly pronouncements here and in the acts of "generosity" that bring him fame. Gullible toward men who, feigning similar attitudes toward officialdom, bilk him of a large portion of his inheritance, Du remains nonchalant to the end about his losses, not deigning to stoop to the pettiness of others. His generosity is praised as noble by like-minded recluses and scholars, while careerist and vulgar officials such as Hanlin academicians and censors heap scorn on him as an irresponsible dreamer and fool, an example of youth gone astray. Criticism from patently hypocritical and venal characters appears at first glance to redound to Du's credit. Yet he no less than his philistine detractors is circumscribed by an inability to view his actions with impartiality, and his total rejection of power and privilege leads him to a reckless embrace of its absence, whatever the consequences. The series of follies that result from his idée fixe cannot but taint the very ideals he so ardently professes.

An analogous failure afflicts the earnest Chi Hengshan. Chi professes a firm conviction that ritual holds the key to the transformation of society, which as we have seen was certainly a widely held conviction among many eighteenth-century scholars. Decrying the corrupted state of contemporary rituals (which as discussed in Chapter 3 largely remained faithful to Zhu Xi even into the eighteenth century), Chi urges their restoration to the spirit of the ancients: "[The founding emperor] Taizu of our dynasty established peace in the realm, and this achievement is no less than that of the [sage emperors] Tang and Wu. But he completely neglected to set up rituals and music.... We will use this [ritual] for people to practice ancient rituals and music. This will foster talent, and also be of assistance to government and education" (*RWHH*, chap. 33, p. 459; *TS*, p. 370). He takes charge of preparations for the event and, following discussions with Du Shaoqing and Zhuang Shaoguang, assembles its various participants. During the performance itself, he like its other participants is mute, but presumably the archaic movements, music, and recitations represent the fruit of his careful research.

Like Du Shaoqing's preoccupation with the unconventional, ritual wholly captivates Chi Hengshan, whose words never stray far from his chosen topic (as he puts it, "ritual, music, military affairs, and agriculture" [*liyue bingnong*]). Chi rather idealistically believes that ritual can bring order to the realm and fulfillment to its subjects. While few Confucians might argue with this contention, the problem is that Chi's interests leave little room for ideas on any other subject. As several commentators note, his obsession with ritual matters makes Chi the quintessential pedant (*yuru*). Chi and those who follow his lead attempt to reify the hoary ideal of ritual propriety, an act that however noble in intent ignores the forces that render this an exercise in futility.[9]

The third of this scholarly trio, Zhuang Shaoguang, is a sophisticated and perspicacious recluse whose views appear less narrowly circumscribed than either Du's or Chi's. Zhuang indeed reconciles Du's levity with the stodginess of Chi—in short, a more balanced figure. He enjoys the pleasures of life in Nanjing in moderation and wears his learning lightly, yet his scholarly achievements have brought him national recognition. After a brief visit to the capital, Zhuang returns to a utopian existence on an island retreat in Xuanwu Lake, where he devotes his days to uninterrupted research.[10] While sharing Du Shaoqing's conviction of the wisdom of remaining out of office, Zhuang avoids Du's headstrong rejection of all intercourse with officialdom. Instead, during his summons to an imperial audience he delivers a realistic assessment of the political situation and manages to avoid office with a minimum of provocation. Nonetheless, though broad-minded and cultivated, Zhuang does not escape the taint of intellectual arrogance. After spending years on research of *Yijing*, he is quoted as belittling an examination essay editor as an "arrogant little dragon" (from the title of a hexagram in the same work; *RWHH*, chap. 49, p. 662; *TS*, p. 540), implying a condescension toward other scholars (or at least toward the somewhat pathetic editor Ma Chunshang) not apparent in his earlier appearances.[11] While embodying the highest possibilities for the *ru* vocation, even Zhuang reveals traces of a will to omniscience and intolerance of competing views that, as I discussed in Chapter 1, was decried by numerous Qing thinkers.[12]

These three scholars stand against the prevailing tide of careerism and obtuseness that afflict the great majority of literati and devote themselves to scholarship untainted by mercenary desires. While examination essay editors, down-and-out poets, and officialdom make easy targets for satirical deflation, these scholars appear to embody the ideals of the literati at their best.[13] Nevertheless, although Du, Chi, and Zhuang transcend the cupidity and crudity of their contemporaries, their very act of transcendence of mundane concerns engenders a subjectivity shared in greater measure by their fellow literati. Like poets, essayists, and *bagu* enthusiasts, these men of scholarship voice versions of literati identity that, however erudite or noble, nonetheless reveal the circumscribed quality of their experiences and prejudices. They thus define the possibilities and constraints of the literati, that is, the difficulty of any individual to transcend the intellectual subjectivity that blinds him (or her) to competing discourses. It appears that even intellectual inquiry of the highest order reflects the conditions endemic to the literati as a whole.

Literature

Only the small number of men who gather in Nanjing prior to the Taibo ritual can be unambiguously identified as *ru* or men of classical learning. By contrast, those men who practice the literary arts of prose and poetry are both much more numerous and distributed over a larger section of the novel, both preceding and following the Taibo ritual. From sophisticated and cultivated literati to humble tradesmen, and from relatively upright men to unscrupulous rogues, poetry and prose find advocates among a wide spectrum of men (and some women) seeking recognition, material reward, or some combination of the two. While classical scholarship attracts men apparently for its intellectual stimulation and perceived value, literary composition is engaged in largely as a vocation promising (though not always delivering) tangible benefits. For many such men literary fame substitutes for the examination status they have failed to achieve.

Poetry and prose also serve as avenues for characters who seek elegance and refinement; nonetheless, even among such men these arts inspire mercenary desires little different from the examination preparation their adherents profess to despise, namely, the appetite for temporal fame and wealth. The youth Qu Xianfu, for example, who incongruously marries an ardent *bagu* enthusiast, Ms. Lu, comes from a family of strong literary inclinations and correspondingly weak training in examination learning. When pressed by his new bride to compose a *bagu* essay, Qu retorts: "Not having been a month yet in your honorable house, I would prefer to write something more cultured. I really have not the patience to write these common [*bagu*] compositions" (*RWHH*, chap. 11, p. 156; *TS*, p. 124). He instead seeks to make a name for himself by composing and publishing poetic essays. Yet such disdain for *bagu* turns to fascination when Qu reinvents himself as an essayist following a series of disappointments.[14] This lack of commitment to literary pursuits is typical of the novel's poets and prose writers, for the choice of literature as a vocation appears to spring largely from frustrated ambitions.[15]

Poetry is associated in particular with the city of Hangzhou, perhaps for topical reasons,[16] for its citizens are said to honor poets above even the highest officials. The city is first described in chapter 16, when the young licentiate Kuang Chaoren meets Jing Lanjiang, proprietor of a turban shop and devotee of poetry. Jing introducesCed Kuang to a world of poets for whom literary fame, and not the examination success to which he has been earnestly devoting his efforts, represents the height of attainment. Among the constellation of literary lights of this city, the doctor Zhao Xuezhai shines as the model of success through poetry. He is said to consort with high officials and leading citizens of the empire, who reportedly treat him with great deference. As Jing Lanjiang crows, "Although Mr. Zhao has not passed the metropolitan examinations, there are tens of books in which his poems have been printed, and these have circulated throughout the empire. Who doesn't know of Mr. Zhao Xuezhai? He must be much more famous than any *jinshi*!" (*RWHH*, chap. 17, p. 246; *TS*, p. 198, translation modified).[17] This success validates the belief of such men that even high official position cannot measure up to the fame achieved through poetic composition.[18]

The poets of Hangzhou celebrate poetry as a means of escape from the obscurity and drudgery of their daily lives as salt runners, merchants, doctors, and menial tradesmen.[19] Itinerant bohemians such as Niu Buyi and his various associates similarly regard poetry as a means of cultivating relationships with the rich and powerful (*RWHH*, chap. 20, p. 282; *TS*, p. 228). While the classical scholars described above seek intellectual fulfillment as well as the realization of utopian ambitions, literary composition inspires both men of lowly status in search of recognition by their contemporaries and officials and wealthy men with pretensions to culture.[20] Completely absent are the sort of ideals that appear to motivate the three men discussed earlier (Du, Chi, and Zhuang). Poets justify their activities by the prestige and material rewards success brings, and not as serious intellectual or artistic endeavors. Moreover, although no evidence is presented in the form of compositions, innuendoes abound suggesting that these various self-styled poets and essayists possess neither talent in nor devotion to their art, apparently reflecting the decline of literary endeavors and of poetry in particular so lamented by Wu Jingzi's friends and contemporaries.

Nevertheless, each return to the motif of a literary career (in chapters 10–11, 15–18, 21–23, and 28–30) suggests the gradual evolution of an independent, and genuinely sophisticated, pursuit of literature on its own merits. Qu Xianfu and his literary colleagues dabble in criticism but fail to give voice to anything resembling justification for such composition. That is left to the poets of Hangzhou, whose efforts though sincere apparently produce only ludicrous results. The poet Niu Buyi appears to possess somewhat higher literary qualifications, while at the same time evincing greater ambitions for his art (chapters 21–22). And with the character of Du Shenqing, whose presence in chapters 28–30 leads directly to the introduction of his cousin Du Shaoqing in chapter 31, the novel provides a credible spokesman for the literary arts as a viable literati vocation.

On the one hand, Du Shenqing is little more than a youthful fop who spends much of his energies in pursuit of "manly" beauty. Yet in a conversation with several men collaborating on a *bagu* essay collection, Du offers excellent, tasteful advice on a poem written by one of them (*RWHH*, chap. 29, pp.398–99; *TS*, pp. 319–20). He himself is said to be a poet of some stature, his talents having been recognized at a special provincial poetry examination in which he took first place.[21] Yet while studiously cultivating a literary elegance, he nonetheless despises the idle pastimes of men searching for the trappings of culture. When poetry is suggested as an afternoon entertainment, he counters, "Sir, this is the worn-out way of poetry societies of our age. In my opinion, it is a vulgar elegance" (*RWHH*, chap. 29, p. 400; *TS*, p. 321). The expression he uses here to refer to poetic fashions, *ya de su* ("elegant to the point of vulgarity"), could easily designate Du's own jaded precocity.

Just as his cousin gives voice to the ideals of *ru* scholarship while simultaneously embodying its weaknesses, Du Shenqing also serves as the unwitting mouthpiece for prejudices of a literary persuasion. Discerning and sensitive in matters of literary taste and judgment, Du Shenqing's particular blindness is his almost complete disregard of moral issues, as illustrated in a discussion of the legitimacy of the Yongle usurpation of 1402. While wandering over historical sites in

Nanjing, Du and several companions come across a memorial temple to Fang Xiaoru, the most prominent victim of the great slaughter that took place upon the Yongle emperor's ascension to the throne. The following conversation ensues:

"What is your opinion of Mr. Fang, sir?" asked Hsiao.
"Fang was an impractical pedant. When there were so many more important matters to discuss, why should he speak only of the rightful succession? To be publicly executed in his court robes was no more than he deserved!" (RWHH, chap. 29, p. 402; TS, p. 323)[22]

For men of literary elegance, the moral rectitude and unbending idealism of men such as Fang Xiaoru were unnecessary distractions. Contempt for the naïveté of scholarly but impractical men such as Fang was in fact widespread among Wu Jingzi's acquaintances.[23] Though somewhat caricatured here, Du Shenqing's lack of patience with the moralistic pedantry of his cousin Du Shaoqing and the latter's associates gives expression to a genuine tendency among literary figures of the time. He, and by implication literary men in general, cede this dimension of literati identity to the *ru* who gather in Nanjing soon after Du Shenqing's departure from the city. Though avoiding the absurdities that result from his cousin's insistence on taking the moral high ground, Du Shenqing fails to integrate his views of literati responsibilities with the temptations of elegant refinement. Both Du Shaoqing and Du Shenqing thus become emblematic of the limitations inherent in pursuing either literary or scholarly identities, however cultivated or principled they may seem.

Examination Studies

Among the various literati vocations portrayed in *Rulin waishi*, examination preparation is the only one to be identified and defended as a bona fide profession. Ma Chunshang, an examination essay editor, expounds what he terms the "way" of examination essay writing, and his opinions are echoed by other characters, who defend it with a vehemence not seen in other matters. The adherents of the study of *bagu* generally share a narrowness and lack of sophistication, even crudity; and their devotion to it ranges from the mildly amusing to the patently absurd. It is no exaggeration to say that as the principal butt of the novel's satire, the study of *bagu* is paradigmatic of much that is wrong with the literati.[24] Nevertheless, over the course of the novel it emerges that the absurdities of an adherence to *bagu* differ in degree but not in kind from those of scholarly and literary pursuits. Each literati "way" develops a following whose biases and hegemonizing tendencies are revealed over the course of its articulation. This is truest of all for the adherents of examination learning.

Bagu's most determined spokesman, Ma Chunshang, defends the essay as the culmination of three thousand years of evolution. In an oft-quoted statement, he claims that "even were the Master [Confucius] to be present today, he too would have to read essays, and prepare for the examinations, instead of saying 'Make few false statements and do little you may regret'" (*RWHH*, chap. 13, p. 190; *TS*, p. 150). The salient feature of *bagu* learning is its narrowness, excluding everything beyond its ken as "miscellaneous readings" (*zalan*) that distract the student from developing a proper and ergo successful *bagu* style. A succession of characters mouth various versions of this formula. Zhou Jin, the protagonist of the first episode of the novel, and a devoted *bagu* proponent, rebukes one of his examinees for daring to practice poetry (though he puts this in the form of a seven-character couplet): "Our emperor stresses essays, why need you speak of Han and Tang [prose and poetry]?" (*RWHH*, chap. 3, p. 39; *TS*, p. 30, translation modified). His parochial views are amplified in the episode that immediately follows this passage, where Zhou's protégé Fan Jin fails to recognize the name Su Shi as that of the most famous writer of the Song dynasty.

Hanlin Compiler Lu and his daughter the fanatical Ms. Lu (chapters 10–11), the *bagu* editors Wei Tishan and Sui Cen'an (*RWHH*, chap. 18, pp. 253–54; *TS*, pp. 253–54), and Zhang Shusheng and other advocates of strict adherence to the examination essay also decry the dangers of "miscellaneous readings." According to Lu, breadth in study can detract from and indeed vitiate one's efforts to write good *bagu* essays; as he tells his daughter, "If you write [*bagu*] essays well, then whatever literary form you use—and this applies even to lyrics or descriptive poems—you will express yourself forcefully and exactly. If, however, you cannot write [*bagu*] essays well, then your writing will be unorthodox and third-rate" (*RWHH*, chap. 11, p. 155; *TS*, p. 123, translation modified). Such characters proclaim this medium to be the font of all learning, a multipurpose key that can guide any endeavor. Thanks to her father's influence, Ms. Lu has no interest in anything other than *bagu.* She and her father fret over her young husband Qu Xianfu's attempts at essay compositions, which are riddled with the traces of his poetry.

As discussed above, with the introduction of each new group of characters over the first half of the novel the literary vocations of poet and essayist gradually gain in sophistication, culminating in the studied indifference of the genuinely talented Du Shenqing. The zeal for *bagu* composition exhibits a parallel waning in later sections of the novel, where its practitioners protest their boredom with the medium. Wu Shu, a licentiate at the Imperial Academy in Nanjing, expresses his impatience with the form even while his essays take first place in every competition. And Yu Yude ("Dr. Yu") although once a teacher of essays admits that he too has no interest whatsoever in the subject (*RWHH*, chap. 36, p. 496; *TS*, p. 402). By the closing sections of the novel even characters who defend the importance of examination study do not give evidence of any enthusiasm toward *bagu*. Moreover, increasingly odious rogues of the last third of the novel, such as the Tang brothers, and the inhabitants of Wuhe County, juxtapose essay composition with buffoonery and debauchery. And among the more cultured scholars and poets of Nanjing and Hangzhou, *bagu* is not merely ignored; they decry its deleterious influence on their fields of interest. Chi Hengshan and Wu Shu see it as having lowered the standards of scholarly competence, a condition they seek to rectify (*RWHH*, chap. 49, p. 662; *TS*, pp. 539–41). Wang Mian warns in the opening chapter that its impending adoption as the principal method of official recruitment will bring about a decline in the morals and learning of the literati. And by the conclusion of the work, examinations are said to have become the only subject in which the literati remain competent, effectively eclipsing all other literati vocations.[25]

Yet while *bagu* does indeed appear to foster narrowness and crudity, there are hints that its effects are perhaps not entirely as pernicious as some characters charge. Ms. Lu, whose great disappointment in her husband Qu Xianfu's deficiencies in essay composition sour their otherwise happy marriage, carries her fervor for *bagu* to ludicrous extremes (she spends entire nights tutoring the couple's hapless young son in essay composition). But she is an exemplary wife and mother, admired for her competence in household affairs. And though gullible, the editor Ma Chunshang generously extends aid on several occasions to men in need. Likewise, Yu Yude, an idealized character hailed as a "true scholar" (*zhenru*), teaches *bagu* without suffering ill effects. With its faithfulness to the ethical rigorism of Song Neo-Confucian teachings, *bagu* seems to encourage—at least in those who take it seriously—the attention to moral scruples that Lü Liuliang emphasized in his teachings. Although *bagu* as it is practiced by most advocates fosters an intellectual narrowness and complacency of unparalleled proportions, within the novel's spectrum of literati vocations it nonetheless occupies a place of modest value.[26]

The problem with *bagu*, then, is precisely the overzealous devotion it inspires in its adherents. This is well illustrated by the story of Zhou Jin, the protagonist of the first section following the prologue, who pursues *bagu* with unflagging devotion in spite of a lifetime of failure in the examinations. Cowering before the provincial candidate Wang Hui, he claims to have read over the latter's successful essays many times, attempting to glean their secrets for success. This faithfulness is eventually rewarded by his sudden rise from lowly *tongsheng* to *jinshi* and officialdom at an advanced age. Sent to the province of Guangdong as commissioner of education, he presides at a county examination where Fan Jin has come to sit for the licentiate test. The following scene ensues:

> The last candidate to enter was thin and sallow, had a grizzled beard and was wearing an old felt hat. Guangdong has a warm climate; still, this was the twelfth month, and yet this candidate had on a linen gown only, so he was shivering with cold as he took his paper and went to his cell.... The man's clothes were so threadbare that a few more holes had appeared since he went into the cell. Commissioner Zhou looked at his own garments—his magnificent crimson robe and gilt belt—then he referred to the register of names, and asked, "You are Fan Jin, aren't you?"
> Kneeling, Fan Jin answered, "Yes, Your Excellency."
> "How old are you this year?"
> "I gave my age as thirty. Actually, I am fifty-four."
> "How many times have you taken the examination?"
> "I first went in for it when I was twenty, and I have taken it over twenty times since then." (*RWHH*, chap. 3, p. 38; *TS*, p. 29, translation modified)

Fan's experiences and current material distress mirror those of Zhou's up until only a few years before. Zhou too suffered years of poverty and repeated failures in the examinations before miraculously succeeding late in life. He immediately feels inclined to treat Fan with special consideration, paying close attention to his essays to try to discern any possible merit. The first and second readings yield only incomprehension. But by the third reading, Zhou sees that Fan's essay "is the most wonderful essay in the world—every word a pearl. This shows how often bad examiners must have suppressed real genius" (*RWHH*, chap. 3, p. 39; *TS*, p. 30). He passes Fan first and places Wei Haogu, a devotee of "poetry, songs, and *fu*" at the bottom of the list.

As the commentator Tianmu Shanqiao (Zhang Wenhu, fl. 1880) observes, Zhou sees himself in Fan: "It is because he himself had suffered, and thus could empathize with others based on his own experiences" (*RWHH*, chap. 3, p. 39). In this incident Zhou cannot see beyond his own particular experiences; and instead of passing the candidate who appears to be most qualified (Wei), he seeks out the one whose experiences mirror his own. While this slavish and narrow adherence to examination dictates borders on a fatuity hardly imaginable in the real world, the intellectual failure of characters such as Zhou and Fan can be seen as the paradigm for the more sophisticated characters who follow. For as I have attempted to demonstrate, not only *bagu* adherents,but poets, scholars, and other more cultured literati founder on a misplaced confidence in their own inherently subjective knowledge and experiences. Their inability to transcend such limitations echoes the eighteenth-century attacks on Neo-Confucian epistemology by Dai Zhen and the corresponding problematization of literati infallibility. In *Rulin waishi*, claims to omniscience by any literati, both the most refined and the least cultured, are the object of a mordant satire.

The examination dunces of *Rulin waishi* manifest a particularly obtuse version of the will to omniscience, mouthing grandiose claims for themselves based on their knowledge of *bagu*. It is encapsulated in the phrase "to speak for the sages" (*dai shengren shuohua*—the rhetorical stance taken by *bagu* writers), which is cited by literati characters as justification for their arrogation of power and wealth. When the two brothers Wang De and Wang Ren are asked by their brother-in-law Yan Zhihe to support his concubine's promotion to main wife, thereby replacing their dying sister, they express some reservations. But after being presented with a substantial gift of silver from Yan, they reply: "The great thing about us scholars is our adherence to principles. If we were writing a [*bagu*] composition to speak for Confucius, we should take exactly the line that we are taking now" (*RWHH*, chap. 5, p. 77; *TS*, p. 59, translation modified). The study of *bagu* has given these hypocritical representatives of Confucius the authority to assert their right to rule over matters of family and state. Later, Du Shenqing, who is particularly patronizing and arrogant toward his social inferiors, derides the clerk Jin Dongya for daring to write a commentary on the Four Books (the textual basis for *bagu* composition): "'A yamen clerk!'

he said to the boy. 'And he leaves his post to take up the interpretation of the classics! Is it for fellows like this to write commentaries on the works of the sages?'" (*RWHH*, chap. 30, p. 412; *TS*, p. 331). This proprietary interest of the literati in the source of their authority—the Confucian classics—is guarded against encroachment, exhibiting an overriding concern for protecting their status and perquisites from their social others.

The various claims made for *bagu* all betray a self-aggrandizing pomposity; but even in this rather narrow field of endeavor, its adherents do not share a unanimity toward its genesis or characteristics. Ma Chunshang provides the following taxonomy of *bagu* development: "The essay is always governed by reasoning. No matter how styles change, the reasoning remains the same. During the reigns of Hongwu and Yongle we find one style, and during the reigns of Chenghua and Hongzhi another; but careful investigation shows that the reasoning remains the same" (*RWHH*, chap. 13, p. 188; *TS*, p. 148, translation modified). A different view of the history of the medium is expressed by the editors Wei Tishan and Sui Cen'an. They see *bagu* as an indicator of historical change:

> Thus from an essay you should be able to see not only the writer's rank and fortune, but also whether the empire is passing through a period of prosperity or decline. The Hongwu and Yongle periods had one set of rules; the Chenghua and Hongzhi periods had another. Each reign has its particular rules which have been handed down from one group of scholars to another, forming an orthodox tradition. (*RWHH*, chap. 18, p. 254; *TS*, p. 204, translation modified)

Although these two passages hardly seem irreconcilable, the editors Sui and Wei mock Ma Chunshang's essays, claiming that he has "ruined" many promising students. Such intolerance toward competing views epitomizes the tendency of *bagu* enthusiasts to exclude all but their own individual tastes. That this intellectual arrogance is based on the most dubious of all literati vocations is only the most extreme example of tendencies shared by the literati as a whole, whatever their ideological predisposition.

The novel's treatment of examination learning can be seen to echo what *bagu* theorists and commentators of the eighteenth century were distancing themselves from—that is, the claims of Lü Liuliang and others concerning the efficacy of the essay as a means of moral cultivation. The essayists make grandiose claims for the power of this medium to bring literary perfection to its devotees, yet this efficacy is not borne out over the course of the novel. True to his views of *bagu* as a medium of "reasoning," Ma Chunshang's own essays are said to be "full of reason [*li*] but lacking in vigor [*qi*]." Kuang Chaoren, who is inspired by Ma's example, is nonetheless his opposite in style: "full of vigor, but lacking in reason." As these various theorists and practitioners proclaim the superiority of their own methods, refusing to admit the possibility of more than one mode of writing, they reveal the perils of relying on any area of knowledge as one's sole guide in intellectual endeavor.

Despite their limitations, Ma Chunshang and his protégé Qu Xianfu are befriended by Du Shaoqing and other cultured literati who have little interest in examination learning. But in his later appearances Ma continues to exhibit the same narrow, uninformed views, and in the company of culturally sophisticated and learned men, he quickly reveals his limits. In their company he is said to have authored a scholarly treatise on *Chunqiu* (Spring and autumn annals), which like his *bagu* essays is praised as "well-reasoned" (*hen you tiaoli*) (*RWHH*, chap. 49, p. 662; *TS*, p. 444). Ms. Lu is also given a similar accolade in her management of household affairs (*RWHH*, chap. 13, p.187; *TS*, p. 147). It appears that examination learning has some place within the spectrum of knowledge; but taking it to be the center of human endeavor, and arrogating power based upon it, is thoroughly satirized in *Rulin waishi*. And in that the practice of *bagu* most obviously manifests literati claims to omniscience, it can be seen as the paradigm for literati failings as a whole.

Art

Artists are a very minor presence in *Rulin waishi*, represented in the body of the novel only by the calligraphers Jin Yuliu and Xin Dongzhi of Yangzhou. These two brag about having treated their salt merchant patrons with contempt, demanding huge sums for writing a few characters (*RWHH*, chap. 28, pp. 380–81; *TS*, pp. 305–6). As discussed in Chapter 2, even in the increasingly "bourgeois" atmosphere of Yangzhou, the acceptance of payment for art apparently remained an issue sensitive enough that painters such as Zheng Xie were still viewed as flaunting literati conventions by ostentatiously seeking payment for their work.[27] The two calligraphers' mockery of merchant wealth is gratuitous, and if anything, they ape the merchant cupidity they profess to despise. Interestingly, this fleeting episode occurs almost exactly halfway through the novel. The only other artists are found in the novel's prologue and epilogue. Wang Mian, whose biography opens the novel, is cast as a painter—and indeed, his posthumous fame rested largely, though not exclusively, on his renderings of plum blossoms. And the final chapter opens with an anecdote in the life of an eccentric calligrapher, Ji Xia'nian.

The strategic position of artists at the beginning, middle, and end of *Rulin waishi* suggests a significance that belies their meager parts. The painter Wang Mian avoids all entanglement with the world and lives a life unsullied by its demands. He personifies the man of education who is nonetheless not a literatus, for he is not tied to any of the conventions or roles of literati life. Ji Xia'nian, the calligrapher in the concluding chapter, also spurns the attentions of educated men, preferring Buddhist monks as his companions, and lives a life of eccentric poverty. Perhaps the persona of the painter and calligrapher attracted the author Wu Jingzi for its possibilities of transcendence of the dichotomy between the literati and their social others. There is evidence that Wu Jingzi may have been directly acquainted with Zheng Xie.[28] And his descriptions of Yangzhou calligraphers and Ji Xia'nian vaguely evoke eccentric figures of eighteenth-century Yangzhou such as Jin Nong and Gao Fenghan. The novel's version of Wang Mian's life illustrates the contours of a literati existence wholly beyond the mold of traditional prescriptions of literati identity. That a painter was selected as the medium for this exploration suggests a freedom from literati inhibitions and preoccupations that no other literati vocation could offer.

Non-literati

The opening and closing chapters of *Rulin waishi* are devoted to the biographies of men who either by choice or necessity abstain completely from literati roles. Wang Mian the painter lives as a hermit in a country village and later dies anonymously in the mountains; the four eccentrics of Nanjing described in chapter 55 include a tailor, a peddler, and a tea-house proprietor. In the body of the novel as well, literati characters are surrounded by and interact with diverse elements of society, including merchants, servants, yamen runners, monks, and tradesmen. Many members of these groups, especially salt merchants, actors, and military officers take on literati affectations and mingle with their social betters to enhance their own prestige or simply to gain access to wealth or status. But those who do not seek such social advancement remain free of the delusions that afflict the judgment of their literati betters. Yamen runners and servants are streetwise and agile in the world of mundane affairs and provide useful though often unheeded advice to their clumsy literati patrons. Merchants as well prove both wiser and more generous than the by turns niggardly or financially reckless literati, who claim to live beyond the sordid world of money. Most notable is their generosity in coming to the aid of literati in distress. For example, when Zhou Jin collapses in frustration over his inability to achieve examination rank, it is his merchant relatives and friends who purchase the degree that enables him to compete in the provincial examinations. Zhuang Zhuojiang, a retired merchant of substantial means, performs various philanthropic deeds, including supplying the impecunious Du Shaoqing with rice.[29]

While manifesting a human decency and altruism found in only a handful of literati characters, commoners are not infrequently made to bear the brunt of literati capriciousness. A number of court cases and legal difficulties punctuate the novel at regular intervals: Yan Zhizhong's suit for his sister-in-law's property (chapter 6), Quan Wuyong's imprisonment (chapter 12), the widow Niu's accusations against Niu Pu (chapter 24), Lu Xinhou's arrest for possession of contraband works (chapter 35), and so forth. In every case, these legal difficulties are cleared up with relative ease, thanks largely to the light treatment given literati offenders by officialdom. But when non-literati are found in violation of the law, or even suspected of misdeeds, they are dealt with harshly. The pimp Wang Yian, for example, is roughed up and threatened by two gruff licentiates for daring to wear a scholar's cap. And salt merchants are subjected to cruel beatings merely on the suspicion of having colluded with pirates during a theft of salt on the Yangtze River (chapter 43). The pervasiveness of this pattern suggests that literati suffer little for offenses much more serious than those for which commoners are shown little mercy.[30]

Among these diverse members of the novel's society, the non-literati occupation given the greatest prominence in *Rulin waishi* is that of the military. Like the literati, martial men also participate in the realm of public affairs and both historically and discursively served as the complement to civil authority. That the civil and military arms of government act in harmony was crucial to the ideal of effective governance in Confucian statecraft. Mutual cooperation between the two wings of the bureaucracy could guarantee peace and stability, while a lack of coordination or conflict was taken as an omen, if not the root cause, of social unrest and official paralysis. Moreover, the qualities of military men were seen as in contrast with, if not antithetical to those of the literati. While the literati manifest civil virtues of culture, literacy, and a knowledge of the arts, the military were expected to embody the forcefulness, courage, and decisiveness of men of action.

Professional military officers of *Rulin waishi* include two characters prominent in the final third of the novel, the commanders Xiao Yunxian and Tang Zou. The major portion of each of their biographies is devoted to their military campaigns in the western and southern border regions. The first campaign, in Qingfeng cheng, is successful in large part because of Xiao's knowledge of local geography, which he gleaned from ancient treatises. He subsequently directs a program of pacification, encouraging agriculture and a basic curriculum of examination studies among the local inhabitants. Tang Zou is the leader of an operation against a group of rebellious Miao tribesmen in the southwest. Outwitting both the rebel Miao tribesmen and a wily local magistrate opposed to the use of military force, Tang restores peace to the wartorn region. Yet in spite of their successes, both Xiao and Tang are demoted, putting to an end at least temporarily their apparently successful careers. In Xiao's case, the authorities levy fines against him while promoting semiliterate colleagues who belittle his wide learning but fail to contribute any ideas during the campaign. Tang is similarly charged with profligate use of state funds and relieved of his duties. Following these disappointments, Xiao moves dejectedly to a new posting in the center of the country, far away from the frontier, while Tang devotes his energies to trying to prepare his dissolute sons for the civil examinations.

These two figures evoke great admiration among the idealistic scholars of Nanjing, who express sympathy for the injustices they have endured. To Du Shaoqing their achievements demonstrate the importance of using men of some education, "literati" (*dushuren*) in military posts. Neither Xiao nor Tang belongs to the rough-and-ready stratum of swaggering warriors; both are cultivated and to a certain degree proficient in literary matters. In their respective campaigns it is not just their valor on the battlefield but their knowledge of texts that proves decisive to victory. Combining civil as well as military talents, these two men appear to represent an ideal integration of civilian and military roles that transcends literati concerns.[31] Yet their presence also signals what appears to be the deleterious influence of literati mores on national defense. For though on good terms with many literati, these martial men suffer apparently because the civil bureaucracy upon whom they must depend fails to appreciate and properly reward their military achievements. Just as the practitioners of the various literati paths described above fail to recognize the validity of rival points of view, the civil bureaucracy as a whole is a force for the perpetuation of literati privilege and prerogatives at the expense of the national interest. The literati monopolization of power that is reflected in the treatment of Xiao Yunxian and Tang Zou brings about an alienation between military and civil and the exclusion of the latter from government. The ultimate denouement of this literati will to dominance is national disaster, namely the fall of the dynasty.

The Literati Ideal

Although these scholars, poets, artists, and examination essay editors display varying degrees of fatuity, ignorance, or worse, these men are nonetheless differentiated in turn from the run-of-the-mill literati who populate the novel. The many aspiring degree candidates, officials, and their hangers-on who represent the majority of the novel's characters dully adhere to a philistine faith in examinations and the preservation of the status quo. By contrast, even the rather uncultured Ma Chunshang and the poets of Hangzhou evince a certain enthusiasm for their chosen professions that, however ludicrous, seems preferable to the crudity of those who trumpet the infallibility of the current system of official recruitment. There is even a certain pathos, perhaps, to the men who, either unsuccessful in or unqualified for the examinations, seek alternative means of achieving some measure of satisfaction, even if for transparently mercenary aims. Among them, a few cultivated literateurs and men of classical learning pursue the sort of broad learning that manifests the highest ideals of literati culture. Nonetheless, even men such as Du Shaoqing, Chi Hengshan, and others of impressive attainments and deep convictions fail to free themselves from the subjectivity and intellectual limitations that differ in degree but not in kind from those of *bagu* enthusiasts. All engage in a vainglorious attempt to achieve an omniscience that leads directly to the absurdities and fallacies satirized by the novel. While the examination system produces men of little learning and even less imagination, the ultimate bane of the literati way of life seems to be the failure of any of its members to recognize their own subjective prejudices.

Indeed, regardless of their particular ideological bent, literati as a whole are prone to pursuing an idée fixe—whether a single-minded careerism or an ephemeral ideal—that ultimately blinds them to the surrounding realities. The Lou brothers of Huzhou squander their wealth by seeking out unrecognized men who share their own resentment at the dynasty for having failed to give them examination degrees, an obsession that blinds them to the idiocy and charlatanry of self-styled recluses such as Yang Zhizhong and Quan Wuyong. While magistrate at Anqing, Xiang Ding presides over the case of Niu Pu, who is rightly accused by Niu Buyi's widow of assuming her husband's identity. But holding to a Confucian skepticism, and apparently reluctant to accuse a man known locally as a poet and friend of officialdom, Xiang fails to bring Niu Pu to justice. Interpreting their surroundings according to their own necessarily subjective experiences, these men fail to make dispassionate judgments of men and events. This is especially evident in the episodes that trace the maturation of the impressionable youths Kuang Chaoren, Niu Pu, and Bao Tingxi. Their young minds undergo corrupting experiences that suggest not a simple moral debasement but the narrowing of their otherwise remarkable native intelligence. Kuang Chaoren in particular enters the novel as a remarkably versatile young man, absorbed in *bagu* essays and poetry, and an eager listener to mentors who offer their guidance. But as he is drawn into an increasingly mercenary and corrupt pursuit of official advancement, his native intelligence turns into befuddlement. When justifying a series of unscrupulous actions, he misquotes literary sources and expresses incoherent and absurd opinions with little attempt made to sort out their convoluted logic (chapters 19–20). Another such character, Ji Weixiao, matures from a successful young licentiate into a libertine whose words never stray far from his chosen motto, "*jishi xingle*" (carpe diem).

The three scholars introduced just prior to the ritual at Taibo Temple manifest literati perspicuity and probity far above that of their contemporaries. Yet even they fail to free themselves from their subjective preconceptions. Immediately following Zhuang Shaoguang's summons to the capital, however, the author inserts the biography of a character who has managed to avoid the delusions that befuddle the literati as a whole. Aside from Wang Mian, who lives in a world removed from that of the rest of the novel (in the *xiezi* or prologue), only the character Yu Yude ("Dr. Yu") transcends the follies to which his contemporaries fall prey. Though an educational intendant at the Nanjing Imperial Academy, he betrays not the slightest hint of the pretentiousness that is said to afflict officialdom almost without exception. Nor does he give evidence of subscribing to any particular views that might narrow his perspective. In this fallen age of *bagu*, with its multitude of prejudices and absurdities, he avoids the opinionated, smug confidence of his contemporaries. His life follows the pattern of many of the novel's characters, namely, of repeated failures in the examinations, with success coming only late in life (at the age of fifty). Yet in spite of his poverty he is not tempted to seek fame or fortune through alternative means, as many characters do. Instead he simply and unpretentiously engages in the occupations commonly held by literati climbing the examination ladder—namely, teaching, and service as a *muliao* or adviser to various officials. He even teaches *bagu* and practices geomancy to make ends meet but with neither the partisanship nor the cupidity that characterize their adherents.[32] Moreover, as an official he treats servants and literati alike with equal respect and deference.

These attributes make his title *boshi* (literally "broad literatus") apt, for he avoids the narrowness and prejudices of all other literati. It is he, and not Zhuang Shaoguang, who is honored as the presiding officiant of the ritual at Taibo Temple and lauded as a "true scholar" (*zhenru*) worthy of emulation.[33] Among the twenty-four literati celebrants of this event only he seems to transcend the narrowness, prejudices, and subjectivity of his contemporaries. And he does so precisely by recognizing the limits on his own individual capacities. He does not seek to interpret his surroundings in any terms but merely observes and reacts appropriately to circumstances. As a result, he achieves an intellectual integrity that eludes the advocates of even the most exalted scholarship, let alone other literati paths.

CHAPTER FIVE

The Decline of Literati Mores

THE REPRESENTATION of the literati in *Rulin waishi* can be described as encyclopedic in scope, encompassing not only men who conform to the roles of scholar, poet, *bagu* essayist, and artist but also numerous characters whose cultural attainments place them somewhere between literati and the general population. The words *rulin* of the novel's title may apply only to the tiny minority of erudite scholars in Nanjing, but as we have seen, these men exemplify the entire literati class. Given the importance of this term, it may not be unreasonable to look to the other half of the title, *waishi*, or "unofficial history," for clues to the interpretation of the novel. This task is more problematic than one might think, however, for while few would argue over the prominence of literati to the novel, *Rulin waishi* generally has not been read as a work of major historical implications.

This is further complicated by the many topical allusions to the life and times of the author of this novel. Although these allusions have not generated the degree of interest that those found in *Honglou meng* have, the Jin He colophon of 1869 has long been accepted as the most important statement of the work's referential dimension. Jin He, a member of a clan in Wu Jingzi's native place of Quanjiao with close ties to the Wus, including Wu Jingzi himself, claims that eighty to ninety percent of the novel's characters and events can be traced to contemporary sources. He Zehan's *Rulin waishi zhenshi benmo kao* documents the extensive correlations between the contents of *Rulin waishi* and writings from the mid-eighteenth century, in particular from the period of Wu Jingzi's adulthood (1720–50). Whatever we may wish to make of these correspondences, it seems irrefutable that the novel was appreciated by Wu's friends and contemporaries at least in part for its contemporary references.

And yet, following the precedent of many works of fiction of the period, this eighteenth-century portrait is framed within a Ming dynasty chronology, roughly between the years 1360 to 1600. References to actual historical figures and events are sparse and relatively inconspicuous. But this chronology is invoked often enough, and in places of particular significance within the text, that it cannot be dismissed as mere staging. Most obviously, it provides a frame that while seemingly marginalized, nonetheless superimposes a diachronic dimension on the novel's episodic structure.[1] This historicity extends the novel's frame of reference beyond what has generally been viewed as a thinly disguised contemporary setting to encompass the historical development of society and the forces within it. Moreover, by employing a frame quite faithful to the historical record, it draws upon events of the Ming period as subtle glosses to the significance of its fictional account. These references suggest a remarkably complex view of Ming history and its relevance to the evolution of the literati of Wu Jingzi's own lifetime.[2]

The choice of the word *waishi* or "unofficial history" in the novel's title is an especially evocative one, given the novel's subject matter.[3] This term can be understood as more or less synonymous with the terms *yeshi* and *baishi*, which designate a very broad category of narrative works that were not officially sponsored. Ranging from chronologies, to personal memoirs, to *biji* collections of anecdotes miscellaneously arranged, as well as patently fictional accounts, *yeshi* and *baishi* imply a freedom from strict adherence to historical veracity. The latter term in particular was also frequently used to refer to popular novels and story collections, effectively blurring the distinction between fact and fiction. What allowed all of these disparate works to be grouped together was an ideological predisposition unconstrained by the documentary standards and political orthodoxy of institutionalized state historiography. They were often employed as repositories of information either unreported in, or at variance with, the official histories.[4] In a society where the recording of history was considered both the duty and prerogative of the state, any version of events that might conflict with the accepted official account could be considered suspect.

The component *ye* of *yeshi* does not necessarily imply the taint of subversion, however, for it often carried connotations simply of the lowly or private, and thus beyond the reach of government historians. However, when the state was determined to impose its own account of sensitive events, and to suppress others, the *yeshi* clearly became vehicles for the expression of alternative views of historical events. This function was particularly evident during the early-to-mid Qing, in part

The Decline of Literati Mores / 111

because of the vestiges of Ming loyalism that simmered for decades, and also as a perhaps inevitable response to the policies of the literary inquisition (*wenzi yu*) adopted by several emperors to suppress what was deemed subversive or anti-Manchu literature. Hence, even more than in earlier periods the *yeshi* of this era were often defined largely in terms of a confrontational attitude toward state-sponsored histories, most notably that of the Ming History Board.[5] The choice of the entire Ming period as the setting for an "unofficial history" could not but have suggested some affinities with such works, particularly in the 1740s (when, it is generally agreed, Wu Jingzi wrote his novel), just after the Ming History was completed in 1739.

The extent to which *Rulin waishi* can be said to contain views subversive of either Manchu legitimacy or the court-approved version of Ming historical events has been debated rather inconclusively. Certainly several issues of great concern to the Qing court are alluded to in the novel: the suppression of works by historical figures unfriendly to or persecuted by previous emperors; the actions of military figures and outlaws both in support of and in opposition to the government; the holding of special examinations such as that sponsored in 1736 by the Qianlong emperor (and to which Wu Jingzi was recommended); and so forth.[6] But whatever its attitude toward such contemporary issues, the novel's historical allusions can be interpreted independently of their topical significance. That the Ming period was a charged subject during the mid-Qing only enhances its power, for in effect, Wu Jingzi locates his history precisely in the period to which many men of his own and previous generations devoted a great deal of thought and historical scholarship.[7] To many, the Ming was a lost opportunity, and its mistakes had resulted in the ignominious subjugation of the Chinese by a barbarian people. Moreover, writers such as Quan Zuwang (1705–55) devoted much of their lives to preserving a record of the heroic deeds of the Ming resistance to the Qing invaders, in the face of Qing efforts to expunge such events from official histories.

While residual Ming loyalism remains an intriguing if somewhat shadowy aspect of the novel's historical dimension, I focus here on the implications of this history for the portrayal of literati intellectual life. Early Qing thinkers who saw a need for serious reform of the literati looked to the Ming for the root causes of the conditions of their own times. *Rulin waishi* broaches several areas of particular interest to Qing thinkers in this regard. These include the establishment of civil service examinations at the beginning of the dynasty, the impact of Wang

112 / *The Deconstruction of Literati Identity*

Yangming's teachings, the literary movements of the Jiajing period, and the decadence and apathy of the Wanli reign. Each of these events and their attendant issues is identified with a particular historical moment within the novel. Broadly speaking, we can identify four more or less distinct stages in the Ming chronology to which the novel adheres. The first is that of the Wang Mian biography of chapter 1. This introductory tale purports to chronicle the life of the historical figure Wang Mian, concluding sometime around the founding of the Ming dynasty in 1368. Identified in its title as a *xiezi* or "wedge," this chapter is set off from the rest of the novel both structurally and temporally. The second stage begins in chapter 2, which is said to take place in the late Chenghua period (1465–87), and continues until chapter 7, which contains an actual historical event of the year 1517, near the end of the Zhengde period. The third group of references are found in chapters 21–35, which mention several dates of the Jiajing reign, spanning the period Jiajing 9–35 (1530–56). Chapter 55, the final chapter, opens with a mention of the date Wanli 23 (1595). In the previous two chapters, however, several references indicate that these final sections are also set in the Wanli period (1573–1620), which I identify as the fourth stage of the chronology.[8]

Hence, although the body of the novel spans a period of roughly a century, with most of the characters and episodes bracketed within two or three generations, this chronology encompasses more or less the entirety of the dynasty. It is, however, far from contiguous; indeed, the four groups of references outlined above do not serve to create the impression of a continuous flow of time, but rather to connect certain events and sections of the text with particular historical circumstances. Following the founding of the dynasty in chapter 1, the first few chapters are situated in the period between the Chenghua reign, noted as a time of stability and prosperity, and the Prince Ning Rebellion, a major crisis that nearly toppled the dynasty. The middle sections of the novel devoted to the gathering together of literati at Nanjing are set in the Jiajing period, that is, the era of the most renowned figures of Ming literature and art. And the final chapters turn to the Wanli reign, a time of political uncertainty at court and what turned into the beginning of the dynasty's precipitous decline.[9]

At least superficially this chronology corresponds with the general contours of the account of literati vocations described above. The early sections of *Rulin waishi* depict the rather simple world of men intent on examination success. Gradually their places are taken by characters of increasingly complex motivations, as well as by men of higher moral, literary, and scholarly attainments, culminating in the ceremony at Taibo Temple. The last third of the novel traces the descent into apathy and decadence of the literati and in its conclusion apparently repudiates literati life. What this historical dimension accomplishes above all else is the superimposition of issues identified by Qing thinkers as crucial to the transformation of the literati over recent history. It remains for us to examine these four sets of references in some detail.

The use of historical references in the main body of the text is for the most part both allusive and elusive. Only in the first "wedge" chapter do historical figures briefly emerge as protagonists. This section consists of the biography of Wang Mian, the late Yuan painter of plum blossoms. Wang is portrayed as an idealized recluse who avoids all political entanglements. Disdainful of the pettiness and careerism of officialdom, he retreats to a mountain hut rather than answer the call to assume a role in the newly established Ming dynasty. In the novel's version of Wang's life, he epitomizes the eremitic ideal of self-contentment, sequestered from the sordid events in the political arena. The first literatus of the novel is a man who rejects all aspects of literati identity, choosing complete anonymity over participation in public life.

Yet this account is in marked contrast to the most widely known versions of Wang's life and career, the biographies by Xu Xian and Song Lian of the late Yuan and early Ming, and Zhu Yizun of the early Qing. These and other texts treat Wang as a "recluse" (*yimin*); but the motives for his retreat from public life and the ultimate denouement of his disengagement are interpreted quite differently from this fictional version. The novel carefully crafts nearly every detail and vignette of Wang's life from preexisting sources, including the above-mentioned biographies, but very little of the original versions is retained intact. The result is a metamorphosis that reflects back on the sources that inspired it, responding to the issues raised by the earlier biographers.

Two of these biographies were authored by illustrious political and literary figures who lived during the founding of the Ming and the Qing and were apparently intended to exert some influence over public opinion. Song Lian's biography, written shortly after Wang's death, adopts a very partisan and engaged tone. Zhu's account, written three centuries later, during the early Qing, is more dispassionate. Xu's biography, written in the last years of the Yuan dynasty, is the longest of the three and perhaps the least concerned with the political events leading up to the founding of the Ming.

Each of these three biographies dwells on the eccentric and even quixotic aspects of Wang's behavior and interprets them as symptoms of frustration toward the unsettled conditions of the late Yuan. In each, Wang finally withdraws from civilized life to the wilds of Jiuli Mountain, where he hopes to avoid the impending chaos of dynastic change. However, each concludes his life on a slightly different note. Whereas Song has Wang won over to the Ming forces who descend on his mountain sanctuary, the other two portray him as a scornful critic of rebels who abduct him unceremoniously from his home. Moreover, Zhu pointedly informs the reader that he follows Xu's account of this episode, and that his primary purpose in writing the biography lay in refuting Song Lian's distortions in the service of Ming loyalty: "Ever since Song Wenxian [Lian]'s biography appeared, people have always regarded Wang as an adviser [of the Ming armies]. But did he ever spend even one day in such a post? After reading Xu Xian's *Baishi jizhuan*, [I have concluded that] Wang probably did not compromise his integrity before he died."[10]

Clearly, the question of whether or not Wang joined the Ming rebels was the most important issue for both Song and Zhu, not only because it reflected on the credibility of the dynasty, but also because it colored the evaluation of Wang's nonconformist temperament. Hence, Song's interpretation of Wang's actions makes of them the more or less straightforward symptoms of frustration of a political outsider with corruption and misgovernment, in effect a "pose" that he could shed upon the advent of an enlightened administration.[11] Zhu, by contrast, objects to the idea that Wang's idealism could be so easily compromised. He instead seems to regard Wang's eccentricity as an expression of some personal, deeply felt beliefs, which could not be abandoned when opportunity came knocking at his door. Wang's final refusal to cooperate with Zhu Yuanzhang's marauding troops thus severs him both from the Ming itself, as well as more broadly from any easy commitment to political participation under prevailing conditions.

Rulin waishi's creation of Wang Mian seems to take its departure from Zhu's biography, pointedly concluding with Zhu Yizun's own closing remark ("Did Wang ever spend a single day as an official?"). But it goes far beyond Zhu in creating a character oblivious to worldly gain and antipathetic to officialdom. In all three biographies Wang is said to have participated unsuccessfully in the provincial examinations and to have traveled to Dadu in search of patronage, before finally giving up such aspirations. After burning his examination essays, he turned to the study of Sunzi's *Bingfa*, and according to Song, he authored a work in imitation of *Zhou li*, that is, expressly for the establishment of a governmental system. Though living on the fringes of acceptability, in none of the three extant biographies is he beyond the pale of social expectations for the literati. In contrast, *Rulin waishi* places Wang in almost total isolation from human contact. From his earliest childhood he is self-taught, requiring neither schooling nor even advice from local scholars to attain a remarkable erudition. He never seeks the company of other educated men, contenting himself with an elderly farmer, Old Qin, whose cows he tends as a young child, and his mother, to whom he is devoted. Even marriage and family life apparently cannot distract him. The ambitions and appetites expressed by those around him seem to meet with an imperturbable silence from a man immersed in a self-contented, almost lyrical reverie. While Song Lian describes Wang's donning a hat and robes modeled on the poet Qu Yuan as a symptom of his political frustration, the novel transforms this into the innocent diversion of a free spirit bent on his own amusement.

Wang was perhaps best known in later ages as a painter of plum blossoms, but Song's biography seems to minimize the importance of his artistic activities, mentioning only perfunctorily his skill in *mogu hua*, a style Wang made famous. Song even has him express remorse for having to stoop to selling his paintings for his livelihood. But in the novel, painting is by far his principal interest, and the issue of receiving payment for his works is conspicuously absent. Instead, income from his painting gives him the leisure to entertain his mother and to live a carefree, unfettered existence isolated from other educated men. This peaceful and bucolic life is shattered, however, when the fame his paintings have achieved brings him to the attention of local notables, a meddling magistrate, and his venal lackey. Only then does his painting come to express political sentiments, of *jici*, or satire of the foolish and crude gentry of Ji'nan, where he has been forced to live in temporary exile. The fame he has achieved in the practice of his art has, in spite of his desire for anonymity, led him to grief, and he must eventually disappear entirely into the mountains to avoid the snares of literati society. In this denouement, Wang is transformed into a victim not of the enveloping chaos, as all three biographies portray him, but of a society that forces its men of talent to submit to the unwelcome shackles of public life. His eremitic retreat from politics under conditions of peace and stability follows as a logical conclusion to the desire for a life led entirely according to one's own inclinations, free of concern for praise or censure. Wang's final escape into complete anonymity comes just as an announcement heralds the establishment of the examination system by the new emperor, that is, the institutionalization of literati ambition.

Wang is not entirely free of concern for the wider world, as he demonstrates in a conversation with the founder of the Ming, Zhu Yuanzhang. In the Xu and Zhu biographies, he lectures the Ming rebels who have abducted him on the importance of treating the inhabitants of Shaoxing with respect. In *Rulin waishi*, by contrast, Zhu Yuanzhang humbly visits Wang's hut in the manner of the sage kings of antiquity, who paid deference to wise recluses. This meeting and Wang's advice to the future emperor are portrayed as an idealized encounter between ruler and subject, entailing neither elaborate ceremony nor obligation on either side. Both here, and in his subsequent warning about the deleterious effects of the newly instituted examination system, Wang's advice is given not in the context of an impending dynastic upheaval but in that of a newly founded dynasty at the advent of its rule. It could even be read as a deliberate revision of the three biographies, suggesting that dangers in the form of social or military unrest pale by comparison to the insidious effects of the examination system on successive generations. Immediately following his prediction, an allusion to *Shuihu zhuan*'s meteors falling to earth (from chapter 1 of that novel, where meteors let out by a venal official spell impending doom) adds a finishing touch to the image of a Pandora's box of troubles let out to plague the future.[12]

In all three biographies Wang is portrayed as prescient and as fervently desiring governmental reform. *Rulin waishi* retains this prescience but fails to include mention of the work cited by Song Lian as the distillation of his ideals, an imitation of *Zhou li*. Though apparently already lost by the seventeenth century, Wang's work inspired what is perhaps the most famous proposal for the reform of governmental institutions, Huang Zongxi's *Ming yi daifang lu*. According to Huang's preface to his treatise, Wang placed great hopes in his plan for the reorganization of political institutions (presumably based on the feudal well-field system of the original work). Huang quotes him as follows: "If I don't die before then, I will present this work to an enlightened ruler. With it we will be able to bring about a sagely administration without difficulty."[13]

It would appear that to Huang and others, who saw the reform of governmental institutions as a prerequisite for social change and the reform of literati mores, Wang served perhaps as a sort of patron saint. It was Wang's image as an aspiring political activist ("He recited his work on government to himself rapturously in the dead of night," says Huang), and not as a mere eccentric, that appealed to them. Influenced by Song Lian's and Liu Ji's accounts of Wang (the latter in a preface to Wang's poetic works),[14] Huang and his coterie of Ming loyalist scholars may have felt drawn to this particular historical figure for several reasons. Like them, Wang had lived in an era of dynastic change, when neither preceding nor succeeding regimes offered especially attractive circumstances in which to serve as officials. He may have been nothing more than a convenient vehicle for their frustrated and conflicted attitudes toward the Ming, for he embodied a sort of lost opportunity at the beginning of the dynasty, to which, had he lived, he might have presented a plan that could have averted some of the tragedies of subsequent history.[15]

By contrast, Zhu Yizun's biography presents a distinctly less sanguine view of the Ming founding than Song Lian's does: "Wang never served as an official for even one day of his life," the remark with which both Zhu's and *Rulin waishi*'s accounts conclude, is perhaps addressed to those who would make of Wang a symbol of loyalist nostalgia for the Ming. Furthermore, Zhu's hope that his version would replace the account already accepted by the Ming History Board seems to make an issue of this particular historical uncertainty. We could even read into this a dispute between Zhu—a poet with few if any ties with or sympathy for Ming loyalist circles—and disciples of Huang Zongxi, notably Wan Sitong and his nephew Wan Sida, on the Ming History Board, that may have reflected broader differences toward the historical record and its preservation.[16]

Rulin waishi follows Zhu Yizun's portrait of Wang more closely than the others, but it does so without casting doubt on the legitimacy of the Ming dynastic succession itself. Zhu Yuanzhang is portrayed as precisely the sort of "enlightened ruler" whom both Song Lian and Huang Zongxi claim Wang longed for, and Wang's withdrawal from an opportunity to serve him springs apparently not from revulsion toward the new government. Rather, Wang is quite simply uninterested in any public role at all. The tragic failure of men to find circumstances in which fulfill their political and moral aspirations, of which Wang is emblematic, in the biographies by Song, Zhu, and Xu turns into a complete rejection of public life. Men of extraordinary talent need not seek the path of social utility but should be able to live a life free from the pettiness and venality of the political fray. Needless to say, this delineation of a figure embodying total emancipation from literati public service obviously holds great import for the novel as a whole. As discussions of the Yongle usurpation, the death of the poet Gao Qi, the Prince Ning rebellion and other topics later in the novel attest, the recurrent question of dynastic legitimacy serves only to obscure the issue of whether, and how, literati commitment to public service is dependent upon the bureaucratic mechanisms that Wang Mian predicts will lead to their corruption.

The fate of the official Wei Su, Wang's unwitting tormentor (Wei's request for a painting disrupts the latter's life for some time), is apparently intended as one illustration of the difficulties of maintaining one's integrity, and one's dignity, in high places. Divorced from the lives of common people such as Wang Mian, he remains ignorant of the injustices committed on his behalf.[17] But he himself falls victim to the dangers of life at the court of Zhu Yuanzhang and is ignominiously exiled to the tomb of a Yuan general (where the historical Wei Su soon died). In Zhu Yizun's biography, Wang Mian accuses Wei of being "devious" (*gui*), apparently a pun on his surname Wei. But the novel transposes this idea to the meaning of the surname itself, that is, "precarious." The same report that promulgates the new examination system also announces Wei's banishment from court, juxtaposing the dangers met by one official with the perils posed by the future system of official recruitment.

The subtle interplay between the text of the novel and the biographies contributes to the particular force of this opening chapter; in He Zehan's words, its meaning lies precisely "in the places where the author has changed his sources."[18] It also contrasts from the rest of the novel in its extensive use of historical materials, which for the most part is studiously avoided thereafter. A gap of over one hundred years separates it from chapter 2, which begins at the end of the Chenghua period. This marks the beginning of what I have referred to as the second historical stage, which is brought to a close by the rebellion of Prince Ning (in the years 1517–18) in chapter 8. Despite their inconspicuousness the references to these two dates serve to bracket these six chapters into a single unit.

Both of these dates are tied to the career of the character Wang Hui, a provincial candidate and later official in Jiangxi. In the late Chenghua period (chapter 2), Wang is a pompous and boorish *juren*, whose visit to a village in Shandong causes a stir among its humble citizens. He appears at the temple where the hapless Zhou Jin, who has failed to progress beyond even the first rank in the examinations, ekes out a meager living tutoring village children. Wang then disappears from the novel until chapters 6 and 7, where he belatedly succeeds in passing the metropolitan examination and receives an official post in Jiangxi. A few years later his career in government is cut short when, captured by Prince Ning, he is forced to assume an appointment in the rebel regime. The rebellion soon ends with the defeat and capture of the prince by Wang Yangming's forces,[19] and Wang Hui ignominiously disappears from the novel until his rediscovery by his son, Guo Li, in chapter 38. Although a minor character, Wang Hui's appearances are tied to the beginning and end of this historical period, that is, the roughly thirty years from the 1480s to 1517 covered in chapters 2 through 8.

In these first episodes of the body of the novel, the scene of action alternates primarily between Shandong and Guangdong, tracing the fortunes of Zhou Jin, Fan Jin, and their acquaintances. Among these members of the gentry of the two provinces, none is portrayed as possessing more than a mere pretense of cultural sophistication, or an interest in goals other than success in the examinations and the power, influence, and wealth that go with it. The deprivation and humiliation endured by Zhou and Fan are not without a certain pathos, but this is undercut by the unimaginative narrow-mindedness (Zhou) and obtuseness (Fan) that surface after their successes. They are the naive products of a total, unswerving faith in the examination system, which leaves them ignorant of anything other than the rather limited knowledge required to achieve success in it.

Wang Hui combines the worst features of the various characters of the sections in which he appears, including both the ignorance of Zhou Jin and Fan Jin and the venality and avarice of men such as Zhang Shusheng, Magistrate Tang, and Licentiate Yan. Whether as a provincial candidate or later as an official, he takes conspicuous advantage of the resources at his disposal. Having endured a humiliatingly lengthy period during which he failed to progress to *jinshi* rank, in chapter 7 Wang attempts to make up for lost time by shamelessly enriching his own purse from official coffers. But following his capture and subsequent flight from the authorities, he evinces no awareness of culpability. He merely recalls a line of prophesy concerning "eight Wangs" (which is actually a joke at his own expense—Wang Ba, or "cuckold") and becomes convinced that his misfortunes are all predestined. But his capitulation to the rebels is very much in character, given his inability to adhere to a modicum of ethical standards.

Following Wang's departure, the novel introduces a circle of disaffected literati who gather in Huzhou at the home of two affluent brothers, the Lous. The relatives and friends of the Lou brothers belong to a cultured stratum of elite Jiangnan families and their associates. It is among these self-styled connoisseurs of poetry and the arts, and patrons of eccentric recluses, that we first hear of dissatisfaction with the examination system, and of suggestions of other modes of life and purposes more worthy of men's efforts. Even some diehard adherents of the examination essay must defend it not simply for its practical value but as an intellectual discipline equal in rigor and depth to other pursuits.

The rebellion that serves to retire Wang Hui from officialdom thus almost imperceptibly shifts the social setting from the simple-minded, examination-bound dunces of its beginnings to the more complex society of the later sections. For Zhou Jin and other examination aspirants, Wang's examination essays serve as models for emulation. And following his capture and escape from the authorities, he becomes the object of sympathy among the men who seek alternatives to examination study. Magistrate Qu, whom Wang replaces as magistrate in Jiangxi, first gives voice to the desire for release from the onerous duties of official life. And the magistrate's grandson Qu Xianfu actually launches his literary career by publishing a work given to him by Wang Hui in gratitude for financial assistance (a work that turns out to be that of another dynastic nemesis, the early Ming poet Gao Qi). Thus does Wang's metamorphosis from examination candidate and official to fugitive and ultimately recluse serve to mark the transition between these two societies, one fervently examination bound, the other populated by men seeking alternative means of fulfillment. The conversation in which Wang's actions and ultimate fate are debated introduces the two Lou brothers, failed degree candidates who subsequently undertake a search for rustic savants languishing for want of recognition.

This juxtaposition of political alienation with the ultimately traitorous activities of Wang Hui seems to hint at some connection between them. For the Lou brothers, Wang's treason is mitigated by the illegitimacy of the dynasty itself; they argue that the only difference between Prince Ning's rebellion and the Yongle emperor's usurpation is that Prince Ning failed and the Yongle emperor succeeded. Provocatively denouncing an ancestor of the present emperor, the Lou brothers conclude that their dynasty does not deserve the loyalty of its servants. But as the narrator explains in an aside, their views are colored by the resentment they feel at their failure to obtain degrees. The two men subsequently set off on a search for like-minded men that results in a series of misadventures, culminating in their disillusionment from all involvement in such activities and a retreat behind the walls of their family compound.

While unobtrusive within the text as a whole, these historical allusions gain significance simply by virtue of the fact that they coincide with a particularly important textual transition. Following this threat to the dynastic succession, in the novel's account the peace and prosperity of the empire is broken only by faint rumblings of disturbances on the frontiers far to the west and south. The great bulk of the novel following this event is peopled by men who express little interest in the affairs of state, either civil and military. By running Wang Hui off into the anonymity of monkhood, Wang Yangming seems in effect to serve as a sort of agent of depoliticization, whose valorous deeds ensure continuing dynastic survival, but also the apathy of men who see little need for action.

This is a clever ploy. At a gathering at the Qu home in chapter 8 (*RWHH*, p. 123; *TS*, p. 96), admiration is expressed for Wang Yangming's brilliant defeat of the prince's forces, which was regarded by many later historians as the crowning achievement of Wang's military career. But in spite of saving the dynasty from a potentially disastrous civil war,[20] Wang Yangming was blamed by many Qing thinkers for indirectly causing, through the influence of his philosophical teachings, the ultimate demise of the dynasty. The controversy between Wang's partisans and detractors grew particularly heated during the early Qing, when the "debates over Zhu [Xi] and Wang [Yangming]" took on a decidedly factional ring.[21] Furthermore, after the Kangxi emperor declared his admiration for the Zhu school, thereby further consolidating its position as the orthodox doctrine, the taint of heterodoxy seems to have bedeviled the remnant of thinkers still loyal to Wang. Even many nonpartisan scholars like Gu Yanwu condemned Wang's teachings as a contributing factor in the tragic events of the late Ming. Among those who still saw something to admire in Wang, and particularly for the thinkers of the early Qing who championed martial values, the tendency was to stress Wang's achievements on the battlefield, that is, precisely what the interlocutors here praise.[22]

This allusion thus seems both to de-emphasize Wang Yangming's role as a purveyor of doctrine, while still strongly implying his centrality to the development of literati mores. Following his pacification of the rebellion in Jiangxi, Wang met with suspicion from the courtiers surrounding the Zhengde emperor, who saw to it that he was given little reward for his deeds.[23] Wang's experiences are thus emblematic of the hazards of serving a court that not only fails to appreciate meritorious deeds but actually attempts to entrap and destroy its servants. It is thus appropriate that his victory is mentioned by characters who begin to give voice to a cynicism and passivity toward political commitment and explore alternative vocations for literati either apathetic toward or unsuccessful in the examinations. Significantly, no mention is made of philosophical debate in any form either here or elsewhere in the novel. Instead it is the other Wang, Wang Hui, with his unbridled ambitions and unabashed venality, who provides the transition from the examination fervor of its beginnings to the birth of competing literati discourses of subsequent sections.[24]

By juxtaposing these events with Ming history, the novel superimposes additional dimensions of meaning to this transition in the text. In the novel's account, the tenacious attachment to the practice of *bagu* among the examination dunces of Shandong and Guangdong coincides with the Chenghua and early Zhengde reigns, that is, what was regarded as the apex of stability and prosperity of the dynasty. The representative figure of these eras, Wang Hui, exposes the fragility of this prosperity when his cynical pursuit of power turns to an equally cynical disillusionment. And while explanations for it may have varied, it appears that there was substantial agreement among later writers that the late Zhengde period marked the beginning of a decisive change in literati commitment to officialdom and the responsibilities of social activism.[25] As for Wang Yangming, the much-maligned loyal servant of the Ming throne, in the novel's account he is absolved of blame for the development of literati malaise. The subsequent emergence of the cacophony of competing literati vocations and ideologies can thus be seen to have its beginnings in the wholehearted faith in examination success manifested by Wang Hui and his ilk.

No further references to Ming historical events are made until chapter 21, where a date of Jiajing 9 is obliquely mentioned. Other dates of this reign follow until chapter 35, where the year Jiajing 35 is given for Zhuang Shaoguang's imperial audience at the capital. These fifteen or so chapters introduce the men who eventually gather in Nanjing for the ceremony at Taibo Temple, that is, the most cultivated and perspicacious of the novel's characters. Fittingly, the Jiajing reign has been viewed by later historians as the zenith of Ming culture, an age of brilliance not equaled by earlier or later periods. By bracketing the apogee of the work within this period, the novel suggests that the convergence of literati in Nanjing is to be read as the cultural fluorescence, indeed the apex, of dynastic as well as literati development. Nonetheless, other than the cameo appearance of the Jiajing emperor, who converses with Zhuang Shaoguang at the conclusion of this section, there is little indication of actual historical events (such as the debates on ritual, the incursions of Japanese pirates, and other issues that preoccupied the court). But similar to the references to Wang Yangming in chapters 7 and 8, historical figures of some importance are alluded to through the medium of a minor character. Zong Ji, a visitor to Nanjing and Yangzhou in chapters 28 and 30, mentions Xie Zhen, Wang Shizhen, and Li Panlong, who were no less than the leading arbiters of literary taste during the Jiajing reign.

Zong makes but three brief appearances in the novel, the first when he pays a visit to the rake Ji Weixiao during the latter's wedding banquet in Yangzhou. He introduces himself as follows: "My humble courtesy name is Muan, and though a native of Huguang, I have been resident for a number of years in the capital, where, along with Xie Maoqin, I have served as a tutor to the Prince of Zhao" (*RWHH*, chap. 28, p. 384; *TS*, p. 308, translation modified).

Xie Zhen (1495–1575) was perhaps the most notorious of the late Ming *shanren* or self-styled "hermits" and was criticized by many, including his literary associates, for his unscrupulous behavior. After breaking with the other members of his literary salon, he spent his last years as a tutor and adviser to various royal princes, in particular the prince of Zhao. One of the most notorious anecdotes of his wanton ways relates the story of Prince Zhao's presentation of one of his own concubines to him after her performance of a song written by Xie.[26] Zong Ji claims to be a relative of Zong Chen, one of the members of the literary group centered on Wang Shizhen.[27] But his name means literally "concubine of the imperial clan," seemingly alluding to the Xie Zhen story. (This is further reinforced by the character *mu* in his courtesy name, since it is identical to the personal name of the prince.) The fact that he enters the novel just as his host, Ji Weixiao, is celebrating the taking of a new concubine supplies further evidence that his presence was intended to evoke this episode in Xie Zhen's career.[28]

As a representative of literary circles, Zong appropriately meets the aesthete Du Shenqing during a subsequent visit to Nanjing. He continues to drop names, claiming to have "participated in poetry gatherings at Prince Zhao's residence with Wang Shizhen, Li Panlong, and other members of the Seven Masters." In the company of Du Shenqing, Zong refers, not to the dissolute Xie Zhen, but to the principal arbiters of taste of the period, Wang Shizhen and his friend Li Panlong. Thus do these allusions to events of the Jiajing reign conclude with the cultural brilliance of the times, in contrast to the previous example of the military exploits of Wang Yangming. Once again this matches the novel's own progression to the scholarly and literary activities of Du Shenqing, Du Shaoqing, and their respective circles of acquaintances.

The final mention of the Jiajing reign is made during Zhuang Shaoguang's audience with the Jiajing emperor in chapter 35. Summoned to the capital for his remarkable learning, Zhuang is asked to give his opinions on matters of state and is even considered for a position at court. But the emperor is counseled to refrain from appointing Zhuang, who has not obtained the *jinshi* degree (and in any event professes to be uninterested in an official career), since this would risk giving hope to others who have failed to rise through the examination system. Zhuang is told to devote himself to writing and returns to a life of seclusion in Nanjing. Thereafter, mundane affairs fail to draw him out of his retreat.[29]

Thus does the novel identify the Jiajing reign as the culmination both of the apathy toward politics first adumbrated in Wang Hui's flight and a corresponding evolution of an unconventionality and cultural sophistication that fosters the growth of literati discourses and lifestyles antipathetic to government service. Such a lack of convergence between the literati and their government is amplified in the final third of the novel, chapters 37 through 55. In these later sections, men of martial abilities and battlefield victories are deprived of their just rewards and demoted. Alienation and bitterness result, setting the stage for the final historical moment of the novel, set in the Wanli period. Chapters 53 through 54 chronicle a fleeting affair between Chen Munan, a young literatus related to the enfeoffed Xu family of Nanjing, and Pinniang, a prostitute. The date Wanli 23 (1595) appears only later, at the beginning of the final chapter; but references in the previous two chapters indicate that they also are set in the Wanli period.[30]

Zhang Wenhu and other commentators remark perceptively that although Chen figures as the protagonist of these chapters, in fact the real subject is the Zhongshan-fu, that is, the enfeoffed descendants of Zhu Yuanzhang's great general Xu Da (1332–85) (*RWHH*, chap. 53, pp. 708–9). Chen relies on the largess of his cousins Third and Ninth Xu, who tolerate his spendthrift ways with remarkable unconcern, to live it up in Nanjing. It is not only their financial support but also the attention he commands through the mere mention of their names, that enables him to impress, and enjoy favor with, his friends. He is literally nothing without the Xus, as the orthographical similarity of the characters in his name Munan to those in the expression *nanke yimeng* or "dream fantasy," suggests. Thus his princely benefactors' departure for Fujian at the close of these chapters leaves a bankrupt and discredited Chen no alternative but to follow them.

The importance of the Zhongshan-fu both to Chen's exploits and to the episode as a whole is signaled by his visit to the garden of the estate almost immediately after his first appearance in chapter 53. As the only representatives in the novel of an ennobled family, the Xus' position is rather unique, for they belong neither to the degree-holding literati nor to the other groups represented in the novel. But since their fortunes are inseparable from the fate of the dynasty, we may associate them with the Ming ruling house. (They are mentioned earlier in the novel as mixing with the members of another ennobled family, the Mus, who with the Guos of Shanxi constituted the "three enfeoffed families" descended from Zhu Yuanzhang's generals.) And since they appear in person only at the conclusion of the novel, we should expect them in some way both to embody the malaise affecting the dynasty and to prefigure the disasters on the horizon. This is confirmed both by the role of the family in the novel and by historical associations and allusions that accompany them.

The estate of the Zhongshan-fu as seen through the eyes of Chen Munan is an opulent palace of vast dimensions, planted with hundreds of flowering plum trees. The extravagance of the garden is in turn matched by comfort indoors: as Chen and his cousin Ninth Xu spend a leisurely afternoon gazing out over the blossoms cloaked in snow, Chen becomes aware of the peculiar warmth of their pavilion and jokingly quotes from a poem, "No one knows of the cold outside." At the conclusion of the party, Xu explains that the "pavilion was built during the lifetime of the previous lord. It is made entirely of pewter, so that when we burn coal inside, it stays as warm as it has been today. How could anywhere on the outside have a place like this?" (*RWHH*, chap. 53, p. 711; *TS*, p. 575, translation modified).

This refuge of warmth and comfort, which excludes the harsh weather on the outside, is yet another of the signs of opulence with which the descendants of Xu Da have surrounded themselves. The implication is that the current occupants of the house are merely basking in the glory of achievements long past, reveling in the self-enclosed luxury of their garden, and failing to prepare their martial skills for the future defense of the empire. Indeed, the final third of the novel has demonstrated that the nation cannot make use of its military talents, thereby bringing about their decline. As a prelude to the debauched degeneracy of Chen Munan, who is in fact helping the Xus to squander their legacy, it is a fitting image, summing up in effect the end of the historical process of decay.

Unlike Wang Mian at the beginning of the novel, the Xus who appear here probably have no historical counterparts. But the choice of this family not only resonates with the founding of the dynasty in chapter 1; for readers of the Qing, it also undoubtedly evoked the image of the last occupant of the estate of the Zhongshan-fu, the pathetic Xu Qingjun. A profligate wastrel of the decadent last years, who after the fall of the Ming was reduced to taking corporal punishment in place of criminals who could pay his surrogate's fee, he perhaps more than any other scion of a once-noble house evoked the pathos of the dynasty's ignominious end.[31] That this last Xu may have been a symbol of the frivolity and indulgence of Nanjing society in the late years of the dynasty is suggested by his appearance in the first act of the drama *Taohua shan* (The peach blossom fan), where he also holds a flower-viewing party.[32]

The conclusion of *Rulin waishi* is set many years before the end of the Ming, however, and instead of having the Xus simply wallowing in luxury at home, it sends them off to Zhangzhou, in Fujian, on an official assignment. The Zhangzhou area is mentioned several times in the novel as a posting for officials on the rise: a retired Nanjing official is said to have served there (chapter 24); and the prefect Xiang Ding is promoted to a post in the area (chapter 26). But in the context of Ming history, Zhangzhou was perhaps best known at the end of the dynasty as the base area for Zheng Chenggong (Coxinga), the Ming loyalist and conqueror of Taiwan. Moreover, by the mid-eighteenth century it seems to have become the area of contact between the Triad Society members on Taiwan, where that secretive organization was first formed, and the mainland. In other words, it was a region associated with Ming loyalist sentiment, both in the immediate aftermath of the dynasty's fall and in the period of Wu Jingzi's adulthood. It is no coincidence, then, that the protagonist in the previous episode of chapters 50 through 52, Feng Mingqi, represents a fictional allusion to the eighteenth-century anti-Manchu renegade Gan Fengchi; both Feng's (Gan's) presence and this move to Fujian adumbrate the future fall of the Ming. By placing these uninspiring servants of the dynasty here at its conclusion, the novel appears to juxtapose Chen Munan's own moral and financial bankruptcy to that of the nation itself, plagued by impotent and apathetic civil and military officials, and the opulent vestiges of a now hollow, faded glory.[33]

Instances of Buddhist abnegation in these last two chapters may also allude to trends that reached their height in the Wanli period. While monks, nuns, Buddhist rites, temples, and festivals appear sporadically throughout the novel, only in these final chapters do some characters actually take Buddhist vows. Specifically, the prostitute Pinniang as well as the "son of Chen Hefu," an admirer of Chen Munan, shave their heads to escape their difficult circumstances. According to Timothy Brook, beginning in the early-to-mid-sixteenth-century Buddhism attracted strong support and interest among gentry alienated from the public realm of officialdom and Confucian discourse: "Buddhism mapped an alternative world, not just of belief, but of action: a world of associational undertakings through which elite status could be cast in high-cultural terms that did not rely on definitions handed down by the state. Buddhism provided the opportunity for spiritual discernment and refinement—'merit' in the social rather than Buddhist sense—to prevail over skills in writing examinations or performance in a perilous bureaucracy."[34] While these allusions to Buddhism do not go beyond mere caricatures of the religion, they appear to mirror the literati's abdication of a public role and cynicism toward public life that were blamed on the spread of Buddhism by conservative Ming and Qing Confucians such as the Donglin partisans. Moreover, this setting corresponds almost exactly to the period when Li Zhi, the most eloquent critic of literati hypocrisy, ostentatiously rejected his Confucian role by shaving his head and adopting Buddhist garb.

It is worth recalling that each of the four phases of Ming historical references highlight literati alienation from and ultimate rejection of political participation. Wang Mian quietly avoids an imperial summons; Wang Hui ignominiously flees from officialdom in any form; the Nanjing scholars Du Shaoqing and friends ostentatiously decline imperial patronage; and the indolent Chen Munan and his friends fail to summon the energy for even a token effort at examination essay composition. In each case these references single out problematic points in Ming dynastic history, such as the Ming founding, the Prince Ning Rebellion, the tumultuous court politics of the Jiajing reign, and the apathy during the Wanli period, that is, eras that were often cited by later historians as major turning points in literati commitment to their public role. Yet each set of references suggests that dynastic malfeasance exerts little if any direct influence on literati commitment or loyalty to the regime.

Nonetheless, this does not prevent those characters who reject governmental participation from adducing dynastic wrongdoing, even illegitimacy, as justification for their attitudes. The founding emperor's persecution of literati, the Yongle usurpation, the Prince Ning Rebellion, court intrigues, and other events are cited by various men as reasons for deciding against, or in some cases for, public service. Indeed, the very words *waishi*, or "unofficial history," of the novel's title can be seen as indirectly raising the question of dynastic legitimacy. According to Sheldon Hsiao-peng Lu, the Chinese historiographic tradition beginning with the *Spring and Autumn Annals* was preoccupied with uncovering the morals inherent in historical events, morals that can essentially be summed up in the notions of legitimacy and illegitimacy. Historiography is a "grand metanarrative of legitimation, [which] aims at rendering human social institutions such as the Patriarch, the Emperor, the Father, the State, or the Law into natural, transparent, and universal relations."[35] Subsuming its history of literati mores within the story of the rise and decline of a single dynasty, *Rulin waishi* implies an inextricable link between the fortunes of the literati and the legitimacy of the institutions and political forces that sustain them.

It should thus not surprise the reader that the question of dynastic legitimacy comes to be adduced as justification for literati reforms at the height of literati dissatisfaction with the status quo, namely, the ritual at Taibo Temple in chapter 37. Chi Hengshan argues for the necessity of such rites on the grounds that the founding Ming emperor did not establish "rites and music," resulting in a serious deficiency, even perhaps illegitimacy, that required remedial action by men such as themselves. This ritual is initiated and planned by the *ru* scholars who seek freedom from the constraints of the examination system and spurn offers of official appointment. Such men avoid the shallowness and absurdities of the examination fervor that sweeps their contemporaries, but as I have suggested above, they bring their own prejudices and shortcomings to these endeavors, whether ritual or otherwise.

In essence, then, in its allusions to Ming history the novel raises the issue of whether dynastic misgovernment through the examination system or other means has contributed to literati malaise. This issue comes to a head in the discussions that lead up to the ritual of chapter 37, in which the advocates of ritual envision it as correcting the mistakes perpetrated at least in part by the dynastic powers themselves. Whether or not their assumptions regarding the dynastic record, and their prescriptions for remedying it, are correct is the question that will be taken up in the next chapter.

CHAPTER SIX

The Use and Abuse of Ritual

THE DEPICTION of the literati vocations of scholarship, literature, and examination learning achieves a denouement of sorts in the first 36 chapters of *Rulin waishi*. Examination-bound literati of naive tastes and aspirations predominate in the chapters prior to the Prince Ning rebellion, with examination essay editors, poets, and hack writers following in that order. In the sections centered on the city of Nanjing (chapters 25–36), we find a series of increasingly cultured representatives of literature, scholarship, and even examination learning, namely Du Shenqing, Du Shaoqing, and their respective groups of associates in Nanjing. Yet beginning in chapter 37 a more heterogeneous mix of military figures, ruffians, and small-town gentry and merchants alternate until the concluding chapters set in the Wanli period. These later chapters suggest very little in the way of an adherence to literati creeds or of any genuine commitment to intellectual pursuits. Instead, these chapters trace a process of decay and decadence that culminates in the sordid tale at the Laibinlou brothel of Nanjing.

A single event marks this transition: namely, the ritual of Taibo Temple in chapter 37. As discussed earlier, preparations for the ritual preoccupy the scholars of Nanjing, who advocate reviving ritual propriety (*li*) to remedy the ills of the day. Following the solemn enactment of chapter 37, the participants of the ritual disperse, and the scene of action moves to distant border regions in the west and later the south, returning only intermittently to the coterie of Nanjing scholars. While another round of rituals (in chapters 47 and 48) echo the ceremonies at Taibo Temple, the events following chapter 37 appear to trace a process of fragmentation and decline that begins in the immediate aftermath of the ritual itself.

Both traditional commentators and modern critics alike have

viewed the ritual at Taibo Temple as the focal point of the book.Among these, Shuen-fu Lin has articulated the influential notion of ritual propriety as a compositional principle by which seemingly disparate episodes of the novel coalesce into a coherent whole.[1] Whatever is made of it, the structural as well as thematic importance of the ritual performance is indisputable. Moreover, given Wu Jingzi's links with the Yan-Li school discussed in Chapter 3, the prominence of ritual is, to put it mildly, highly suggestive.[2] In an eighteenth-century novel of literati manners it would be surprising if no mention were made of the ideological ramifications of ritual current in that period. Yet this does not answer the questions that have been posed by many scholars concerning its significance within the narrative. Why is this event situated at the moment of transition between the rise and decline of literati culture? Why does the novel articulate a vision of literati self-renewal through ritual, only to document its failure in subsequent events? Does this denouement vitiate the goals of a ritual program itself, or does it suggest merely the failure of the novel's protagonists to implement it? We can seek answers to these questions by examining the motif of ritual in the novel as a whole, and in particular its prominence in the sections immediately preceding and following the Taibo ritual.[3]

As discussed in Part I, ritual propriety (*li*) along with cultural refinement and writing (*wen*) were attractive to Qing thinkers who attempted to reject or rectify various elements of the Neo-Confucian tradition.[4] Such diverse figures as Gu Yanwu, Huang Zongxi, Zhang Boxing, and Dai Zhen sought to reassert the primacy of cultural and ritual forms as an antidote to what was perceived to be the vacuity and crudity of Ming thought and culture. Ritual offered a medium of concrete study sanctioned by the Confucian tradition and accessible both as a scholarly discipline, and a means of self-cultivation and social praxis. Similarly, the notion of *wen* received renewed attention from Qing figures as a civilizing ideal that was perceived to have been neglected in favor of moral truths. Kai-wing Chow sees in the elevation of both *wen* and *li* a powerful reassertion of native cultural identity, even "a token condemnation of the 'barbarian' regime," during the first several decades of Qing rule.[5] While such nativist sentiments probably weakened considerably in subsequent years, by the eighteenth century they had evolved into what Angela Zito has called the "hyperdevelopment of devotion to *wen*," manifested in a broad range of discourses both on ritual and other scholarly subjects, to include the visual arts.[6] By the Qianlong and Jiaqing eras ritualist programs similar in many respects to Yan Yuan's, but generally with a much stronger emphasis on the explication of ritual texts (*wen*), were accepted by virtually every leading thinker of the day.

The Taibo ritual of *Rulin waishi* appears to allude to the general preoccupation with this subject among literati of the period. Chi Hengshan, its principal organizer and architect, echoes many of Wu Jingzi's contemporaries in envisioning the revival of ancient rites as a panacea for the social ills of the times, a means by which his contemporaries could re-create the harmony of an ancient age. Preparations for its enactment engage the attention of the men who gather in Nanjing, in particular the three scholars Du Shaoqing, Chi, and Zhuang Shaoguang.[7] And although it fails to exercise much if any benign influence, those who come to the city in later times acknowledge its importance by paying homage to the site and its ritual implements.

Although the novel uses the term *li* primarily in the sense of ritual enactment, it should be understood as inseparable from the symbolic domain of ritual propriety, that is, the standard of social interaction through which harmonious, hierarchically ordered relations were maintained. As such its implications extend beyond the preparations for and enactment of the Taibo ritual alone to encompass virtually the entire range of literati behavior. The novel first explicitly broaches the topic of *li* in this sense, namely, as the observance and violation of normative rules of propriety. Indeed, in its broadest dimensions *li* as both ritual and ritual propriety preoccupies not merely the scholars who advocate its dissemination; nearly every literati character in the novel in some way consciously manipulates the forms of social interaction that are the essence of ritual propriety.

In the opening scene of the body of the novel, the preeminence of ritual concerns is foreshadowed in the preparations for a banquet to welcome Zhou Jin as village tutor, preparations dominated by a discussion of the propriety of seating arrangements. The attendees debate who should be shown greater deference—the guest most senior in age, or the one with the higher examination degree (Zhou, though older, is outranked by another guest, a licentiate). This sort of punctiliousness at first glance appears to parody the elaborate seating arrangements found in the novel to which *Rulin waishi* exhibits some indebtedness, namely *Shuihu zhuan*.[8] But the issue of propriety and its relationship to examination status first broached here turns into a recurrent topic of conversation throughout the novel. Again and again literati characters ponder the propriety of terms of address, seating arrangements, and other minutiae as these bear upon status, power, and wealth, thereby foregrounding the ritual implications of the literati pursuit of "fame and fortune" (*gongming fugui*) decried in the novel's opening poem.

It could be said, in fact, that ritual propriety as an issue of concern and debate follows a clear pattern of amplification over the course of the novel. In the early chapters set in Shandong and Guangdong, ritual events such as weddings and funerals provide occasions in which literati like the Yan and Wang brothers, Zhang Shusheng, and Mei Jiu flaunt their (often spurious) expertise in ritual minutiae. On the whole, the attitude of these men toward ritual requirements is one of indifference or annoyance—as when, for example, both Fan Jin and later Xun Mei attempt to avoid the requisite period of mourning for deceased kin. In later chapters, the more cultured families of Jiangnan, such as the Lou brothers, and their cousins the Qus, generally hold to a higher standard in matters of decorum. This greater conscientiousness takes a slightly ludicrous turn in incidents such as Quan Wuyong's arrest in a fracas over his mourning cap[9] or Ma Chunshang's scrupulous avoidance of eye contact with women during a tour of the West Lake in Hangzhou.

The lengthy sections depicting the lives of Kuang Chaoren and Niu Pu (chapters 15–23) introduce ever more serious violations of propriety as these characters mature into unscrupulous rogues. Caught up in the quest for recognition, the conduct of Kuang and Niu toward their families, friends, and erstwhile benefactors turns increasingly outrageous. Niu Pu's simple and good-hearted father-in-law, Bu Chongli (homophonous with "does not honor propriety"), dies just at the point when Niu degenerates into an incorrigible recreant. At his death (in chapter 22) Bu dreams that his name appears on a list of 35 people, apparently alluding to the number of participants of the Taibo ritual (twenty-four literati and twelve musicians). Although the ritual is still fifteen chapters away, subsequent sections soon broach the topic of a ritualist agenda for literati renewal.

Beginning in chapter 24 the increasingly intimate relations between actors and literati chronicled there evoke much discussion of the impropriety of such mingling. Niu Pu's biography concludes when he finds a new home as son-in-law to a kindly actor, who has rescued him from the cesspool (both literal and figural) into which he had been cast. Under the influence of Du Shenqing and other pruriently motivated literati who fraternize with attractive young actors, the normative hierarchy between these two groups eventually breaks down. In later episodes, Bao Tingxi and members of his theatrical company joke freely with Du Shenqing, Du Shaoqing and other literati. That the weakening and eventual disappearance of restraint in relations between the two groups takes place simultaneously with the discussions of Chi Hengshan, Zhuang Shaoguang, and Du Shaoqing over the revival of ancient ritual suggests a connection between them. Although these scholars do not patronize actors, they disparage contemporary customs with a defiance of normative standards of propriety reminiscent of that of Du Shenqing. Du Shaoqing in particular revels in transgressing the bounds of public decorum, engaging in free-spirited revelry in public places that alternately embarrasses and amuses passers-by. He and his associates regard their violations as acts of defiance not against true propriety but merely in reaction to the philistine conformism of their day, a conformism that is personified by hypocrites such as Du's detractor (and aficionado of actors) Hanlin Academician Gao. But the symmetry between Du's revelry and that of his cousin Du Shenqing, who sponsors a "beauty contest" for young actors (chapter 30), suggests an underlying equivalence in their tendency to subvert ritual propriety.

If this is so, then the exaltation of ritual by Du Shaoqing and his cohorts cannot but be problematic.[10] On its surface, the Taibo ritual's carefully choreographed movements suggest harmony and order, that is, the essence of ritual propriety. Yet the increasingly riotous behavior of Du and his friends can be seen as effectively subverting this aim. Instead of remedying the failure of literati to adhere to a common and consistent standard of propriety, the ritual program of literati renewal advocated by Du Shaoqing appears to reflect, and even to be implicated in, such shortcomings. If even the proponents of this program of reform cannot reconcile the various contradictions inherent in their behavior, how well can one expect average men to fare?[11]

Such a reading of the representation of ritual in *Rulin waishi* gains support from the events of the final third of the novel. These later chapters have been judged somewhat inferior to the rest of the work by a wide range of critics. Some readers even reject the authenticity of several sections, believing them to be later additions to Wu Jingzi's original manuscript.[12] While the first 36 chapters achieve a certain degree of internal cohesion and coherence, subsequent sections appear to manifest a disorderly, even chaotic randomness. Spatially, they move rapidly between events in Nanjing and other locations in Jiangnan and distant border regions. This disorder can of course be interpreted as but another symptom of the breakdown of literati mores.[13] Signs of impending disruption and decadence are steadily amplified over the final 18 chapters, evincing what many scholars have referred to as the vertiginous descent characteristic of satirical narratives. Sensuality and debauchery, frustration and impotent rage, ineptitude, and other signs of decline abound.

In these circumstances, transgressions against ritual propriety intensify in seriousness and scope. Moreover, the advocacy of ritual as an ideology of literati renewal traces a parallel devolution, from the noble reformism of the Taibo ritualists, into the focal point of a series of increasingly acrimonious disputes over mundane matters. The interest in propriety here takes the form of a hypocritical self-righteousness that adheres to the letter rather than the spirit of such rules and comes to be manifested quite literally in the prominence of the written word (*wen*) as an instrument by which literati achieve their aims. While Du Shaoqing and his associates err in failing to reconcile their ritualist agenda with their own public conduct, in these later sections increasing punctiliousness toward the forms of social relations overtakes substance, resulting in the transformation of ritual fervor into the barely disguised pursuit of literati self-interest.

It might of course be argued that such a decline does not necessarily follow naturally from the advocacy of ritual renewal but simply reflects the failure of the literati as a whole to implement ritual renewal adequately. In the opinion of the more idealistic characters of these chapters, the increasing decadence of their times reflects the failure not of ritual but of the literati of this later era to follow it properly. Such idealists express admiration for Dr. Yu's transforming influence, who by his mere presence is said to have prevented men from acting with impropriety. Conveniently forgetting the excesses and imperfections of the past, they abhor the crudity of their contemporaries and fellow townsmen, whom they accuse of having given up even the pretense of civilization in the pursuit of sensual gratification.

Nonetheless, the very idealists who proclaim themselves to be the heirs to the ritualism of earlier days demonstrate a compulsion for the trappings of propriety that is only hinted at in earlier sections. Whether or not confidence in the efficacy of ritual to affect social mores is justified, the apparent impotence of ritual to achieve the aims ascribed by its advocates implies at the very least that such faith is misplaced. Indeed, by the novel's conclusion the ritual idealism that inspires the scholars of Nanjing degenerates into an ineffectual mouthing of moral pieties that have little relevance to events.[14]

It bears pointing out that the effacement of ritual as a rallying cry for literati reform occurs within the context of a weakening of the various "creeds" of literati life over these sections. Examination learning, literary composition, scholarship, and other literati pursuits continue to claim adherents in the chapters following the Taibo ritual. Nonetheless, the character of those who undertake such pursuits and the nature of their attitudes toward such vocations undergo significant changes that mirror those toward ritual. For example, the practice of *bagu* actually appears to spread ever wider, even to remote border regions, yet its practitioners remain virtually silent over their commitment to it. Likewise, while a few men of these chapters pursue interests in scholarship and literature, little remains of the fervor or loyalty evinced in earlier chapters. In essence, it could be said that these literati vocations lose the ability to reverse the general apathy toward intellectual pursuits of any sort that afflicts the literati as a whole.

It remains to demonstrate in more concrete terms how the events of the final third of *Rulin waishi* implicate ritual concerns in the general decline of literati mores traced in its pages. I would like to single out three problematic events as illustrative of the tendencies inherent in the espousal of ritual reform. These are Shen Qiongzhi's marriage to the salt merchant Song Weifu; the legal difficulties of Yu Youda over a case of bribery; and the suicide of Wang Yuhui's widowed daughter. Although other examples of literati ritual fervor and fallibility complement them, these particular incidents appear to epitomize the inability of ritual propriety to check the decline of literati mores traced in these chapters. Each of these events revolves around what appears to be the fulfillment of noble ritual aims, including those of chastity, filial duty, and interment of the dead. Yet each calls into question not only the literati commitment to ritual but the very tenability of ritual as a means of literati renewal.

Critics have long been divided over the evaluation of Shen Qiongzhi, a young woman who flees from a marriage to a wealthy salt merchant. She has been variously interpreted as noble-minded or scheming, a courageous rebel against merchant excesses or a virago of questionable motives. In the words of the *Woxian caotang* commentator, her willingness to live beyond the bounds of respectable society (she sets up as a seamstress in Nanjing after her escape) mark her as "unconventional" (*qi*). As Du Shaoqing (who defends her against attempts by her merchant husband to have her apprehended) remarks, she possesses an uncommon boldness to stand up to the demands of the rich and powerful. But upon closer inspection her defiance smacks less of courage than of a willingness to flaunt standards of female propriety that largely recapitulates Du Shaoqing's own behavior.

Shen is the daughter of Shen Danian, the teacher of *bagu* appointed by Xiao Yunxian in the border region of Qingfeng cheng. Upon his return to Jiangnan, Shen marries his daughter to the salt merchant Song Weifu for the rather exorbitant dowry of 500 taels of silver. They have been told that she will become the principal wife of Song's household, but even before the wedding both father and daughter suspect that this will not be the case. As feared, it is soon revealed to her that she will be installed as a concubine among many others. Rather than demand an end to the wedding, however, Shen decides to enjoy the luxurious quarters assigned to her even while planning her escape: "I doubt if he [Song Weifu] appreciates as secluded and elegant a place as this. Perhaps I'll enjoy it for a few days [before leaving]" (*RWHH*, chap. 40, pp. 556–57; *TS*, p. 448, translation modified). She even makes off with some valuable items on her way out. Citing her status as the offspring of a literati family, as well as her own literary skills, she feels no compunction for her contempt toward Song. When later apprehended in Nanjing, she explains to the magistrate there that she had never intended to marry Song in the first place: "How could I, a talented woman with some literary abilities, marry an oaf like that!" (*RWHH*, chap. 41, p. 568; *TS*, p. 459, translation modified). This seems to hint that she and her father planned the marriage as a hoax from the beginning, with the aim of extorting a very considerable dowry.

Shen's treatment of Song is particularly damning in the light of the general tendency of Yangzhou salt merchants to be victimized by avaricious literati. The merchant Wan Xuezhai is treated with condescension by Niu Yupu, an oafish and ungrateful hack writer in his employ (chapters 22–23), while calligraphers and their cronies mock their wealthy patrons even as they shamelessly exploit them. Moreover, the power of salt merchants decried by men such as Du Shaoqing proves to be less extensive than he alleges. Soon after the Shen Qiongzhi episode Wan Xuezhai's servants are subjected to a brutal beating by an irate magistrate, one that contrasts with the light treatment given Shen Qiongzhi and other literati offenders against the law (*RWHH*, chap. 43, p. 586; *TS*, p. 476).

Even the salt merchants' apparent abuse of the practice of concubinage (Song Weifu is said to take seven or eight new concubines each year), the defiance of which endears Shen to Du Shaoqing, falls short of fully excusing her actions.[15] It is no salt merchants but one of Du Shaoqing's cronies, Ji Weixiao, who champions concubinage as a way of life, and the depravity it apparently engenders is most evident in his character. Shen is outraged at having been brought into Song's household in the incongruous position of a self-proclaimed woman of literary talents servicing the sexual needs of a purveyor of salt. But instead of seeking redress she simply runs off to Nanjing, where as a seamstress and occasional poetess she is taunted by the local population as a fallen woman.

That Shen Qiongzhi's quest for freedom from conventional propriety is analogous to Du Shaoqing's own proclivity to flaunt public mores is suggested in a brief conversation that serves as an interlude to Shen's story. Gazing lazily upon late spring scenery, Du Shaoqing and a companion encounter Zhuang Shaoguang's clansman, Zhuang Zhuojiang. The latter has retired in the city after a successful career as a merchant, devoting his energy to various worthy causes. He is described to Du as a patron of the literati, a friend to other merchants in need, and altogether an inspiring model of integrity and generosity. Furthermore, he has single-handedly undertaken the repair of a temple to a Jin general. All these good deeds contrast starkly with Du's recklessness, which has brought him to the brink of destitution without having effected much if any good. Zhuang still remains after his many deeds a wealthy man, able to continue his acts of charity, even coming to the aid of Du in time of need. Immediately after this encounter, Du visits Shen Qiongzhi's shop and praises her courageous defiance of salt merchants. At first glance, Du's contempt for vulgar morality would seem to elevate Shen's actions above mere opportunism. Yet by juxtaposing these two characters with the restrained and judicious conduct of the merchant Zhuang Zhuojiang, a patron of ritual enterprises with apparently little need for literati ritualist expertise, Shen's excesses smack of a gratuitous violation of decorum in pursuit of literati privilege. In effect, she perverts the ritualist aims of her nobleminded protector, turning them into the very instrument of her own pursuit of wealth and status.

The denouement of ritualist fervor comes in the rather lengthy sections that trace the peripatetic lives of two brothers, Yu Youda and Yu Youhe (chapters 44–48). Like Du Shaoqing and Shen Qiongzhi these two characters vent their ire against salt merchants, in this case the malign influence exerted on the mores of their native place by powerful Huizhou merchant families. Most particularly, they blame the nouveaux riches of their county for having brought ritual decorum there to a low ebb, a condition they fight valiantly, though in vain, to remedy. This preoccupation with ritual also takes the form of drawn-out preparations for the interment of the Yus' parents, still unburied twenty years after their deaths, as well as a ritual performed in honor of chaste widows.

In contrast to the public character of the setting of Taibo Temple, the Yu brothers lack a ritualist agenda for reform of the literati. In fact, their interest in rites and decorum takes the form of a somewhat ostentatious punctiliousness in the observance of proper forms of address. That these trivialities fail to instill an enduring commitment to ethical probity is indicated by a relatively inconspicuous incident recounted here. The elder brother Yu Youhe becomes embroiled in a potentially disastrous legal case and spends much of these chapters eluding prosecution. Fortuitously offered an assignment to serve as a middleman in the extralegal settlement of a murder case, Yu Youhe receives payment of 130-odd taels of silver for his services. This event is described so briefly that it seems to merit little notice; but soon thereafter, a shadowy figure, Feng Ying (literally "Wind and Shadows") and Yu are both named in a suit brought by the victim's family. By a stroke of good luck, the warrant for Yu's arrest mistakenly names not Yu Youhe but his brother, Yu Youda, since their given names differ by just a single stroke (Te 特 and Chi 持). Because Yu Youda has an alibi—he was attending an examination at the time the bribe was paid—he is able to evade prosecution. He sends word to his brother to wait in Nanjing until things have quieted down, and before long the case seems to evaporate.

Coming close on the heels of this affair, Yu Youhe's railings against the indifference to propriety of his fellow townsmen ring hollow. Equaling and even surpassing Shen Qiongzhi's irascibility, Yu Youhe works himself into a fury of indignation over the improprieties of his townsmen, while Yu Youda sanctimoniously scolds the local magistrate for daring to indict his brother on corruption charges. Yet only through subterfuge, and what appears to be the sympathy of the local magistrate, is Yu Youhe is saved from potentially embarrassing, and thoroughly justified, charges. The Yus' compunction in matters such as the propriety of forms of address (he rails at a provincial graduate for referring to the examination status of an uncle) does not apply when his own interests—or freedom—is at stake. Whether viewed as hypocrisy, or merely the inability to perceive the contradictions between their ideals and the actions to which they resort, such behavior undermines the lofty standard of ritual rectitude loudly proclaimed by these men.

The Yus' interest in ritual propriety reaches a crescendo in the enactment of rites for a virtuous widow of their clan. In separate precincts of the same ancestral temple, the Fang and Peng clans simultaneously celebrate with great fanfare their own rites in honor of a female ancestor of the Fangs. The quiet grace of the Yus' rites contrasts starkly with the gaudy display of the Fangs, whose parading of their high-ranking relations is apparently designed to impress their townsmen. Viewing the ceremonies from above, the leading officiant of the Fang clan converses with a local matron as she absent-mindedly plucks lice from her scalp, "plopping them into her mouth one by one." Such scenes elicit visceral disgust from their more cultured neighbors, who self-righteously conclude that "propriety, honor, and shame have completely disappeared" (*RWHH*, chap. 47, p. 642; *TS*, p. 524) from their community. Yet following ritual prescriptions to the letter has not prevented the Yus from conveniently abandoning their scruples in legal matters, suggesting an inability to translate ritual exactitude to ethical rectitude.[16]

The rites in Wuhe are soon followed by yet another ritual honoring a chaste widow, this time in Huizhou Prefecture, to which Yu Youhe moves to assume a post as an educational official. This widow is the daughter of Wang Yuhui, an aging scholar befriended by the Yus who has spent his life writing three essays on government, education, and morals. With little time left over to attend to practical affairs, he is apparently far from prosperous but prides himself on having placed learning and moral principles above more mundane matters. When his young daughter declares her intention to commit suicide after losing her husband, he applauds her bravery as a "death on a good topic" and appears oblivious to her suffering and quick demise. Yet once the gravity of his actions becomes apparent, Wang's grief leads him to regret having encouraged her. He excuses himself from the rites held in his daughter's honor and embarks on a journey to seek the solace of unfamiliar surroundings.

Wang can be viewed as a permutation of the scholar Chi Hengshan, the guiding force behind the Taibo ritual. Both are described by commentators as "pedants" (*yuru*), that is, scholars long on lofty ideals but short on practicality and common sense. Even the stubbornly idealistic Yu brothers express shock at Wang's encouragement of his daughter's decision to end her life in the service of some intangible "topic." It seems only fitting that his daughter chooses to die by starvation (the most common form of widow suicide in Huizhou),[17] since it epitomizes the neglect of material concerns that has characterized Wang's own life. In the chapters set in Wuhe county immediately preceding this episode, abstinence from eating and drinking is already linked with the refusal to bow to contemporary custom. While the Yu brothers languish in poverty and are described as unable to eat for their anger, their philistine neighbors indulge in repeated feasting and drunkenness. The Wang daughter's starvation in the service of chastity marks the consummation of this alienation between the fervor of ritual purists and the corporeal excesses of the majority. Yet instead of validating the former, this incident impugns the wisdom of pursuing ritualist agendas even when motivated by the most noble of intentions.

That a devotion to the ritual over the material results ultimately in death ironically prefigures Dai Zhen's pithy summation of the misuse of principle by Neo-Confucian idealists, namely, "to kill using *li*" (*yi li sha ren*). Needless to say, eighteenth-century thinkers largely concurred that the alienation of the abstract from the concrete could be ameliorated rather than exacerbated by the observance of ritual propriety. *Rulin waishi* seems to insist that the reverse is true. By insisting on the punctilious attention to the forms of ritual propriety, the denizens of this last stage of the novel's account encourage their abstraction from the concrete verities of life. These several episodes all imply fundamental problems in the exaltation of ritual as a panacea for literati renewal.

The penultimate episodes of the novel, in chapters 49 through 54, chronicle the descent of literati into ineffectuality and decadence in the Wanli era of the late Ming. Here, the ritual fervor that only a chapter before inspired Wang Yuhui to condone his daughter's death, disappears without a trace. Their protagonist, Fourth Feng (Feng Silaodie), is a martially adept, happy-go-lucky drifter (allegedly modeled on the anti-Manchu renegade Gan Fengchi)[18] who acts with a barely disguised contempt for the literati and their institutions. Unlike the military figures Xiao Yunxian and Tang Zou, Feng shows no trace of deference toward his literati interlocutors, intimidating even high officials with his quick-witted decisiveness. He wastes no time on social niceties, quickly getting to the bottom of a legal case, that of Secretary Wan, that a group of officials has entrusted to him. It turns out that Wan has been masquerading as a "secretary" when in fact he has no official rank at all. In a gesture of contempt toward literati institutions, he offers to turn Wan into a "real" secretary through bribes, influence, and sheer audacity. He is ultimately successful in this endeavor, helped less by the venality of officialdom than by the mediocrity and laziness of the men who adjudicate the case.

Secretary Wan's troubles can be seen as a pitiful conclusion to the literati desire for a vocation that confers some measure of income and respectability. The simple truth about him is that he turned impostor not out of a self-aggrandizing thirst for fame or power but simply to make ends meet at home. He differs from his more successful friend Hanlin Academician Gao only in being less fortunate, for Gao manifests a fatuity and ineptitude equal to those of the most ludicrous characters of the novel.[19] During his journey on Wan's behalf, Feng has occasion to incidentally restore the fortunes of two merchants, one the victim of a seductress and the other of a fast-talking salesman. All benefit from Feng's ability to see, and state, the truth of each situation, and to act decisively and without regard for social hierarchy or decorum. Needless to say, the juxtaposition of the purchase of an official position and the return of a merchant's capital has the effect of placing all on the same plane, equating Wan's desire for office with the sexual and financial desires that ensnared the other victims. Moreover, allusions to Hong Hanxian, a trickster who earlier in the novel fools the *bagu* editor Ma Chunshang into believing that charcoal can be turned into gold, further reinforce the deflating implication that neither official service, nor *bagu* essays, nor even high-minded idealism rises above corporeal needs.

Does this denouement imply that literati devotion to ritual, literature, scholarship, and examination study is vitiated by the reality of human desires shared by all, literati and non-literati alike? As discussed in Chapter 4, of the many characters of the body of the novel only Yu Yude exemplifies the possibilities for the transcendence of literati foibles in the "fallen age" predicted by Wang Mian.[20] Though a participant in the Taibo ritual, he does not share the fervor of its sponsors, for while exemplifying ritual propriety through his conduct, he does not seek in its articulation a creed to be exploited in the service of literati interests. He alone among the scholars, poets, examination enthusiasts, and other sundry literati conspicuously declines to assert the superiority of any one literati vocation over all others. But this is precisely his greatest strength, for the various competing discourses of examination study, cultural pursuits, learning, and ritual give rise to prejudices and preconceptions that afflict their adherents to varying degrees. In the final third of the novel, the wisdom of Yu Yude's example is confirmed negatively by the characters who give voice to an increasingly narrow-minded, superficial attention to ritual exactitude. Literally and figuratively, they consistently display a tendency to subsume the complex conditions of their world under a set of categories ultimately inadequate to the task, resulting in their own irrelevance.

Here it seems appropriate to ask whether or not the apparent repudiation of literati ideals outlined above corresponds to a genuine rejection of the literati as an institution; or, whether the novel's animosity toward its subjects is perhaps comparable to the exaggeration common to examples of Western satire. As noted in Chapter 3, Cheng Tingzuo as well as other acquaintances and relatives of Wu, came into contact with, and even espoused, the doctrines of Yan Yuan and Li Gong, the authors of a major reconceptualization of literati tasks and interests. A number of recent critics of the novel have noted the similarity of the phrase *liyue bingnong* ("rites, music, military, and agriculture") used by the character Chi Hengshan and others, to Yan Yuan's curriculum of the Six Arts. Some argue that the phrase is a deliberate allusion to Yan-Li philosophy, thereby making Chi Hengshan the mouthpiece for such doctrines. Yet regardless of whether or not this can be proven, it is not difficult to discern the relevance of Yan-Li ideas to Wu's novel. The notion of the literati as a corporate body, no individual of which can hope to achieve the sort of unifying vision promised by orthodox doctrines, is clearly echoed in the novel's depiction of literati vocations. Moreover, the intellectualization of human nature advocated by Cheng Tingzuo and others obviously has some bearing on much of the novel's satire.

Where the novel appears to part company with the discourses of literati self-renewal of its time is over the question of precisely how this revival should be effected, or even whether it should be attempted at all. For while Yan and Li as well as many of their contemporaries viewed ritual practice and empirically based scholarship as panaceas for literati ills, such a conclusion does not follow from the representation of ritual in *Rulin waishi*. To the contrary, instead of reforming literati abuses, the dissemination of a ritualist agenda of reform both manifests and even contributes to the descent of the literati in the last third of the novel. Among influential figures of eighteenth-century scholarship, perhaps only Zhang Xuecheng and Weng Fanggang came close to this degree of skepticism regarding the value of ritual study. One can only marvel at the iconoclasm of a novelist who in the heyday of the fervor for ritual viewed this trend as fraught with the very problems that its proponents attempted to ameliorate.[21]

In this regard it might be helpful to recall the events of the early Qianlong reign, when by most accounts Wu Jingzi began writing his novel. The character Zhuang Shaoguang's summons to the capital in chapter 35 has been widely interpreted as alluding to the *boxue hongci* examination of 1736. Zhuang's reputed model Cheng Tingzuo participated in this examination, as did a number of other friends and acquaintances of Wu Jingzi. Wu himself was recommended but failed to progress beyond the preliminary tests. Although many writers have speculated over the reasons for this failure, Chen Meilin demonstrates fairly conclusively that health (Wu was a diabetic and prone to extended bouts of illness) was probably the principal factor. Yet apparently Wu's alienation from and apathy toward political participation grew during subsequent years, for when the Qianlong emperor assembled Nanjing literati for an audience during his first southern tour in 1749, Wu pointedly refused to attend.

In *Rulin waishi*, the enactment of the Taibo ritual immediately follows Zhuang's return from the capital, perhaps indirectly alluding to the Qianlong emperor's establishment of a board for the compilation of an imperially sponsored edition of the three ritual classics in the second year of his reign. The new emperor's enthusiasm for ritual studies obviously bore some relation to the interests of Wu Jingzi's contemporaries and can be interpreted at least in part as an attempt to appropriate it for the enhancement of imperial prestige. According to Kai-wing Chow, the compilation of these editions, which continued for well over a decade, became a watershed event in the development of Han Studies, marking the beginning of the clear preference for Han exegesis that grew pronounced by the late 1760s.[22] Yet while such state-sponsored scholarship, especially the slightly later *Siku quanshu* project, spurred the growth of evidential studies, it may have also aroused the suspicions of reclusive scholars such as Wu Jingzi and his associates. Two of the three directors of the project, Zhang Tingyu and Ortai, were bitter rivals whose disputes allegedly form the background to Zhuang Shaoguang's refusal to engage in factional politics in *Rulin waishi*.

The Use and Abuse of Ritual / 145

Interestingly, perhaps the closest analog to the catalog of literati failings in *Rulin waishi* can be found in a provocative essay written a few decades after the novel by Yuan Mei, *On the Origin of the Literati* (*Yuan shi*). According to Yuan, the problem with the literati lay in the lax standards of literacy and scholarship that had made the status too easy to attain. Hence, "those whose talents are adequate only to farming, crafts, or trade have become literati; while some who are inadequate even to those professions have also become literati. Once they have attained this status they do not labor with their limbs and cannot distinguish the five grains, yet brazenly hope to become high officials. ... Alas, it is not that the world has no literati, but that the [true ones] are mixed with those who appear to be but are not in fact." Thus, in Yuan's view, the ancients understood the importance of keeping the number of learned men low, so that the people were content to engage in occupations useful to society.[23]

Rulin waishi can also be understood as the chronicle of men who advocate and engage in literati vocations principally as the means to higher status and eschew less prestigious paths such as farming or trade of more tangible benefit to society. Their unquenchable thirst for "fame and fortune" (*gongming fugui*) prevents them from recognizing the ludicrousness that such pursuits have brought them to. In the final episodes of the novel the humble poets, writers, and examination candidates who gather around the Laibinlou brothel reinforce such themes. Fancying themselves to be men of culture, Chen Munan, Ding Yanzhi, and Chen the Monk live a parasitic existence while mindlessly aping literati ways. That such men would do better by remaining content with more fruitful occupations and foregoing the temptations of literati status, is echoed in the epilogue in chapter 55. Its four plebeian talents pointedly avoid seeking any of the perquisites of literati status, enjoying pleasures of literary and other arts purely on their own terms rather than as means to an end. They thereby avoid the delusions brought on by those who, seeking to capitalize on literati prestige, come to trumpet hegemonizing discourses that only further delude their advocates.

Perhaps Wu Jingzi agreed with Yuan Mei that recognition by the state awarded to men of learning and culture remained a valid goal for those few gifted enough to achieve high standards and wise enough to avoid the self-aggrandizement so tempting to the literati of their own day. Yet the novel illustrates only the negative consequences brought about both by the state co-optation of intellectuals and their resistance to such corrupting influences. The way out of this impasse, and the reassertion of literati intellectual identity in reinvigorated form, remains the problem with which subsequent generations would be forced to grapple. Ultimately, of course, the problem was made irrelevant by the collapse of the imperial order at the end of the Qing dynasty.

PART III

Fictional Reconstructions of Literati Identity

The preceding three chapters have attempted to demonstrate how the representation of the literati in *Rulin waishi* reflects the intellectualist tenor of Qing discourse and transposes issues of literati identity and the scholarly arguments in which they are embedded into the medium of vernacular fiction. These concerns are expressed in *Rulin waishi* primarily in a satirical mode, and focus on the intellectual failures and absurdities of its constellation of literati characters and vocations. As I have observed, this consistently ironic representation of the literati was not emulated by successors; indeed, *Rulin waishi* is commonly held to be the only satirical novel in all of premodern Chinese fiction. Not until the *qianze xiaoshuo*, or "novels of chastisement," written in the final decades of the Qing dynasty do literati institutions and practices evoke a satire comparable to this work. But while the depth and range of *Rulin waishi*'s indictment of literati society remained rare in mid-Qing fiction, the literati were nonetheless the subject of deep and abiding interest in eighteenth- and nineteenth-century examples of the genre.

While distinct from *Rulin waishi* in a number of ways, we find an analogous fascination with the literati and their institutions in examples of the so-called scholarly novels of the Qianlong and Jiaqing period.[1] During the heyday of the philological movement in the late-eighteenth and early-nineteenth centuries, vernacular as well as classical fiction came to some extent under the spell of the general preoccupation with scholarly endeavors. The novel *Jinghua yuan* is the best known, and arguably the best, of the works by what have been called "scholar-novelists," that is, writers of at least some intellectual stature who imbued their fiction with evidence of their scholarly interests.[2] Other novels also attest to the degree to which the dissemination of learned inquiry found expression in this genre. Not surprisingly, such fiction manifests an interest not only in scholarly knowledge but also in the human practitioners of scholarship, namely, the literati.

In the following two chapters I will single out two such novels as particularly intriguing examples of the interrogation of literati concerns that took place during the mid-Qing period. Both *Jinghua yuan* and its predecessor *Yesou puyan* have long been regarded as the principal examples of scholarly fiction written in the vernacular medium. Although *Yesou puyan* was composed several decades before *Jinghua yuan*, there is no evidence that the author of *Jinghua yuan* read *Yesou puyan*, or that either of their authors were influenced by *Rulin waishi*.[3] Each chronicles the accumulation of a vast body of knowledge by literati, or their surrogates, whose thirst for erudition mirrors the scholarly trends of the day. Both also exhibit a preoccupation with a range of literati experiences beyond scholarship alone, in particular the attainment of personal recognition and political success. Although their extensive cataloging of learned pursuits taxes the patience of most readers, the erudition found in both novels serves as an unlikely but nonetheless effective instrument for the interrogation of contemporary mores and customs. In more succinct terms, scholarly knowledge is explored for its function in defining literati identity and tasks.

CHAPTER SEVEN

Yesou puyan: A Confucian-Feminist Utopia?

As DISCUSSED in Part II, in *Rulin waishi* the hoary ideals of public service, ritual propriety, and learning fail to counteract the corrupting influences of worldly glory and riches. Indeed these very ideals are shown to be themselves problematic. Only through repudiation and renunciation of literati life do a few men find a measure of freedom from its delusions. By contrast, *Yesou puyan* resurrects the notion that literati political participation is a precondition to sorely needed social reform. Indeed, political recognition and participation are given prominence in *Yesou puyan* as motifs of both structural and thematic significance.

Such recognition falls under the rubric of *yu* (literally, "encounter"), which in the narrow sense of literati political success can mean simply recognition of individual talents through the examination system. But at a more generalized level, it implies recognition of moral and intellectual qualities through a wide range of means, enabling the literati to realize in the public sphere the ideals to which they are committed. *Yesou puyan* is constructed around the notion that personal encounters are laden with fateful significance and determine both the individual's course in life and the broader moral and political aims of the literati as a whole.

The term *yu* does not occupy a place of particular prominence in Chinese philosophical discourse. On the contrary, its earliest apearances fail to evoke doctrinal associations. In the *Analects*, for example, it conveys little beyond the element of chance in human contact.[1] But in spite of its near invisibility, by the Warring States period it seems to have assumed greater significance for certain thinkers. In *Mencius* (1B.10), for example, it denotes a meeting (or rather the lack of one) between a sovereign and a potential recruit to his government (in this case, between Teng Huan Gong and Mencius himself); elsewhere, it implies not only contact but also mutual entente, a "meeting of minds," between ruler and subject (see *Mencius* 4B.30). Not coincidentally, during Mencius's era the *shi* began to assume roles of importance in administration and diplomacy; the appreciation of their talents and advice by rulers as well as by other *shi* simultaneously came to occupy a place of prominence in Confucian discourse.[2] For these emerging actors of the political landscape, the encounter with an appreciative lord became an indispensable precondition to political participation and worldly success.

As early as the Spring and Autumn period *yu* seems to have carried implications of accident, and these took increasing prominence in later texts. Xunzi was apparently the first to use the term to describe the vagaries of political fortune. This he sums up in the passage, "Whether one meets with success, or not, is a function of timing."[3] This interest in the uncertainties of personal fortune is echoed by the Han philosopher Wang Chong, in his work *Lun heng*. Wang is generally noted for his rationalistic refutation of the system of beliefs based on the Five Phases (*wu xing*), which held that heavenly and earthly or human phenomena were inextricably linked in a deterministic totality. He is also perhaps the sole thinker to elevate the "encounter" to the status of a philosophical concept, indeed as a sort of cosmic principle of unpredictability. Rejecting the elaborate, all-embracing categories of the Five Phases and their associated cosmology, he ascribes the course of history to the convergence of pivotal human figures, that is, the "coincidental meetings" that bring such men the power to influence events. Even sages rise in response to the needs of the moment; in his words, "Sagely rulers come to power in hurried and accidental moments; good ministers are promoted above others in times when they are needed."[4]

Wang Chong was regarded as an iconoclast for precisely these ideas, for he defied the prevailing view from the Han dynasty on that human morality is part and parcel of the natural order. As I said in Chapter 1, orthodox Neo-Confucians placed great stress on affirming the moral integrity of the universe, what Thomas Metzger calls the support of an "immense power transcending the immediate ego," which would "transform the world."[5] The ups and downs of personal fortune, that is, of whether or not one met with success in political or temporal domains, could be disregarded as long as a belief in the cosmological foundation supporting one's moral commitment remained intact. The strong fascination with the aleatory elements of personal fortune apparent in *Yesou puyan* appears to reflect challenges to such beliefs, paralleling the breakdown of the cosmological unities of Neo-Confucian orthodoxy. (As we shall see, the issue of whether the moral integrity of the universe can still guide human endeavors becomes a topic of debate in *Jinghua yuan*, appropriately in a discussion of the significance of Wang Chong's ideas.)

In essence, *Yesou puyan* employs the motif of "accidental meetings" as a narrative trope that restores faith in what had degenerated into a chaotic and immoral political order. Such chance encounters bring together alienated but idealistic men and women, who together bring about political reform and achieve both personal fulfillment and the edification of their contemporaries. But en route to their respective utopian conclusions, the novel chronicles the disequilibrium that such chance meetings effect among literati protagonists, first and foremost in the realm of literati knowledge. The conventional means by which the literati gain the recognition of others, namely, the examination system, is demonstrated to have failed to promote men of talent, and otherwise bright and noble-minded literati are lulled into an unwarranted complacency by the false promises of current practices. Their examination failures have the effect of bringing the protagonists to the uncomfortable realization that, like recognition itself, complete intellectual or moral certitude is but a chimerical ideal, unattainable and indeed undesirable.

We might describe *Yesou puyan*, and indeed *Jinghua yuan* as well, as explorations of the contours of literati knowledge in a world characterized by chronic epistemological uncertainty, not unlike the intellectual world described in Chapter 1. Although the range of characters in *Yesou puyan* runs the gamut from servants and thieves to animals, demons, and even a wide assortment of foreigners, it is the literati failure to achieve recognition that is paradigmatic of other social ills. Through this failure and resulting compensatory efforts to find meaning in their misfortunes, literati come to terms with the impossibility of ever achieving full or absolute "success" and, correspondingly, moral or intellectual certitude. Moreover, though both novels can be said to explore the role of the literati in bringing about the Confucian ideal of a just and moral society, they give vent to an ambivalence toward their social prominence. In *Yesou puyan*, the literati are denied sole responsibility for effecting social reform and renewal, which require collective action beyond the scope of the elite alone. *Jinghua yuan*, on the other

152 / *Fictional Reconstructions of Literati Identity*

hand, addresses the problems of reconciling literati ideological roles with the heterogeneity of its constituent members and the corresponding difficulty of imposing uniform expectations on all. In spite of their scholarly character, neither work accords homage to literary or scholarly skills as the sole criteria for social usefulness; rather, a much wider body of knowledge must be tapped by the literati, whose diverse intellectual powers must be exercised in an ever expanding domain of knowledge. The often tediously detailed exposition of these forms of knowledge constitutes much of the scholarly content of these two novels.[6]

Women, Water, and the Salvation of the Empire

Yesou puyan[7] has never enjoyed a wide readership, among either scholars of Chinese fiction or the general population. Unlike *Rulin waishi* or *Jinghua yuan*, it fails to present a perceptive critique or even an entertaining portrait of traditional social practices; instead, this novel (which remained unpublished for over a century after its completion) champions ad nauseum a stridently orthodox version of the Cheng-Zhu school of Neo-Confucianism.[8] As discussed in Chapter 3, its author, Xia Jingqu, was along with his kinsman Xia Zonglan the protégé of their fellow townsman Yang Mingshi, a prominent champion of Cheng-Zhu teachings during the first decades of the eighteenth century. Both Lu Xun and Zhao Jingshen have inferred that the novel's impassioned defense of orthodox Song teachings reflects the influence of Yang upon the author.[9] Whatever its source, an obsession with defending Neo-Confucian teachings against their ideological opponents, whether Buddhist, Taoist, or non-orthodox Confucian, pervades the novel's monumental expanse (152 or 154 chapters, depending on the edition) with a rather tedious consistency. Its protagonist, Wen Suchen, dedicates his life in the opening chapter to the eradication of heterodoxies; and he does not rest until near the end of the novel when every vestige of them has disappeared. This grand spiritual and intellectual cleansing of China (and eventually the rest of the world as well) provides a unifying thread tying together an often bewilderingly complex series of subplots.

To this intellectual dimension are added elements of romance and adventure. In his discussion of the novel in *A Brief History of Chinese Fiction*, Lu Xun observes that *Yesou puyan* can be seen as a very elaborate reworking of the *caizi jiaren* romances of the seventeenth century.[10]

Like the heroes of that genre, Wen Suchen finds himself involved in a series of romantic entanglements that provide numerous occasions for the display of uncommon chastity in the face of temptation, as well as for the exercise of his prodigious literary and scholarly talents. But unlike the protagonists of most romances, whose valorous deeds generally prepare for the consummation of married union, Wen's marriages to five concubines set the stage for and are integrated into his grand scheme of ridding the world of non-orthodox doctrines. Relations between the sexes for both Wen and the other major characters culminate, not in connubial bliss alone, but in the creation of a small army of progeny who eventually carry out Wen's ambitions in the last forty or so chapters.[11]

We might say, then, that *Yesou puyan* can be described as a sort of extended, intellectualized elaboration of the romance tradition, to which military adventure and a great deal of supernatural elements are added. Its various strands are blended into a narrative focused very closely on its literati characters, and specifically on its protagonist, Wen, who represents a sort of model of new possibilities for the failed or unenfranchised literatus unrecognized by his contemporaries. A lowly licentiate, he fails the prefectural examination for daring to speak out against the corruption of his time but eventually rises to glory as the adviser and intimate of the future Xiaozong emperor. Yet although ultimately showered with honors and high posts, Wen remains throughout the novel at some distance from official ranks, not deigning to participate in the official examination system that could bring him bureaucratic status.[12] Instead, he finds fulfillment by working as a sort of free-lance agent of the forces of good, traveling unobtrusively through the empire and returning to his home at irregular intervals to attend to family affairs. Although he eventually rejects the "knight-errant" (*renxia*) tradition, he seems to represent a sort of composite of literati and military, or *wen* and *wu* ideals. This marriage of martial and literary qualities is one of his most important features, allowing Wen to transcend the limitations of the conventional literati and consort with the rough-and-ready men and women that inhabit the social universe beyond elite circles.[13]

His unwavering allegiance to the crown prince, later emperor, involves Wen in a long series of adventures and valorous deeds on behalf of the crown, thus suggesting a strong commitment to the ideal of public service. Nevertheless, Wen's most obvious loyalties lie toward his widowed mother, Mme Shui. This redoubtable matron presides over the expanding Wen household, where her sagely domestic administration brings into being a miniature utopia of harmony and health. Eventually, the progeny who are reared within this matriarchy emerge as the political leaders of the succeeding generations, who finally succeed in rooting out the pernicious forces against which Wen Suchen battles. In fact, although Wen's prodigious talents are credited for many of the benefits he and his descendants bring about, ultimate responsibility seems to rest with his mother, who in moral scrupulousness and encyclopedic learning outshines even that of her remarkable son.[14]

Hence, although the greater part of the narrative describes Wen Suchen's heroic deeds, his mother looms behind him as the symbolic center of the novel. Mme Shui is no merely ordinary exemplar of widow chastity but a paragon of Confucian virtue. Through her careful exercise of power within the female compound (there are no male relatives in a position to override her authority) she is able to achieve there what the contemporary rulers of China have so conspicuously failed to do: that is, to bring about the full exercise of human talents in the service of the common good. Wen's various wives possess unique aptitudes and skills (Wen trains them in the Four Arts of poetry, archery, mathematics, and medicine), and Mme Shui recognizes and guides the development of the gifts of each. Moreover, her omniscience is recognized not only by her own family but also by all the men of her son's acquaintance (who represent most of the worthy men of the empire), and finally by the imperial family itself, all of whom defer to her judgment in matters great and small. Her court lectures on the orthodox Song interpretations of the Confucian classics, of which she is an indefatigable advocate, result at the end of the novel in the reestablishment of their unassailable position as state orthodoxy. In the apotheosis of Confucian sages and their mothers at the novel's conclusion, she is honored as the guiding inspiration for the revitalization of Confucianism in the contemporary world (of the mid-Ming).[15]

It is thus the novel's feminine domain that serves as the paradigm for its Confucian utopianism. For in spite of her rigidly orthodox ideology, Mme Shui's management of the domestic realm suggests both the causes of and solutions to the state of imbalance afflicting the world at large. Wen Suchen restores the nation to health by ridding it of an unholy alliance of Buddhist, Taoist, and other nefarious forces conspiring to destroy it; but these heterodox conspiracies find their most conspicuous manifestation in sexual aberrations, most of which involve

A Confucian-Feminist Utopia? / 155

the debasement and corruption of women. Mme Shui brings about a model domestic environment wherein women not only escape the degradation and dangers to which they are vulnerable but achieve an intellectual fulfillment that is eventually emulated in the realm at large. Her charges in effect serve as the counterparts of, and perhaps proxies for the unrecognized male talent of the political world, yet they also delineate a distinctly novel adaptation of literati vocations and identities to a world of narrowed and uncertain possibilities. As the author of this transformation, Mme Shui, like her son, apparently embodies human talent at its utmost development, but her gender distinguishes the manifestations of her talents from those of her son's. As I will explain shortly, the major events of the novel gain meaning in the light of her figural as well as literal significance, for her centrality to the narrative is reinforced by its plethora of imagery drawn from Five Phases symbolism.[16]

First of all, let us address the means by which the novel draws its parallels between domestic, feminine concerns and the problems of governance in the empire. After failing the prefectural examination in chapter 1, Wen Suchen sets out on a series of fact-finding missions to determine the extent to which the corruption of court officialdom has affected the empire. He soon finds that a massive, empire-wide conspiracy has united eunuchs, evil ministers, rebellious royal princes, foreigners, and other nefarious elements together with the Buddhist and Taoist clergy to subvert imperial authority. Barely concealed beneath this lust for power and wealth simmers a wanton sexual debauchery, acts of which are more often than not committed in the Buddhist and Taoist temples scattered throughout the country. Wen soon confirms his conviction that by denying normal marital relations between men and women, the celibacy and alchemical techniques of Buddhism and Taoism have perverted and grossly distorted sexual appetites, thereby corrupting society from the highest to the lowest rungs.[17]

Wen's heroic deeds follow a typical pattern over much of the novel. He generally tracks down the perpetrators of treasonous crimes in local temples, where he finds tens or even hundreds of half-naked, distraught female prisoners cowering in their recesses and dungeons. These victims explain to their rescuer that they were lured or kidnaped there to satisfy the insatiable sexual appetites of the local clergy or their allies. Indeed, most of Wen's principal acts of heroism are directed toward saving women from their dissolute and usually treasonous rav-

156 / *Fictional Reconstructions of Literati Identity*

ishers and returning them to their families and legitimate (and therefore chaste) admirers. At the apex of this pattern of debauchery and corruption is the imperial court itself, where imperial consorts under the influence of heterodox beliefs have seduced the emperor and thereby dangerously depleted his vitality. To rectify these menaces to the social order at its highest level, Wen intervenes in palace politics, thereby restoring the health of the imperial family.[18] That the blame both for the emperor's sexual misconduct and for the plots aimed at enthroning the debauched Prince of Jing is laid at the feet of the eunuch Jin Zhi only further attests to the novel's implication that political and societal troubles reflect sexual misconduct and even dysfunction.[19]

This coalition of forces has brought about stagnation in the imperial bureaucracy, for by promoting their cronies and squeezing out upright officials, they have blocked the rise of genuinely talented and scrupulous men. Excluded from its ranks, Wen is thus limited by default to action outside the domain of officialdom. As he investigates the goings-on of Buddhists and Taoists and their cohorts, he finds himself time and again the rescuer of women in distress. The first three of his concubines, Liu Xuangu, Shen Su'e, and Ren Xiangling, all come to be betrothed to him as a result of acts of heroism on behalf of women in the clutches of male abductors. But since it is precisely in the realm of male-female sexual relations that this unrest is most prominently manifested, Wen's attention to female problems, and the rearing of a gargantuan family (with descendants numbering in the hundreds), figure as the most prominent of his concerns.[20]

Unlike much of traditional Chinese erotic fiction, which tends to be dominated by seductresses and succubi who lead men down the path to ruin, women in *Yesou puyan* are, as I have mentioned, generally portrayed as the victims of male profligacy rather than its willing participants. Although the novel features a number of strong-willed, decisive women, female characters as a whole rather passively submit to the male influences surrounding them, whether those be good or evil. This portrayal seems to make them the embodiment of the cosmological principle of *yin* or female passivity, which in the allegorical subtext of the novel is synonymous with the forces of darkness, heterodox-inspired delusions, and everything else against which Wen Suchen is fighting. Wen resorts to an almost Manichaean use of *yin-yang* imagery to justify the suppression of heterodoxy; only with the elimination of all *yin*, he says, can the light of truth, which is identified with *yang*, reign supreme. Although women constitute the principal victims of the forces of *yin*, their passivity and malleability imply a potential complicity with the nefarious forces of *yin*. We might interpret this as reflecting an ambiguous or even misogynous antipathy toward aspects of the female psyche, an attitude for which the novel displays a great deal of evidence.[21] But at any rate, that upheavals generated within the female, domestic realm are resolved by Mme Shui would seem to indicate that she indeed provides the key to understanding the novel's female realm.

Although perhaps the least recognizably feminine of all the novel's women characters, Mme Shui's name identifies her with the Five Phases element most closely associated with *yin*, the female principle. *Shui*, or water, has long been associated with the qualities attributed to *yin*, especially those of passivity, yielding, and quiescence.[22] *Laozi* presents perhaps the earliest and most eloquent eulogy to these attributes, and Taoist adulation of them was expressed in art, literature, and philosophy throughout subsequent millennia.[23] Consistent with *Yesou puyan*'s anti-Taoist rhetoric, water is the natural element that poses the greatest danger to Wen Suchen, his friends, and their allies. In the landscape over which Wen is frequently a traveler, water in the form of rivers, lakes, and oceans is a locus of difficulty and the source of most major disasters. These bodies of water are prone to tempestuous upheavals that disrupt and often literally engulf the characters who gather near them. They moreover bring about a loss of equilibrium to the men and women accustomed to life on land and react violently to misdeeds committed on their shores by powerful men, often with disastrous consequences.[24] The drownings, capsizings, and other water-related mishaps that befall the heroes and especially the heroines of the novel also serve an important structural purpose, for they often begin each train of events in which Wen becomes involved. Significantly, women are especially vulnerable to the instability of watery realms.[25] Wen, whose swordsmanship and superhuman strength make him impervious to human assault nevertheless often falls victim to unanticipated consequences of exposure to aqueous environs, most notably in his several bouts with illness. Even his weakness for tears and nervous sweating are frequently described in imagery evocative of the moisture evident elsewhere in the landscape.[26]

Moreover, water's dangers include its tendency to delude and obscure the natural luminescence of the mind. Wen Suchen adduces the example of water more than once as an analogy for the power of deluding heterodoxy, in contrast to the fire-like radiance of Confucianism. Delusion, he says, is like a morning fog that gives rise to mirages, creating dangers for ships at sea. "The correct *qi* [material ether] of the mind is like a burning fire," he tells a group of imperial consorts, "the heat of which cannot be violated" (chap. 108, p. 933). Although fire is also frequently descriptive of excessive male virility and the lustful perversions of monks and Taoists, the power of orthodoxy to bring about correct thinking is unequivocally associated with *yang* and the element of fire.[27]

The first episode of Wen Suchen's travels, that is, his adventure at the West Lake in Hangzhou, is perhaps the best example of the unsettling effects of aqueous disasters. In addition to linking the various female-related elements of the plot to the political dimensions of Wen's mission, it also sets in motion a chain of events whose significance reverberates almost to the end of the novel. Wen decides to start his journey there to investigate its plethora of Buddhist and Taoist clergy, and his first impression of the city confirms his commitment to eradicating these heterodoxies. In the midst of an afternoon squall, he observes heavily made-up women who have taken cover under a pavilion being ogled at by the monk Ben'an. Disgusted by both seducer and the objects of his attention, he braves the downpour to seek a more comfortable shelter. This act of moral defiance brings him to the attention of a bystander, old Wei, who invites Wen onto his boat to share a cup of wine and warm himself. Wen quickly finds an excuse for launching into his first diatribe against Buddhism, conveniently addressing charges at a monk in their company. Aroused to anger by Wen's lack of deference, the monk departs; and the violence of his temper is soon succeeded by a tidal current that throws the boat's passengers into the water. Wen eventually rescues Wei Luanchui, old Wei's daughter, not from the water itself, but from the clutches of an abductor attempting to take her back to his lair beside the lake.

During the torrential rains and flooding that accompany the tide, Wen battles a dragon (*jiaolong*), the mythological creature believed to regulate rivers, lakes, and other waters. After a brief skirmish in which he manages to blind the animal, Wen learns that it was displaced from its normal habitat by the eunuch Jin Zhi, the architect of subsequent treacheries, who is building a new mausoleum for his ancestors there (in the hope of tapping the power of a *longxue*, or "dragon lair," which according to geomantic practices could bring a family success in the examinations).[28] This watery unrest is thus unequivocally attributed to

A Confucian-Feminist Utopia? / 159

the misgovernment being perpetrated by corrupt elements in Peking. Moreover, the dragon, which symbolizes, among other things, imperial power, flees the realm entirely, a situation analogous to the reigning emperor's inability to restrain his officers from corruption. This malfeasance threatens the entire population, but most directly, it menaces women; Luanchui's seducer is, along with the lascivious monks of the area, a member of the Jin clique.[29] The links between imperial misconduct and the profligacy of the armies of lackeys vying for power are subsequently made explicit, when the emperor's own sexual indulgences are described. Eunuchs, monks, and unscrupulous ministers all encourage the Xianzong emperor to deplete his sexual vitality and *yang* essence. (Eventually, Wen prescribes sleeping beside young boys, whose *yang* is strongest, to treat the loss of the emperor's male vitality.)

In this initial disturbance, it is the loss of a controlling male presence, symbolized by the dragon, which leads to the resulting upheavals on the waters of the West Lake. Eunuchs, whose lack of male functionality makes them, with a few exceptions, the natural allies of the dark forces of heterodoxy, similarly act to delude and take advantage of male power in a variety of ways. (One of Wen's acts of heroism is to save a young boy from castration by his eunuch jailers. See chapter 50, p. 446.) The mishaps at the West Lake thus serve to conflate the various dimensions of social, political, and ideological unrest, encompassed within the rubric of sexual relations and *yin-yang* cosmology. In a word, the disturbances in the natural realm reflect the imbalance between *yin* and *yang*, or male and female components of the human realm, which in turn finds its expression in the political troubles threatening to erupt into chaos.

Yet while seemingly portending inauspicious events, the disruption brought about by the unexpected plunge into the waters of the West Lake turns out to be an accident of good fortune for Wen Suchen. For in addition to alerting him to the nature of the dangers he faces, it brings into being a long and politically fruitful (though wholly platonic) friendship with Wei Luanchui, as well as the circumstances that result in his marriages to his three concubines Su'e, Xuangu, and Xianglin. Watery disasters such as this one function in fact very much like the forces of corruption that block Wen's path up the examination ladder, for by steering him, and others, in new and unanticipated directions, they inadvertently bring about good fortune and eventually the changes that are sorely needed. Water's unpredictability, it seems, is the instigator of renewal and change in the clogged, stagnant conditions that prevail over the realm.[30] In fact, it is the very agent in these cases of unexpected "meetings," or *yu*, between Wen and his supporters, which eventually bring into existence the coalition of forces that defeats his enemies.[31]

Herein, then, lies the significance of the novel's employment of natural motifs centered on water in its delineation of the problems Wen Suchen and his allies face in overcoming the ills of their age. Both women and the talented men kept in a state of powerlessness by a corrupt elite threaten to bubble over with discontent, for they are deprived of all vehicles of expression and of the means to be of use to their society. Mme Shui, as the character most sensitive to the dangers that such pools of unrecognized talent pose, channels the rich but potentially threatening human resources of the female domain into socially constructive activities. Wen's wives eventually experience their greatest satisfaction in putting the talents nurtured by Mme Shui to use. Throughout his career as informal mentor to and later senior adviser in the court of the Xiaozong emperor, Wen finds many occasions to call upon the various skills of his wives. And just as Wen trained them in their respective vocations, each one in turn becomes a teacher to her children, passing on her knowledge to the next generation. These progeny then go out into the world to carry out Wen's various plans for the pacification of the empire and its neighbors. Hence, although most women cannot serve the empire as men do, they achieve social usefulness vicariously through their (male) children.[32]

What is notable about the recognition of human talent, or what I have called *yu*, in *Yesou puyan* is its widening of relevance beyond the sphere of the literati alone, to include the female realm. In other words, the desire for social recognition and the deployment of human talents is portrayed as a universal human need shared by women and men alike. During his days of wandering among the masses as an unrecognized genius, Wen Suchen is ceaselessly on the lookout for human talent in all social spheres and frequently laments the fate of non-literati and women who go unrecognized (*buyu*) among their contemporaries.[33] On the one hand, this would seem to represent a sort of "Confucianization" of society as a whole, by inferring noble aims and public sentiments to the majority of the population excluded from literati ranks. Apparently, Mme Shui's long-winded lectures to the women of her family on arcane passages of the Confucian classics are meant to suggest the relevance of such subjects to non-literati life. Yet this expansion of the "pool" of human resources far beyond the narrow confines of the literati can also be interpreted as a sign of the lessened importance of this elite in the totality of human society. For all its trumpeting of Wen Suchen's immense personal gifts and achievements, like his mother his greatest power rests in his ability to bring the collectivity of human effort to fruition. For this, Wen relies not only on his literati friends but on his servants, illiterates, and even subhuman acquaintances and admirers, all of whom contribute to the gargantuan task of destroying heterodoxy and subversion.[34] Clearly, literati in *Yesou puyan* are not reduced to irrelevance in the social universe. But in spite of its stridently orthodox ideology, the novel seems to have revised their role as guiding forces of its social collectivity.

The Mind of a Confucian Dreamer

The world Wen Suchen and his mother leave to their descendants at the conclusion of the novel is cleared of the dangers that threatened them and the empire as a whole. Most importantly, this includes the total eradication of the heterodoxies of Buddhism and Taoism and the conversion of the entire world to Confucian doctrines. That Wen Suchen's struggle for recognition is centered on an ideological confrontation between orthodox and heterodox doctrines is an indication of the importance of the intellectual dimension of his cause. Mme Shui and her coterie of male and female devotees espouse a highly doctrinaire, purified version of Neo-Confucianism as the antidote to social corruption; nevertheless, the Four Arts in which Wen's wives specialize sound suspiciously like the arts of Yan Yuan and other early Qing thinkers.[35] Moreover, the wives' male progeny, though all favored with literary skills sufficient to get them through the imperial examinations, make their mark on the world largely through their talents in their respective individual arts. Indeed, like the aqueous terrain that never fails to surprise and unsettle the travelers who venture over it, the domain of literati knowledge proves much less predictable than the novel's faithful adherence to Cheng-Zhu doctrines would seem to suggest.

First of all, it should be pointed out that although unfailingly ready with an answer for any question posed to her, Mme Shui does suffer the occasional intellectual lapse. She must at times defer to the judgment and opinions of those around her, whose knowledge of specialized subjects she increasingly relies upon to solve the problems that confront the family and state. Her rationalistic bent is moreover belied by an occasionally pronounced emotional weakness, the unsteady and disconcerting qualities of which are linked to the female, aqueous traits of which she is the symbolic center. In the section following the routing of Buddhist and Taoist forces, she is moved by these events to call for a series of ceremonial events, including a household ritual, banquets, and various forms of entertainment. During the enactment of a solemn ritual she dwells on the centrality of the emotions (*qing*) to human life (chap. 145, p. 1122).[36] And at the performance of a theatrical rendering of the Wen family saga (which she at first condemns as frivolous), she breaks down into a torrent of tears, which prompts others to call her the "mistress of emotion" (*qingzhu*). "Words of sorrow and bitterness move people's deepest natures," she proclaims, "allowing them to cry. Only this is truly satisfying!" (chap. 146, p. 1132).

The apparent security and clear-cut nature of the Neo-Confucian orthodoxy presented in the novel is destabilized by the involvement of women such as Mme Shui, who bring to such studies their own unmistakably feminine sensibilities and emotions. As I have argued above, the incorporation of females and other disenfranchised elements of the social landscape into a purified Confucian polity represents a major element in the rectification of current disorder. In addition to accommodating such social elements into their intellectual world, the literati of the novel must also acknowledge the presence of feminine and non-literati domains of knowledge. The incorporation of such elements into literati intellectual endeavors includes not only an expansion of such knowledge but also the reevaluation of the body of literati knowledge and beliefs that have resulted in the current state of doctrinal confusion. Wen and his allies argue for a massive intellectual housecleaning of sorts, to ferret out the layers of error and falsehood that have come to be accepted over the centuries. Like the philologists of the Qianlong era, they seek truth through a return to the purity of original texts—although in the novel, it is Song Neo-Confucian doctrine that is affirmed as the proper means of understanding the classics.[37]

At first glance, the influence of delusion appears to be concentrated within the ranks of the nefarious purveyors of heterodoxy and their allies. The world of *Yesou puyan* is a largely one-dimensional one of diametrically opposed forces of good and evil, orthodox and heterodox, and its characters choose unambiguously and apparently largely unreflectively between these alternatives. Men of probity and noble intentions line up behind Wen Suchen to fight the nefarious cliques colluding with Jin Zhi and Prince Jing. These men, who share with Wen an emotional impulsiveness (*rechang*) and an irrepressible moral outrage at the corruption that surrounds them, find themselves persecuted by the treasonous forces whose influence they try to contain. A devotion to Confucian learning also distinguishes this cadre of allies against corruption from their enemies, whose arsenal of weapons includes magical powers wielded by nefarious monks and Taoist immortals.

And yet these men of good intentions are not immune to falling into the trap of tolerating or even occasionally sympathizing with or abetting the advocates of heterodoxy. While usually irreproachable, they err by failing to understand the nature of the beliefs against which they are doing battle. In such situations Wen Suchen and the women of his household instruct these wayward men, guiding them back onto the straight and narrow path through doctrinal explication. For as long as a single man or woman remains ignorant of the true doctrines of Confucianism, the utopian program of ideological purification cannot be realized. The heterodoxies that afflict the nation ultimately derive their power not from lust for sexual pleasures or raw power alone but from the misconceptions that inhibit correct understanding, particularly among the literati who are charged with maintaining social mores. Using highly learned and often quite elaborate arguments, Wen Suchen expends much energy in enlightening men and women of the deceptive nature of heterodox doctrines.

Dongfang Qiao is but one of many examples of upright men who have been led astray by heterodoxy. A wealthy landowner in Jiangxi and father-in-law of Wen's female confidante Wei Luanchui, he provides Wen's family with a safe haven from their enemies for a good portion of the novel. The valley in which his estate lies is a veritable paradise, surrounded by hills that shield it from the outside world (it is referred to as Taoyuan Zhuang, Peach Garden Farm, in a reference to Tao Yuanming's famous ode about a utopian village cut off from the world). In this bucolic setting far from the distractions of political intrigues Dongfang has apparently turned to Taoist views for inspiration. During a friendly chat with Wen Suchen, he expresses admiration for the Taoist classics *Laozi* and *Zhuangzi*, which he argues are close in spirit to Confucianism and related to it historically.

According to Wen, Dongfang's error stems from his gullibility concerning fallacious accounts of the historical roots of these doctrines. Confucianism and Taoism are diametrically opposed and completely unrelated, Wen reminds him, in spite of certain historical links be-

164 / *Fictional Reconstructions of Literati Identity*

tween them such as the Yellow Emperor (Huangdi), who was honored by Confucius and Taoists alike. One must avoid the tendency to accept received wisdom that is not grounded in the facts, Wen argues; otherwise, baseless accretions (*fuhui*) tend to arise, leading to the growth of all sorts of unfounded legends and beliefs. While men such as Dongfang approach Taoist doctrines with innocent intentions, the effect of such beliefs is to poison historical fact with innumerable falsehoods and superstitions. What begin as mere stories eventually become accepted as fact by subsequent generations. As Wen puts it, "One person propagates [such legends] in the beginning, and a hundred echo him in later ages. The curious then follow, gathering them up and transmitting them into the future. How can they be believed?" (chap. 62, p. 535). Moreover, the corruption and distortion of historical truth lead indirectly to the beginnings of popular rebellions such as those inspired by the White Lotus cult (p. 536).[38]

Two relatively brief sermons are all that is needed for Dongfang Qiao to thoroughly repudiate his Taoist beliefs. Thanks to Wen's timely advice, Dongfang is said to become a "great Confucian scholar" (*juru*) in his later years, putting his intellectual talents to proper use. The Taoist beliefs of another otherwise intelligent and gifted literatus, Lian Cheng, prove much harder to dispel. The spoiled son of a high official serving at the capital, he is attracted to Taoism for its sexual techniques, and the depravity it encourages in his household leads to a number of misfortunes. His prurient interest is focused on Wen's fiancee Liu Xuangu, who, while awaiting her nuptials, has been forced to seek temporary refuge in Lian's home. Encouraged by his debauched Taoist teachers, Lian plots to lure her into his bed, but each attempt only results in ever-worsening disasters, including the deaths of a maid and a concubine. This series of calamities brings Lian to the brink of death, but change finally comes in the form of a sudden awakening to the truth, inspired by a poem extolling orthodoxy by Liu Xuangu. "This is truly a sage among women!" he sighs on reading it. "I, Lian Cheng, have committed a mortal sin for vainly wishing to seduce her!" (chap. 32, p. 291). As Lian's wife gratefully acknowledges to Liu, "My husband and I have been moved to the depths of our hearts by your teachings through poetry. My husband deeply regrets his past transgressions, and now fears you like a god, and respects you like a teacher" (p. 295).[39] This example suggests that even when heterodox doctrines have brought corruption and debauchery to their adherents, salvation is possible not so much through the renunciation of desire but through the recognition of error. Like Dongfang Qiao, Lian Cheng redeems his sins by realizing the nature of his mistakes and returning to the Confucian fold.[40]

The sad tendency of mortals to ignore, whether willfully or not, the full scope and implications of doctrinal issues leaves literati vulnerable to such errors. As Mme Shui cites in her explication of the phrase *gewu*, men and women must dedicate themselves to the unabated quest for knowledge, and not the obstruction of desire as figures such as Wang Yangming had argued, to achieve the understanding (*zhi zhi*) essential to a moral life. Scholarship thus becomes not just an aspect of literati training but the very basis for the proper nurturing of morals both among the literati and in the broader social world of the nation as a whole. As Wen explains to Dongfang Qiao, faithfulness to historical fact and the avoidance of unsubstantiated beliefs and superstitions are essential to guard against the insidious effects of "accretions" (*fuhui*) that repeatedly threaten to corrupt the minds of men.

In a similar example, two renowned scholars (Dai Tingzhen and Liu Shiyong) submit for Wen's comments a number of historical dramas they have composed for the edification of the theater-going population. In the interest of inculcating proper moral standards, they have taken liberties with the facts, fabricating moral endings that mete out justice but are at odds with the written record. Thus founding emperors such as Liu Bang of the Han, Li Shimin of the Tang, and Zhao Kuangyin of the Song are castigated and made to suffer for sins committed against parents and brothers. Wen applauds the efforts of these two scholars to use their extensive learning for educational purposes. Yet he cautions them against distorting historical fact even if for wholly noble aims. Puritanical absolutism that strays from faithful adherence to fact, however uninspiring and sordid that reality may be, is a mistaken path. While praising the lofty integrity of these two scholars, Wen urges them to rejoin human society and eschew their impractical and pedantic fixation with reversing history. "Birds and beasts cannot but join their flocks and herds," he counsels. "If I do not consort with my fellow men, then with whom do I consort?" (chap. 84, p. 725). Without an understanding of human society in its currently debased state, scholars quickly fall into mere pedantry, which as Mme Shui repeatedly warns has prevented the literati from exercising their proper role in leading their nation and sovereign away from error.[41]

Hence, while the actual forces of heterodoxy are easily identified, their insidious dangers are obscured by the confusion that has grown out of the writings of centuries of ill-informed and misguided literati. Moreover, this confusion of the issues has assumed the dimensions of a vast and confusing labyrinth of problems that can baffle even the most intelligent and learned of men; reliance on any one individual's inevitably incomplete knowledge can cause difficulties for even the most well-intentioned of literati. Wen's generous and normally tolerant friend Bai Yulian, for example, feels justified in having punished a female servant who gave birth to a child three years after last seeing her husband. Insisting on her innocence, the woman committed suicide in protest against her accusers and has returned as a ghost to haunt him and his family. Asked for assistance in getting to the bottom of the case, Wen determines that she was wrongly accused and seeks to have her name cleared of the smear of infidelity. With his extensive knowledge of ancient anomalies and portents, he discovers that even as bizarre an event as this has a rational explanation (she was impregnated by the "male essence" [*yangqi*] of her young son's urine while using a bed pan). "The vastness of heaven and earth encompasses both normal and anomalous [phenomena]. In ancient times there were also [women] without husbands who had children. Now that I have looked into all the details of this case, it conforms with the events of the ancients" (chap. 77, p. 654).

Confucianism is heralded throughout the novel as a corrective to Buddhist and Taoist error; yet one of the major problems of contemporary Confucians is their skepticism toward phenomena and beliefs beyond the ken of a rather narrow rationalism. Over the course of the novel, the belief in spirits and ghosts, the uncanny, dreams, portents, and other popular superstitions are shown to have some rational basis in fact.[42] One notable example is that of Xianglie Niangniang, a deity revered by coastal fishermen for her powers of protection during stormy weather. She is said to be the spirit of a woman (Huang Tie'niang) who died in defense of her chastity. In the face of skepticism among his friends, Wen defends the plausibility of such phenomena through the Neo-Confucian doctrine of *qi*: "The belief in Xianglie Niangniang has an origin [in fact]. People come into being endowed with the *qi* of Heaven and Earth, and after death their *qi* returns to the Great Void. Only sagely, loyal, filial, or chaste individuals possess the righteous *qi* which, great and firm, fills heaven and earth with its force. In life they are human, in death they become deities. This is what Confucius meant in saying 'their *qi* rises above and becomes high, bright, and commiserating'" (chap. 72, p. 609).[43]

This irrepressible curiosity about natural as well as preternatural phenomena is a significant aspect of Wen's superior intellect; by contrast, most of his literati colleagues are inhibited by their Confucian-inspired skepticism about the existence of rationally unsettling phenomena. (His friends and colleagues at first scoff at the implausibility of Xianglie Niangniang; yet they are jolted into acknowledging her by the news that the official Huangfu Jinxiang has been saved from a storm by this very deity. See chap. 84, p. 717.) The belief in and respect for the uncanny, as well as sensitivity to intuitive perception that falls outside mundane reality, is also evidenced in Wen's frequent appeals to prognostication. During his travels throughout the country to determine the status of the enemy and seek out allies (*wuse yingxiong*, or "find heroes"), Wen frequently disguises himself as an itinerant fortune-teller, even relying on the income gained therein to support himself when his funds run low.[44] He and his friends take local gods and deities quite seriously, as when Hong Changqing seeks the aid of the deity Yuewang to locate Wen's mother and wives in hiding in Jiangxi (chap. 37, p. 338). An open-mindeness toward oracles, deities, and other supernatural phenomena, which a more narrowly circumscribed rationalism fails to account for, actually saves Wen and his allies from peril on numerous occasions.[45]

But while the scope of knowledge is expanded to incorporate such uncanny phenomena, the characters also take pains to repudiate mere superstitions spread by "irresponsible men of letters" (*wenren langzi*), who seek fame and entertainment through their writings at the expense of truth. Wen warns repeatedly against putting any credence in superstitions such as the "boys' songs" (*tongyao*) that were believed to hold political import (p. 1094).[46] Fate, he argues, is not a mysterious force inaccessible to human effort, for sheer human will can reverse what may appear to be inevitable. On the eve of departure on one of his many fact-finding missions, the wine in Wen's cup turns to blood, causing alarm among his wives. But by interpreting such a portent as favorable, Wen transforms its seemingly inauspicious meaning. As Mme Shui explains, "[Wine] turning to blood is normally a strange event. But Yujia [Wen Suchen] doesn't take it as strange, and hence its strangeness disappears" (chap. 65, p. 560).[47]

In short, then, knowledge is the key to the social transformation of the literati and of society as a whole. Only by recognizing the full range of phenomena and the nearly inexhaustible possibilities for its exploration can literati find their true vocation as intellectual leaders.

This uncertain terrain is fraught with danger, and even Wen Suchen can on occasion fall into complacency. When he admits to a confidence in his ability to avoid corruption by the honors that may be bestowed upon him, Mme Shui turns livid with rage: "Anything that is not yet in existence, is still empty. One must first experience something, before one can gain a solid appreciation of it. . . . One must experience such a reality, and engage in it in concrete life, before one can say one possesses such capabilities . . . one should never noisily proclaim oneself to be capable" (chap. 59, p. 513). Much of Mme Shui's instructions are directed toward upsetting the easy self-satisfaction of her charges and acquaintances, who occasionally fall into the misplaced belief that they have achieved complete or even adequate knowledge of any particular area. She advocates unremitting intellectual endeavor and relentless vigilance against the sort of complacency that robs people of respect for the immense difficulties of a steadfast devotion to seeking knowledge of the world.

As I have argued above, Mme Shui's sex and her position as the symbolic center of the novel's use of water-related imagery make her an especially appropriate vehicle for such vigilance. Attuned to the inherent insecurity and unsettling potentialities of the human as well as natural landscape, she and other women of the novel aid their male counterparts by pulling them back from any relaxation of intellectual vigilance. And although she champions Confucianism as the pinnacle of thought, Mme Shui also speaks for the intuitive and feminine forms of understanding, whose immediacy makes them indispensable to men as well as women. Just prior to a severe windstorm in the area of Jiangxi where the Wen family has taken refuge, the members of the household all predict that great havoc will result in the surrounding countryside, based on various signs. Mme Shui praises the itchiness felt by a young servant girl as the best of these methods of observation:

> I predicted this based on the principles of things; Yujia proved it in heavenly phenomena. Among my daughters-in-law, some based it upon supposition, some used technical skill, some found [evidence in] records, and some related it to what they have heard. But none are equal to [the maid] Qiuxiang's ability to know this through her own body. The human body is a small universe, and even ignorant men and women partake of knowledge and ability [through it]. This is where heaven and men mutually interact and affect one another. Compared to the methods of prediction of Yujia and the others, [Qiuxiang's] is near and verifiable, clear and proven. (chap. 64, p. 551)[48]

A Confucian-Feminist Utopia? / 169

Knowledge of intuitive, even irrational origins, shared by all members of the social spectrum, is validated for its proximity to the concrete, lived experiences of the community of humankind. Contrasting with such common sense is the pedantry of outmoded Confucians (*yuru*), whose scholarly meditations are divorced from the mundane world and thus irrelevant to it. The literati can maintain their social utility only by mixing with the various elements of the social landscape of the novel, a skill at which Wen Suchen is particularly adept. For such mundane knowledge complements literati textual skills in achieving and perpetuating the Confucian ideals of social order and harmony. This is especially true of the most significant lacuna in literati expertise, that is, the martial abilities and derring-do of the outlaws, generals, and heroes whose cooperation Wen solicits. As I have discussed in the case of *Rulin waishi*, men (and women) of martial abilities possess a directness and willingness to act lacking among the literati as a whole. Wen and many of his closest friends overcome this shortcoming by themselves becoming competent in martial skills and turning their attention to military strategy. As the novel's representation of the literati ideal, Wen and his friends apparently exemplify the duty of educated men to seek training in military as well as civil arts; as one couplet puts it, "Without learning, one is definitely not a hero; only with pluck can one be a sage" (chap. 63, p. 549). Failing that, however, the literati must allow martial men to find the place and means through which to give expression to their talents. Otherwise, their alienation from society will result in brigandage and social decay. And repulsive or crude behavior (such as that of the swarthy Tie Gai and other swashbuckling heroes [chap. 23, p. 214]) alienates cultured and refined literati, thus preventing the often invaluable abilities of such men from finding social use. Literati would do better to emulate the honesty and directness of such figures, according to Mme Shui. For the literati are obligated by Confucian duty to speak out frankly and directly on matters of nation and society. Only their courage can stem the tide of corruption in government that threatens the health of the nation.

In the concluding sections of the novel, with the complete eradication of the alliance of heterodox and subversive cliques, the emperor calls for the "collection of airs" (*cai feng*), a time-honored tool for inviting criticism of government policies. But in the utopian state that has come about, there are no criticisms to be found: "In our time customs have surpassed those of [the sage emperors] Tang and Yu, and not a single man has not found his proper place. Hence in the songs expressing the peoples' intentions, there is only praise, and no blame" (chap. 140, p. 1254). In this contented utopia that China has become, both men and women find the means to be of use to their society, and no trace of resentment remains. Literati lead this collectivity, but their leadership can be assured only through unremitting commitment to continued intellectual growth and with the collective participation of the entire body politic.

CHAPTER EIGHT

The Philological Musings of *Jinghua yuan*

MUCH BETTER KNOWN as an example of scholarly fiction than *Yesou puyan* is *Jinghua yuan* by Li Ruzhen,[1] written in the first decades of the nineteenth century. This work also bears the strong imprint of the scholarly interests of its author, who unlike the obscure Xia Jingqu seems to have achieved some limited renown in learned circles of his day. It also betrays an analogous preoccupation with literati concerns, preeminent among them the achievement of recognition through public service, or what I have called *yu*. But while Confucian in conception *Jinghua yuan* exhibits a much greater catholicity in its use of non-Confucian traditions, drawing substantially from Taoist and Buddhist mythology and doctrines.[2] Esoteric knowledge of alchemical techniques instrumental in attaining immortality is complemented by a wide spectrum of literary and scholarly subjects, all discussed in often tedious detail by its cast of erudite characters. Set during Wu Zetian's usurpation of the Tang in the seventh and eighth centuries, the disruption of the normative political order provides a background of political disorder similar in broad outline to that of *Yesou puyan*. Early in the novel calls are made for action by brave men to restore the rightful occupant to the throne, and this task is finally achieved at the novel's conclusion.

But although the usurpation results in difficulties for the officials and their families still loyal to the Tang house, the female assumption of power serves as the catalyst for unprecedented developments among Wu's female subjects. In contrast to the myriad dangers to the empire posed by proponents of heterodoxy and their nefarious allies in *Yesou puyan*, China under Wu Zetian's rule enjoys exceptional peace and prosperity. For though guilty of excesses, Wu's administration promulgates sixteen measures for the relief of the long-suffering women of her realm, and thanks to such good deeds, according to the astrologers who seek signs of her fall, her reign will continue for a total of sixteen years. Essentially, then, for the novel this period of female rule, however aberrant and unsustainable it may be in the overall scheme of the natural order, provides the opportunity for an emergence of female talent unencumbered by the strictures of the normative patriarchal social and political order. Unlike *Yesou puyan*, whose learned heroines achieve intellectual and social fulfillment primarily through Wen Suchen, no single male figure guides or inspires the talented girls of *Jinghua yuan*. Moreover, romantic involvement with the opposite sex is still premature for these girls, who though first tutored in literati learning by fathers and other male relatives, develop and train their various talents largely within the female domain.

Since Hu Shih and other early-twentieth-century reformers first argued that *Jinghua yuan* presents liberal and reformist views on the position of women in Chinese society, scholars have debated the meaning of the novel's "feminism."[3] Its treatment of issues such as footbinding, concubinage, and the education of women suggests that it is at least in places seriously concerned with the social inequities endured by women. And although its fictional version of the interregnum from male dominance does not prove to be a permanent solution to the ills brought on by entrenched social customs, at the very least the novel implies that the inversion of male-female relations does not necessarily lead to unmitigated disaster (in contrast to traditional views of female political ascendancy, especially the reign of Wu Zetian). Many of its most famous episodes are devoted to the exposure of male arrogance and hypocrisy and to exploring the comic possibilities of the reversal of sexual roles. While not denying the importance of such issues, however, my aim in this discussion will be to scrutinize the novel's reversal of gender roles in the context of its treatment of literati concerns.[4]

Like *Yesou puyan*, *Jinghua yuan* exhibits both structural and thematic evidence of an abiding concern with recognition and fulfillment of political and moral aims through chance meetings—namely, the narrativization of *yu* and its attendant implications. Its male protagonist, Tang Ao, suffers disappointment in the examinations at the beginning of the novel and embarks on a voyage that brings him into fortuitous encounters with many of the young women who later converge at the capital to compete in a special "examination for talented females" (*cainü ke*). The preparations for these examinations, and the festivities called to celebrate their successful conclusion, take up nearly half the novel.[5] Both before and afterwards, their participants discuss the significance and implications of the achievement of recognition through such means. But there is little indication of anything resembling the overriding moral purpose that preoccupies the like-minded men and women who converge in *Yesou puyan* to work for the spiritual cleansing of China and the world. The women of *Yesou puyan* come to profess most if not all of the moral and political concerns of their male literati counterparts. Wen Suchen's wives may be denied direct participation in political affairs, but they share his concerns for the routing of the forces of heterodoxy and sedition, whose corruption and sexual perversions threaten the female realm even more than the male. But in *Jinghua yuan*, the talented girls are largely uninterested in the ethical dimensions of literati life. Nor does this suspension of moral obligations merely reflect a willingness to temporarily compromise ethical principles in the interest of personal advancement; rather, the freedom from such constraints is portrayed as a significant, and wholly positive, element of the novel's feminization of the literati experience.

It is paradoxical that in a work that purports to describe the defeat of a usurper and restoration of the fallen house, loyalty counts for so little. For the crusade to restore the Tang that serves as the novel's frame tale seems to vitiate the heroines' easy willingness to pay homage to the usurper of the rightful dynasty. What for male literati presents a serious ethical dilemma is barely remarked on by the girls, who express no qualms about seeking examination success under such conditions. Although many of these girls later participate in the restoration of the Tang, none expresses any interest in this goal, in spite of the difficulties suffered by many of their families as a result of the usurpation. In short, the ethical ideals and norms of the male political order fail to inspire even a perfunctory loyalty in these girls.[6] Instead, they appear to honor the empress for her sponsorship of their scholarly activities, and the injustices brought about by her excesses elicit only indifference among them. Not a single girl declines the opportunity to participate in the examinations held for talented girls by Wu at the capital. Moreover, the men do not expect the women to do otherwise; when a lone voice of disapproval from a male relative is heard, he expresses concern not over moral issues but only at the unorthodox and unprecedented nature of this event (*Jinghua yuan*, chap. 58, p. 432). In a word, it seems that participation in such examinations is devoid of political or moral content; as Wu Zetian's edict pronounces, its sole purpose is to bestow recognition upon the talented women of the empire, who until this time had been relegated to obscurity (chap. 57, p. 418). As such, it provides the opportunity for the celebration of learning in and of itself, something that the rightful dynasty did not deign to sponsor.[7]

Although the examinations in Chang'an appear to follow the model of male literati examinations,[8] the range of knowledge displayed by its participants extends far beyond conventional literati learning to encompass a cornucopia of information on mundane as well as scholarly subjects. C. T. Hsia has remarked that the author's enthusiasm for such knowledge reflects his "enchantment" with traditional Chinese culture.[9] But while the novel does appear to glorify the classical erudition of its girls, the esoteric knowledge that comes to preoccupy them, particularly in later chapters, is remarkable for its inclusiveness, as well as for its disregard for the normative hierarchy of literati knowledge. Among literary genres, only poetry elicits the girls' interest. Literary ability presumably determines their fate in the examinations, and they recite examples of their prowess in a number of genres. Yet while orthodox literati learning—namely, classics, literature, philosophy, history, and other textual scholarship—certainly occupies a prominent place in their discussions, it is embedded within the context of games that make no distinction between classical erudition and trivia, scatological jokes, puns, riddles and other amusements. The moral urgency that pervades the discussions of classical texts in *Yesou puyan* is completely absent here; and amid its scenes of revelry, a vast array of often mundane and trivial information is accorded parity with more conventional examples of textual erudition. In short, the girls seem to celebrate knowledge for its intellectual content, with little reference to its purposes, and knowledge itself seems neither antithetical to nor wholly dependent upon moral aims such as the restoration of the Tang for its validity.

Men are conspicuously absent from this scholarly banter, for most such discussions take place in exclusively feminine company. In the novel's scheme of things, the ascendance of women as the intellectual equals of men has as its corollary the effacement of male intellectuality. This unprecedented opportunity for women to pursue intellectual fulfillment in the public sphere comes at a time when most men have abandoned traditional literati pursuits. The young heroes who eventually restore the Tang to power hone their martial skills in preparation for battle and show no talent in or inclination for literature or learning.

They seem content to leave such studies to their female relatives, who eagerly fill the void. Hence, we can observe two mutually opposing developments that extend through the entire course of the novel: the feminization of intellectuality, and its liberation from Confucian ethical and political exigencies; and the corresponding effacement of men, who become preoccupied with the demands of political loyalty.

Gender Reversal and the Revival of Literati Intellectuality

As I have already suggested, the broad pattern of gender displacement and reversal in *Jinghua yuan* exhibits a clearly symmetrical pattern, and moreover one that serves as the most obvious structural principle of the entire novel. The displacement of male characters by the young girls emerges only gradually, extending over the work's first half. Although the novel begins with two frame tales, one set among female deities and the other among the denizens of Wu Zetian's palace, the protagonists of its first half are predominantly male. These consist of the three male travelers, Tang Ao, Lin Zhiyang, and Duo Jiugong, and the (primarily) male characters they encounter in the exotic lands described in chapters 7 through 42. A few of the girls who later participate in the examination for women are introduced here, but the future dominance of women is adumbrated only in a few key sections.

This begins to change with the beginning of the second maritime expedition (chapters 43–53), which is instigated and led by Tang Ao's daughter Tang Xiaoshan. Although searching for her father (who has disappeared to seek Taoist enlightenment), Tang Xiaoshan ends up collecting a number of the future participants in the female examinations, which have just been announced in chapter 42. Once they return to China and begin their journey to the capital (chapters 53–62), the girls become increasingly self-reliant and are soon able to look after their own well-being and interests. In fact, in their last significant encounter with men (male loyalists of the Tang, in chapters 56–57), the men escape Wu Zetian's clutches only with the aid of women from Tang Xiaoshan's group of travelers. The last milestone in this process of male effacement comes with the examinations in chapter 68, after which men disappear entirely for 25 chapters.[10]

Although women come to dominate the novel roughly after its midpoint at chapter 50, the section that most fully broaches the motif of gender reversal and explores its metaphorical implications is the pe-

176 / *Fictional Reconstructions of Literati Identity*

nultimate episode of the first journey, when Tang Ao and his companions visit Nüerguo, the Country of Women, in chapters 32 through 37. I would thus like to examine it in some detail for its clues to the use of this motif in the novel as a whole. By the time they arrive at this nation, the three travelers have seen many lands, where the customs and bodily forms of the inhabitants are generally permutations, idealized versions, or perversions of those back home. Here, local customs differ from those of China in only one respect—the reversal of sex roles. The ascendancy of women is adumbrated earlier in the journey, when for example Tang and Duo are embarrassed over their faulty knowledge of scholarly subjects by two scholarly girls in Heichiguo, in chapters 16 through 19. Tang is furthermore rescued on two separate occasions (in chapters 9 and 24) by martially adept young women who, after fleeing China, have had to take up hunting and brigandage to care for their families. In Nüerguo women exercise political and social domination over their male countrymen, foreshadowing the transformation of women into examination candidates in subsequent episodes.

Lin Zhiyang, Tang's merchant brother-in-law, visits this nation primarily to supply it with cosmetics, for which its inhabitants have a great weakness. "Its people are inordinately fond of dressing up their women. Whether rich or poor, whenever they speak of women's clothing and adornments, their interest invariably quickens. They care not whether they have the resources for them" (chap. 32, p. 231). This propensity for covering their women (=men) with cumbersome attire is described as "constricting" (*jushu*) for Lin Zhiyang, whose good looks inadvertently lead to his abduction and selection as a consort by the king (=queen) of the land. Over the course of Lin's forced initiation into the customs of this country, which culminates in the binding of his feet, he alludes to the significance of his position. As the bindings are first applied to his feet, Lin screams that he feels like a licentiate forced to return to taking the annual examinations, after years of study abroad (*youxue*) in other regions. And when he removes them, he sighs that his relief is that of being exempted from this requirement.[11]

The physical constriction of women suffered by Lin Zhiyang is analogous, then, to the personal frustration stemming from the restrictive requirements placed on literati by the examination system, the social effects of which also include an impractical fascination with the accouterments of status. (The girls who later converge in Chang'an continue to allude to this metaphor when, joking about the tightness of their foot bindings, they pun the word for "feet" [*jiao*] with that meaning "examination status" [*jia*] [chap. 72, p. 534].) On the collective level, another stultifying, oppressive condition afflicts the nation of Nüerguo as a whole. That is the festering problem of water conservancy, which has brought the nation's waterways to the brink of disaster. The major river has become dangerously clogged by the debris and refuse allowed to accumulate in its bed and threatens to inundate the city. Tools or "instruments" used in practical work are banned, however, and thus the river has not been dredged. It is in urgent need of "clearing" (*shu*), a task in which none of the inhabitants can be of use. Tang Ao offers his services in exchange for Lin Zhiyang's release and, fashioning tools from the steel he has brought with him (as ballast for what he feared would be rough seas) from China, instructs the local inhabitants in their use. Although these men (=women) have little experience in practical affairs, their manual dexterity and eagerness to learn ensure eventual success. They are described as intelligent, industrious, and efficient, much better than the real men back home.

This stagnation appears to reflect the same predicament of which Lin Zhiyang complains, namely, the restrictive system that hinders the flow of human talents and energies into useful and satisfying outlets. As noted above, the dangers posed by tumultuous waters in *Yesou puyan* are closely identified there with the metaphorical position of women as a neglected, protean pool of human potentiality bubbling over with suppressed energies. This episode seems to offer an analogous allegory, for without the "instruments" with which to employ it in useful and relevant ways, the increasing pools of unused talents pose a threat to the health of Nüerguo. By relieving the nation of this danger (and thereby gaining Lin's release), Tang saves it from certain disaster, and presumably such "clearing" heralds the improved use of human talents and energies there. Soon thereafter, the novel turns to the preparations for precisely the sorts of opportunities for the expression of talent for which its gifted girls yearn, namely, the examinations in Chang'an and their aftermath.

The journey of Tang, Lin, and Duo comes to a conclusion shortly after the episode at Nüerguo, and thereafter the young women of the novel assume the role of examination-bound literati, supplanting their male counterparts. By chapter 50 the girls have displaced men in the realm of public affairs, and like their male counterparts they become preoccupied with the pursuit of examination success. Compared to the neglect under which they languished during previous administrations, Wu Zetian's establishment of pharmacies and other institutions for their benefit and, most important, her examinations for the promotion of learning among the women of the empire, provide opportunities long denied to women. Like the "tools" that bring fulfillment to the inhabitants of Nüerguo, recognition even from a tyrannical usurper seems to promise the revitalization and "clearing" of dormant minds.

The problem with this means of intellectual fulfillment lies precisely in its mimicry of the male literati route to success, namely, literary examinations. As we have seen, the constricting practices of footbinding and other female attire applied to Lin Zhiyang in Nüerguo allude to the problematic aspects of the examination system, namely, its stifling of natural talents and intelligence. Following the visit to Nüerguo, the literati vocation of examination study is appropriated by the novel's talented young girls. Particularly after their return to China in chapter 53, the girls become susceptible to the competitiveness of male literati life. As they travel north to Chang'an, Tang Xiaoshan (whose change of name to Tang Guichen, or "female minister of the Tang" in chapter 50 revives the ideal of loyalty even as it retires it as a concern of any importance to the girls) and her female friends turn their full attention to their studies. Their eagerness to succeed in the palace examinations is described in the same language as that used for the more conventional male preserve of examination success, or *gongming*.

That literary examinations become the vehicle for fulfillment among women thus seems to suggest at least a grain of irony. For all the entertainment and personal satisfaction that their participation in the examinations provides the girls, it also engenders among them precisely the sort of petty concern for temporal success that plagues male literati. Participants live a parodic travesty of the male experience of success and failure, rejoicing and even going temporarily mad over their examination success and plunging into the depths of despair over setbacks or failure.[12] In short, when women are afforded opportunities for recognition, they appear no less prone to the follies inherent in such pursuits than their male counterparts.

Near the end of the novel, the Taoist nun Daogu sums up the pursuit of worldly success as a competitive love of winning (*zhengqiang*) that obscures the inconsequentiality of human affairs: "[People fail to realize that] human life, with its schemes and worries, the risking of all for victory, wonders and prodigies, life and death, is nothing more than a game of *go*. Only because they cannot recognize the snares of this trap, are they fooled by it" (chap. 90, p. 689). The novel's allegorical frame tale begins with a game of *go*, when a longing for victory, and the shame of defeat, set in motion the chain of events that are played out over the novel. The nun seems to be warning that the desire for examination success poses dangers to the girls commensurate with those found among men. Nonetheless, while many of the talented girls become temporarily entranced by worldly honors, this interest recedes once they have achieved success, their *gongming*. By the conclusion of the novel, the girls appear to have thoroughly dispelled the insidious effects of examination competition and desire for bureaucratic emoluments.

The Failure of the Institutions of Learning

Such a conclusion suggests that the feminization of intellectual endeavors acts as a corrective to abuses prevalent in the male literati world of examination participation. Although such abuses come into play before and during the girls' examinations, and are in fact given most detailed treatment in the Country of Women, it is the foreign countries visited during Tang Ao's journey which provide the principal vehicle for the satire of male literati pursuits, and most particularly, the examination system. Specifically, the consequences of the institutionalization of literary and scholarly knowledge, and its role in the social order of contemporary China, are the butt of much trenchant ridicule in these chapters. Through the adventures of the three travelers, learning as it is practiced and patronized in the island nations to which they venture is gradually but unmistakably revealed to be fraught with problems that undermine what appear to be utopian societies. Hence, before further discussing the specific features of the novel's femininization of intellectual pursuits, I would like to briefly summarize its allegorical treatment of literati values transplanted to distant maritime climes.

Just as Wen Suchen reacts to his failure and disappointment in the examinations by setting off on quests for knowledge more valuable than that needed to write examination essays, Tang Ao similarly leaves with his brother-in-law Lin Zhiyang on a trip abroad after being stripped of a metropolitan degree by Empress Wu. He is less interested in joining any noble causes, however, than in trying to assuage his shame at having to return home without an examination degree in hand. This adventure turns into the discovery of a world of which Tang, whose energies have been devoted to literary work, is largely ignorant. Only Duo Jiugong, a former licentiate who went to work on

180 / *Fictional Reconstructions of Literati Identity*

the high seas to make ends meet, and the merchant Lin know anything of the distant and obscure lands to which they set out for trade and sightseeing. Tang manifests the exemplary ethical standards expected of educated men, but his mind is said to be cluttered with essays, poetry, and other odds and ends of "useless" learning (which he expels with the aid of an herbal laxative). He lacks the practical knowledge and experience required in voyages for trade, and only rarely does his advice turn out to be genuinely useful to his companions. Moreover, in contrast to the more altruistic Wen Suchen, he seeks knowledge of the realms they visit apparently for selfish reasons, namely, to obtain the elixir of immortality. In his exodus from China and abandonment of the literati vocation, Tang Ao manifests a disengagement from society apparently meant to suggest a permanent state. For him, it is not merely a matter of turning from impractical to practical knowledge; he appears to have embarked on a search for a mode of life and thought beyond the roles available to him within China.

The first stop on the journey to foreign lands is at Junziguo ("the Nation of Gentlemen"), an unqualified Confucian utopia where the highest virtues of propriety and yielding (*lirang*) reign supreme. The travelers interview two inhabitants, the brothers Wu He and Wu Ren, who are descended from no less than the patron saint of propriety, Taibo (who as we recall is honored by the men of Nanjing in *Rulin waishi*). They explain to Tang that their nation's customs derive entirely from written works imported from China, whose lofty ideals are credited with having transformed their nation. By putting the ideals of its philosophers into effect far from the corrupting influences of home, this nation has succeeded in creating what Chinese philosophers have only dreamed of doing. The moral perfection of this land is complemented by the love of learning found in Heichiguo, where the travelers arrive soon after leaving Junziguo. The redoubtable dark-skinned young women there immerse themselves in classical scholarship with a dedication unequaled by even the most ardent of Chinese philologists. Like the Wu brothers, these women honor the traditions that have been disseminated among them from their Chinese source and wonder why Tang Ao and his compatriots do not follow them with the devotion they expect of Chinese scholars.

This unquestioned belief in the ideals of Confucian civilization, first adumbrated in Junziguo, Heichiguo, and other nations visited at the beginning of the journey, begins to go awry at the journey's midpoint in Shushiguo (chaps. 24–25). This nation of pedants enforces a Confucianization of its entire population, whose citizens both great and humble alike must exhibit proficiency in their respective occupations through participation in examinations. The travelers' informants, who speak a literary gibberish, explain their nation's customs by reference to a Neo-Confucian doctrine that propounds "changing one's nature" through study: "Books can change the physical nature. If people abide by the teachings of the sages, then those who commit evil and falsehood will diminish in number" (chap. 24, p. 170). This optimistic confidence in the latent nobility of humankind corresponds to the official dogma of the (Qing) Chinese state, which champions the study of the Confucian classics. And the shortcomings of the nation are the embodiment of precisely those epithets used to deride pedants at home, namely, of "sourness." Their wine is vinegar, their food, pickled, and the inhabitants crippled by an unjustified faith in scholarly study.[13]

Beneath this attention to the superficial trappings of a Confucian order lies the suggestion that true human talent receives little recognition, an implication mirrored in the indifference of the local power broker, the royal son-in-law, toward his aide Xu Chengzhi. The son of Xu Jingye, a loyal minister who gave his life in the service of the Tang, Xu has taken refuge in Shushiguo since fleeing China. He is appreciated by the royal son-in-law, and promised a position of importance, he anticipates the prospects of a satisfying life there. But after three years of waiting (that is, the interval between examinations in China), he comes to the realization that his patron, ever suspicious of him, is insincere in his offer. Neither will he let him leave the nation, however, thus keeping him in a state of "uselessness." And when Situ Wuer, the palace woman promised to him in marriage, has been beaten and put up for sale after warning him of his patron's ill temper, she is ignored by the local population, who are too stingy (another meaning of "sour") to purchase her even for a few coppers. Only Tang's efforts save both Xu and Situ from languishing in this nation, which has no use for either of them.

Ominously, Shushiguo is located adjacent to Liangmianguo, or "Two-faced Nation," inhabited by rapacious pirates. In what is perhaps the most famous episode of the novel, its inhabitants display the *haoranjin*, a scarf that hides men's true hideousness behind a polite and pleasing demeanor. During their brief visit there, Lin, the merchant, is shown the true face behind the mask, while Tang, in scholar's attire, is treated with obsequious flattery. When they switch clothes, Tang is treated as Lin was, and vice versa (chap. 26, p. 183). The juxtaposition of the rapacious pirates of Liangmianguo with the follies of Shushiguo suggests an equation between brute violence and the duplicity that marks the treatment accorded the young Xu in Shushiguo. For the former is only the most extreme example of an aggressive, even violent pursuit of power hidden behind a thin veneer of civility that claims both male as well as female victims. Before female talent can safely emerge, it seems that such male habits must be subjected to a thorough deflation and unmasking. During a subsequent visit to Liangmianguo in chapter 50, the same pirate attempts to abduct Tang Xiaoshan and her companions but is humbled by his shrewish wife, who berates the pirate for his duplicitous treatment of her (he inadvertently confesses his wish to take his captives as concubines). Having destroyed this personification of the worst excesses of male aggression and duplicity, the girls can subsequently gather without fear of further threats. (This underlying import is adumbrated in the first half of chapter 50, when the two girls Tang Xiaoshan and Yin Ruohua [the Heir Apparent in Nüerguo] are saved from a voracious tiger by a gentle, docile horse.) The novel then enters into an epoch when women are unencumbered by any obligations toward men.

The progressively more absurd ramifications of Confucian social practices are developed in the second half of the journey, in countries such as Bolüguo, Zhijiaguo, and Qisheguo. Each nation's inhabitants suffer from some manifestation of the unintended consequences of the institutionalization of Confucian learning. Thus do the people of Bolüguo ("the Country of a Hundred Worries") fear fame so much that they live to an advanced age in a somnambulist stupor. In Zhijiaguo ("the Country of Excellent Wisdom"), however, the inhabitants exhaust themselves in frenetic intellectual endeavors that make them old before their time. And in Qisheguo ("the Country of Split-tongues"), where the special split tongue of the inhabitants makes them especially suited to linguistic studies, the secret of their phonology is guarded so strictly that the penalty for disclosure is castration.

Ultimately, then, the bane of the male literati world as transfigured in the South Seas appears to be the tendency for Confucian ideals such as learning and propriety to be corrupted by the institutions set up to promote them, first and foremost of which is the examination system. Again we return to the apparent contradiction that while serving as a catalyst for a fervent devotion to intellectual endeavors in women, examinations corrupt men and alienate them from literary pursuits. To interpret this apparent dichotomy of experience we must again revisit the motif of gender reversal. For the process through which women turn into examination candidates entails not only the actual assumption of literati roles by women but also the feminization of intellectual pursuits. Once they have appropriated the field of literati knowledge as their own, the girls who converge at Chang'an transform it from the stultifying preserve of moralizing pedants and careerists, such as those of the nations of the South Seas, into the source of joy and playfulness.

Perhaps the most important element in this transformation lies not in the examinations themselves, which differ little in format from the standard male curriculum of literary subjects. Rather, the girls' chief examiner, Bian Bin, serves as the catalyst for the transcendence of examination learning. For Bian apparently prizes a diversity of skills extending far beyond the uniformity and rigidity of examination essays. He seeks to promote talent in a wide range of arts and disciplines: "Throughout his life he greatly respected people of culture," the novel describes him. "He treasured not only people of literary abilities, but also those skilled in the lute, *go*, calligraphy or painting, medicine, divination, astrology, or physiognomy. As long as someone excelled in even a single subject, he treated him with the greatest deference" (chap. 64, p. 468). These pursuits, along with a number of others, turn out to be the subjects of the girls' discussions during the subsequent banquet scenes. Hence, although Bian is charged with promoting the girls based on their literary performance, he apparently serves as the guiding influence that channels their talents into the wide range of avocations to which they are attracted.

As the girls' chief examiner, Bian Bin is given responsibility for the selection and ranking of the girls. Yet his role of recognizing and promoting talent does not end with the examinations, for he also furnishes the venue for the girls' banquet called in celebration of their success, that is, his family garden in the capital. This luxuriant compound, planted with the hundred flowers of whom the girls are human incarnations, recalls the vast garden of *Honglou meng*, where talented girls and women also assemble for literary diversions. Like its literary predecessor, the Bian family garden of *Jinghua yuan* inspires elegant repartee among the female talents that assemble there. But it contrasts with the former in doubling as a source of income. Sections of it are devoted to growing vegetables, which are sold to finance the upkeep and expansion of the property. This self-sustaining independence frees it from the fortunes of (male) officialdom; nor does it become the refuge of boys (such as Baoyu) seeking an escape from the onerous responsibilities of male literati life. Its economic self-sufficiency pointedly distinguishes it from the Jia family property, which drains the family finances and contributes to the final collapse of the clan in the earlier novel.[14]

Thus freed of any dependence on literati examinations or official position, the Bian compound seems well suited to the exploration of knowledge without regard for its political or moral uses. Moreover, the recent history of the Bians reinforces the theme of self-reliance, and the dispensability of bureaucratic emoluments, in maintaining the family's fortunes. The great-grandparents of Bian Bin, Bian Hua ("flower," or "luxurious") and his wife (née She, literally "extravagant") are said to have spent their patrimony on high living, leaving their son and daughter-in-law penniless. Bian Jian (literally "parsimonious") must overcome the impracticality of his Confucian education to revive the family. He does so with his wife's (née Qin, "industrious") aid by selling eggs and other farm products in a simple but sensible business. In addition to displaying great commercial acumen, Bian Jian and his wife perform numerous good deeds, such as aiding their neighbors and relations during times of need. Bian Bin continues this family tradition of good works by donating half of his estate to the national coffers during a famine. Combining public altruism with a practical attention to maintaining their source of income, the Bians appear to personify the very highest ideals of literati conduct. While committed to public service, however, the Bian family and their garden are not dependent on the official world and can survive quite well without it.

It is in this setting, where examination success is secondary to practical needs and fundamental moral obligations, that the girls' exploration of knowledge reaches its zenith. Bian's ability to foster playful and exuberant intellectual inquiry is hinted at in the opening scenes of the banquet, where he participates in the first riddle, a pun that prefigures much of the succeeding games. But such nurturing is only effective in the case of girls; Bian's only son, Bian Bi, matures into manhood without the benefit of his father's guidance. This son fell victim to a cold at the age of three,[15] and presuming him dead, his family gave his body to a mendicant Taoist. The boy resurfaces in chapter 95, where he joins the band of young men seeking to overthrow Wu Zetian. He owes his life to an unsuccessful examination candidate, Shi Sheng, who was recognized for his talents and given employment by Bian Bin. Shi decided not to return the boy to his family after his recovery, for although Bian Bin excels at promoting talent, "Rich families fear that their small children will suffer a chill, and hence are too protective," Shi explains (chap. 95, p. 728). While girls apparently thrive under the tutelage of a man such as Bian Bin, boys need the stricter discipline of martial rigor. Shi Sheng has Bian study reading and writing only in his early years, to be followed by a curriculum of archery and horsemanship, in preparation for a military career. Like the other young men of the novel, he abandons civil for military arts that will serve the purpose of bringing about Wu Zetian's downfall. Moreover, the pursuit of literary skills appears to be deleterious to male health. Raised in mountainous retreats and military households, their virile talents can be nurtured for use on the battlefield. Since literary aptitude and recondite learning count for little in war, Bian Bin's garden of scholarly diversions is ill suited to the fostering of male talent.

These experiences suggest, then, that men who leave the Confucian fold entirely are able to foster their talents primarily because they escape the deleterious influence of literati institutions. Such men seek utility in the wider world of political engagement and become preoccupied with the moral imperatives of loyalty to the sovereign. Women, on the other hand, are free of such constraints and can foster their individual gifts and aptitudes within this institutional setting. Hence, while examinations perpetuate a destructive careerism and competitiveness in men, for women they serve as an instrument to achieve recognition for their native talents and intelligence, in turn inspiring them to give full rein to their interests. Examinations are in fact the catalyst that spurs the girls to seek engagement in learning and to bring their intellects to fruition. Nonetheless, as I alluded earlier, this intellectual inquiry extends far beyond the domain of orthodox literati learning. From the elegant diversions of music, divination, *go*, and card games, to mathematical problems, riddles, fishing, and various outdoor sports, to scatological jokes, riddles, and puns, entertainment is the order of the day. And while indulging their appetite for light-hearted revelry, the girls engage in discussions of an immense range of scholarly minutiae. These discussions of knowledge return again and again to the issue of the nature and uses of knowledge and its role in defining the tasks of the literati.

Women and Philology

Thus far I have attempted to illuminate the novel's use of gender reversal as the representation of an alternative to the institutional and social ills of examination learning and its corruption of intellectual life. The female examinations serve to stimulate women by "recognizing" their individual talents and providing opportunities for their expression, yet still allowing them to avoid the stifling influence of careerism as well as stultifying moral teleologies. While this re-gendering of the examination experience can be seen as directed toward institutional issues, it also incorporates what was perhaps the most important intellectual debate of the author's time, namely the question of the relevance of philological scholarship to the Confucian tradition.[16] In the novel this debate finds its main expression in the subject that attracts serious as well as playful interest throughout the novel, namely, phonology. In the fictional metamorphosis of such issues, the nature of language, whether written, read, spoken, or heard, serves as a particularly important point of contrast between male literati learning and its feminized variant.

An obsession with problems of language is adumbrated almost from the beginning of the novel, among male as well as female characters. Tang Ao is baffled by questions on the Tang dynasty rhyming system known as *qieyun* (and on which the dictionary of the same name, *Qieyun*, is based); he and Duo Jiugong discuss the origins of the names of the foreign countries; and he goes to great lengths to obtain the rhyming dictionary of Qisheguo. The riddle of determining precisely how to analyze words according to their phonetic components of vowels and consonants seems to take on a particular urgency for Tang and his companions. Although the travelers eventually obtain the key to the phonetic scheme in Qisheguo, its very simplicity baffles them. They have been told that in that country, the secret of phonology is treasured as the means by which that country maintains its prestige among the other nations of the world. Without such prowess it would not be able to "get one head above others" (*churen toudi*). This characteristically male interest in knowledge as an instrument of gaining and enhancing power is transposed to specifically linguistic issues, embodied in the novel notion of phonological prowess.

Such mercenary interest in language as a means to temporal ends is largely absent in the young women, who take pleasure in linguistic knowledge for its own sake. In fact, the girls express their disdain for the male preoccupation with ends in the very first scholarly exchange of the novel, when Tang Ao and Duo Jiugong visit the redoubtable girls of Heichiguo, Tingting (Lu Zixuan) and Honghong (Li Hongwei). As mentioned above, among the nations visited by Tang and his companions the girls of Heichiguo personify a zeal for learning unequaled by their peers; later, Tang Xiaoshan returns to this nation with the express purpose of recruiting the especially formidable Tingting for the examinations in Chang'an. When Yin Ruohua, the heir apparent in Nüerguo, is summoned back to her country to assume the throne in chapter 68, these two girls of Heichiguo, along with the phonologically gifted Zhi Lanyin of Qisheguo, are selected to accompany her there as advisers. Among the many erudite females of the novel they have attained the apex of scholarly achievement, an example to be emulated by the other girls. This prominence, as well as their lengthy scholarly musings, signal their exemplary status as the crème de la crème of the female talents.

When the three male travelers first arrive in Heichiguo, Lin Zhiyang finds to his great dismay that its women are completely uninterested in feminine accouterments such as cosmetics or jewelry. Though of dark and (ergo) unappealing complexions, they pay no attention to appearance, devoting their whole attention to scholarship alone. The rulers of their country hold examinations for girls similar to those called by Wu Zetian, and preparations preoccupy the nation's talented women during their youth and young adulthood. As in China, success is said to bring great honor and prestige to families and future husbands. This love of learning contrasts with the attitudes toward learning shown by the men of the neighboring countries Baiminguo and Shushiguo, through which the travelers pass after leaving Heichiguo. Tang Ao assumes from the fair skins of the inhabitants of these latter nations that they too are well versed in Confucian teachings. But though strenuous efforts are made to promote classical studies among their populations, these men turn out to have little aptitude in this area. In Baiminguo, Confucian tutors completely misunderstand relatively simple classical texts, while Shushiguo is, as was discussed above, a land of pedants where speech is mangled by the use of classical particles. In marked contrast to Heichiguo, the superficial trappings of a Confucian attention to learning and culture are marred by the inability of their (male) citizens to master even the language of the texts.

The exchange between the travelers Tang Ao and Duo Jiugong and the two girls Honghong and Tingting serves to introduce the issues that come to the fore in subsequent chapters. It begins when Duo and Tang inadvertently stumble upon the girls' school and are presented with a request for guidance. The travelers, who are recognized by their robes and demeanor to be Chinese scholars, are presumed to be highly

188 / *Fictional Reconstructions of Literati Identity*

learned, and starved for intellectual companionship, the two girls eagerly quiz them on a series of textual points. As the topic shifts from one problem to the next, it quickly turns into a battle of wits between Tingting and Duo Jiugong. Although intimidated by Tingting's formidable learning, Duo ridicules the girls' niggling attention to what he considers to be minor issues: "You young ladies try to find fault with everything, and wildly criticize. Please do not blame this old man for speaking bluntly: this sort of behavior is audacious, and your irresponsible words simply betray your ignorance of human affairs!" (chap. 17, p. 120). Tingting, on the other hand, rebukes Duo's attempts to dismiss their arguments as insignificant:

> In a word, learning must be pursued on the basis of facts, so that reasonable opinions can be backed up by proof. If you merely grab at shadows and appearances, with no fixed opinions, then naturally you will be cast about on the waves, without anything to follow. You great sages suffer precisely from this shortcoming, and insist that you know everything even when you haven't the slightest inkling, fooling people with your braggadocio. Don't you think you regard others as ignorant of texts [*wen*]? (Chap. 18, p. 125)

The girls of Heichiguo express a philological approach to scholarship that makes them mouthpieces for eighteenth- and nineteenth-century evidential scholars; first and foremost, they argue that opinions on scholarly questions be grounded in a thorough grasp of the language of texts and backed up by convincing proof. Daring to question received opinion on scholarly issues, they ridicule Duo Jiugong's conservative adherence to orthodox traditions of scholarship. After Tingting rattles off an interminable list of the possible readings of a single character, Duo mocks the careful attention to language held dear by the Heichiguo girls as follows: "The [readings of] characters are trifling matters. Often a single character will have many readings, so how can I remember them all? And anyway, memorizing a few obscure characters cannot count as learning. This is all [appropriate to] lessons for small children, but if one takes it too far, it becomes distasteful" (chap. 16, p. 112). He discounts the practicality of investigating historical phonology (p. 115) and accuses the girls of profaning the classics (chap. 17, p. 116). In short, he completely rejects the validity of their attention to textual detail.

Duo's criticisms of Lu Tingting are little more than a parodied version of the reaction against evidential scholarship that gained momentum in the late Qianlong and Jiaqing periods. But although satirized here, these discussions conclude with an argument that restores some credibility into his position. Tang Ao remarks that the sort of scholarship that questions orthodox doctrines need not necessarily diminish the latter's philosophical insights. He cites the writings of Zhu Xi (anachronistically, of course) and Mencius as examples of the dictum "Do not let writings harm one's words, do not let words harm one's intentions." In spite of mistakes or unacceptable elements in their works, we should not allow these to obscure the larger significance of their philosophical contributions, he pronounces. If one only picks out their linguistic errors, echoes Duo, then "[detractors] could argue that if even such small matters have not been carefully researched, then the rest must be even worse. Such people do not realize that the merits of these philosophers are numerous, and of an utterly different order [from phonology]" (chap. 19, p. 130). One should view them within the context of their historical circumstances, Tang Ao adds, instead of simply judging them by contemporary philological standards.[17]

The tension between these two different tendencies—that is, a close attention to textual or linguistic issues on the one hand, and ethical or philosophical concerns on the other—echoes the disputes between adherents of Song Neo-Confucianism, or what was called "philosophy" (*yili*), and evidential scholarship during the Qianlong and Jiaqing reigns discussed in Part I. Here, it serves as the first indication of the gendering of knowledge that I have already discussed: namely, it identifies interest in linguistic and textual minutiae with women, while portraying men as impatient with such studies, excusing themselves on the ground that ethical truths or meaning need not depend on linguistic accuracy. The fascination with language voiced here by Tingting is steadily amplified as the girls assume increasing prominence. By chapter 50, when the girls begin to devote their energies to examination preparation, their discussions turn increasingly to questions of language, such as the origin and use of words, punning, and double entendres.

Name, Fame, and the Gendering of Knowledge

These intellectual dimensions of the gendering of knowledge need not be viewed as wholly distinct from the institutional context of examination participation discussed earlier. For by the mid-Qing period Song Neo-Confucian orthodox scholarship had become more or less synonymous with examination learning. Although advocates of textual studies did not as a group eschew participation in the examination system, the opposition between these two forms and styles of knowledge and understanding reflected differing perceptions of the nature of political and intellectual commitment.[18] The increasingly professionalized scholarly elites of the evidential studies movement were hardly averse to the attainment of bureaucratic status through the examination system. Indeed, many of its leading exponents, such as Zhu Yun, Ji Yun, and others attained high rank in government. It is thus telling that in *Jinghua yuan*, the very topic that appears to separate men and women, that is, the place of language in intellectual inquiry, also forms the common ground that unites them. For although the girls' fascination with language is expressed largely through the playful punning and wordplays of their extended post-examination revelry, it encompasses more than simply the phonological properties of language. Even while avoiding the male preoccupation with political or career goals, many of the girls hope to achieve lasting fame through success on the examinations and scholarly achievements. In the novel's scheme of things, women as well as men seek "name" (*ming*), that is, both the fundamental function of language to make the world intelligible, and the measure of temporal success.

Needless to say, the term "name" has great resonance in Confucian thought, spanning the gamut of ethical, political, and linguistic concerns. In the doctrine of the rectification of names (*zhengming*), the aims of linguistic accuracy and political stability are wedded in a seamless whole, and this very indivisibility manifests an abiding belief in their mutual interdependence.[19] Yet the inherent difficulty of implementing it—i.e., of turning back the clock to a time of simple linguistic usage— made it one of the most problematic of all Confucian doctrines. In the Qianlong and Jiaqing periods, "name" was a charged topic in scholarly discourse. As discussed in Chapter 2, Dai Zhen and other advocates of philological research prided themselves on confining their scholarly inquiry to "names and institutions" (*mingwu dushu*), which they saw as an antidote to the vacuity of previous Confucian scholarship. Yet detractors of evidential studies pilloried its practitioners precisely because of this limitation to what they called a merely superficial knowledge of names without "meaning" (*yili*). As we shall see, the girls of *Jinghua yuan* come to terms with the polemic against evidential studies by recognizing the inherent instability of the realm of "name," both as knowledge of the concrete world of phenomena and as the moral and political "principles of duty" (*yili*) advocated by the critics of philology.

Their male counterparts, however, achieve neither the ethical aims they so cherish nor the intellectual rigor they so sorely lack.

The relationship between names and their referents, or more broadly between signifier and signified, emerges early in the novel, as a topic of discussion between Tang Ao and Duo Jiugong during the first journey. Observing the numerous fantastic and bizarre flora and fauna of the South Seas, they discuss the appropriateness of names to the objects to which they have been attached. As the well-informed reader of Li Ruzhen's day fully appreciated, the journey sections of *Jinghua yuan*, to include the names of the countries, and those of their inhabitants, flora, and fauna, are inspired almost entirely by terse entries found in the ancient geographical treatise, *Shanhai jing*, and other quasi-mythological texts.[20] Clearly, the issue of naming has a great deal to do with the use of this text in particular.

Several annotated editions of *Shanhai jing* appeared during the eighteenth and nineteenth centuries, notably one compiled under the auspices of the prominent official and philologist Bi Yuan.[21] Like the journey sections of *Jinghua yuan*, *Shanhai jing* provides a wealth of information on the geography, flora and fauna, and customs of the world beyond China, most of it highly fanciful. Bi Yuan and others of his circle were apparently determined to assert, against a tradition of skepticism toward its veracity going back to Sima Qian, that *Shanhai jing* faithfully represents the world as seen by its reputed author, Yu, the legendary sage and first "geographer" of China. As Sun Xingyan's preface to Bi's annotated edition puts it, the work provided an invaluable source for knowledge of the natural world of that time:

> Mr. [Bi] also told me: Confucius said, "One should know the names of numerous birds, animals, plants, and trees." No [text] has more of these than *Shanhai jing*. [The pharmacological text] *Shennong bencao* records the nature of medicinal herbs in great detail, and this book can serve to corroborate it. To be able to name things one encounters—this is something the scholar should do.... To my sympathetic contemporaries, I hope that they will expand their knowledge of different phenomena [through this work].[22]

However far-fetched they might seem, the names given in the *Shanhai jing* describe the "reality" of the world in its prelapsarian state and deserve careful study. The *Shanhai jing* could in fact serve as a model for the pursuit of knowledge in an ancient age before men became constrained by the limits of conventional literati scholarship.[23] Through it scholars could, he implies, expand the scope of their knowledge of the world of natural phenomena and geography beyond the narrow confines of literary or classical learning. This task entails first and foremost the learning of names, the proper source of literati knowledge.

In *Jinghua yuan* the exploration of the world beyond China turns repeatedly to the question of names and their relationship to the phenomena they describe. As the travelers encounter these bizarre and exotic conditions, they frequently reflect on the textual sources of their own knowledge of such phenomena, the "names" encountered in their studies. At the conclusion of Tang Ao's journey, the problem of naming is given a summary of sorts in an extended discussion of its various ramifications. At the last nation visited by the three travelers, Xuanyuanguo, the monarchs of the thirty or so countries through which they have just passed assemble for the birthday celebrations of its king. Attending a banquet held in view of the travelers, the royalty exchange views on the vexing problems that plague their various kingdoms. The Long-armed and Long-legged men could cooperate with one another, it is suggested, in fishing, and other occupations. In fact, says the king of Shushiguo, just such an arrangement is mentioned in the work *Shanhai jing*: "Who would have known that the King of the Country of Long-arms would coincidentally say this today. It is as if he intentionally made up this story, to give rise to the many clever discussions of my fellow kings" (chap. 39, p. 274).

We can read this comment as a wry remark on the origin of the entire journey section of the novel: all of its episodes are indeed stories "made up" from cryptic sources, most of them mere names, found in *Shanhai jing*. This leads the kings to discuss the function of naming, that is, the attachment of verbal constructions to external phenomena. Inadvertently, they pose a question that puts their own reality into doubt, for they debate the issue of whether words merely reflect some existing reality or can actually become the source from which new realities come into being. The king of Qisheguo complains to the others of the injustice his country has been subjected to by being given what he refers to as a "detestable" name. Even worse is the other name for his country, "Fansheguo" (literally tongue-twisting [argumentative] country), which, he protests, it shares with a variety of bird. His interlocutors insist that this in itself should not be objectionable. After all, says the king of Junziguo, Emperor Wang of Shu's personal name (Zigui) is identical with the name for the cuckoo: "There are many cases of naming [different things] by the same name, and no harm is done by it" (chap. 39, p. 274). But his example ingenuously proves the opposite of what he seems to intend. Emperor Wang was said by popular legend to have been transformed into a cuckoo after his death, and thus the identity of names can hardly be said to be accidental. It seems that names have far more to do with the creation of meaning than meets the eye.

To eliminate the embarrassment of an inelegant name, the king of Changrenguo proposes that Qisheguo be renamed "Changsheguo" (long-tongued, or gossiping and garrulous country). That would have the added merit of making them relations (*lianzong*), by virtue of sharing the character *chang*, meaning "long." This diverts the interlocutors into the social ramifications of naming, that is, the manipulation of names to create relationships for the exchange of power and wealth. The gist of the conversation points to the tangible consequences brought about by what at first glance seem to be purely arbitrary associations of names with their objects, in this case people. Qisheguo's inhabitants seek to maintain the prestige they have achieved through their phonological prowess, and their penchant for manipulating such abilities in the service of worldly goals prefigures the girls' interest in names as both the basis for knowledge and the determinant of worldly success. Yet unlike the novel's talented girls, who seek knowledge through collective discussion, this nation closely guards the secret of its linguistic gymnastics, that is, the knowledge that all words are merely the product of sounds combined together. Such a proprietary interest in phonology allows the people of Qisheguo to achieve recognition, but once the world recognizes the true properties of language, its men of learning fear that it will become more difficult to dazzle their contemporaries and make a "name" for themselves.

By this point in the journey, the travelers have already discussed both aspects of name, as the naming function of words that is the source of knowledge, and as the recognition or temporal success that Tang Ao has repudiated. These two dimensions are not at first joined in any explicit way; but following this fanciful debate, they are conflated in ways that suggest the inherent parallels between the uses of language and the attainment of social position. This culminates in the final drinking game of chapters 82 through 93, which turns into a contest of the girls' knowledge of names. At this event, the infinite potential of "name" to produce entertaining puns and fictions, indeed the very instability of language, is juxtaposed with somber reflections on the corresponding inability to bring fame into accord with its referent, that is, the virtue, intelligence, and achievements of the human subject

194 / *Fictional Reconstructions of Literati Identity*

to whom it accrues. Like the often arbitrary relationship between names and their referents, the attainment of worldly fame is vulnerable to factors beyond human control. For the girls of the novel, their own future, both as lasting fame and as the denouement to their earthly lives, is subject to the karmic workings of *yuan*, that is, a fatalistic notion of preordained human destiny with few if any of the political or moral associations of Confucian-inspired notions such as *yu*.

A second discussion of the nature of names occurs at the opening of the post-examination banquet, appropriately called to celebrate the girls' success (*gongming*, literally "merit and fame") (chap. 69–70, pp. 513–18). Tang Xiaoshan tells her fellow examinees about the two nations Changrenguo ("Country of Long [Tall] People") and Xiaorenguo ("Country of Little [Petty] People"), where Lin Zhiyang did a great business in two commodities, wine barrels and cocoons respectively. The people of Xiaorenguo have the nasty habit of confusing names and insist on calling things by names other than the accepted ones. Their fondness for cocoons (which they use to make hats) reflects the desire to spin yarns of confusion that envelop their subjects' heads in tangled messes (chap. 19, p. 139). The people of Changrenguo, on the other hand, are fond of snuff and use empty wine barrels (whose contents were consumed by Tang and Lin during their journey) as snuff bottles attached at their waists. The king of this country, as we recall, advocated changing Qisheguo's name during the debate among the kings in chapter 39, which would have allowed the two countries to reap the benefits of kinship. And in the ensuing conversation about varieties of snuff, it becomes clear that this habit represents a wordplay on the subject of examination success. The names of snuff (and the means of obtaining it) popular among the girls all allude to the various unpalatable means of obtaining an examination degree—"cheating," hackneyed, and so forth. And the giants of Changrenguo are compared to a mythical giant named *Wulu*, a substitution for the expression *wudao*, "without the Way," or immoral and treacherous (chap. 20, pp. 138–39).

As in the discussion at Xuanyuanguo quoted earlier, these remarks allude to the (male) tendency toward obfuscation in the use of language and the pursuit of temporal success by any means, however treacherous or hypocritical. The girls have convened to celebrate their own success in Wu Zetian's special examinations, and like successful male candidates they are preoccupied with their own future fortunes. After introducing her father's journey with these two vignettes, Tang

Xiaoshan recounts the story of his retreat to Xiao Penglai and of her own adventures there with Yin Ruohua. She concludes with a line of prophecy from the inscription in the *Qihong ting*, or Pavilion for Lamenting Beauties, about the disparity of fortune among the hundred talented girls: "Who said that no one at the banquet will suffer a cruel fate," she quotes (chap. 70, p. 519). This deeply disturbs the girls present, for their happiness over their examination success seems marred by the possibility that some celebrants will be less fortunate than others. Some object that it does not seem to tally with the age-old adage that "evil is punished, and virtue rewarded," threatening their faith in the moral justice of the universe. Wang Chong's work *Lun heng* is cited as the locus classicus for the morally neutral view that personal fate is whimsical and not necessarily in correlation with moral worth. But the moralistic Shi Lanyan insists that Wang's theories do not refer to the human world (*luo*) at all but only to the lower forms of life. As a wealth of classical sources of high antiquity illustrate, she insists, evil is punished and virtue rewarded, everyone receives their just desserts (*guo*), and "sages make it to the top" (chap. 71, p. 523).

The pun between the "human" world of *luo* (倮) and "karmic result," *guo* (果), has already occurred in an earlier incident, when Tang and her companions are captured by four fruit demons (another meaning of *guo*) (chaps. 45–46, pp. 333–37). In that episode, two of the four demons who abduct the girls attempt to impersonate Confucius's disciples Zeng Xi and Yan Yuan by assuming their forms. But because these sagely men made an indelible mark on history, their fame was transmitted to posterity, which prevents the demons from assuming their likenesses (they retain the appearance of dried fruit). The same Taoist nun who later appears at the drinking party (and here identifies herself as the Fairy of the Hundred Fruits [*Baiguo Xianren*]), explains: "Their fame has been transmitted into eternity, and though dead they still live on. How could these demons have been able to imitate their forms? This is what is meant by the expression 'evil cannot overpower the right.'" (chap. 46, p. 337).[24] This affirmation of the power of fame to distinguish between virtue and its enemies, and to transmit the moral worth of the sages into the future, echoes the Confucian belief that concern for reputation, like the maintenance of clear relationships between words and meanings, enforces a stabilizing accountability on human society.[25]

Indeed, the pursuit of temporal fame as an instrument for the achievement of laudable social and moral aims receives unqualified approbation from many of the girls. As Lu Tingting explains upon being selected to serve as an official in Nüerguo:

> Today's imperial command to accompany Ruohua back to her country is truly an opportunity that comes but once in a thousand years. In the future when Ruohua becomes king, we will work together with loyalty and devotion. We may establish rites and music, or stimulate beneficial practices while eliminating corruption; remove cruel overlords and bring peace to the people, or promote the wise and banish flatterers; pay careful attention to punishments and names, or expend our energies on legal matters. By so doing, we will help her to become a wise ruler of her nation, and ourselves achieve fame as female ministers, leaving a good name for posterity. Is this not a happy story?" (Chap. 68, p. 505)

The arrogance and complacency fostered by the examination system are the object of much laughter and joking among the talented girls; yet the deployment of learning through public service and fame for the accomplishments achieved therein are defended as worthy goals for those who choose to take the path of government service.

On the one hand, then, female scholars like their male counterparts appear to be motivated by analogous desires for social utility and worldly recognition, desires that the Taoist fairy-nun Baiguo Xianzi cautions inhibit the apprehension of the emptiness and purposelessness of human affairs (chap. 90, p. 689). But the banquet in Bian Bin's garden affords them an opportunity to revive and bring to fruition the intellectual curiosity that first led them on the path of examination study, a curiosity that men apparently lose permanently in the examination process. The feminization of literati knowledge that is effected by these examinations matures into the liberation of intellectuality from the stultifying pursuit of temporal aims that plagues the male world. Beginning with the disaffection toward Wu Zetian's regime of Tang Ao and many of his associates in the bureaucracy, the political and moral concerns of men lead them toward martial endeavors; women thus find themselves in the position of guardians of the cultural tradition. They are successful in managing this role precisely because they treat it as a game, to be pursued largely for its own sake. While recognizing the moral and political dimensions of the pursuit of fame, they are not distracted by them, but instead turn to their true interests in the skills and games played during the banquet scenes. Therein lies the beauty of a fully feminized knowledge—that is, the recognition of its value as a play of forms, whose complexity need not be subsumed under any overarching moral programs or distorted by the overweening pursuit of worldly glory.

The Perils of Naming

It is intriguing that when male political authority is restored in the novel's conclusion, the men who reappear there do not emulate their female counterparts. These final chapters describe the storming by martial young men of four mythical passes guarding the capital, resulting in Wu Zetian's abdication. They adopt an allegorical mode similar to that of the first six chapters, which chronicle mythical events among female deities. While the opening chapters adumbrate the ascendancy of the hundred talented girls, these describe the closure of this gender reversal in battles between Wu Zetian's four brothers and a number of young men dedicated to restoring the Tang house. The Four Passes are named for the Four Vices of drunkenness, licentiousness, greed, and irascibility,[26] but although Wu Zetian and a few male characters indulge in some such excesses, these have little to do with the principal events of the novel.[27] Their significance can be found in their relation to the literati desire for recognition, for they are referred to collectively as *zizhu zhen* ("self-destructive traps"), that is, by the same words that describe the temporal success which the Taoist nun Daogu condemns as the root of delusion in both the heavenly and earthly realms.

But it is not simply that these young heroes fail to find pleasure in the intellectual diversions of their talented female counterparts. As in Shushiguo, Baiminguo, and other nations of (male) pedants encountered by the travelers, the men of these chapters grow infatuated with the trappings of learning without its substance. Here, however, instead of the examination study followed in those nations, it is the philological study of names that is corrupted by the male thirst for recognition; knowledge of "name" is overpowered by, and subsumed under, the desire for "fame." In this final summation of literati aims and aspirations, these men restore the normative political order without retaining the intellectual curiosity celebrated by their female counterparts, manifesting the re-imposition of careerism and moral self-righteousness onto the intellectual landscape refashioned by the girls' philological endeavors. The reversion of literati knowledge to its normative male state thus revives the deleterious conditions from which the girls managed to briefly rescue it.

198 / *Fictional Reconstructions of Literati Identity*

As the battles between Tang loyalists and Wu's forces rage, we find a sort of mimicry of the intellectual games of the preceding banquet scenes. At first glance, the Four Passes appear to continue the playful exploration of language of previous chapters, for they create a literalized landscape brimming with puns, allusions, and wordplays. The attackers of each pass enter a phantasmagoria where they are presented with long lists of names (of beautiful women, liquor, money, and so forth) and a series of literary allusions and puns associated with each. The Tang loyalists (who are referred to as members of the "Wen [=writing/language] camp," from the name of their commander) are bewitched by this plethora of words, and a number of them sink into a trance from which they cannot be revived. Such names are in several cases presented in the form of mock scholarly investigations; but instead of intellectual stimulation, these names inspire self-destructive impulses in their attackers, who are soon engulfed in clouds of confusion.

The return of the normative male order reaches its climax in the last and most formidable of the four, Caibei Pass, representing the vice of greed (*cai*, literally, wealth). Wealth is homophonous and nearly identical orthographically with the word for "talent" (*cai*), and the two words are linked at several points in the narrative. At the conclusion of the examinations for talented girls (*cainü ke*), the narrator comments that in spite of her adoration of the talented girls she has assembled, Wu Zetian still finds wealth more enticing than talent (instead of keeping them in China, she sends Yin Ruohua and her talented female advisers back to Nüerguo, in gratitude for sumptuous gifts from the king of that land) (chap. 68, p. 507). And in Junziguo, where talents appear to achieve fulfillment through service to the exemplary ruler of that land, there is a *caiqi* or "aura of wealth" that attracts predatory fishermen to its shores. As both the determinant and mark of literati status, wealth signals the final stage in the re-imposition of the male literati order.

In Caibei Pass, the Tang loyalist Zhang Hong finds himself in a gleaming valley filled with splendor and opulence. "In as lovely a place as this," he thinks to himself, "if I could find a secluded dwelling to spend some time, I won't have lived in vain" (chap. 99, p. 757). He then meets an old man named Wang Lao, who presents him with a lengthy list (*mingdan*) of names for money. There ensues an arcane and witty discussion of the various names and their history and suitability—indeed, probably the most elaborate scholarly dissertation in the entire novel. Zhang Hong becomes enraptured by these "names," and in a condensed version of the tale of Lu Sheng, lives a life of evanescent glory in the twinkling of an eye. His story concludes with the following realization:

> If he had only known that a hundred years are as ephemeral as this, he would have realized the futility of his actions. But saying this now was useless, so he traced his path back to the years when he was on the ascent. When he came before the hole of money [of covetousness], he stuck his head through to have a look outside. Unexpectedly the hole shrank and took hold of his neck, so that he could neither push in nor pull out. (Chap. 99, pp. 762–63)

For those who become entranced by the illusory rewards of worldly recognition, the best antidote apparently lies in a healthy respect for temporality and the transience of human life. As Yin Ruohua comments on Tang Xiaoshan's pride in her ability to decipher the inscription at the Pavilion for Lamenting Beauties: "That you understand it is fine, but that I don't is not necessarily bad. In sum, when the moment of mutability arrives, it is not just the ignorant like me who will turn to dust, with nothing to show for my efforts. Even you who know will be no different. Do you have the elixir of immortality?" (chap. 49, p. 362). Seeking worldly success as a goal in and of itself corrupts and destroys its unwitting victims. The love of learning and quest for knowledge that motivates the hundred girls to seek glory in the capital brings them to appreciate and even cherish the unpredictability and arbitrariness of name in both its senses. For as the tendency of language to overflow into a riot of polysemous play, ever eluding any attempts to achieve final or absolute knowledge, it is the source of their amusement. Understanding and reveling in these qualities thus tempers the girls' ardor for the achievement of worldly glory.

In the supernatural frame tale with which the novel begins, Baihua Xianzi, Tang Xiaoshan's heavenly form, arouses Chang'e's jealousy largely on account of the fame she enjoys among immortals. Such feelings motivate Chang'e to provoke Baihua Xianzi at their initial confrontation at the Immortal Peach Garden, and because both Chang'e and Baihua Xianzi are too proud to back down, the hundred flowers are temporarily expelled to earth. Similarly, in the mortal world the belief in an inevitable and unalterable relation between words and their referents, or fame and human worth, only spells delusion. Tang Ao's Taoist enlightenment and escape to Xiao Penglai midway through the novel represents a liberation from the delusion that examination degrees or other worldly success is awarded to the virtuous. And the linguistic play that follows the girls' success demonstrates the often fickle relation of words to meaning, and of fame to human deeds or moral worth. Fame is not so detached from reality that it fails to prevent human beings from acting without regard for their reputations. But neither is it fixed indelibly to the social institutions that have resulted in the numerous excesses and perversions given expression in the nations of the South Seas. Hence, the desire for personal success and recognition does not figure as the instrument of moral regeneration in *Jinghua yuan*, as it does in *Yesou puyan*. And in fact, in the realms of intellectual endeavor in which the talented women of the novel excel, such concerns take second place to an intellectual curiosity that, while not at odds with Confucian moral dictates, is nonetheless unencumbered by them.

The fickleness of fame, and name, and its tendency to assume a life all its own, detached from its referents, might be said to be the principal conceit of *Jinghua yuan*. In *Yesou puyan*, worldly fame—both its denial as well as its achievement—serves as the means by which its heroes achieve both personal success and the moral transformation of the realm to which they dedicate their lives. For *Jinghua yuan*, however, both fame and name are both troublingly problematic realms that repeatedly threaten to detach all sense of certitude from the human or, more specifically, the literati world, which is based on the erroneous premise that both can be relied upon unthinkingly. For those who seek absolute certitude in linguistic exactitude or fame and emoluments through temporal success, the novel seems to offer a cautionary tale.[28] Hence, the workings of fate (*yuan*) presented in it are eminently more disconcerting than those of individual destiny developed in *Yesou puyan*, where the encounters between characters accord with the ideal that even the most accidental and unfortunate of events can be transformed through human effort into the means of attaining noble moral aims. By contrast, *Jinghua yuan* appears to question the epistemological basis of a social and political system that has led the literati to believe in the omnipotence of their ideals, which are, in the end, as unstable as the words used to express them.

Scholarship and Trivial Pursuits

As we have seen, the analysis of literati mores in *Jinghua yuan* centers on the potential conflict between temporal success through its institutional expression in the examinations and the spirit of intellectual inquiry celebrated by its female cast. The first half of the novel traces the institutionalization of personal fame through the perversions and distortions of Confucian ideals, and the corresponding abasement of learning, found in the nations described in Tang Ao's journey. In the domain of feminine talent that emerges in its second half, however, the quest for recognition actually serves as a stimulus to serious intellectual interests. For the girls, the desire for personal success and need for intellectual satisfaction can be equally salutary. That such compatibility of aims is impossible in the male world is confirmed in the novel's conclusion, where men can do no better than make a mockery of the knowledge so successfully explored by the girls. It seems, then, that the contradiction between personal ambition and intellectual inquiry is completely neutralized only within the confines of the Bian garden; outside it, the desire for personal glory continues to pervade the male world of both China and its imitators abroad. As we have seen, the restoration of the Tang with which *Jinghua yuan* concludes revives in new form the abuses to which their own experiences have offered a resolution. In a word, the philological study of names pursued by the girls ultimately is corrupted by the male pursuit of fame, apparently dooming the brief interregnum of intellectual creativity celebrated in the banquet of chapters 69 through 93.

The relevance of this narrative to the intellectual world of the later Jiaqing period, when Li Ruzhen was composing his novel, is clear. Although many of the great figures of the evidential studies movement were still active in the first two decades of the nineteenth century, its prime had clearly passed. The most trenchant polemic against Han Learning, Fang Dongshu's *Hanxue shangdui*, appeared in this era. But while intellectually Han Learning may have been weakening, the political dominance of its leaders seems to have resulted in the ever widening dissemination of its influence in the nation as a whole. As Benjamin Elman has recently demonstrated, Han Learning began to be reflected in the examination system only in the late-eighteenth and early-nineteenth centuries. By the Jiaqing period training in Han Learning was incorporated into the examination curriculum, and hence came to be seen as indispensable by aspirants to office. Li Ruzhen's account thus appears to give expression to the concern and skepticism he may have harbored about such developments. For at the very least, the novel can be read as a cautionary account directed toward his fellow Han Learning devotees on the potential for corruption of the ideals they held dear.

I have tried to demonstrate some of the ways in which both *Yesou puyan* and *Jinghua yuan* manifest the intellectual concerns that are a hallmark of mid-Qing discourse. Their accounts of the literati quest for recognition both accord prominence to the pursuit of knowledge—whether it be of literary or classical texts, exotic phenomena of foreign lands, preternatural forces, or the intricacies of games, divination, and the fine arts. In *Jinghua yuan*, however, intellectual endeavors overshadow (male) political and moral aims, as the talented girls seek knowledge of specialized and seemingly trivial subjects with little if any application to the conventional realms of literati expertise. This intellectual engagement unencumbered by an "agenda" reaches full expression in a world entirely separate from male literati endeavors. By contrast, both men and women of *Yesou puyan* train in skills seen as contributing to the realization of their utopian political projects. Erudition in that novel comes only rarely in the form of diversion and entertainment. More often than not, its scholarly expositions are delivered with an earnestness, even messianic fervor, that leaves most modern readers cold.

As I have suggested, the motif of play pervades *Jinghua yuan*'s treatment of literati learning, most particularly its later chapters. While the moralizing pedants of the journey chapters stifle the creative energies of the inhabitants of the South Seas, girls see learning as opportunity for joking and amusement. In the banquet chapters, mathematical problems, riddles, card games, prognostication, music, and even physical sports occupy the girls, who express little interest in more staid topics of conversation. Their engrossment in play reaches its culmination in the twelve-chapter-long drinking game with which these chapters conclude, where nearly every exchange is peppered with riddles, puns, and witticisms. That such entertainment epitomizes learning at its best is in fact adumbrated even in the male world, where in spite of the distractions of temporal success and moral seriousness, men are by no means indifferent toward the lighter side of learning. Though less consumed by such diversions than their female counterparts, the male protagonists Duo Jiugong and Tang Ao also take pleasure in discussing the arcane textual sources of their journey to the South Seas. Like the girls' merrymaking, the wit and humor of these two men stand the prosaic world of male examination learning on its head.

The banquet scenes begin, as I have said, with somber reflections on the tragic dimensions of human life and the inevitability of a disparity between the fortunes of the various girls. Indeed, up until the examinations and their aftermath the girls have not been devoid of seriousness. Tingting, Honghong, Tang Xiaoshan, and other learned girls debate questions of classical philology and discusse the exotic flora, fauna, and medicines of the world beyond China, with great earnestness in chapters 16–19, 46–48, 52–54, and elsewhere. But once the festivities of the banquet get under way in chapter 70, the girls' knowledge becomes framed within the context of the games they play during these extended discussions. Moreover, although we might question the degree to which such games entertain the reader, it is clear that they absorb the attention of their players. Far from serving as mere interludes between erudite discussions, such entertainment dissolves the barriers between learning and play, and in fact becomes the objects of scholarly attention itself. Moreover, by subsuming scholarship within such a framework of games, the girls find their attention turning beyond the specific content of knowledge, to the nature of its formal dimensions, its "methodology," so to speak.[29]

The first ten or so chapters of the banquet are taken up with various board and card games, music, divination, mathematics, and other diversions. This relaxing session appears to offer a much-needed respite from the tension of the examinations. Yet these games serve to introduce and amplify the theme of play as an essential vehicle of, and metaphor for, literati learning. For example, the card game known as *madiao* is said to exist in a simplified popular version known as *chandiao*. It is explained that "when *madiao* was first created, careless people or those lacking in concentration were not allowed to watch . . . otherwise, they would have destroyed the beauty of the game" (chap. 73, p. 543). Games should be played with maximum concentration and skill; creativity and the development of a personal style are also critical. If in the game of *go*, for example, one simply copies the playing styles of others, then

> It is like someone trying to write an essay, who plagiarizes old compositions. So that others don't recognize them, he adds a few of his own opinions, trying to bring this jumbled mix together in some sensible manner to cover up the facts from others. Such people don't realize that such an essay is like a person who wears brocade and silk on his body, but a straw hat on his head and straw sandals on his feet. Such finery only makes him more ludicrous. (Chap. 73, p. 537)

As in the allegorical frame tale, mere winning should not be allowed to dominate any competition. In archery, simply seeking to score a bull's-eye is wrongheaded. Rather, one needs to perfect one's posture: "Often people shoot for diversion, in order to stretch the muscles, stimulate the circulation, heal chronic illnesses, and increase the appetite. It is good for people. But if one does not pay attention to the stance, then even Zizhi [an archer] . . . might be injured" (chap. 79, p. 586). For many of these avocations, the novel goes into great detail in explaining the rules for and current state of the art. For example, in a discussion of prognostication, one girl gives a lengthy lesson on the instrument known as *tiandi pan* ("heaven and earth board"), which she says has been a stumbling block for many attempting to learn the art: "Because people of the past were unable to clearly explicate the basics [of divination], learners could not understand its subtleties, and hence were ignorant of them" (chap. 75, p. 557).

Despite their seeming insignificance, these avocations possess formal intricacy that is worthy of serious study. Of relevance here are Ling Tingkan's remarks quoted earlier that the understanding of human nature must be preceded by an intimate familiarity with detailed measurements, gestures, movements, and vessels of ritual—that is, the formal qualities of learning. Yet technical knowledge is not the only object of such games and diversions. In the dice game known as *shuanglu*, the origin of its use of two dice is explained as follows: "The intent is to urge harmony between brothers. If brothers are of the same mind and heart, then others cannot take advantage of them; but if each has his own opinion, and cannot be harmonious, then they become isolated. How otherwise can people attack them?" To which another girl adds: "This goes to show that every act of the ancients was meant to bring people to the proper path. Even in games, they inserted a moral message. But people only crave entertainment, without knowing the meaning of these games" (chap. 74, pp. 546–47). The ethical dimension of human life clearly has a place within the spectrum of intellectual endeavors and should not be slighted.

In fact, knowledge of ethical principles (*yili*) so prized by the practitioners of orthodox learning can also become the instrument for validating new and potentially disquieting areas of inquiry, such as the scientific and mathematical subjects championed by Ling Tingkan, Ruan Yuan, and their fellow compilers of the biographical work *Chouren zhuan*. A number of mathematical problems entertain the girls over the course of their merrymaking, several of which incorporate elements of European origin. In the midst of calculating weights and volumes, for example, the girls see a bright flash of lightning in the distance. Mi Lanfen, the most mathematically proficient member of the group, having determined the time differential between the lightening and thunder, calculates the lightening to have struck ten and a half li to the south. Soon thereafter, a servant returns from the area to report that the lightening had struck and killed a local scoundrel, to the inhabitants' great relief. Mi's calculations turn out to be exactly right, repudiating the doubts of some of the more conservative girls over the reliability of such "new-fangled" knowledge (chap. 79, pp. 589–90). These scientific and mathematical observations serve a dual purpose: both demonstrating the possibility of knowledge based upon methodologies and assumptions without basis in the classics and, at the same time, reassuringly confirming the age-old belief that evildoers are punished by heaven in the form of thunder.[30]

As discussed above, many of the games of the banquet, as well as the repartee and witticisms earlier in the novel, turn on the phonological and other linguistic properties of words. Riddles, rhyming and alliteration, homophones, and other such verbal gymnastics exercise the girls' playful intelligence, as they compete with one another in interminable rounds of jokes. The girls' fascination with language, first broached in the exchange between Duo Jiugong and the two girls of Heichiguo, here is given its ultimate expression in a wide-ranging discussion of the principal issues and discoveries in phonology, orthography, and even semantics as of Li Ruzhen's time. This culminates in the final drinking game of chapters 82 through 93, a deceptively simple contest testing the girls' abilities in rhyming and alliteration. The girls are required to cite an alliterative or rhyming pair of characters on a set topic, from a pre-Tang text not yet used by the others. The progress of the game itself mirrors the gradual amplification of the motif of language and its use and misuse over the course of the novel. While it begins with paeans to the hoary virtues of loyalty and filial piety, the girls soon move on to a potpourri of knowledge and an irreverence toward conventional proprieties of language, that mirrors the increasing irrepressibility of "name."

Perhaps the most representative of all the various games are the riddles that punctuate the party in a number of places. The festivities begin when one girl asks her companions to guess a sentence from either *The Analects* or *Mencius* based on the clue "*hongqi baojie*—the red flag announces victory." Various phrases with the words "victory" are offered, until one girl finally realizes that the word for victory (*ke*) is in fact a name (in *Ke bao yu jun*—"Ke tells the lord"). This and the next riddle (*shi er you*—"serving with distinction") play on the punning qualities of language and are cited as the ideal form of riddle: "One uses a personal name as an empty word, while the other uses an empty word as a personal name. Both exhaust the possibilities of literary cleverness.... The best riddles borrow words [i.e., pun]; straightforward riddles are of secondary value" (chap. 80, p. 593). Also favored are the so-called "riddles of splitting characters," that is, those that hinge on internal elements within one or more characters. Rather ingenuously, the girls claim to seek simplicity in such riddles and praise allusions that are "clear and obvious," that do not require knowledge of abstruse texts such as *Shanhai jing*. And indeed, as this and numerous other examples demonstrate, it is "literary cleverness," that is, the creative use of language, rather than mere erudition that piques the girls' interest. This exploration of knowledge as the endless play of form is summed up by the narrator in his concluding remarks, when he says of his work that he has "used *wen* as a game" (*yi wen wei xi*).

Conclusion

THIS BOOK has attempted to demonstrate the relevance of a movement to revise and even redefine literati identity as it had come to be constituted in late imperial China to three novels: Wu Jingzi's *Rulin waishi*, Xia Jingqu's *Yesou puyan*, and Li Ruzhen's *Jinghua yuan*. Each of these novels can be situated within the context of what I have called discourses of literati self-renewal, specifically the scholarly and ritual programs of the Yan-Li school, Changzhou practical studies, and evidential scholarship, as well as the broad literary and intellectual trends of the mid-Qing period. Although each novel bears the imprint of these discourses, their treatment of the trials and tribulations of literati status does not by any means reproduce such discourses either wholly or uncritically. Indeed, Wu Jingzi and his fellow novelists appear to have sought the freedom of what Li Ruzhen called the "play of *wen*" to probe literati intellectuality and political participation in a medium quite different from other discursive forms. While the quality of their results ranges from the masterful satire of *Rulin waishi* to the moral sententiousness of *Yesou puyan* and tedious pedantry of parts of *Jinghua yuan*, as a group these writers made contributions to the development of fiction in the late imperial period that form a significant chapter in literary history.

Of these three novels, *Rulin waishi* offers what is indisputably the most searching critique of literati mores. Not only are the status quo of the examination system and its attendant careerism and opportunism subjected to a mordant satire, but various alternative routes to literati "success," including even the idealistic redefinition of literati roles by committed reformers, receive their share of satirical barbs. While apparently drawing on the programs of literati "self-reinvention" espoused by the author's associates and contemporaries, *Rulin waishi* nonetheless throws into doubt the possibility of reconciling the conflicting components of literati identity into anything of long-term viability or coherence—in other words, the possibility of reviving the literati as a social institution of genuine benefit to society as a whole.

The three dimensions of *Rulin waishi* discussed in Part II work in concert to introduce ever deepening degrees of skepticism toward attempts to reform literati mores. The first thirty or so chapters present a carefully balanced constellation of vocations and identities, including examination study and essay editing, literary or aesthetic dilettantism, self-styled eremitism, and erudite scholarship. Each version of literati identity is represented by a range of characters whose weaknesses and faults serve as evidence of tendencies inherent in these vocations. Examination study encourages superficial and uninformed scholarship, as well as a philistinism blind to the value of culture divorced from the immediate goals of social advancement. Poetry and prose on the other hand foster complacency and an oddly misplaced snobbery among their advocates, who like Zheng Xie's bogeymen Wang Wei and Zhao Mengfu seek the status and perquisites of cultural endeavors with no commitment to or awareness of their practical benefits. Even scholarly research that champions a revised social ethic is marred by the pedantry of men accustomed to regarding their own often idiosyncratic ideals as beyond question or criticism. In this cacophony of competing voices, no particular intellectual position or vocation is valorized over another.

In *Rulin waishi*, we can find much that parallels the intellectual debates and ideological programs to which Wu Jingzi was exposed. While far from endorsing the creed enunciated by Yan Yuan and Li Gong for literati revitalization, *Rulin waishi* nonetheless reflects a corporate view of the literati similar to that of Yan Yuan and Li Gong. As its representation of literati vocations shifts from one perspective to another, playing off one version of literati identity against another, the novel could even be said to offer a narrativization of the views of Yan-Li and some of their contemporaries regarding the essentially incomplete and limited nature of individual human endowments. Moreover, Cheng Tingzuo's exposition of the primacy of mental capacity over moral attainment, further elaborated by Dai Zhen, finds strong echoes in the relentlessly intellectualist satire of literati manners, in which one literati character after another founders on his or her own inherently narrow interpretation of the plethora of social phenomena. Through these tactics each vocation is exposed as inherently limiting in its exclusion of and antipathy toward competing discourses. This includes even those characters who would appear to give voice to the concerns of evidential studies, such as Zhuang Shaoguang and Chi Hengshan, let alone the many lesser scholars of the novel.

Given Wu Jingzi's reputation during his lifetime as a literary stylist and poet of some ability, it is intriguing that the novel's literary men number among the most ludicrous of its characters. Although there is no evidence that Wu knew Yuan Mei directly, he was certainly well acquainted with the latter's circle of literary professionals during the last decade or so of his life. And though hardly of Yuan's stature or resources, Wu appears to have lived very much as Yuan did, as a poet and essayist who garnered much of his income through his writings. In this he perhaps shared Zheng Xie's derisive attitude toward those who sought social advancement above and beyond mere income through such activities. For Wu Jingzi, the antics of those who disguised their greed beneath cultural or literary affectations apparently deserved a ridicule harsher and more unremitting than any other group of literati.

Perhaps most discomfiting in terms of locating *Rulin waishi* within the discursive field of its time is its problematization of the discourses of ritual. The creed of ritual activism enunciated by the novel's scholarly characters, which culminates in their enactment of the rites at Taibo Temple in chapter 37, presents the novel's sole plan for remedying contemporary social malaise. This would seem to reflect the emergent discourses of ritualism so much in evidence by the early Qianlong era. Nonetheless, as I indicated in Chapter 6, the novel's treatment of ritual suggests potential flaws in these discourses, flaws that are mapped out in greatest detail in the final third of the novel. For the precipitous decline in literati mores that follows the ritual appears to be far from unrelated to the idealistic activism of its proponents. Such cynicism toward the efficacy of ritual as an instrument of social change finds few echoes during the period of Wu Jingzi's adulthood, perhaps the high-water mark of ritualist fervor.

The ritualism espoused by Chi Hengshan and his fellow scholars is first and foremost a program of ritual enactment, of bringing the forms and movements of the rites to perfection, rather than one of philosophical debate. As such, it is quite consistent with what Kai-wing Chow describes as the dominant tendency of Qing ritualists to stress "praxis" (*xi*), and the corresponding abandonment of what he calls the "didactic mode" (*jiangxue*) of moral autonomy of the individual that characterized Ming thought. Li Fu, one of the compilers of the imperial rites project of the early Qianlong period, was an early advocate of the view that "once the performative structures of ritual were restored, the moral meanings would reveal themselves transparently," and hence that speculation on such meanings was to be avoided.[1] In *Rulin waishi*, the espousal of a ritualist program and even the enactment of rites appear indeed to entirely eschew their "moral meanings" in favor of a devotion to an almost totally mute performative dimension.[2]

If the ritualism of *Rulin waishi* is suited to the need for praxis that so many men of Wu Jingzi's generation advocated, its abject failure to accomplish the goals to which it is addressed raises serious problems of interpretation. Is it simply the pedantry or deficiencies of its advocates or the misunderstandings of subsequent generations that result in the debasement of these ideals? As I have suggested, the events that follow the Taibo Temple rites of chapter 37 appear to reflect an inability to abide by ritual at the mundane level of quotidian life, ranging from the cynical manipulation of literati privilege and "ritual expertise" to a failure to resolve the various contradictions between ritual advocacy and material needs and desires. Moreover, the novel as a whole draws attention to ritual propriety in its broadest dimensions as a zone of conflict between literati and their social others, presenting opportunities for corruption and the abuse of power. Essentially then, even an otherwise well-intentioned program of ritual reform cannot compensate for a neglect of ritual propriety in mundane affairs, and the ever-widening disjunction between ritual and everyday life only contributes to the malaise to which ritualism is addressed. For those of Wu Jingzi's contemporaries bent on carrying out such programs even in the absence of adherence to a modicum of propriety, the novel can be said to offer a cautionary tale.

As for *Yesou puyan*, the conservative tenor of Xia Jingqu's views on scholarship and literati identity can be ascribed to a number of factors, temporal, geographic, and biographical in nature. First is Xia's origins in Jiangyin County, a bastion of examination study where commitment to orthodox Song Neo-Confucianism had not diminished even by the mid-to-late eighteenth century. Moreover, although Xia traveled extensively during his lifetime, it was primarily to peripheral areas such as Shaanxi, Yunnan, and elsewhere where evidential studies were barely known. His mentors included the staunchly orthodox Yang Mingshi, Gao Bin, and Sun Jiagan, while a possible antagonist very well may have been the most prominent eighteenth-century defender of the school of the Mind, Li Fu. Moreover, Xia's formative years were spent in the late Kangxi and Yongzheng eras, when the principal scholarly schism remained that between the Zhu Xi and Wang Yangming schools of Neo-Confucianism, and not between Han and Song textual exegesis. Xia's near contemporaries Jiang Yong and Shen Tong, both leading figures in the rise of Han Learning, remained faithful to Neo-Confucian doctrines throughout their lives.

Yet while in many ways reactionary in tone and perhaps anachronistic in its attachment to Neo-Confucian dogma, the case can be made that *Yesou puyan* does in fact seriously address significant issues relevant to Han Learning. In its delineation of the role of the literati under conditions of increasing difficulty and alienation from political participation, the novel simultaneously creates both a model of the omnipotent literati male and the social landscape within which literati must seek a more constricted and limited version of this overarching model. Collective effort that involves not merely a small male elite but the broad spectrum of humankind is necessary to root out the evils and delusions that afflict the polity. Within this social nexus literati must devote themselves to unremitting intellectual effort and to recognizing the insights and talents of non-literati such as women, foreigners, and various semihuman creatures. The mind is easily led astray by false knowledge and thus must be vigilant in seeking out the "concrete and verifiable fact," rather than useless abstractions. Preconceived ideas, notably over the rationality of mundane existence and the workings of preternatural phenomena, must be overcome in a search for and acceptance of human society in its totality.

Through its revitalized orthodoxy, *Yesou puyan* reconstructs the possibility of a literati identity during the difficult times of the mideighteenth century—difficult, that is, for lowly and unenfranchised literati such as the author. Yet this reconstruction can also be seen as responding to the very issues that men such as Dai Zhen had attempted to resolve through his excursions into moral philosophy, namely, the ever-widening gap between the pursuit of knowledge of form and the moral and political responsibilities of the literati as a social elite. To the question of whether a literatus fully devoted to the investigation of the phenomenal world could still seek moral coherence or "meaning" (*yili*), *Yesou puyan* responds quite enthusiastically in the affirmative. It repairs the strains in this relationship with a zeal for encyclopedic learning that seems designed to match that of the devotees of evidential studies, demonstrating in the very act of writing itself the possibility of achieving moral aims while busily building up the mountain of arcana that fills the many pages of *Yesou puyan*.

Needless to say, Li Ruzhen's *Jinghua yuan* represents the scholarly mainstream of Han Learning much more faithfully than does *Yesou puyan*, and it is perhaps in part its topical relevance to the debates of the nineteenth century that earned it a wide readership throughout the late Qing. But like *Yesou puyan*, it also attempts to bridge the gap between the conflicting demands of Han and Song, or textual/philological and moral/philosophical thought, in ways that draw upon the strengths of each. While *Yesou puyan* can be said to incorporate the methods of Han Learning into a revitalized Neo-Confucianism, *Jinghua yuan* proposes rather the reverse—namely, the assimilation of orthodoxy into the framework and worldview of evidential studies. Li Ruzhen attempts to articulate a new relationship between the social and political duties incumbent upon literati status and intellectual life, issues that so preoccupied his generation.

In its delineation of these tensions, *Jinghua yuan* appears to have largely followed the opinions of Li Ruzhen's mentor, Ling Tingkan, on the dispute between Han Learning and Song orthodoxy. As discussed in Chapter 3, Ling castigated the idea that Han and Song learning were compatible, arguing instead that the best way to achieve the aims of philosophical truth was through a single-minded devotion to the methods and principles of philology, and in particular of phonology and its insights into the history of linguistic change. Compromise over such issues could only result in the perpetuation of the errors introduced by Song speculative philosophers, errors that Ling and his fellow scholars were at pains to systematically weed out of classical exegesis. However well-intentioned and seemingly insightful Song philosophy might be, its errors could not but impugn the entire edifice of thought and scholarly endeavor which rested upon it.

To be sure, the allegorizing of the Han-Song disputes by *Jinghua yuan* extends its range beyond the ethereal world of scholarship to encompass more mundane concerns. Most notably, this debate includes—one might even say focuses upon—the issue of careerism and its attendant desires as determinants of literati intellectuality. In its story of female ascendance, male and female styles and forms of knowledge bifurcate over the issue of the individual's use of learning for personal gain. Males, who by and large serve as the spokesmen for orthodox thought, remain wedded to learning as a commodity to be exchanged for, and ultimately corrupted by, the "name" to which they aspire. Women as idealized in the later sections of the novel manage to achieve both the playful exploration of knowledge and scholarship and a realistic assessment of, and commitment to, moral principles— that is, the preservation of a literati identity in its broad contours without compromising their intellectual integrity. By and large, women achieve the goals of both the Han and Song schools: state service, moral commitment, and intellectual acuity, while recognizing nonetheless the contingencies inherent in all three areas of literati life. As such this novel promises a true utopia that, however fleetingly, evokes the possibility of a resolution of the debates that had raged for nearly a century.

Both *Yesou puyan* and *Jinghua yuan* provide ample evidence of their respective authors' interests in the scholarly and intellectual currents of their day. Moreover, even the scant biographical data we possess on Xia Jingqu and Li Ruzhen reveal more about their intellectual affiliations than does the now rather extensive reconstruction of Wu Jingzi's life. While it cannot be proved definitively, the paucity of evidence for Wu Jingzi may reflect his lack of interest in seeking such affiliations, or even a skepticism toward his contemporaries, whether advocates of Yan-Li thought or evidential scholars. Certainly the evidence from *Rulin waishi* supports such a conjecture. Yet as I have tried to demonstrate, through its exploration of ritualism as an instrument of literati renewal, Wu's novel also delineates the central issue over which each of these two literary successors would take divergent tacks: namely, that of whether the literati should seek meaning in the reintegration of form with meaning, and of moral and political duties with intellectual commitment (as in *Yesou puyan*), or instead to accept the perhaps unavoidable tension between the various dimensions of literati life, and follow the path most appropriate to each individual endowment (*Jinghua yuan*). *Rulin waishi* hints at the magnitude of this quandary but does not offer any resolution beyond the dissolution of literati identity itself.

A word needs to be said here about the alleged feminism of *Jinghua yuan*. Various claims have been made both for and against the notion that this novel presents a genuine argument for the revision or even rejection of social practices such as footbinding, concubinage, prejudice against the education of women, and other traditions restrictive of women's freedoms. While Lin Yutang, Hu Shih, Ono Kazuko, and others have supported the idea that Li Ruzhen espoused a protean version of twentieth-century feminism, others such as Frederick Brandauer and C. T. Hsia have cautioned against adopting any sanguine views of Li Ruzhen's progressive tendencies. Recently, Qingyun Wu has added another view that largely concurs with Hu Shih and Lin Yutang, arguing that *Jinghua yuan* indeed advocates nothing less than the full enfranchisement of women as the equals of men in learning, government, and family life. To Wu, the feminization of literati knowledge that I have argued to be a principal structural feature of the novel should in fact be understood quite literally, as the empowerment of women in all fields of literati endeavor.[3]

While I do not necessarily take issue with all of Wu's conclusions, I find it difficult to endorse the view of *Jinghua yuan* as an unqualified call for the reevaluation of women's social position. Instead, I believe we should view it within the context of its fictional predecessors such as *Yesou puyan*, *Xingshi yinyuan zhuan*, *Lin Lan Xiang*, and numerous other works that include the elevation of women. In the words of Keith McMahon, this conspicuous motif of Qing fiction implicitly challenges male dominance in various spheres, but its significance is open to a range of interpretation: it may be "the critique of and compensation for bad male behavior, the feminization and purification (or atonement) of the alienated male self, the projection of greater self-determination for the female self, or the idealization of compassionate, monogamous love."[4] In the case of *Jinghua yuan*, its gendering of the dispute between Han and Song Learning may in some but certainly not in all of its dimensions suggest direct application to gender inequality. Its learned women offer a model for the emergence of a new and healthier relationship between the divergent demands of literati identity, but as I have attempted to demonstrate, this is a model of figural more than literal relevance.

The three novels treated in this book manifest what appears to be a progressive amplification of the representation and reflection of the scholarly issues of their eras. Indeed, with the exception of *Rulin waishi*, they are clearly more "learned" than any fiction either before or since. All three novels can be described as heavily reliant upon underlying intellectual themes, rather than the presentation of events, for their structural integrity. Whereas the novel in both Europe and China of the seventeenth and eighteenth centuries can be described as to some extent "event"-centered[5] these three works exhibit compositional unity at the level of intellectual coherence. In *Rulin waishi* this could be summarized as the search for an all-embracing concept, or merely a career, that could accommodate literati ambitions and pretensions. For both *Yesou puyan* and *Jinghua yuan* alike this intellectualism turns toward the resolution of the conflict between the styles and content of the Han and Song schools of scholarship.

It is an intriguing coincidence that the great works of philosophical fiction in western Europe appeared almost simultaneously with these Chinese novels, namely, the classics of this genre by Swift, Montesquieu, Voltaire, and Johnson. According to Frederick Keener these works are united by the "central topic [of] the increasing qualification of eighteenth century philosophy by psychology" and the quest for self-knowledge: "For a knowledgeable person of the eighteenth century to know himself in some degree, he had to experience the genesis of his thinking, lest his thoughts be no more than the automatic consequences of unrecognized and uncontrolled inner forces."[6] The philosophical tales portray characters "attaining freedom from false mental associations," thereby understanding the "chain of events in their minds and the world." Such descriptions seem remarkably apt for the Chinese works under study here. Like the philosophical and scholarly works cited in Part I, they too turn to the cognitive and affective workings of the mind as the key to literati malaise and rejuvenation. In *Rulin waishi*'s satire, it is the failure to understand the genesis of one's own "unrecognized and uncontrolled inner forces" that mars the otherwise laudable efforts of its scholars to reform their society. Wen Suchen struggles mightily against what are indeed quite analogous to "false mental associations" (*fuhui*) that obscure the origins and true state of the phenomenal world. The girls of *Jinghua yuan* are similarly drawn to the "associational element in mental life," but their interest in the exploration of the unstable properties of language satirizes less than it celebrates. They repudiate not such associations themselves, but the belief in a necessary relation between what are in the end highly unstable and contingent words, mere "names."

On the level of literary form, the three works discussed here have more in common with other examples of Qing fiction than *Candide*, *Rasselas*, *Gulliver's Travels*, or *Lettres persanes* have with their counterparts in English and French fiction. The latter have in fact been thought of as "tales" rather than novels per se largely for their failure to adhere to the conventions of the novel. While satirical distortion and the episodicity characteristic of Western tales is also present in all three of these Chinese works, the latter nonetheless remain closely wedded to the formal conventions of vernacular Chinese fiction. The question of why these works retain the pretense of historicity even in fantasies such as the travel sections of *Jinghua yuan* can perhaps be ascribed to the power of historical writing in the Chinese tradition. As Nakano Miyoko puts it, in spite of the plethora of supernatural phenomena in much of Chinese fiction, it ultimately remained into modern times "a literature without gods or demons," wedded to temporal and spatial specificity.[7] Only in relatively short works such as *Zhong Kui zhuan* do we find a combination of the fantastic with satire reminiscent of the Western works cited above.[8]

By introducing the possibility of comparison between these three Chinese works and the philosophical tales of Enlightenment Europe, I have inadvertently raised what some have adduced as a fundamental difference between Chinese and Western fiction. As the list of European authors attests, fiction was used by some of the most influential figures in letters and thought of their time as a medium for the expression of social or philosophical criticism. While these Western tales were widely read and disseminated by their contemporaries, however, no Chinese work of vernacular fiction achieved a comparable position within elite circles. Indeed, the leading exponents of evidential studies, the intellectual movement that I have suggested bears the most affinities with the fiction under study, generally looked with scorn upon vernacular literature as a whole, and in contrast to the acceptance it had achieved among many late Ming literati, they rarely deigned to comment upon or perhaps even to read it. As a largely marginalized genre during the Qing period, employed by disaffected members of the increasingly numerous middle-to-lower strata of gentry society, there is little to suggest that these works were viewed as in any way compatible to loftier realms of intellectual or literary discourse. One of the assumptions of this book has been that in fact fiction shares much common ground with the more highly valued genres of scholarly and literary discourse. Nevertheless, it is evident that the great bulk of Chinese vernacular fiction does not partake of the fascination with scholarly debate found in the works treated here.

While demonstrating the relevance of these examples of Qing fiction to their discursive contexts, I have paid relatively little attention to their significance to vernacular fiction as a whole. The substantial engagement of these three works with intellectual issues of their day appears to justify considering them as distinct from both their forebears and from other works of the Qianlong and Jiaqing eras. As I have suggested, they share certain features with the philosophical novel of European literature. On the other hand, they can also be seen as a logical if extreme development of certain tendencies present in literati fiction of the Ming and early Qing periods.

We can find significant precedents to the works under study here in the early Qing period, which also witnessed an increasing interest in vernacular fiction as a medium for the exploration of philosophical or ideological issues. Ellen Widmer has demonstrated how in the first decades of Qing rule Ming loyalists such as Chen Chen, the author of *Shuihu houzhuan*, turned to fiction for its allegorical potential in venting hostility to the Manchus. There were obvious social and political reasons for this: "Occupations that might have been viewed as leisurely under other circumstances—religious contemplation, printing, scholarly research, and music—often took on the seriousness of a career for many of Ch'en's friends, something that would not have happened so easily if there had been official positions to pursue. Fiction was in the same category for some people but not for all."[9] While cautioning that "in the troubled times at the end of the Ming, connections between intellectuals and fiction were more often a marriage of convenience than a heartfelt commitment," she nonetheless points to the many works of this period that allude at least indirectly to the important intellectual and political issues of the day. In a similar vein, Robert Hegel has suggested that the seventeenth century marks the stage at which vernacular fiction had evolved into a "vehicle for self-expression."[10]

In stylistic terms, the abstract, spare narrative style found in both *Rulin waishi* and *Jinghua yuan* was anticipated in some of the short stories of the playwright Li Yu. As Patrick Hanan describes them, Li's fictional characters "tend to illustrate ideas and attitudes" rather than full-fledged personae. In his plays as well, "his process of composition must have begun with a daring idea, which he then explored in all its delicious improbability."[11] Li's operational principle was what he called the "path of thought" (*touxu*), which played down the proliferation of detail in the interest of compositional clarity. We find numerous analogies to these features in *Rulin waishi* in particular.

Generally speaking, however, the degree to which influences from earlier fiction can be discerned in these works is debatable. Of these three only *Rulin waishi* alludes to a previous work (*Shuihu zhuan*) in ways that suggest any significant influence. The same cannot be said of *Yesou puyan*, which voices adamant hostility to fiction (much of it is written in a mixture of abstruse and recondite language far removed from the colloquial styles typical of the genre), or of *Jinghua yuan*, which, aside from possible borrowing from the slightly earlier *Honglou meng* (1792/1793) and *Lü mudan* (1800), looks back to such ancient texts as *Shanhai jing*. This contrasts with the early Qing fiction mentioned above, for many significant examples of that period consist of sequels to and adaptations of the great Ming novels. This was of course also the period when the greatest commentaries to the Ming novels were produced. Jin Shengtan, Mao Zonggang, and Zhang Zhupo wrote and published their commentaries to three of the four Ming masterworks (*Sanguo yanyi*, *Shuihu zhuan*, *Xiyou ji*, and *Jin Ping Mei* between the 1630s to the 1660s, precisely when the writers, such as Chen Chen and Dong Yue, were most active, and it is clear from their writing that they had read these commentaries and in some cases borrowed from them.

The lack of discernible influence upon the three novels under study here does not, however, suggest a radical departure from the tradition of *zhanghui xiaoshuo* ("fiction in volumes and chapters"). Rather the status of vernacular fiction appears to have undergone a significant decline by the mid-to-late Kangxi period that weakened if not entirely severed the links between Ming literati fiction and its successors of the eighteenth century. Under the increasingly conservative ideological climate of the 1680s on, when active resistance to the Manchu regime had all but disappeared, the acceptability of vernacular fiction, and particularly the traditions of the Ming novel and short story, as a medium of expression in literati circles appears to have considerably diminished. Nor did the sexual explicitness and, for lack of a better term, populism of much of sixteenth- and early-seventeenth-century fiction endear it to the decidedly less tolerant arbiters of Kangxi culture. Indeed, as Wang Liqi has amply demonstrated, by the late seventeenth century condemnations of fiction and drama had greatly intensified in tone, scope, and frequency, a tendency that was to continue throughout the eighteenth and well into the nineteenth centuries.[12] Such statements need not be taken at face value, of course, for it appears that a certain hypocrisy prevailed. But at any rate, one result of this fall from grace seems to have been the reduced relevance of the Ming masterworks as significant models for emulation by writers of Qing fiction.[13]

If the Qianlong and Jiaqing eras were a time when, at least in elite circles, the prestige of vernacular literature reached perhaps its lowest ebb ever, then the scholarly erudition of these novels under study can be seen as a compensatory feature, partially mitigating the low prestige to which the genre had sunk. These are not the only novels to include such features, but they are certainly by far the most noteworthy.[14] This is not to say, however, that no other fiction of this era shares some of the features that have been identified here as characteristic of these novels. Indeed, in nearly all the major works of eighteenth-century fiction, literati and their concerns and interests assume a prominence greater than in previous fiction. Here I would like to cite just a few of examples of novels comparable to the objects of study.

Xingshi yinyuan zhuan (A marriage tale to awaken the world), although currently still impossible to date with certainty, seems in all likelihood to be the product of the mid-to-late Kangxi period (the earliest known reference to it, in a Japanese catalog, is dated 1732, and references exist to editions of 1764–65). A brilliant satire of bureaucratic ineptitude in a provincial backwater of Shandong, it has received notice in recent years for its treatment of shrewish women. *Lüye xianzong* (Immortal traces in green fields) (prefaces by the author are dated 1764 and 1771) by Li Baichuan (of whom no records are known) shows the clearest affinities with the three works treated here. For although avowedly Taoist in inspiration, like both *Yesou puyan* and *Jinghua yuan* its plot follows a pattern of struggle against and final victory over nefarious political forces by persecuted and unenfranchised literati.

No discussion of eighteenth-century literati fiction would be complete without touching upon *Honglou meng*, the preeminent work of its period, and arguably of the entire tradition. Comparisons between *Honglou meng* (The dream of the red chamber) and *Rulin waishi* abound (including even the realm of geography: both Wu Jingzi and Cao Xueqin lived in Nanjing during the Yongzheng reign, and both novels contain allusions to some of the famous gardens and landmarks of the city during that period). Moreover, readers have long pointed out what appear to be allusions to *Honglou meng* to be found in *Jinghua yuan*, even reading the latter work as a "response" of sorts to its eminent predecessor. Yet while in many ways comparable to the three works discussed in this book, I will argue that intellectually and even culturally it reflects a tradition of Chinese fiction very different from what I have described here.

We can locate a number of thematic as well as structural aspects of these novels that find striking parallels to the three works discussed above. All three are 100 to 120 chapters long[15] and were written in the period from the late seventeenth to the mid-eighteenth centuries, that is, close in time to both *Rulin waishi* and *Yesou puyan*, although slightly earlier than *Jinghua yuan*. All three foreground literati experiences such as examination taking, bureaucratic service, and the pursuit of learning of various kinds. Moreover, as in *Yesou puyan* and *Jinghua yuan* domestic life reflects the centrality of literati concerns in ways foreshadowing if not entirely analogous to those later novels. To simplify this discussion, I would like to focus upon two areas for comparison: examinations and the attainment of bureaucratic status; and the treatment of literati learning and erudition in its broadest sense.

First and perhaps foremost is the broad range of issues pertaining to the examination system. *Rulin waishi, Yesou puyan,* and *Jinghua yuan* all devote considerable attention to exploring the appropriateness of the examinations, both as a means of selecting officials for government service and as the primary mechanism of literati social mobility. All three of these novels satirize both examiners and examinees and introduce utopian solutions to the dilemmas created or exacerbated by the status quo. *Xingshi yinyuan zhuan, Lüye xianzong,* and *Honglou meng* also chronicle substantial debate and dissatisfaction over this institution and rival these three in the intensity of their satire of the examination system. Yet none of them offers any more than a hint of a resolution to the issues raised or proposes any alternatives to them. In short, they seem content with attacking excesses and incongruities without articulating corrective measures.

Xingshi yinyuan zhuan presents a portrait of official recruitment that while frequently of burlesque dimensions, agrees in large measure with the assessment of our three novels. Its men of true talent are uninterested in examination learning; the learned scholar Xing Gaomen, for example, "did not expend his energies on perfecting his examination essays, feeling that it was enough to be able to get by. Instead, he spent his time in research in classics, philosophy, and history, in the process becoming a well-rounded scholar. He was unlike those louts who stick to a single volume of the Four Books, or a few lousy examination essays, for their whole lives, and are completely ignorant of other things" (*Xingshi yinyuan zhuan,* chap. 15, p. 152).[16] Correspondingly, examination learning has failed miserably to promote talent: "Successful essays have definite styles. Today, the indiscriminate use [of quotations] and bizarre fashions grow more pronounced with each examination, yet they are able to please the chief examiners" (chap. 74, p. 782).

Even the system of purchasing degrees (*najian*), which does not attract much notice in fiction until the satirical novels of the mid-to-late nineteenth century, comes under attack in *Xingshi yinyuan zhuan*. An illiterate farmer is recommended by his neighbors for such a degree and protests that he can hardly afford to feed himself, let alone raise the amount needed for such an undertaking. But the avaricious magistrate sees illiteracy as no hindrance to office: "Because you do not recognize even a single character, you have been recommended for promotion. If you did know some characters, then you should be recommended for peasant status" (chap. 42, p. 452). Such burlesque exaggeration is common throughout this novel, where magistrates, court officials, indeed nearly all literati, display gross incompetence in literary matters. Officials brag that they can barely read, having paid someone else to get them through the examinations (chap. 50, pp. 536–38). And nearly all officialdom is in the pay of the nefarious eunuch Liu Jin, who is blamed early in the novel for the capture of the Yingzong emperor by Mongol marauders. Even after death, opportunities are ample for corruption by venal officials sent to serve in the heavenly bureaucracy (chap. 42).

The frame of political intrigue we find in *Lüye xianzong* is closely analogous to those of *Xingshi yinyuan zhuan*, *Yesou puyan*, and *Jinghua yuan*. As in the latter novels, men of talent and learning are prevented from achieving success in the examinations and government service by a corrupt clique of evil ministers, in this case the powerful Ming grand minister Yan Song and his notorious son, Yan Shifan. Examinations perpetuate Yan's hold on power by promoting his cronies, and upright and talented members of the literati, alienated from government, seek other means of achieving social utility. Nonetheless, although the literati heroes of the novel eventually win official recognition and appointment, their tale of success is subsumed within a larger allegory of Taoist enlightenment that leads to their transcendence of temporal existence. Although they and their allies battle hordes of venal officials, sorcerers, rebels, and Japanese pirates, for which they are appointed to high posts, these men do not articulate alternatives to the standard route of examination success such as those in *Yesou puyan* or *Jinghua yuan*.

Corruption in *Lüye xianzong* is rife at all levels of society, but the worst offenders of public mores are various characters identified as literati degree candidates. The imperial academy student Hu (Hu Jiansheng) forces another's wife to marry him, bragging about his illiteracy to her: "Although you Madame can spout lots of classical particles, I don't understand a single line of literary speech" (chap. 16, p. 109).[17] Another lascivious literatus finds himself sexually aroused while practicing his examination essays (chap. 60, p. 633). Among officialdom, the possession of an examination degree is exalted to the complete exclusion of genuine talent. After the heroes Lin Dai and Zhu Wenwei have saved the empire from a murderous assault by Japanese invaders who have sacked countless cities and defeated the high officials and generals sent to subdue them, a banquet is given in their honor. Yet the supercilious official Hu Zongxian snubs them, refusing even to seat them at his table, when he learns that they lack examination degrees (chap. 59, p. 625). Conversely, those successful in the examinations possess neither skills needed in times of trouble nor even a modicum of personal probity. One particularly egregious example, the magistrate Feng Bopi ("Bark-stripping [i.e. exploitative] Feng"), extorts money even from beggars (chap. 34,, pp. 241–42).

Honglou meng is very different from any of the other novels discussed in this book. Although in Gao E's sequel Jia Baoyu is said to pass the metropolitan examinations shortly before his final disappearance from the novel, he gives little indication of any interest in such advancement before that time. Indeed, aside from his father Jia Zheng, the rather wooden personification of Confucian duty, none of the male Jias or their associates voice any concern with passing examinations or serving the state. The Jia family compound and the grand garden to which its members seek amusement for the body of the novel serves as a refuge from such demands. In fact, the only character who pursues anything resembling a typical literati career path is the rather uncouth Jia Yucun, who remains both literally and figuratively an outsider to the Jia compound.

This of course hardly suggests that *Honglou meng* fails to allude to the moral or worldly demands incumbent upon male literati. The characters and events within the Jia household suggest numerous parallels with the outside male world that have been explored in some depth by Martin Huang and others. Yet in contrast to *Xingshi yinyuan zhuan*, *Yesou puyan*, and *Jinghua yuan*, *Honglou meng* can be said to invert the correlation between political dysfunction and literati participation described in those novels. This is not to say that political corruption and literati ineptitude are entirely absent as objects of satire and derision (Jia Yucun is perhaps the most prominent example of this). Rather, in *Honglou meng* corruption springs first and foremost from within the household, and by implication the literati themselves. The principal vehicle for airing such views is of course Jia Baoyu, whose distaste for participation in the larger male world arises from an assessment of the character of the literati as a whole. In an oft-quoted speech to his maid Xiren, Baoyu says that

> on the strength of having read a couple of books and got up a text or two by heart, [the scholars] began to cry stinking fish as soon as they found the smallest thing at Court not as they thought it should be, in the hope of winning themselves an imperishable reputation for honesty; then, if the Court didn't immediately change its policy, they would work themselves into a passion and promptly get themselves killed. You won't, surely, say that they died because they had to? . . . [A]ll those death-with-honour characters you have so high an opinion of were thinking only of their own personal fame and glory. They weren't really thinking of their loyal duty to their sovereign at all.[18]

Such sentiments have led commentators such as Yu-kung Kao to compare Baoyu to *Rulin waishi*'s Du Shaoqing. Both are repelled by the mercenary careerists who surround them and rebel by immersing themselves in literary, scholarly, or aesthetic pursuits. Indeed, in this respect these two novels are quite comparable. *Rulin waishi* chronicles not a literati struggle against nefarious forces of corruption, but the implication of the elite in their own decline through the very ideals they come to espouse. As Baoyu puts it, literati blame the state for problems that are largely of their own making, the result of their own inordinate desire for fame and fortune.

Nonetheless, there is a crucial difference between these two novels in their delineation of literati angst. Whatever Du Shaoqing may say about his disdain for political power, he reaffirms his own membership in the *ru* through his espousal of and participation in ritual. Baoyu, by contrast, remains throughout the novel a literatus in cultural but not social terms, an outsider to the corporate body of literati, the presence of whom clearly defines all of the other novels considered in this study. This fact bears obvious relation to the nature of the society it is so clearly a reflection of, that of the bannermen of the early-to-mid eighteenth century. This also helps to explain the near-total silence of *Honglou meng* on matters of eighteenth-century scholarly trends, the absence of which also distinguishes this novel from the others considered here.[19]

We know virtually nothing about the circumstances or lives of the authors of *Xingshi yinyuan zhuan* or *Lüye xianzong*. Hence, there is little if any evidence that could tie these two works to an identifiable intellectual or literary figure, milieu, or movement such as can be done for

Wu Jingzi, Xia Jingqu, and Li Ruzhen. Moreover, the novels themselves suggest that whatever intellectual affiliations their authors may have had, they did not use fiction as a vehicle for the expression of scholarly or intellectual issues per se. This is despite the fact that both Cao Xueqin and Li Baichuan wrote their novels during the heyday of evidential scholarship in the mid-Qianlong period.

Nonetheless, although lacking in scholarly erudition these novels nonetheless bear traces of the intellectualization of the literati self-image discussed in previous chapters. As touched upon earlier, *Xingshi yinyuan* is particularly brilliant in its satirical portraits of literati pedantry and incompetence. Officials render faulty and even absurd judgments, yet claim to be immune from error, and in general very few characters in this work rise above literary mediocrity or even mere incompetence. In *Lüye xianzong*, its protagonist Leng Yubing faces three possible choices during his spiritual quest for self-knowledge: Confucian learning, banditry, and Taoist cultivation. The first he finds the easiest to reject, for the licentiate who argues its merits presents little more than a parodied version of Confucian moral platitudes (*Lüye xianzong*, chap. 6). None of the novel's scholars can counter the more compelling goal of worldly renunciation to which all of the novel's protagonists eventually gravitate. Officials and small-town pedants speak in a literary gibberish, and while espousing noble ideals, their conduct betrays a crude hypocrisy. In essence, it appears that Confucian learning brings its practitioners to a state of impractical pedantry. Even when motivated to act nobly they are unable to respond effectively to the crises confronting the state.

Once again, *Honglou meng* defies categorization, for while it reflects an immense body of literary knowledge, this novel does not lend itself to comparison with either *Yesou puyan* or *Jinghua yuan* in their use of scholarly erudition. Having said this, however, it is also apparent that the banquet scenes in *Jinghua yuan*, and especially the amusements played there such as riddles, rhyming games, and poetry contests, may conceivably have been inspired by the earlier work. The question is to what extent the literary banter and games of *Honglou meng* function in ways that presage or parallel *Jinghua yuan*.

One example of potential borrowing is the well-known episode of Granny Liu's second visit to the Jia compound in chapters 39 through 42. During the height of the festivities inspired by Liu's antics, the maid Yuanyang presides over a rhyming game that tests the various participants' abilities in couplet (*duilian*) composition. Grandmother Jia,

Aunt Xue, Xue Baochai, Shi Xiangyun, and Lin Daiyu all acquit themselves with grace and wit, while Granny Liu predictably makes a fool of herself with various uncouth phrases (soon to be followed by a wine-induced nap in the garden). Throughout this game, Yuanyang plays the role of judge to the hilt, insisting upon adherence to correct rhyme, and punishing Granny Liu with cups of wine. In the banquet scenes of *Jinghua yuan*, the maid Wang Yu'er also presides over rhyming contests, enforcing the rules of these games and flaunting her own knowledge of phonology and etymology. In her irrepressible exuberance she recalls the mischievousness of Yuanyang. Nonetheless, like the other women of *Jinghua yuan* Wang Yu'er carries her quest for linguistic prowess to far greater lengths, launching into ruminations on various questions of phonology that extend, with interruptions, over several chapters (chaps. 84–87).

In short, these and other examples suggest that *Honglou meng* introduces learning more often than not as a vehicle for the juxtaposition of cultural and social levels, or for the exploration and intensification of lyrical states. In *Jinghua yuan*, by contrast, the foils with whom the learned girls interact consist almost entirely of other literati—namely, men such as Tang Ao and Duo Jiugong—who are not uneducated, merely uninformed about scholarly issues of their day. In this as well *Honglou meng* appears to be very much the product of the bannerman society to which its author belonged, into which the learned discourse of Jiangnan literati circles seems to have penetrated barely, if at all, in the mid-eighteenth century.

It could even be argued that *Honglou meng*'s undisputed position as the crowning achievement of Chinese narrative art is predicated on its transcendence of the immediate issues of Qing scholarship, culture, and even social institutions such as the examination system. *Honglou meng* extends its gaze back upon the entire literary tradition, thereby avoiding the tired pedantry with which so much of Qing literature can be faulted. It is, moreover, much more indebted to earlier works of fiction such as *Jin Ping Mei* than any of the other works under study here. In sum, *Honglou meng*'s greatness may lie in its avoidance of specifically eighteenth-century concerns, thus achieving a universality that few other works of this period can begin to approach. It is a literati novel largely in aesthetic and cultural terms, rather than in the philosophical or social dimensions that are explored in other fiction and discursive works of its time.

In this book I have attempted to trace the contours of mid-Qing images of the literati through two broadly distinct categories of writings, that is, works of vernacular fiction on the one hand, and discursive/critical writings on the other. It is my hope that the juxtaposition of these various writings has achieved an effect greater than that of their individual parts, namely, to trace the contours of the literati self-image during the Qianlong and Jiaqing reigns. In many respects these two categories of writings complement each other rather well. While discursive essays on scholarship, literature, and art reveal much about how literati perceived their occupations and interests, fiction represents a panoply of literati discourses within their larger social and historical frameworks. Works of fiction can in fact be seen to situate many of the issues and debates chronicled in Part I in a context larger than their respective discursive regimes. And as I have attempted to demonstrate, these novels present themselves precisely as that: representations of literati discourses competing with one another in an increasingly confusing and disorderly world.

For the writers of these three novels, the literati were afflicted by a malaise serious enough to demand a rethinking of their social and intellectual tasks. The discursive writings treated in Chapter 1 also suggest a certain crisis of self-confidence, even of identity. But the other side of this rethinking of a number of significant issues is an almost exhilarating explosion of intellectual activity. While it may be true that philologically minded thinkers ultimately conceived of a circumscribed and somewhat authoritarian intellectual domain freed from the polluting influences of heterodox doctrines, many scholars, writers, and artists sought freedom from the dictates of what they perceived to be the oppressive moral and epistemological imperatives of orthodox thought. Genuine objectivity may have proven chimerical, but culture of the Qianlong and Jiaqing periods seems to have achieved a bona fide widening and pluralization of thought, even as many writers sought ideological purity.

From the perspective of many historians, the High Qing period marks the culmination of what Mark Elvin has called the "high-level equilibrium trap" of Chinese civilization. Stasis, ossification, and an almost rococo aesthetic are the words that come to mind to describe Qianlong and Jiaqing visual art, theater, architecture, and other forms of expression. In Angela Zito's words, the "proliferation of surface decoration on porcelain, furniture, wall, and clothing reached an apogee of excess under Qianlong." She equates this with a larger cultural trend toward the "hyperdevelopment of devotion to *wen*," to the point of "fetishizing writing."[20] In a similar vein, Richard Vinograd has discerned what he calls a pervasive disillusionment, a "physical presence and psychological absence" in the portraits of the Qianlong era. Even the works of relatively creative painters such as Jin Nong and Luo Ping seem "cognizant of issues of artifice, fiction, inauthenticity, and disillusionment to an unprecedented degree."[21] Such an interest in artifice seems closely consonant with what Zito has characterized as the impulse of *wen* to emphasize surface over substance, form over content: "Discourses on painting, medicine, and ritual converge in emphasizing the site of this emergent pattern as an ever-shifting boundary or surface, which is then accessible as various forms of knowledge."[22]

For Qianlong and Jiaqing scholars the world of form held the promise of a potentially infinite wealth of knowledge, unencumbered by the "single thread" unifying its disparate elements. That such a situation made the tasks of the literati more onerous is evident in a number of discourses, for in spite of their time-honored role as (in Zito's words) "inscribers of culture" for the imperium, the increasing heterogeneity of the epistemological and social landscape, and the diversification of the literati themselves, militated against any easy acceptance of the dictates of orthodox thought. That a certain political apathy and even alienation may have played some part in this narrowing of literati aims and expectations is certainly plausible.[23] But as I hope to have demonstrated, the proliferation of cultural forms, both as *wen* and as other "patterns," seems to be integral to the reevaluation of the literati self-image of this period.[24]

The three works of fiction treated in this book can be viewed sequentially as artifacts in this history of the proliferation of *wen*, offering a narrative of its ramifications for the literati and their tasks that complements other discourses. Their interest lies in part in the comprehensiveness of this vision, for each attempts a wide-ranging catalog of literati pursuits, aims, and uncertainties in their respective historical moments. Having already engaged each one on its own terms, we can conclude by reading the three together as a single narrative, the narrative of literati self-representation in the last great age of indigenous Chinese civilization before its fateful encounter with the West.

The Woxian caotang preface to *Rulin waishi* is dated in the first year of the Qianlong reign, when the author Wu Jingzi was recommended to the special Hongxue boci examination held at the capital. Zhuang Shaoguang's summons in chapter 35 appears to allude to this event; but perhaps even more telling of its link to this specific event is the enactment of the ritual at Taibo Temple. As the brainchild of Chi Hengshan, the novel's spokesman for the "creed" of ritualism, the event is heralded as a moment of signal significance for the literati. But the pure emptiness of its enactment suggests the fascination that its surface forms—the ritual patterns of gesture, dance, and incantation—exert upon its celebrants. The scholars who advocate the propagation of ritual seek meaning beyond such forms, yet fail to fully integrate the various dimensions of ritual with the life they lead outside the temple grounds. Only Dr. Yu, the "true scholar" who presides over this event, is unencumbered by a desire to go beyond its surfaces. He and other characters who unburden themselves of literati identity transcend the complex interplay of *wen* and meaning, surface and intention, that ultimately beguiles the literati who cling to them.

By the time of *Yesou puyan*, presumably written in the middle decades of the Qianlong reign, the great figures of evidential studies were in their prime, and the proliferation of *wen* in scholarship had reached its zenith. This novel's zeal to strip away the accretions of Buddhist and Taoist heterodoxies from the minds of men and women parallels the "purist hermeneutics" of mid-Qing classical scholars bent on retrieving ancient meanings of texts. Wen Suchen and his cohorts attempt to reconnect form with meaning through the restoration, not of the prelapsarian purity of an ancient age, however, but of the Neo-Confucian unities threatened by precisely such purist tendencies. The result is a sort of fictional monument to the excessive fascination with *wen* found in other discourses, whose profusion of surfaces, like an intricately carved ivory tusk, threaten to undermine the integrity of the structure itself.

The rococo convolutions of *Yesou puyan* find a resolution of sorts in *Jinghua yuan*, whose formal perfection has not been matched before or since in Chinese fiction.[25] This novel marks a convenient terminus for this study, since its publication coincided with the end of the Qian-Jia era. But even if this were not the case, it appears to give voice to what many men of the period strove to accomplish, that is, the liberation of form from substance, of intellect from morality, and of political ambition from scholarly inquiry. Through its feminization of literati knowledge, the reader is presented with a paradigm that encompasses these various dualisms, namely, that of gender difference. The reversal of normative gender hierarchies serves as a model for the suspension of the normative hierarchy of substance over form, or morality over intellect, thereby demonstrating the possibility of a resolution to the polarizing debates of the early nineteenth century.

The crises that afflicted the Chinese nation during the mid-to-late nineteenth century appear to have made irrelevant many of the pressing questions that exercised men during the Qian-Jia era. Once the very survival of the political order became an open question, the relevance of the literati to and their place in it did not excite the same degree of interest that we find in pre–Opium War fiction. Works of the mid-nineteenth century and later no longer problematize the literati and their concerns. In the homoerotic novel *Pinhua baojian* (The precious mirror for the ranking of flowers) (1849), for example, the protagonist Tian Chunhang is generally agreed to be a thinly disguised portrait of the eighteenth-century philologist Bi Yuan, but there is little evidence of his scholarly interests. Talented young literati dutifully take examinations, and old men amuse themselves with pedantic banter, but little attention is given to any of the questions explored with such intensity by their literary forebears.

This situation changed somewhat near the end of the Qing period with the appearance of the so-called *qianze xiaoshuo* or "novels of chastisement." Written during the disastrous final years of the dynasty, works such as *Guanchang xianxing ji* (Officials reveal their true forms) describe the breakdown of social mores at all levels of society but most particularly among the bureaucracy and rural gentry. Yet their largely negative representation of the literati does not problematize the contours of literati identity so much as the simple failure of its representatives to live up to the ethical standards they profess. Moreover, they somewhat wistfully chronicle the increasing irrelevance of the literati to the political life of the nation. It was left to subsequent generations of writers to probe the remnants of literati society, which by the Republican and Communist eras were little more than whipping-boys for the newly emerging ideologies of those times.

Appendix

APPENDIX

Editions of the Novels

Rulin waishi

A number of issues related to the authenticity of portions of the novel (in particular, parts of chapters 38 through 47 and chapter 56), the history of its publication, and the years during which the author composed it have spawned controversy among scholars. A good summary of these is given in the preface by Li Hanqiu to *Rulin waishi huijiao huiping ben* (Shanghai: Gudian wenxue chubanshe, 1984).

Although the nineteenth-century collophon of the novel by Jin He suggests that it was printed as early as the 1760s, all known manuscript and published versions of *Rulin waishi* apparently derive from the earliest extant edition, the 56-chapter Woxian caotang edition of 1803 (see Li Hanqiu, *Rulin waishi yanjiu ziliao*, pp. 1–15). Incorporating some minor alterations made to this standard text by two generations of the Pan family of Wujiang, several editions printed in Suzhou during the 1860s constitute the principal variorum texts to the Woxian caotang edition. Later editions tend to follow the Suzhou text, including the so-called Conghao zhai editions. Two editions published by the Qixingtang in 1869 and 1888 interpolate four chapters between chapters 41 and 42 of the other versions, giving them a total of 60 chapters. But modern scholars have uniformly rejected its editors' claim that these are the work of Wu Jingzi. Chapter 56 was included in all versions of the novel until the 1950s, when some editions began to delete it. This trend has recently been reversed, however, as the debate over its authenticity continues.

Several commentaries to the novel appeared in its nineteenth-century editions, including that of the original Woxian caotang edition, those in the Qixing tang editions, and two by Zhang Wenhu, a well-known late Qing classical scholar. Moreover, a commentary by Huang Xiaotian, only recently discovered in a late-nineteenth-century manuscript, has been published separately, since its discovery was too late to be included in the compendium *Rulin waishi huijiao huiping ben* (1986). While the other commentaries all date from the nineteenth century, the date of the preface to the Woxian caotang edition (1736) seems to suggest the possibility that its end-chapter commentary was composed substantially earlier than the date of publication (1803).

Yesou puyan

Two Qing printed recensions of *Yesou puyan* are extant. Both were published in the Guangxu period, approximately one hundred years after the death of the author Xia Jingqu. Pertinent information about them is as follows:

Piling huizhenlou edition, published in 1881; 152 chapters, interlinear commentary, as well as lengthy end-chapter commentary.

Shenbaoguan edition, published in 1882; 154 chapters, end-chapter commentary (identical to that in the Piling huizhenlou edition).

These two editions differ in several important respects. While the Shenbaoguan edition contains two additional chapters, it also deletes a number of sexually explicit passages and has been viewed by Sun Kaidi, Zhao Jingshen, and Lu Xun as less reliable than the Piling huizhenlou edition. The latter appears to contain a number of lacunae as well, however, and omits entire chapters (which it explains were "lost" in the manuscripts available to its editors). A slightly later edition of 1905 published by Guangdong Shiyin shuju appears to largely follow the Shenbaoguan version.

A recent article by Ouyang Jian, "*Yesou puyan* banben bianxi" (*Ming Qing xiaoshuo yanjiu* 1 [1988]: 181–95) compares the two editions in some detail, arguing that the additions to the Shenbaoguan edition faithfully represent the original text (presumably that of Xia Jingqu) that served as the basis for both editions.

Jinghua yuan

Jinghua yuan was printed in numerous editions throughout the period from the late Jiaqing to the Guangxu periods. The earliest extant version of the novel, a handwritten copy now in the Peking University Library, dates possibly from the late Jiaqing period. It is virtually identical to the "Suzhou" editions of 1818 and 1821. Another edition of this period is that printed in Taohongzhen, near Nanjing, in 1817–18.

The Jiezi yuan ("Mustard Seed Garden") version first appeared in 1828 and incorporates a fair number of textual emendations of the earlier editions. Based on correspondence, prefaces, and poetry written by the author and his friends, it has been argued that its changes are the result of the author's revisions made during the years after the publication of the first editions. Later editions of the novel for the most part follow this revised version. (For a discussion of the differences between the earlier and later versions, see Sun Jiaxun's *Jinghua yuan gongan bianyi* [Jinan: Qilu shushe, 1984].) Many Guangdong publishers put out the novel in the mid-nineteenth century, including Yingde tang (1842), Yuande tang (1842), and an unnamed Fuoshan publisher (1858).

Interlinear commentary by several of the author's friends is included in the Jicheng tang edition. Each item is followed by an attribution, the majority being those of Xu Xiangling and Fan Bowen.

Reference Matter

Notes

Introduction

1. Wu Jingzi, *Rulin waishi huijiao huiping ben*, ed. Li Hanqui, chap. 46, p. 623; translation modified from Hsien-i Yang and Gladys Yang, *The Scholars*, pp. 508–9. Hereafter *Rulin waishi* is abbreviated as *RWHH* and *The Scholars* as *TS*.

2. Tao Qian, "Guiqu laixi ci," in *Tao Yuanming shiwen huiping*, pp. 326–27.

3. It is certainly conceivable to interpret Yu's desire to retire from office as an expression of the time-honored traditions of Confucian eremites. But in the context of his life and actions this rejection of bureaucratic appointment appears to reflect a fundamental alienation not only from public personae but from all facets of literati identity.

4. Lu Xun, *Zhongguo xiaoshuo wenji*, p. 230.

5. Jean-François Billeter, "Contribution à une sociologie historique du mandarinat," p. 8.

6. *Jinghua yuan* was first printed in 1821 but was substantially revised in what became the standard version of 1828. See Appendix for details.

7. I have chosen to use the translation "literati" to refer to the educated members of traditional Chinese society. Although the term is sometimes used to apply only to the rather narrow Chinese designation *wenshi*, or "literary men," I mean for it to correspond to the term *shi* (or *shidaifu*), meaning the entire range of educated males during the imperial period. The latter term can be identified with the classification *shenshi* (or *jinshen*), or what has been called the "gentry," that is, men possessing a "title, grade, degree, or official rank" conferring certain legal privileges. See Chung-li Chang, *The Chinese Gentry*, p. 3. But by choosing "literati" over "gentry" I wish to stress the cultural rather than legal or political dimensions of the classification. In the novel *Rulin waishi* several variants of these terms appear; among them is *dushuren* (readers of books), which seems to most closely approximate the sense of "literati." This designation apparently enjoyed wide currency during the Qing. See Chang, p. 4.

8. See Yu Ying-shih, "Zhongguo jinshi zongjiao lunli yu shangren jingshen," in *Zhongguo sixiang chuantong de xiandai quanshi*, pp. 259–404, and Chen

Xuewen, "Mingdai zhongye yilai qinong qiru congshang fengqi he zhongshang sichao de chuxian," pp. 21–30.

9. See Ping-ti Ho, *The Ladder of Success in Imperial China*, pp. 4–7 ff.

10. By the Ming and Qing periods, according to Ho, the areas tested by the examination system had narrowed down to "a knowledge of classics, stereotypical theories of administration, and literary attainments" (*Ladder of Success*, p. 11).

11. In addition to the degrees awarded through competitive civil service examinations, it was also possible in the Ming and Qing to purchase certain degrees from the imperial government. For a comparison of the two types of degree status, see Chang, *Chinese Gentry*, pp. 6–32 ff., and Ho, *Ladder of Success*, pp. 30–34, 47–49. Needless to say, wealth and kinship ties also counted for a great deal in securing the latter type of degree.

12. Yu Ying-shih points out that the word *junzi* became indistinguishable from *shi* and other synonyms for the literati as well as other members of the political elite. Moreover, although it was appropriated by Confucius and his followers as an ideal of the morally perspicacious man, its earlier connotations of high political or social rank never disappeared entirely. See Yu Ying-shih, "Rujia junzi de lixiang," in *Zhongguo sixiang chuantong de xiandai quanshi*, p. 145 ff.

13. Yu Ying-shih, "Some Preliminary Observations on the Rise of Ch'ing Confucian Intellectualism," pp. 105–36.

14. Some prominent modern historians have stressed the continuity of Song, Ming, and Qing thought and view Qing intellectualism as an outgrowth of Neo-Confucian scholarly traditions. See Qian Mu, *Zhongguo jinsanbai nian xueshu shi*, and Yu-lan Fung, *A History of Chinese Philosophy*, vol. 2.

15. Billeter, "Contribution," p. 12.

16. Fiction was not highly regarded in traditional Confucian discourse (it was called *zixu wuyou*, "patent untruth"). Interestingly, Chinese scholars have led the way in treating the novel as a document of social history. Such an approach has inspired the best comprehensive treatment to date on the societal implications of the novel's satire, Paul Ropp's *Dissent in Eighteenth-Century China*. As Ropp has convincingly demonstrated, its critique of social problems such as the examination system, the subjugation of women, geomancy, and superstitious practices is shared by a broad range of writings of the Qing period. My readings of the three novels treated in this book attempt to broaden as well as deepen the insights of Ropp and others toward the reappraisal of literati identity as it had evolved by the late imperial period.

17. See C. T. Hsia, *The Classic Chinese Novel*, p. 237 ff., and Wang Dexiu, "Yinggai yong xin de guannian he biaozhun pingjia *Rulin waishi*," pp. 100–109. Chen Meilin points out that Wu Jingzi's position as the chief heir (*zongzi*) of a declining branch of the Wu family (which had not produced any high officials for several decades) appears to have made him particularly sensitive toward the nouveau riche of his native area. He does indeed exhibit a strong con-

sciousness of his lineage's prestige in his prose poem "Yijia fu." See Chen Meilin, *Wu Jingzi pingzhuan*, p. 73 ff.

18. See Robert Hegel's *The Novel in Seventeenth-Century China*. Hegel traces the rise of fiction expressive of specifically literati concerns to seventeenth-century writers such as Yuan Yuling, Dong Yue, and Li Yu. Like many novelists of the eighteenth and nineteenth centuries, the authors of this era found themselves turning to fiction because, "although trained to expect positions of leadership as their due, these men found that route either strewn with pitfalls or closed to them" (p. 226).

19. This is not say that the great sixteenth-century novels do not explore literati concerns. As Andrew Plaks has argued so persuasively, the great examples of Ming fiction give expression to artists who were "groping for identity as *wen-jen*" (men of *wen*) and reflect the debates over cultivation and self-realization raging in late-Ming elite intellectual circles. See Andrew Plaks, *Ssu ta ch'i-shu*, p. 51.

20. Among Wu's closest friends and acquaintances were a number of poets, Cheng Jinfang, Yan Changming, Wang Youzeng, Chen Yi, Jin Zhaoyan, and his own cousin Wu Qing; although he himself achieved renown as a classical scholar, Wu's friend Cheng Tingzuo tried his hand at dramaturgy. As I will demonstrate in Chapter 2 in particular, views found in these men's writings, particularly in those of Cheng Tingzuo, are relevant to aspects of *Rulin waishi*.

21. In recent years researchers have discovered a number of new clues to the life of Wu Jingzi and his circle of friends and associates in Nanjing and elsewhere. But none of these discoveries has significantly altered the information on his life found in his own poetry collection (*Wenmu shanfang ji*), the biography by his contemporary Cheng Jinfang, and a few other prefaces and short pieces. Whatever we may wish to make of it, there is convincing evidence suggesting that he must have had at least a passing familiarity with the thought of Yan Yuan and Li Gong, and that he was acquainted with a number of minor scholars and literary figures of the Jiangnan region. The most comprehensive treatment of Wu's life and times, and their relationship to the novel, is Chen Meilin's biography *Wu Jingzi pingzhuan*. Chen makes a number of bold assertions concerning Wu's probable ideological predisposition. I have not referred to these in my analysis of the novel, in part because they still remain speculative, and in part because the novel can be understood through a broad reading of its contemporary discourses without relying on conjectures concerning Wu's affiliations with specific thinkers or writers.

22. Li Ruzhen was a student of the evidential scholar Ling Tingkan, perhaps the most eminent of the late-eighteenth- and early-nineteenth-century proponents of Dai Zhen's philological methodologies. See Hummel, *Eminent Chinese of the Ch'ing Period* (hereafter *ECCP*), pp. 472–73, 514–15.

Chapter 1

1. Jiao Xun, *Diaogulou ji*, juan 8, p. 153. ("Juan" is hereafter abbreviated as "j.")

2. The two poems are "Xiao Bian" (no. 197) and "Mian" (no. 237).
3. Zhu Xi, *Shi jizhuan*, j. 12, p. 9b.
4. Benjamin Elman, *From Philosophy to Philology*, esp. chaps. 2 and 3.
5. Kai-wing Chow has argued persuasively that while evidential scholarship had the effect of eroding the commitment to Confucian ethics, its seemingly objective methodology was applied in ways that merely exchanged one set of ethical precepts for another, more elitist one. Its practitioners' "intellectualism was not meant to question the élite's social and intellectual superiority; it rather sought to reverse the populist tendency so prominent in Late Ming Confucianism" ("Purist Hermeneutics and Ritualist Ethics in Mid-Ch'ing Confucianism," pp. 179–204). While this may have been true for many thinkers, particularly during the early Qing, Chow apparently discounts the stridency of Qing criticisms of the deleterious role Cheng-Zhu thought had played as a class ideology.
6. By "orthodoxy" I refer primarily to what W. T. de Bary has referred to as the "philosophical orthodoxy" of Cheng-Zhu scholarship. But as I shall argue, its intimate association with the state's "rigid and centralized system of bureaucratic training and recruitment" can hardly be separated from the philosophical criticisms of it that grew strident during the seventeenth and eighteenth centuries. See de Bary, *Neo-Confucian Orthodoxy and the Learning of the Mind and Heart*, pp. 50–57. For an enlightening discussion of the Cheng-Zhu school's canonization as the official state orthodoxy, see Thomas A. Wilson, *Genealogy of the Way*, especially chap. 1.
7. Rodney Taylor has argued that Confucianism as a whole must be taken more seriously as a doctrine rich in religious sentiment: "All too infrequently have Confucian teachings and their roots been presented in the framework of a religious superstructure that views humankind a potential mirror of the ways of T'ien, Heaven, the source of religious authority within the Confucian tradition. It is, however, from a religious context that Confucians have traditionally called upon political rulers to emulate the Way of Heaven for the betterment of humankind" (*The Religious Dimensions of Confucianism*, p. 7).
8. A. C. Graham, *Two Chinese Philosophers*, pp. 37, 113ff.
9. De Bary summarizes Zhu Xi's contribution to the formulation of Neo-Confucian teachings as follows: "In the long run [he] succeeded in redefining literati learning, so that 'cultivating the moral self' became the only possible basis for realizing the literati responsibility (both) for maintaining the political order and transmitting the culture" (William de Bary and John W. Chafee, eds., *Neo-Confucian Education*, p. 7).
10. The most influential work on this subject includes Yu Ying-shih's "Some Preliminary Observations" and *Lishi yu sixiang*; Yamanoi Yū, *Min Shin shisō no kenkyū*, esp. pp. 245–60ff.; and Mizoguchi Yūzō, *Zen kindai shisō no kussetsu to tenkai*.
11. See Kai-wing Chow, *The Rise of Confucian Ritualism in Late Imperial China*, especially chaps. 3 and 4.

12. Elman, *From Philosophy to Philology*, p. 27 ff.
13. John Dardess, *Confucianism and Autocracy*, pp. 22–77.
14. Frederic Wakeman notes that Jiangnan gentry in particular were "crushed and humiliated" by events such as the tax-arrears cases of 1660–61. He quotes a gazetteer of the Suzhou area as saying that "as a result the cunning and reckless rogues among the masses saw that there was nothing to fear from members of the gentry and treated them with contempt. The gentry members as well bowed their heads in acquiescence, and customs at once changed." See Wakeman, *The Great Enterprise*, p. 1074.
15. See Susan Mann's *Local Merchants and the Chinese Bureaucracy, 1750–1950*.
16. Alexander Woodside, "The Divorce between the Political Center and Educational Creativity in Late Imperial China," p. 473.
17. Susan Naquin and Evelyn Rawski, *Chinese Society in the Eighteenth Century*, pp. 56–58, 222–25 ff.
18. Willard J. Peterson, *Bitter Gourd*, pp. 166–67.
19. Zhang Xuecheng, "Yuan dao: zhong," in *Wenshi tongyi*, p. 131.
20. Zhang Shunshui, *Qingdai Yangzhou xueji*, pp. 4–25 ff.
21. See Elman, *From Philosophy to Philology*, p. 123 ff.
22. In the mid-seventeenth century Fang Yizhi discussed the wide heterogeneity of literatus as a social classification. In his "Shi lun," he states that "the literati and commoners are most numerous. Manners and morals depend for the most part upon the literati. If successful, they can be high officials. If humble, they are little different from the commoners. If they do not practice good, then the world will follow them, and customs will stray into error" (*Jigutang wenji*, j. 2, pp. 13a–b). The desire to reassert the moral integrity of the literati and their role as moral leaders of their communities is particularly strong among late Ming movements such as the Donglin.
23. Zhu Xi, *Daxue zhangju*, j. 1, p. 2.
24. See Han-sheng Chiu, "Zhu Xi's Doctrine of Principle," pp. 116–35. The importance of this particular gloss is attested to by the fact that *The Great Learning* was viewed by Zhu and his successors as the primary manual of study among the Four Books. See Wing-tsit Chan, "Chu Hsi and Yuan Neo-Confucianism," pp. 214–15.
25. Wei Xi, "Ping lun," in *Wei Shuzi wenchao*, j. 1, p. 6a.
26. See John Henderson, *The Development and Decline of Chinese Cosmology*, pp. 175–207, 253 ff.
27. Ibid.
28. Zhu Xi, *Daxue zhangju*, j. 1, p. 1.
29. Chen Que's criticism of the *Daxue* contains particularly trenchant remarks on the notion of the "completion of knowledge." See Chen Que, "Daxue Bian: 2," in *Chen Que ji*, p. 560.
30. Huang Zongxi's preface to his *Mingru xuean* seems to echo such sentiments. In it Huang recognizes the limitations of any one ideology to encompass the diversity of possibilities inherent in human consciousness.

31. According to Henderson, this state of affairs did not continue past the eighteenth century:

> The obituary of correlative cosmology in China, even so far as high intellectual history is concerned, could hardly have been written as early as the end of the seventeenth century. For a number of prominent mid- and late-Ch'ing scholars rehabilitated certain aspects of correlative thought. Ironically, one of the chief bases of seventeenth-century cosmological criticism, the revival of classicism, also contributed to the mid-Ch'ing renewal of correlative ideas ... [classicists] discovered that anticipations of certain ideas associated with correlative cosmology, especially the notion of resonant interaction between astronomical and political entities, were embedded even in the earliest stratum of the classics. (*Chinese Cosmology*, p. 197)

32. De Bary, *Mind and Heart*, p. 216.

33. The early Daoxue thinkers were particularly concerned with the declining moral standards of the literati faced with such circumstances. According to Peter Bol, "It was into this world of a self-aggrandizing elite relatively immune to government control that Tao-hsueh came. It offered a vision of learning that helped the elite to survive without office and thus supported the independence of the shih from the government; but at the same time it explained how it was possible and why it was necessary for the shih as individuals to discipline themselves" (*"This Culture of Ours,"* p. 342).

34. As R. Kent Guy points out, this rethinking does not seem to have included fundamental institutional reform: "Living in a prosperous and secure age when there were few overt challenges to central authority, eighteenth century thinkers saw little need to contemplate institutional reform" ("The Development of the Evidential Research Movement," p. 114). It appears to have taken the numerous crises of the nineteenth century to spur writers into rethinking the literati's role as political leaders. While echoing many of the views of eighteenth-century thinkers, Yun Jing is much more strident in his condemnation of literati failures in the realm of public administration: "Scholars go to extremes in honoring the sages, yet are negligent in investigating the ordinary people. They dare to follow the past, yet fear to join the trends of the day. They obstinately believe in specialization and denigrate broad investigation. How can this be enough to understand the sages?" ("Sandai yinge lun 8," in *Dayun shanfang quanji*, j. 1, p. 11). Benjamin Elman notes that Yun defines the literati as "no more than" a managerial class (*Classicism, Politics, and Kinship*, p. 101).

35. According to Cynthia J. Brokaw, aside from Dai Zhen (on whom more below), few evidential scholars still believed in the possibility of sagehood: "For them, philology was not the training of a sage but simply an end in itself. ... The philologist could hope to learn the true meaning of the language of the Classics, but this knowledge would not reveal the Way of heaven or the responsibilities of sagehood." See Brokaw, "Tai Chen and Learning in the Confucian Tradition," p. 279.

36. Jiao Xun, "Liang zhi lun," in *Diaogulou ji*, j. 8, p. 123.
37. Huang Zongxi sounded an early note for this when he proposed an alternative to the examination system. See his *Mingyi daifang lu*, pp. 14–19; translated in William T. de Bary, *Waiting for the Dawn*, pp. 111–21).
38. Murase Yuya, *Tai Shin no tetsugaku*, p. 133.
39. Fang Yizhi, "Daoyi," in *Dongxi jun*, p. 82.
40. Ibid., pp. 84, 88.
41. Ibid., p. 89.
42. See Ch'i-ch'ao Liang, *Intellectual Trends of the Ch'ing Period*, p. 67ff. In spite of the predominance of classical studies, the early eighteenth century in particular witnesssed strong tendencies toward a questioning of the authenticity, and hence authority, of many canonical texts.
43. Fang Yizhi, *Dongxi jun*, p. 85. The popularity of Buddhist doctrines among Fang and many of his contemporaries such as Li Zhi has been treated in depth by Timothy Brook in his *Praying for Power*. Some of the implications of this turn toward Buddhism will be discussed in Chapter 5.
44. Fang's slightly younger contemporary, the playwright Li Yu, shared this enthusiasm for the arts writ small. His famous treatise *Xianqing ouji* is, in the words of Patrick Hanan, "devoted to showing that even the lowliest arts and activities can be endlessly refined" (*The Invention of Li Yu*, p. 63).
45. It might be noted in passing that late Ming figures such as Wang Gen, who had proclaimed the equality of all occupations, including even the most menial, were the object of derision in the Qing. By contrast, thinkers of the Qing made no attempt to discover profundity in menial tasks; but they recognized and applauded the worth of what had long been scorned as avocations—games, music, and other leisure pursuits.

Chapter 2

1. Hu Shih, "Yan-Li xuepai de Cheng Tingzuo," pp. 1a–16a.
2. Yu Ying-shih, *Lishi yu sixiang*, p. 161ff.; Murase, *Tai Shin no tetsugaku*, p. 90ff.
3. Jiang Fan, *Hanxue shicheng ji*, j. 6, p. 7b.
4. Dai Zhen, "Yu mou shu," in *Mengzi ziyi shuzheng*, p. 174.
5. Ibid., j. xia, p. 45.
6. Hashimoto Takakatsu, "*Mōshi jigi soshō nitsuite*," p. 768. Indeed, Zhang Xuecheng asserts that its championing of the passions was primarily intended as advice for those engaged in government, and not for application to self-cultivation. See Qian Mu, *Zhongguo jinsanbai nian xueshu shi*, p. 359.
7. Dai Zhen, *Mengzi ziyi shuzheng*, j. zhong, p. 29.
8. Ibid., p. 28.
9. Qian Mu, *Zhongguo jinsanbai nian xueshu shi*, p. 364.
10. Dai Zhen, *Mengzi ziyi shuzheng*, j. shang, p. 15.
11. Ibid.
12. See Lü Zuqian, *Jinsi lu*, j. 2, p. 398. As Brokaw notes, "Tai decries the mystical element of Chu Hsi's sagehood. . . . [The sage] never achieves the re-

ligious consciousness of his unity of all things celebrated by Sung and Ming Neo-Confucians" ("Tai Chen," p. 282).

13. Dai Zhen, *Mengzi ziyi shuzheng*, j. shang, p. 4.

14. Dai Zhen, *Xu yan*, j. zhong, in *Mengzi ziyi shuzheng*, p. 110.

15. Dai Zhen, *Mengzi ziyi shuzheng*, j. xia, p. 49.

16. *Chunqiu Zuozhuan zhu*, "Xiang gong 25," p. 1106.

17. Dai attacks specifically the tendency of post-Song scholars to revere the notion of principle, treating it as if it actually existed in some concrete sense. See *Mengzi ziyi shuzheng*, p. 13.

18. Ibid., j. shang, p. 3; also p. 7: "Principle and righteousness are none other than the correct exercise of judgment; this is what is called *yili*."

19. Duan Yucai, *Dai Dongyuan xiansheng nianpu*, in Dai Zhen, *Mengzi ziyi shuzheng*, p. 244.

20. For example, in his "Yu Fang Xiyuan shu," in Dai Zhen, *Mengzi ziyi shuzheng*, p. 143. It may be making too much of Dai Zhen's arguments for the independence of the three disciplines to give literary composition an equal place with the others. But this is nevertheless implied.

21. See for example the remark by the renowned philologist Qian Daxin (1728–1804): "Once the 'recorded sayings' became a popular [form of writing], then Confucians' words became crude and unpolished. [It was thought that] if one had virtue, he didn't need to bother with words" (in *Shijiazhai yangxin lu*, j. 18, p. 422). Indeed, a sign of the changing times was the shift in attitudes toward rusticity. While writers of the late Ming often appreciated the unaffected simplicity of "men of the wilds," illiterates, and hermits—see, for example, the biographies of Daoists and drunkards by Yuan Zhongdao and Yuan Hongdao or Chen Jiru's *Yanqi youshi*—in the Qing the uncouth generally lost all positive associations of moral probity and became merely neutral and in any event generally receded from the interests of scholars and literary men. See, for example, Wang Fuzhi, *Sijie*, p. 7.

22. It could be objected that late-Ming literary theorists such as Yuan Hongdao were far more appreciative of individual expression in literature than their less colorful successors. Yet the denigration of literary craftsmanship and learning, the advocacy of unadorned content, and above all the transcendent notions of authenticity (*zhen*) and spontaneity (*qu*) which characterize the Gongan school are, in the last analysis, wholly dependent on Neo-Confucian metaphysics and its ubiquitous neglect of form. For Yuan and his followers, literature had an ultimate aim and that was the effacement of the conscious self, self-transcendence rather than the self-conscious recording of the moment. For example, Yuan Hongdao describes literary creation in the following terms:

> When one first tries one's hand [at writing] it is as if [someone else] is pulling at one's arm. Later, one reaches the point where the words are eliminated. Then, reason takes its leave as well. Finally, one's consciousness of the act of writing suddenly disappears. This is like water, which reaches its fullest expression in tranquility, or the plantain, which finds its extreme in

emptiness. When as if by chance one hits on the right circumstances, then the lines suddenly come forth. ("Xing Suyuan cun gao yin," in *Yuan Hongdao ji jianjiao*, j. 54, pp. 1570–71)

The contrast with a significant number of Qing literary theorists is striking, for the latter felt little interest in naturalness as an aesthetic criterion. Many held that literary merit was to be judged by standards that were of themselves temporally determinate, and thus neither absolute not universal in their validity.

23. Guo Shaoyu, "Mingdai de wenren jituan," in *Zhaoyushi gudian wenxue lunji*, 1: 86.

24. As Zhang Xuecheng put it, "To discover the Way through literature—what harm is there in this? When Confucius and Mencius spoke of the Way, when did they ever depart from *wen*?" See his "Yu Lin Xiucai," in *Zhang shi yishu*, vol. 1, j. 9, pp. 345–47.

25. Yuan Mei, "Zai da Tao Guancha shu," in *Xiaocang shanfang wenji*, j. 16, p. 548.

26. Shen Deqian wrote a preface to the literary collection of Jin Zhaoyan, a relative and fellow townsman of Wu Jingzi. Moreover, another disciple, Xue Xue, appears to be alluded to by the character Zhao Xuezhai in *Rulin waishi*. It thus seems quite possible that Wu Jingzi was aware of Ye Xie's work, if not necessarily familiar with the details of his theories.

27. Shen Heng's evaluation of Ye's achievement can be considered a fair assessment of his strengths: "Since ancient times, great craftsmen [of poetry] have generally written only desultory and fragmentary remarks on the fine points of poetic composition. They have never come up with an original theory of poetry that probes its riddles and enlightens [the minds of its readers]. ... Ye, however, has done this" (Shen's preface to *Yuan shi*, quoted in Ye Xie, *Yuan shi*, p. 563). Stephen Owen also points out the uniqueness of Ye in the tradition of poetic criticism: "In the context of traditional literary thought, perhaps the greatest weakness of Yeh Hsieh's poetics is his discussion of the role of mind in writing: for him the quality of the individual mind of the writer is *not* what is known through reading poetry; rather mind is valued purely in its capacity for knowing and conveying knowledge of the outer world" (*Readings in Chinese Literary Thought*, p. 512).

28. Ye Xie, *Yuan shi*, j. 2, p. 584.

29. Ibid., j. 2, p. 580.

30. The playwright Li Yu (1611–82) is perhaps the boldest of the exponents of originality. As Patrick Hanan puts it, for Li Yu "newness is a term of approbation for everything in the world, but doubly so for literature" (*Invention*, p. 95).

31. Ye Xie, *Yuan shi*, j. 1, p. 567.

32. See ibid., j. 4, p. 601, for Ye's discussion of Han and Wei poetry.

33. Ibid., j. 3, p. 596.

34. Ibid., j. 2, p. 584.

35. Ibid., j. 1, p. 576.

36. See, for example, Li E's preface to his poetry collection *Fanxie shantang ji*, p. 2a.

37. See Wang Yingzhi, *Qingren shilun yanjiu*, pp. 282, 284 ff.

38. In Yan Yu's oft-quoted statement about the role of knowledge in poetry, he ambiguously but perhaps perceptively seems to warn of the dangers of learning while still asserting its importance. See Yan Yu, *Canglang shihua*, pp. 11–12. Ye Xie praises Yan Yu's insistence on the importance of learning for the poet, but he is still harsh on Yan's naive faith in rules themselves, without appreciation for the need for discrimination in their use:

> Yan says that the study of poetry requires knowledge, and this is correct. Since one has knowledge, he should place before him all the poetry of the Han, Wei, Six Dynasties, the entire Tang, and the Song. He will then be able to judge for himself what to choose, and what to use as his models. This is what is known as stretching out a hand to take something, and each choice is the right one. . . . I think that, if one has discrimination, then even though he follows exactly in the steps of the Han, Wei, and High Tang, these poetic demons will all be wisdom, and all one's works will be [in the mode of] the Han, Wei, and High Tang. Yan Yu's words are hopelessly misguided, and their intent contradictory. (Ye, *Yuan shi*, j. 2, p. 583).

39. See Ye Xie on the relativity of "new" and "old," in *Yuan shi*, j. 3, p. 593. As Stephen Owen points out, Ye "demonstrates that the concept [of rules] is far more complex than it appears in the crude positions, both pro and con, taken by conventional literary polemicists. . . . Not only does Yeh Hsieh provide a larger philosophical model that subsumes the notion of 'rules' (*fa*), his model also integrates the operations of poetry with the operations of the natural world outside of poetry" (*Readings*, pp. 497–98).

40. Ye, *Yuan shi*, j. 1, p. 576.

41. Zhang Xuecheng, "Wen li," in *Wenshi tongyi*, j. 2, p. 290.

42. Liu Dakui, *Lunwen ouji*, p. 431.

43. Yao Nai, "Da Weng Xueshi shu," in *Xibao xuan quanji*, j. 6, p. 63. See also, in the same collection, "Fu Qin Jun Shan shu," j. 22, p. 224: "Literature is a skill, and is not equivalent to the Way. But the ancient works approach the Way. Later, literature gradually grew distant from the Way."

44. Yao Nai, "Da Weng Xueshi shu," in *Xibao Xuan quanji*, j. 6, p. 63.

45. Yao Nai, "Dunzhuo tang shiji xu," in *Xibao xuan quanji*, j. 4, p. 36.

46. See Zhang Xuecheng's "Yu Liang Shaofu zhuan Du Shushan shiwen xu," in *Zhangshi yishu*, vol. 5, waiji 2 (j. 29), pp. 56–57: "One learns to reach the Way, but writing is the form given to the material ether."

47. Yuan Mei, *Xu Shipin*: "Boxi," p. 147.

48. Zhang Xuecheng summed it up quite well in the following words:

> Men of learning inevitably say that they take the ancients as their teachers. But they do not understand that the ancients cannot be imitated everywhere, nor can later authors be tossed aside entirely. In the observance of generic conventions, standards, and rules of prosody, the ancients did not

need to bother about slight deviations from them. But nowadays, historical circumstances are such that they cannot but be strictly adhered to. ("Ping Shen Meicun guwen," in *Zhangshi yishu*, vol. 8, buyi [supp.], pp. 30–34).

49. Qian Mu observes that "during their youth Huizhou scholars often engaged in lowly occupations due to poverty. Hence, their style of scholarship valued the concrete, and shared common ground with the arts" (*Zhongguo jinsanbai nian xueshu shi*, p. 310). For the social background of Huizhou scholars, see Ōtani Toshio, "Yōshū-Chōshū gakujutsu kō-sono shakaiteki kanren," pp. 313–45.

50. According to Susan Bush, the distinctions between scholarly and professional painting became

> increasingly blurred in late Ming and Ch'ing times. Scholars' painting was revitalized once more by Tung Ch'i-ch'ang. His tradition, carried on by Wang Shih-min, and transmitted to Wang Yuan-ch'i was the dominant style of the Ch'ing Painting Bureau; thus the academy painters now worked in the scholars' mode. Furthermore, one of the Wangs, Wang Hui, seems essentially to have been a professional painter who supported himself through the patronage of scholar-officials. (*The Chinese Literati on Painting*, pp. 156–57)

51. Ibid., p. 171.

52. Shi Tao settled in Yangzhou in 1696 and lived there until his death in 1717. He was regarded by many eighteenth-century painters of Yangzhou, including Zheng, as their "leading light." See Karl-Heinz Pohl, *Cheng Pan-ch'iao*, p. 24. But as Xue Yongnian argues, even in terms of painting styles, the Yangzhou painters repudiated many of the conventions of literati art: "The Eight Eccentrics of Yangzhou made innovations that were characterized by a distancing from orthodox art. Although these were not manifested in all of their works, these innovations reflect a change of aesthetic values in painting, manifesting themselves in the evolution of eighteenth-century painting idioms and stylistic innovation." See Xue Yongnian, "Yangshou baguai dui zhengtong yishu de shuli," p. 130; also see Shen Xiankai, *Zheng Bangiao yanjiu*, pp. 98–107.

53. Dong Qichang, *Huachashi lun hua*, in Yu Jianhua, *Zhongguo hualun leibian*, p. 720.

54. Ibid.

55. Yang Xin, *Yangzhou baguai*, p. 18. My interpretation of Zheng's aesthetics is indebted to Yang's analysis. Ginger Cheng-chi Hsu also argues that eighteenth-century Yangzhou painters created an aesthetic quite distinct from that of the literati school. Theirs "is an art that deals with immediately recognizable motifs and acquires a new quality of visual appeal" ("Merchant Patronage of Eighteenth-Century Yangzhou Painting," p. 215).

56. In the last of his "Letters to Younger Cousin Mo," Zheng Xie concludes that "calligraphy and painting are elegant matters, but they are also vulgar. A man of ambition who cannot achieve anything of worth to the world, or contribute to the people's welfare, and simply revels in the pleasures of the brush

and ink—if this is not vulgar, what is?" (*Yangzhou baguai shiwen ji*, pp. 264–65).
57. Wang Yuanqi, in Yu Jianhua, *Zhongguo hualun leibian*, p. 832.
58. Zheng Xie, "Hua zhu," in *Banqiao ji*, p. 162.
59. Ibid.
60. Ibid.
61. Zheng Xie, "Cong lan ji ci tu," in *Yangzhou baguai shiwen ji*, p. 274.
62. Zheng Xie, "Weixian shu zhong yu shedi di wu shu," in *Yangzhou baguai shiwen ji*, p. 265.
63. Ginger Hsu attributes the uniqueness of Yangzhou painting to the nature of patronage by the local merchant community. While sixteenth-century Anhui merchant patrons were "satisfied with what the artists presented them" (works largely within the orthodox school of literati landscape painting), Yangzhou merchants sought out art richer in narrative content. "With fewer preconceived ideas [the Yangzhou merchants] seemed to have been more open in accepting or discovering new modes of painting." She interprets this as a transitional stage in the process toward commercialization and commodification of painting. Hsu, "Merchant Patronage," p. 220.
64. Vicki Weinstein, "Eccentricity in Yang-chow, 1710–1765," pp. 126–60. Also Yu Jianhua, *Zhongguo hualun leibian*, p. 1110.
65. As Pohl puts it, Zheng "was dissatisfied with the new social developments in Yang-chou, if not to say indignant at the trivial preoccupations of the low class scholars and artists who made themselves dependent on 'vulgar' merchants, in short, at the whole nouveau riche culture" (*Cheng Pan-ch'iao*, p. 60).
66. Zheng Xie, "Banqiao zixu," in *Banqiao ji*, p. 185.
67. Zheng Xie, "Weixian shu zhong yu shedi Mo di er shu: shu hou you yi zhi," in *Yangzhou baguai shiwen ji*, p. 262.
68. Ibid.
69. Yun Shouping, *Ouxiangguan huapu*, in *Ouxiangguan ji*, j. 6, p. 5b.
70. *Yangzhou baguai shiwen ji*, p. 264.
71. Lü Liuliang, "Yu Wu Yuzhang shu," in *Lü Wancun xiansheng wenji*, j. 4, pp. 289–306. His interpretation closely follows the Mencian doctrine of *zhiyan* (*Mencius* VIB: "Gongsun Chou," shang: D. C. Lau translation, p. 120ff).
72. Lü Liuliang, *Sishu jiangyi*, j. 38, p. 9a.
73. According to Chen Zuwu, examination essay editing merely provided a convenient vehicle for Lü Liuliang's social criticism during a time of intolerance. In a letter Lü disclaims any commitment to the medium: "I have merely borrowed the art of the day [*bagu*] to vent my crazed words, like the groans of a diseased man that flow spontaneously from his pain." See Chen Zuwu, *Qingchu xueshu xibianlu*, p. 135.
74. Lü Liuliang, "Yu Wu Yuzhang dier shu," in *Lü Wancun xiansheng wenji*, j. 4, p. 302.
75. Fang Bao, "Chu Lizhi wengao xu," in *Fang Bao ji*, j. 4, pp. 95–96.
76. Fang Bao was also the editor of an important anthology of examination essays, the imperially sponsored *Qinding sishuwen* (1737). According to R. Kent

Guy, he seems to have been charged with defining a set of standards for the essay at a time when "judgment of examination essays could readily be perceived as subjective rather than objective in character" ("Fang Pao and the Ch'in-ting ssu-shu wen," p. 176).

77. Dai Zhen, "Fengyi Shuyuan bei," in *Dai Zhen wenji*, j. 11, p. 174.

78. See, for example, Yao Nai, "Tingyun tang yiwen xu" and "Taoshan sishu yi xu," in *Xibao xuan quan ji*, pj. 4, . 39 and j. 20. p. 208.

79. Yao Nai, "Xiangdang wenze ya xu," in *Xibao xuan quan ji*, j. 4, p. 43.

80. Liu Dakui, "Fang Xiyuan shiwen xu," in *Liu Haifeng xiansheng wenji*, j. 3, pp. 16b–17b.

81. Ibid. Qian Zhonglian points out that Tongcheng writers were often rather disparaging of examination essays. See Qian Zhonglian, *Mengtiaoan Qingdai wenxue lunji*, pp. 78–82.

82. Jiao Xun, *Diaogulou ji*, j. 8, pp. 154–55.

83. In spite of his antipathy toward the examination essay, Zhang Xuecheng was not blind to positive features such as those admired by Jiao Xun. See his "Yan gong xia," in *Zhangshi yishu*, vol. 1, j. 4, p. 124.

84. Dai Mingshi, "Song Songnan zhiyi xu," in *Nanshan ji*, j. 4, pp. 113–14. According to He Guanbiao, Dai Mingshi attempted to use *bagu* as a tool for political and social reform, largely because he could do so without fear of arousing official ire. See He Guanbiao, *Mingmo Qingchu xueshu sixiang yanjiu*, pp. 303–31.

85. Guan Shiming, quoted in Lu Qian, *Baguwen xiaoshi*, p. 83.

86. Nevertheless, *bagu* composition may still have been considered by the majority as an activity best suited for training the undisciplined and less intelligent. Consider the following memorial from the Board of Rites, dated 1744, concerning curriculum in the academies: "Heads of academies should select outstanding students for comprehensive, detailed instruction in the classics, history, and works on government. They can devote their remaining energies to the study of parallel composition and prosody. As for the less intelligent, they should be taught essay composition first, and be made to master a single classic. Only later should they be allowed to move to the other classics" (quoted in Wang Dezhao, *Qingdai keju zhidu yanjiu*, p. 111).

87. Shang Yanliu, *Qingdai keju kaoshi shulu*, pp. 241–42; Lu Qian, *Baguwen xiaoshi*, p. 63 ff.

88. For a discussion of the relation between intellectual change and its sociopolitical dimensions during the late Ming and early Qing, see Mizoguchi Yuzo, "Lun Mingmo Qingchu."

89. Ji Yun, "Jiachen Huishi Lu xu," in *Ji Xiaolan shiwen ji*, p. 37.

90. See Yu Ying-shih, *Zhongguo sixiang chuantong de xiandai quanshi*, p. 469 ff.

91. Zhang Xuecheng, "Lijiao," in *Zhangshi yishu*, vol. 1, j. 1, pp. 25–29.

92. Zhang Xuecheng, "Da Shen Fengxi lun xue," in *Zhangshi yishu*, vol. 1, j. 9, pp. 327–31.

93. Zhang Xuecheng, "Zhi nan," in *Zhangshi yishu*, vol. 1, j. 4, pp. 135–37.

94. As David Nivison paraphrases Zhang, the true scholar "assimilates the

learning of the ancients and then produces himself a body of work that is a unique contribution to the world and a monument to his genius" (*The Life and Thought of Chang Hsueh-ch'eng*, p. 173).

95. Zhang Xuecheng, *Wenshi tongyi*, p. 131.

96. Ibid.

97. Zhang Xuecheng, "Yan gong xia," in *Zhangshi yishu*, vol. 1, j. 4, p. 124.

98. Zhang Xuecheng, "Tianyu," in *Wenshi tongyi*, j. 3, pp. 310–11. Zhang implies in this essay that all doctrines, whatever their shortcomings, have their time and place and arise in response to concrete historical circumstances. Hence, even if Confucius were to be reborn in the time of later thinkers, he would not, Zhang says, have changed the teachings of men such as Han Yu or Zhu Xi.

99. Benjamin Elman, "Philosophy (*I-li*) versus Philology (*K'ao-cheng*)—The *jen-hsin tao-hsin* Debate," p. 214. Elman quotes Zhuang Cunyu to the effect that the Old Text of the *Shangshu* should be retained, whatever doubts existed about its authenticity, for its value in upholding moral standards.

Chapter 3

1. See Chen Meilin, *Wu Jingzi pingzhuan*, p. 389.

2. Yan Yuan and Li Gong were greatly admired by many late Qing figures such as Zhang Binglin and Xu Shichang. Zhang commented that Yan Yuan and Dai Zhen were the two greatest scholars of the Qing period (Zhang is quoted to this effect in Xiao Shafu and Li Jinquan, *Zhongguo zhexue shi*, p. 266).

3. Elman, *From Philosophy to Philology*, p. 119. During the Southern Song dynasty, the Yongjia school of scholarship combined a strong interest in ritual and other studies with a militant utilitarianism. See Huang Zongxi, "Xue Li zhiyi xu," in *Nanlei wending qianji*, j. 1, pp. 1b–2a; also his *Song Yuan xuean*, j. 49 and 50. Though not a product of this school, Chen Liang, a native of the region, seems to have been tangentially associated with a number of its representatives. They engaged in evidential scholarship quite close in spirit, if not in method, to Qing philology.

4. Yan Yuan, *Cun xing bian*, j. 2, pp. 8b–9a, in Yan Yuan and Li Gong, *Yan-Li yishu*).

5. Ibid., j. 1, pp. 8a–8b. He insisted that the great men of antiquity revered for their accomplishments were simply "organization men," so to speak, who coordinated the efforts of a corps of experts:

> Yu's taming of the river was not the result of Yu laboring alone. It must have been accomplished by all men of the land who had ability in hydrology working together. Yu brought their efforts together for completion. Likewise, Boyi's responsibility for ritual did not mean that he alone was in charge of all rites under heaven. The men of the land well-versed in ritual must have been appointed to supervise its various branches. Boyi brought them together. (ibid., pp. 5b–6a)

6. Ibid., j. 2, p. 8a.

7. Dai Wang, *Yanshi xueji*, p. 33.

8. As for Zhu Xi's position regarding ritual, it was, like his positions on many other issues, complex and full of potential contradictions. On the fundamental points he and Yan were essentially in agreement. He stressed their value as praxis, and identified their distinctive feature as a minuteness (*suosui*), and substantiality. He even praised the Six Arts as a valuable pedagogical tool. And contrary to later characterizations of him, he urged that the rites be practiced in whatever form possible, however corrupted and removed from the ancient forms they had become. He attacked those who exalted the ancient rituals only as an excuse to despise current customs, for he considered them to be the product of historical circumstances. "For the rituals," he says,

> time is the most important factor. If the sages and worthies were here now to create new ones, even they would not follow the ancient rites to the letter. I suspect that [such people] merely use the ancient rites as an excuse to destroy or discredit all ritual based on current customs. As long as one is careful not to go against the [ancient] prescriptions, and not let them become too simple, then that will be enough. (quoted in Li Guangdi, ed., *Zhuzi lizuan*, j. 1 ["Zong lun"])

But in the later uses of Zhu's doctrines by succeeding generations, this aspect of his thought was neglected under the increasing emphasis on principle. Zhu himself was skeptical of the feasibility of popularizing the rites on any great scale: "It is not difficult to practice the rites in lofty places; the difficulty lies in bringing them into use at the base of society" (ibid.). Hence, Zhu's own ambivalence on the subject, combined with his pervasive tendency to denigrate practical study, probably contributed to the fall into oblivion of these particular instructions on ritual.

9. Dai Wang, *Yanshi xueji*, pp. 37–38. See also Zheng Taixie, "Gan Gen no reiron," pp. 755–73.

10. Li Gong seems to have taken a somewhat more moderate, perhaps even ambivalent position on Zhu Xi's *Family Ritual* than Yan Yuan did. According to Patricia Ebrey, while he continued to criticize their shortcomings, his "disagreements with Chu Hsi seem on the whole trivial." In her view, this probably reflected the fact while he and other Qing scholars found fault with many specific details of the *Family Ritual*, it was difficult to completely supplant its status as a liturgical text used by large numbers of people. See Ebrey, *Confucianism and Family Ritual in Imperial China*, p. 193. On the other hand, Kai-wing Chow notes that Yan Yuan actually continued to follow Zhu Xi's prescriptions even late in his life. See Chow, *Rise of Confucian Ritualism*, p. 66.

11. Li Gong, *Zhou Yi zhuan zhu*, j. 8; also Li's "Yuan dao," in *Shugu houji*, j. 12, pp. 28a–29b.

12. Dai Wang, *Yanshi xueji*, p. 197.

13. Li Gong, "Liyue: 10," in *Pingshu ding*, j. 14, pp. 1a–4b, in Yan and Li, *Yan-Li yishu*.

14. Dai Wang, *Yanshi xueji*, p. 160 (quoting *Analects* 12.2).

15. See Yan Yuan's *Cun xue bian*, j. 2, pp. 4b–5a, for his interpretation of the phrase from the *Great Learning*, *zhi zhishan* ("extending virtue").

16. Qiu Chun, "Yan Yuan de jiaoyu sixiang," p. 68 ff.

17. Yan Yuan, *Sishu zhengwu*, j. 1, p. 2b, in Yan Yuan and Li Gong, *Yan Li congshu*, p. 47.

18. Feng Chen, *Li Shugu xiansheng nianpu*, under "67 sui," j. 5, pp. 45b–49a; in Yan and Li, *Yan-Li yishu*. The question of Li's importance in scholarly activities of the late Kangxi and Yongzheng periods will have to await the research of specialists on the subject. According to Kai-wing Chow, Li Gong was an ambivalent participant in the critical scholarship of the late Kangxi period, "caught between the need to purge heterodox elements from exegetical traditions predominantly shaped by Neo-Confucianism, and the recognition of the ominous import of critical scholarship" (*Rise of Confucian Ritualism*, p. 66). He was without doubt a controversial figure and seems to have aroused the ire of the redoubtable Li Guangdi (a staunch advocate of Cheng-Zhu orthodoxy), if Dai Wang is to be believed. But according to Li's own testimony, he gained, at least for a short time, a wide following for the educational program of Yan Yuan.

19. Hui Dong may have provided the avenue through which Cheng Tingzuo's thought (and Yan-Li teachings) reached Dai Zhen. On Hui Dong's respect for Cheng, see Hui's preface to Cheng's *Wanshu dingyi*. Some transmission of ideas from Yan through Cheng to Dai, as postulated both by Dai Wang and Hu Shi, seems plausible. For a comparison of Cheng's thought with that of Dai Zhen, see Yamanoi, *Min Shin shisō no kenkyū*, pp. 199–216, and Zhang Shunwei, *Qing ren wenji bielu*, p. 133.

20. Dai Wang, *Yanshi xueji*, p. 152.

21. Richard Wilhelm claims that mid-Qing orthodox scholars also evinced an interest in human psychology. Although he cites no examples, it seems likely that these trends were not limited only to the most iconoclastic of Han Learning scholars and may even have extended into the most conservative groups of the Confucian community. See Wilhelm, "Imperial Confucianism," pp. 243–67.

22. Cheng Tingzuo, "Yuan xin," in *Qingxi wenji*, j. 7, pp. 10a–11a.

23. Cheng Tingzuo, "Yuan xing," in *Qingxi wenji*, j. 7, pp. 12a–12b.

24. Wang Zhong, for example, thought Xunzi to be the greatest man after Confucius. Others such as Ling Tingkan professed admiration for Xunzi and seem to have hoped for some reconciliation of Mencius's and Xunzi's doctrines. See Qian Mu, *Zhongguo jinsanbai nian xueshu shi*, pp. 435–52, 491–508.

25. See Shimada Kenji, *Chūgoku ni okeru kindai shii no zasetsu*, p. 129.

26. This can be considered as essentially complementary to the sixteen-character formulation taken from the chapter *Dayu mo* of the *Shang Shu* (Classic of history), namely, the passage which expounds on the division between the "mind of man" and the "mind of the way." See Elman, "The *jen-hsin tao-hsin* Debate," pp. 175–222.

27. Cheng Tingzuo, "Lunyu shuo," quoted in Qian Mu, *Zhongguo jinsanbai nian xueshu shi*, p. 255.
28. Ibid.
29. Cheng Tingzuo, "Yi lun: 2," ibid., j. 1, pp. 1a–1b.
30. Cheng Tingzuo, "Li yue lun, shang," ibid., j. 3, pp. 1a–3b.
31. There is no evidence that Wu Jingzi pursued the study of mathematics or scientific subjects. But some of his acquaintances did, and his eldest son, Wu Lang, achieved renown for a treatise on mathematics.
32. According to gazetteers and other fragmentary evidence, Wu's circle of friends appear on the whole to have shared his aversion to officeholding and examinations. They were members of Nanjing and Yangzhou urban milieus described in such works as Li Dou's *Yangzhou huafanglu* (1795) and included scientists such as Zhou Qu and Lin Zhu, the painters Wang Sushan and Wang Qi, the physician-poet Yao Ying, and tailor and *go* aficionado Wu Heng. All are described as having consciously avoided examination competition, selling their various services with little if any thought of the scruples that inhibited literati of former eras from the commodification of culture. See Chen Meilin, *Wu Jingzi pingzhuan*, pp. 379–402. Moreover, Wu Jingzi's eldest son Wu Lang wrote a poem dated 1740 titled "Climbing to Jiming Temple with Zheng Banqiao [Zheng Xie] to View Houhu" (in Wu Lang, *Shanting ji*, j. 1, p. 12b). Although there are no other records of their association, this implies that Wu Jingzi probably also knew Zheng personally during the early Qianlong period, when he was writing *Rulin waishi*. Although as we have seen, Zheng scorned the self-styled bohemians who rejected government service entirely, it was during this period that he himself gave up his official career to devote his remaining years to his art.
33. According to Chen Meilin, evidence from *Rulin waishi* and other sources suggests that Wu may have been influenced by the classicist Mao Qiling, who at one point collaborated closely with Li Gong on the compilation of treatises on ritual. But on the whole Chen finds Wu to be largely uninformed of recent advances in *Odes* scholarship (*Wu Jingzi pingzhuan*, p. 408).
34. Jin Zhaoyan, "Dinglang xiaozhuan," in *Zongting guwen chao*, j. 3, pp. 6a–8a. It is worth noting that in addition to his fame as the author of a guide to actors of the Peking stage (*Qinyun xieying pu*), Yan Changming was widely recognized for his scholarly achievements. In the 1770s he worked in Xi'an under Bi Yuan's patronage with some of the most illustrious figures of the time, namely Zhang Xuecheng, Sun Xingyan, and Hong Liangji, among others. See his biography by Qian Daxin appended to Yan Changming's poetry collection, *Yan Dongyou shiji*.
35. See Kai-Wing Chow, "Discourse, Examinations, and Local Elites," p. 139ff. Alexander Woodside also observes a tendency among scholars of culturally peripheral areas to seek a return to earlier identities: "Far from wishing to find new identities, literati (*ju* [*ru*]) were more concerned with repossessing and mastering the rich range of aristocratic and post-aristocratic identities that

their educational tradition already permitted them, so that their value could be more fundamentally understood by their rulers, rather than merely accommodated by them" ("The Divorce between the Political Center and Educational Creativity in Late Imperial China," p. 475).

36. Elman, *Classicism, Politics, and Kinship*, p. 98.

37. Guy, *The Emperor's Four Treasuries*, pp. 46–47.

38. According to the late-Ming gazetteer of Jiangyin County, the customs of Jiangyin were close to those of Suzhou Prefecture: "But in general Wu's customs are cultured, while Piling's [Jiangyin] are simpler. The prefectural seat of Jiangyin is particularly famed for its simplicity." The account goes on to describe how the people shunned large homes, fine clothes, or any ostentatious display of wealth. Moreover, although thrifty the people of the area did not turn to commerce; "profit-making techniques are few." The county was noted mainly for the high rate of success of its scholars in the imperial examinations. Unlike Yangzhou and Hangzhou, where merchant families provided many of the resources and funding for the pursuit of Han Learning scholarly research, Wujiang in particular seems to have been less susceptible to the lure of evidential research. See *Jiangyin xianzhi*, p. 58, 60ff.

39. Wing-tsit Chan, "The *Hsing-li ching-i* and the Ch'eng-Chu School," p. 572.

40. Elman, *Classicism, Politics, and Kinship*, p. 76.

41. Catherine Jami, "Learning Mathematical Sciences during the Early to Mid-Ch'ing," pp. 243, 247.

42. See Cheng Jinfang, "Yu Jia Mianzhuang shu: 3," in *Mianxingtang ji*, j. 3, pp. 5a–5b.

43. Guy, *The Emperor's Four Treasuries*, p. 96.

44. Ling Tingkan, "Dai Dongyuan xiansheng shi luezhuan," in *Ling Cizhong xiansheng wenji*, j. 35, p. 1b.

45. Guy, *The Emperor's Four Treasuries*, p. 94.

46. Ling Tingkan, "Haowu shuo xia," in *Ling Cizhong xiansheng wenji*, j. 16, p. 6a.

47. Ling Tingkan, "Shangxima Weng Tanxi shi shu," ibid., j. 22, p. 10a.

48. Ling Tingkan, "Yu Hu Jingting shu," ibid., j. 23, p. 9b.

49. Ling Tingkan, "Da Niu Ciyuan xiaolian shu," ibid., j. 22, p. 14a.

50. Like his friend Jiao Xun, Ling Tingkan did not disdain the examination essay, but regarded it as an art to be mastered. "To think of oneself as a cultivated man [*wenren*] without having mastered an art is shameful" ("Chao zhujing ba," ibid., j. 30, p. 1b). He also took great interest in pursuits such as chess, songs, and the history of chops. Concerning chops, he cites Wang Mian as an important figure: "During the Han, jade and silver, gold or copper was used to make them. In the Yuan, Wang Mian first introduced stone. People of later times regarded it as a minor art [*xiao ji*], equivalent to objets d'arts or other curios. How ignorant!" ("Cheng Yinxi yinpu xu," ibid., j. 27, p. 16a).

51. Ling Tingkan, "Fu Zhang Zhuoting shu," ibid., j. 22, p. 3b: "You and I

both studied commerce in our youth. Hence our discussions never departed from what we practiced."

52. Ling Tingkan, "Yu Jiao Litang lun husanjiao shu," ibid., j. 24, p. 4a.

53. Li Tiangang notes that in spite of his cultural chauvinism, Dai Zhen's work on Mencius may in fact have been inspired by Jesuit writings such as those by Matteo Ricci. In the Kangxi period, a number of scholars from Dai's home area of Huizhou discussed western science with Nicolas Smogolenski, a Jesuit residing in Nanjing. And Li argues that Dai's repudiation of the Neo-Confucian doctrine of principle can be traced to similar arguments by Matteo Ricci in the work *Tianzhu shiyi*, which was widely available during the Qing: "Dai Zhen's scholarly world already included Europe, and although at first glance wholly foreign, still he strove to include and understand the other, and to construct 'common principles' based on experiences, feelings, and intellect shared by all humanity." See Li Tiangang, *Mengzi ziyi shuzheng* yu *Tianzhu shiyi*," pp. 200–222.

54. Ling Tingkan, "Fu Sun Yuanru guancha shu," ibid., j. 24, pp. 12b–13a.

55. Ling Tingkan, "Shu Wang Tiaowen shu zhongxing ji hou," ibid., j. 31, p. 8a.

56. Ling Tingkan, "Shu Huangshi tongshi fafan hou," ibid., j. 31, pp. 16ab.

57. Ling Tingkan, "Yu Ruan Boyuan gexue lun *Huafang lu* shu," ibid., j. 23, p. 11b. Ling Tingkan worked with Ruan Yuan in editing the *Chouren zhuan*, or the biographies of scientists compiled by Ruan. Ruan was acutely aware of the contributions of Europeans to the development of Chinese science, and included 37 Europeans in this work; later, in a compilation published in Guangdong during the 1830s he printed a lengthy exegesis of a classical work written by a Japanese scholar.

58. Perhaps Ling Tingkan typified what Cynthia Brokaw has described as a pervasive trend among philologists of the mid-Qing period: "For them, philology was not the training of a sage but simply an end in itself.... The philologist could hope to learn the true meaning of the language of the Classics, but this knowledge would not reveal the Way of Heaven or the responsibilities of sagehood" ("Tai Chen," p. 279).

59. Hsin-sheng Kao, *Li Ju-chen*, p. 18.

Part II

1. For example, Wou King-tseu's French translation is titled *Chronique indiscrète des mandarins*; the only complete English translation, by Hsien-i Yang and Gladys Yang, is titled *The Scholars*.

2. It may not be coincidental that most *rulin zhuan* focus less on scholarship per se than on the relationship between state policies of sponsorship and the state of scholarship in their given periods. Quite a few examples of *rulin zhuan* treat of the use of classical learning in the examination curricula at least tangentially. In this they follow the example of Sima Qian's *Shiji*, which includes an acount of the rise of official recruitment based on classical learning during

the reign of Emperor Wu of the Han (140–87 B.C.). Wu Jingzi may in fact have been deliberately alluding to the *Shiji*, for he was reputed to have had a strong interest in the work, and to have authored a treatise on it (see Ping Buqing, *Xiawai junxie*, p. 74). Moreover, at least some Qing commentators read the *Shiji* biography as a highly ambivalent account of the cooptation of scholars by the state (see, for example, Fang Bao, "Du rulin zhuan hou," in *Fang Bao ji*, j. 2, pp. 52–53). Regardless of Wu's intentions, traditional readers were probably led by its title to associate the novel with at least some of these biographies and their themes.

3. My use of "polyphony" is a reference to the Bakhtinian notion of the representation of alien discourse. Although I will not pursue the parallels between *Rulin waishi* and the many examples cited in Bakhtin's works (such as "Problems of Dostoevsky's Poetics," "From the Prehistory of the Novel," and others), his theories of novelistic discourse are particularly applicable to this novel. For like the great dialogic novels of Western literature Bakhtin cites, *Rulin waishi* represents the speech and the ideologies of its characters as qualified and externalized, "historically relative, delimited and incomplete." See Mikhail Bakhtin, *Problems of Dostoevski's Poetics*, p. 45 ff.

Chapter 4

1. It could of course be argued that these features are shared by Chinese narrative as a whole and do not represent a departure from the mainstream of the fiction tradition. See Keith McMahon, *Causality and Containment in Seventeenth-Century Chinese Fiction*, especially chap. 2, and Plaks, "Towards a Critical Theory," pp. 310–25. While this is undeniable, *Rulin waishi* manipulates the conventions of chance in ways that accentuate such aspects of Chinese narrative art.

2. This is not to say that recurrent motifs are absent, for they certainly come into play in events such as the taking of examinations, the holding of banquets, ritual celebrations, and so forth. But it is not too much of a distortion to say that the cyclical patterns of recurrence that impart a strong sense of symmetry to works such as *Jin Ping Mei* are weak if not entirely lacking in *Rulin waishi*.

3. Gilbert Highet, *The Anatomy of Satire*, p. 27 ff. Michael Seidel describes satirical narrative as the subversion of the accumulation of narrative potential from an original source, or "dispensation" (*The Satiric Dispensation*, p. 31). Ronald Paulson also notes the lack of interest in beginnings or endings or in organic change (*The Fictions of Satire*, p. 57).

4. Du Shaoqing is praised by several characters of the novel for his abilities in poetry and prose. But although a man of wide interests, the opinions he expresses are primarily on the subject of *Shijing*. Moreover, his role in this section is to introduce scholarly concerns later amplified in the chapters preceding the Taibo ritual.

5. Just prior to his discussions of poetry, Du Shaoqing examines a manuscript of notes on the *Four Books* by his neighbor Jin Dongya. Du is taken aback

by Jin's rather ribald interpretation of an unremarkable passage from the *Analects*: "As the saying goes, 'People won't eat goat testicles but they don't care if the goat lives or dies,' so Zengzi would not eat [them]" (*RWHH*, chap. 34, p. 468; *TS*, p. 376).
   6. Zhu Xi, *Shi jizhuan*, p. 19.
   7. Ibid., p. 51.
   8. As many commentators have already pointed out, a poem by Jin Zhaoyan addressed to Wu Jingzi appears to confirm that the views expressed here are those of Wu himself. This attitude of skepticism toward Zhu Xi's interpretation of the sexually redolent poems in the classic is echoed by Wu's friend Cheng Jinfang, who writes that

> in my opinion at that time [of the Airs] the institution of marriage was just taking form, and a harmonious atmosphere pervaded [male-female] relations. Officials in charge of music made these poems, to be performed during the consummation of marriage, and for many generations they were used in the bedchamber without interruption. . . . My friend Dai Dongyuan [Dai Zhen] is well-versed in this classic, and his opinion on these poems agrees with mine. ("Du Guanju," in Cheng Jinfang, *Mianxingtang ji*, j. 4, pp. 8b–10a)

Cheng Tingzuo also argues to the effect that only the music to which the Airs of Zheng were set was licentious: "Hence, Zheng had a licentious sound, but no licentious poems" (see "Shilun 5," in Cheng Tingzuo, *Qingxi wenji*, j. 1, pp. 18a–20b). But elsewhere, Cheng Jinfang criticizes the extremes to which the critics of Song traditions had gone, abandoning Zhu Xi for an equally rigid adherence to Han exegetical traditions (see "Zhengxue lun 4," in Cheng Jinfang, *Mianxingtang ji*, j. 3, pp. 14a–15a). Wu Jingzi was most likely well acquainted with Hui's views, which were shared by Wu's patron Lu Jianzeng (1690–1768).
   9. The theme of obsession (*pi*) and its prominence in fiction and art of the late Ming and early Qing periods have been brilliantly analyzed by Judith Zeitlin in her study of *Liaozhai zhiyi*. While Chi Hengshan's immersion in ritual seems indeed to bear some resemblance to the notion of obsession discussed by Zeitlin, my use of the latter term is not meant to allude to its seventeenth-century connotations. For conspicuously absent in *Rulin waishi* is the "glorification" that Zeitlin finds to be a crucial element of tales of obsession in Feng Menglong's story collections as well as *Liaozhai zhiyi* (Zeitlin, *Historian of the Strange*, p. 90ff). The obsessions manifested by literati characters in Wu Jingzi's work instead manifest a narrowness of understanding that, while not without salutary effects, prevents them from achieving the intellectual wholeness toward which they aspire.
   10. This island retreat appears to allude to a dramatic work authored by Zhuang's model, the scholar Cheng Tingzuo, called "Lianhua dao chuanqi" ("The Romance of the Island of Lotus Flowers"). According to Jin Zhaoyan's preface, this work does not give voice to the sort of eremitic scholasticism practiced by Zhuang Shaoguang. Rather, he claims that "if Mr. Cheng had

achieved his ambitions, and carried out his learning [in public life], then the many achievements of the Island of Lotus Flowers would be glorified in painting and histories. But he had no choice but to carefully entrust them to the realm of the fictional imagination" (Jin Zhaoyan, *Zongting guwen chao*, j. 6, p. 15b).

11. Zhuang's model Cheng Tingzuo decries precisely the tendency for literati to become circumscribed by their own views and disciplines:

> Since the Warring States period there have been three changes in scholars. During the Han they took refuge in philology and exegesis. After the Wei and Jin they competed in literary composition and rhyme. In the Song and Yuan those who claimed to study the Way took discourse on human nature and heaven to be the ultimate. These three each took their own studies to be the only one, and tried to put them into practice, with little success. ("Hongfan lun shang," in Cheng Tingzuo, *Qingxi wenji*, j. 1, pp. 6a–7a)

12. An incident occurs on Zhuang's journey to the capital during which, surrounded by armed bandits, he is described as "speechless with fright" (*RWHH*, chap. 34, p. 474; *TS*, p. 383). Although seemingly insignificant, this lack of pluck exhibits a flaw in the literati decried by many Qing writers, namely their inadequacy in martial affairs. Indeed, this incident appears to give voice to the complaint of Wu Jingzi's friend Cheng Jinfang:

> Literati of the Southeast devote themselves exclusively to literary affairs. When they meet with bandits and robbers, their color pales, their hands tremble, and they cannot move. Yet still they look down on all such matters [as archery and horsemanship], and feel fully satisfied with their achievements, believing that they study the Way of the Confucians. Alas, is the Way of Confucians so narrow as this? Some say that Zhang Zifang [Zhang Liang] helped the Han defeat Chu [sic] even though he looked like a woman. And that Kongming [Zhuge Liang] directed his armies from his chariot wearing a silk scarf and using a feather fan, sustaining Shu for decades. Why, such men ask, should literati seek renown for their prowess or courage? I say that these men were great generals. If one lacks their talents, then one should study the arts [of war], to protect one's person and serve the nation's needs. Can one not do this? Archery and riding were certainly not neglected by ancient men who studied the Way. ("Zhengxue lun 7," in Cheng Jinfang, *Mianxingtang ji*, j. 1, pp. 16b–17a)

Cheng Tingzuo himself worried that the "separation of civil and military" had brought about a decline in governance (see his "Hongfan lun xia," in *Qingxi wenji*, j. 1, pp. 8a–9a).

13. See for example, Gao Yuhou, "*Rulin waishi* 'zhenru' xingxiang xinyi," pp. 119–27. Gao argues that in spite of their imperfections, these figures represent a modification of the literati ideal, in contrast to their corrupt and careerist foils.

14. One of the livelier moments of the novel comes when Qu's uncles the

Lou brothers are visited by Iron-armed Zhang late one evening. Zhang presents them with a bloody bag, claiming that it contains the head of his enemy. He then requests 500 taels of silver, which he promises to repay in a few days' time. Zhang never returns, and the Lous decide to open the bag, only to discover the rotting head of a pig. This episode ends their interest in consorting with the bohemians of their region, and they close their doors to future visitors.

15. The decline of poetry was attributed to the demands of the examination system by a number of men of Wu Jingzi's generation. His fellow townsman Jin Zhaoyan laments that in recent times men have had to choose between poetry and examinations:

> Since the Ming when examination essays were used to select officials, poetry has become a minor art for learned men. Talented men used their remaining energies to engage in it, but very few were able to master it. How could this be the result of people's individual talents being unequal to the task? The road to advancement had no connection to poetry, and hence people simply followed their natural talents [without putting effort into it]. ("Fang Mi'an shi xu," in Jin Zhaoyan, *Zongting guwen chao*, j. 4, pp. 4b–6b)

Jin praises the special examination of 1736, to which Wu Jingzi was recommended, for featuring poetry as a prominent component: "Our reigning emperor has revived poetry by imitating the Tang examinations [which used poetry]. Hence even in distant backwaters there is no place where people do not study versification" ("Xu Yuexi shi xu," in *Zongting guwen chao*, j. 5, pp. 15a–b. In a similar vein, Liu Dakui laments the lowly status of poets in a society where only examination degrees are valued: "There is no one among officialdom of today who can compare to [the poet Wang Zao]. Alas, is Zaiyang [Wang Zao] to be poor for his whole life?" Liu attributes this to the prestige of the examination system. See "Wang Zaiyang shixu," in *Liu Haifeng xiansheng wenji*, j. 2, pp. 25b–26b.

16. Hangzhou was home to a number of prominent poets of the eighteenth century, most notably Li E and Yuan Mei (a native of the city though he later lived mainly in Nanjing). It seems to have been the scene of a number of poetic controversies between adherents of rival schools. See *ECCP*, p. 137 ff.

17. Zhao Xuezhai may be alluding to the physician-poet Xue Xue, who was a pupil of Ye Xie, and author of the treatise on poetry, *Yipiao shihua* (Zhao's name Xue is identical to that of Xue). Yuan Mei praises Xue's abilities in both poetry and medicine in his *Suiyuan shihua* (p. 136). But in a letter to Xue's son following the death of his father, Yuan laments his family's insistence on having him remembered for his literary and philosophical activities rather than for his apparently remarkable talents in medicine:

> Medicine is an art, and it is especially difficult. Shennong began it, the Yellow Emperor promoted it, the Duke of Zhou sent ministers to receive it, because its way is connected to the spirits and sages. Why is it that medicine has died out, whereas philosophical discourse continues to thrive? This is

because the effects of medicine can be seen immediately, and hence not even one among a hundred physicians achieves fame; but philosophical discourse has no basis, and hence rustic scholars abound. You do not honor your father in what he excelled at above a hundred others, but debase him among those that can be seen all around us. That is a mistake! (Yuan Mei, *Xiaocang shanfang wenji*, j. 19, p. 1553)

18. In spite of its seeming crudity, this position represents an only slightly parodied version of the deeply held belief that literature in general, and poetry in particular, is the means by which men become "known." See Owen, *Readings*, pp. 19–32ff. Wu Jingzi's acquaintance Chen Yi (Chen Guyu) compiled and published a series of poetry anthologies (in which he included Wu's poems) titled *Suo zhi ji*, or "A Collection of People I have Known." In a preface to this work, the dramatist and poet Jiang Shiquan pronounces the theme of the anthology to be "knowing": "[Chen] has come by good fortune to know poets who are poor in acquaintances. How can he bear to let their poetry disappear?" (*Suo zhi ji: chuji*, p. 1a).

19. One of these poets, Zhi E, is barely mentioned in the narrative until a humiliating discovery—the disclosure that he is actually a mere salt runner masquerading as a licentiate. But his name bears a striking resemblance to Li E, that is, one of the foremost poets of the era. Moreover, his style-name, Moqing, is identical to that of Li E's friend and patron Pu Moqing, scion of a wealthy Hangzhou family. This suggests at least the possibility of allusions to some of the more important literary figures of the day.

20. As Qian Daxin complains about his contemporaries, "Low-ranking literati eagerly pursue glory through position; while high-ranking literati eagerly seek the arrogance of fame" (see "Ming jian," in Qian Daxin, *Qianyantang wenji*, j. 17, p. 268).

21. Wu Qing, the model for Du Shenqing, was apparently famous primarily for his poetry. See Liu Dakui's preface to his poetry collection, "Wu Qingran shi xu," in Liu, *Liu Haifeng xiansheng ji*, j. 2, pp. 21a–22b.

22. A number of critics have read this passage, along with other references to the Yongle usurpation, as indications that the novel as a whole negates the cardinal Confucian virtue of loyalty. See Fan Ning, "*Rulin waishi* de lunli sixiang," p. 114ff. While it is clear that service to the state does not transcend a crass careerism for the great majority of the novel's characters, this does not necessarily entail the revision of such Confucian ethical virtues. Rather, the problem lies in Du Shenqing's rather extreme views on the subject, which like the opposing views of the Lou brothers fail to account for the complexity of the issues involved and reflect his inability to transcend his own prejudices.

23. Disdain for Fang seems to have been common to men of poetic and literary talents among Wu Jingzi's friends and contemporaries. Yuan Mei, for example, decries the tragedy of Fang's pedantic bent as follows: "[Wang] Jinggong and Fang Zhengxue both brought catastrophe to the world with this book [*Zhou li*], yet those who fought against them in their respective eras argued the issues on their terms. There was not even one or two heroic men

who pointed out that this work is a forgery, and not the work of the sages, which would have destroyed the basis for their programs" ("Da Li Mutang lun li shu," in Yuan Mei, *Xiaocang shanfang wenji*, j. 15, p. 1455). Cheng Jinfang ridiculed these two in similar terms: "Wang Jinggong and Fang Zhengxue were too faithful to the past, and too confident of their own infallibility. They brought catastrophe on their families and nation. We should take care in such matters" ("Du *Rizhi lu*," in Cheng Jinfang, *Mianxingtang ji*, j. 4, p. 23a).

24. Beginning in chapter 23, the novel introduces a series of actors, in particular Bao Wenqing and his adopted son Bao Tingxi, whose role amounts to that of foils for the literati. It is significant that the literati who most appreciate the company of actors, even enjoying their sexual favors (i.e., Hanlin Academician Gao, the brothers Tang, and Du Shenqing), are also portrayed as advocates of and avid practitioners of *bagu*. For at least by the early seventeenth century (with the publication of Zang Maoxun's *Yuanqu xuan*), the mimesis of the sages that is the defining feature of *bagu* was linked with the stage, and to many the medium suffered from this association. As Yuan Mei puts it,

> Since antiquity, writing on prescribed topics has not been valued. This is even more true of *bagu*, which cuts and pastes together the words of the sages, thereby defiling them! Moreover, since antiquity essays have expressed one's own beliefs and convictions. Never did writers assume the role of actors and speak on behalf of others. Only *bagu* and the theater value the imitation of another's voice.... This is why this form of writing is so lowly ("Da Dai Jingxian jinshi lun shiwen," quoted in Wu Hongyi and Ye Qingbing, *Qingdai wenxue piping ziliao huibian*, p. 473; this essay does not appear in the standard edition of Yuan's collected works).

25. Such criticisms are close in tone to various remarks by Zhang Xuecheng on the subject of examination learning. He too saw it as having lowered the standards of scholarship by encouraging a shallow and superficial learning. Complaining that his interlocutor's primer for young students fails to throw off the influence of *bagu* primers, he tells him that "young boys will expend their efforts only on attaining literary polish from an early age, so that they will let mere cleverness rule them. They will have difficulty entering the Way. However, the difference between ancient studies and vulgar studies is not in writing. It is in the difference between having something to say, and having nothing to say" ("Da Zhou Lianggu lun kemengshu," in Zhang Xuecheng, *Zhangshi yishu*, vol. 1, j. 9, pp. 339–40). And in a passage often cited by students of *Rulin waishi*, he cites the early Qianlong period as a time when *bagu* had passed as real learning in many localities. ("Da Shen Fengxi lunxue," ibid., j. 9, pp. 327–31). But elsewhere Zhang decries not *bagu* itself but the insistence on taking this or any other literary form as the only truth: "Some proclaim that the world must adhere to their own individual understanding. People may follow me. But if we bring the ancients back from the dead to question them about this, they would say: 'This is not what I have proclaimed. Is this not an insult to me?'" Moreover, Zhang has praise for anthologists such as Gui

Youguang, whose elaborately annotated editions of texts attempted to elucidate literary style for the edification of examination aspirants, among others ("Wen li," ibid., j. 3, pp. 286–95).

26. Perhaps Wu Jingzi's views on *bagu* were not far removed from those of Jin Zhaoyan. In a preface to a collection of *bagu* essays, Jin writes that

> alas, if [their author, Wang Bantang] had not devoted deep thought and gained insight through them, how could they have turned out [as good as] this? The butcher who cuts up a cow, a peddler who catches cicadas, or a wheelwright who fashions a wheel—these minor arts were used by Zhuangzi to speak of the Tao. Hence, if one uses one's energies without distraction in a single place, there is nothing one cannot do. ("Wang Bantang zhiyi xu," in Jin Zhaoyan, *Zongting guwen chao*, j. 6, pp. 3a–4a)

Even while lamenting the deleterious influence of examination studies on scholarship and morals, Cheng Tingzuo admits their usefulness: "I must say that the ruler cannot abandon methods [of recruitment] in establishing government. But we cannot rely solely on methods." Aside from its encouragement of shallowness and competitiveness, examination learning fails simply because it cannot motivate those with deep scholarly or literary interests:

> Examination writings are studied by those literati who seek advancement. It is not learning. Since those literati know that the intent of educators is only this, then how will they be willing to abandon what they need in order to engage in learning for themselves and give up an official career? The examinations are inadequate to exhaust the talents of the world, and within the schools people are allowed to decide whether they are intelligent and wise, or whether they will engage in learning or not. I suspect this is what distinguishes us from the ancients. ("Shang Li Mutang xiansheng lun shuyuan shu," in Cheng Tingzuo, *Qingxi wenji*, j. 9, pp. 18a–20a)

27. See Yang Xin, *Yangzhou baguai*, p. 125.
28. See Wu Lang, *Shanting ji*, j. 2, p. 6a.
29. Jin Zhaoyan wrote several laudatory biographies of actors, street sweepers, and other men of lowly station. On the actor Dinglang, he says, "People such as Dinglang are truly natural. Mr. Yujing says that his elegance is unparalleled. Mr. Dongxin [the painter Jin Nong] says that he suspects that there are hundreds of volumes of books in his mind. Both are referring to his superior tone" ("Dinglang xiaozhuan," in Jin Zhaoyan, *Zongting guwen chao*, j. 3, pp. 12b–15a). And in "Pu Mizi zhuan" (j. 4, pp. 2a–4a), the biography of a streetcleaner turned storyteller, he says that although Pu "did not read books, he loved to perform good deeds. Whenever he saw members of a family doing harm to each other, or friends forsaking each other, he would do his best to try to persuade them to reconcile." This inclination toward altruism helped to turn Pu into a storyteller, a vocation that he used to promote morality among

the population: "Pu never wore brocade clothing, nor did he eat fish. When he saw meat or seafood delicacies on the table, he never touched them, saying, 'How can a man of poverty take away from the good fortune of later generations?'" It seems possible that Pu might have served as a model for the character Bao Tingxi in the novel, who also takes care never to presume to be the equal of his literati patrons.

30. Chen Meilin rightly points out the many negative aspects of the portrayal of salt merchants (*Wu Jingzi pingzhuan*, pp. 477–81), particularly the crudity of the Fang clan of Wuhe. But the satire of these men appears to focus on their aping of literati lifestyles, rather than on their conspicuous consumption and excesses. For a sympathetic view of salt merchants (in particular of their contribution to the anti-Qing resistance at the fall of the Ming) by Wang Zhong, a scholar often viewed as hostile toward merchants, see his biography in Li Dou, *Yangzhou huafang lu* (j. 6, pp. 145–50).

31. The juxtaposition of civil and military skills is signaled by the appearance of the character Wu Shu at the conclusion of chapter 36. Wu's name suggests something of his significance, for it consists of the characters for military (*wu*) and written (*shu*), or a close approximation to *wen* (civil). He is said to be an accomplished literary craftsman, a master of *bagu*, and enlivens the social gatherings of these last chapters with his grace and wit. While thus emblematic of literati qualities, he is also linked to the military characters of these chapters, introducing both the martially gifted Guo Li (Wang Hui's son) and Xiao Yunxian to the Nanjing literati.

32. The model for Yu, Wu Peiyuan, seems to have been particularly proud of his abilities in geomancy. In his literary collection (*Huixin caotang ji*), he refers to an incident in which a high official consulted him on geomantic matters. See his "He Xiangguo eryue wangri yuanyun si shou, 3," in Wu Peiyuan, *Huixin caotang ji*, j. 2, p. 8b.

33. Although the novel uses this sobriquet to describe Yu Yude alone, some critics have taken it to refer to the other scholars in Nanjing, such as Zhuang Shaoguang, Du Shaoqing, and Chi Hengshan. In the view of Gao Yuhou, all of these men manifest the attribute of "sincerity" or "truthfulness" implied by the term *zhen* (Gao Yuhou, "*Rulin waishi*," pp. 119–27). Nonetheless, I believe that while these characters do indeed possess such attributes as sincerity and integrity, the use of this term for Yu alone is quite deliberate.

Chapter 5

1. Chinese critics of the early twentieth century such as Hu Shi, Lu Xun, and others often disparaged the structural looseness of *Rulin waishi*, an attitude that as Lin Shuen-fu argues was influenced by Western models of narrative. More recently, critics have attempted to make sense of its structural integrity in a number of ways. But in my view the fact remains that by virtue of its subject matter the novel is structurally "looser" than other examples of longer Chinese fiction. Hence, the use of the historical frame adds a temporal-

ity that, in the words of Paul Ricoeur, is crucial to "the structural identity of the narrative function, as well as . . . the truth claim of every narrative work" (*Time and Narrative*, p. 3).

2. One can find a similar use of historical setting in a number of works of Western literature. For an influential account of such narratives, see Georg Lukacs, *The Historical Novel*, chapts. 1–3.

3. Among other Qing novels set in the mid-Ming period, only *Nüxian waishi* (Unofficial history of female immortals) includes the word "history" in its title. Others such as *Lüye xianzong* and *Yesou puyan* share a similar time frame, that is, the sixteenth to seventeenth centuries, but do not allude to this in their titles.

4. In a preface to the late Ming miscellany *Baishi huibian*, Zhou Kongjiao draws the distinction as follows:

> Histories are works that record words and events. The nation does not lack for history, and history does not lack for officials. Hence in ancient times there were "left histories and right histories," "inner histories and outer histories." Their styles derived from the four ancient histories, and they were stored in gilt cabinets and stone rooms, and honored with the word "official." Those that arose from mountainous retreats and the stories of old men, that were unreliable and unverifiable were disparaged, and hence called "bai." Bai means that their words are insignificant. But there are official histories that merge into unofficial, and there are unofficial histories that aid the official records. (p. 1b)

5. See Harold L. Kahn, *Monarch in the Emperor's Eyes*, p. 33 ff.

6. *Yeshi* on the subject of the Yongle usurpation (1402–04) proliferated during the Yongzheng and Qianlong periods. They were widely interpreted as referring to the succession crisis of the late Kangxi period and the rumors that circulated concerning the means by which Yongzheng ascended the throne. The Yongle usurpation emerges in *Rulin waishi* as a charged topic of discussion, where the troubling implications of this historical issue must have echoed those of contemporary *yeshi* writings and served to link the novel to such semi-historical and apocryphal works. As to the question of whether or not the novel reflects anti-Manchu sentiments, the novel provides few clues. Wu Zuxiang suggests that such content is carefully "veiled" (*yinxiu*) (Wu Zuxiang, "Guanyu Wu Jingzi de minzu sixiang wenti," pp. 1–4). While it may be difficult to demonstrate conclusively, there is evidence suggesting the existence of veiled allusions to one of the causes célèbres of anti-Qing nationalism, the exhumation of Lü Liuliang. See Stephen Roddy, "*Rulin waishi* and the Representation of the Literati in Qing Fiction," pp. 144–57.

7. *Rulin waishi* contains an episode of the suppression of the early Ming poet Gao Qi's works (in chapter 35) that has been understood by some as an allusion to the Dai Mingshi case. As I mentioned in Chapter 2, Dai was executed in 1712 for alleged anti-Manchu writings and activities. Like other Ming

loyalists and their descendants, he was also the author of a history of the Ming period (which does not survive).

8. In his "Three Levels of Composition of the *Rulin waishi*" Zbigniew Slupski notes that the novel "can be divided into four segments which differ from one another as regards the subject matter, types of comedy, and style employed in each" (p. 47). These criteria include the use of satire and farce, the gathering of positive figures, overstatement, and the social strata of the characters. The boundaries between segments he identifies correspond closely, though not exactly, to the four stages of history outlined here. Slupski sees this segmentation as expressing changing attitudes of the author toward his subject matter, thus forming what he calls the novel's "level of lyrical autobiography." Other critics of the novel, such as Wu Zuxiang, Lin Shuen-fu, and Kao Yu-kung, also place emphasis on delineating similar schemes of segmentation. This tendency seems to reflect the centrality of the historical and diachronic processes to *Rulin waishi*.

9. This chronology imposes a configuration that appears to coincide with what Andrew Plaks has described as a pervasive pattern of Chinese narrative—that is, its tendency to trace both the rise and fluorescence as well as the decline of empire, family, and individual. See Plaks, *Ssu-ta ch'i-shu*, p. 34 ff; also "Towards a Critical Theory," pp. 338–39.

10. In Li Hanqiu, ed., *Rulin waishi yanjiu ziliao*, p. 45.

11. See Matsumura Kō, "Ō Men den kō," p. 167 ff. Matsumura argues that Song and Liu Ji (who authored a preface to Wang Mian's poetry collection) used Wang as a sort of tool in their pro-Ming propaganda effort to garner support among the literati, a segment of whom were wary of committing themselves to Zhu Yuanzhang. Certainly Liu's evaluation of Wang's eccentricity mirrors that of Song Lian, stressing the political satire (*ci*) he finds in Wang's exuberant verse. Liu's preface attacks the proponents of poetry as an individualistic mode of self-fulfillment (*zishi*), arguing that the public, political function of poetry as first enunciated in the *Great Preface* (to the *Shi jing*) should be restored. Liu seems not, however, to have subscribed to the view that Wang served Zhu Yuanzhang's armies during his final days. But he feels confident that Wang would have been active in public affairs under the new dynasty. "If Master Wang had lived into the illustrious Ming, would he have dared to defy Confucius's dictum and [remained silent on affairs of state] like a stone or tree?" Wang's example thus served to illustrate the proper bounds of eremitic disengagement from public life. See Liu Ji, "Wang Yuanzhang shiji xu," in Liu Ji, *Chengyibo wenji*, j. 5, pp. 4b–6a.

12. Ogawa Tamaki, *Chūgoku shōsetsu shi no kenkyū*, pp. 184–85.

13. Huang Zongxi, *Ming yi daifang lu*, p. 1; translated in de Bary, *Waiting for the Dawn*, pp. 89–90.

14. According to Liu Ji, Wang Mian's works express a deeply felt desire to participate in government, something Liu assures us he would have done had he lived into the Ming (Liu Ji, *Chengyibo wenji*, j. 5, pp. 4b–6a). And Wang is

quoted by another Ming author as having urged his descendants to write with moral aims:

> Wang Mian was uninhibited, and scornful of his contemporaries. He once said: "Men who do not become renowned for their virtue or achievements should use writing to achieve posterity. How can one live without benefit and die without being known [to the world]?" His descendants Wuzhao, Keneng, and others held to this admonition. They memorized all of his writings and could recite them easily. . . . Nearly one hundred years later, [Wang's great-grandson] Yunqi had his works printed, thereby realizing Wang's lifelong wish. His admonishments and satire, present beneath his words, can now be seen by men. (Bai Gui, "Shijuan hou," in *Lidai huajia shiwen ji*, p. 76)

15. While eliminating the frustrated political activism portrayed by the other biographies, *Rulin waishi* nonetheless cleverly transposes Wang Mian'sconcern for institutions to the subject of the examination system. Furthermore, this characterization of Wang as a skeptical critic of the examinations is not wholly inconsistent with Huang Zongxi's views on the subject. Huang himself criticizes the prevailing methods of official recruitment and argues that criteria should be broadened and diversified to incorporate a wide range of human talents and skills into government.

16. The divisiveness over how to interpret Wang Mian's disengagement is echoed in another issue that surfaces at several points in the novel, namely, the Yongle usurpation and martyrdom of Fang Xiaoru. Here again there seems to have been a major difference of opinion between Zhu Yizun and other members of the Ming History Board. According to the nineteenth-century scholar Ruan Yuan, Zhu sought to minimize negative elements of the account, even attempting to suggest that the Jianwen emperor actually agreed to abdicate in his elder brother's favor. And like Du Shenqing in the novel, he also discounts the veracity of the claims that "nine grades" of relations and friends of the Fang clan were slaughtered by Yongle. According to the nineteenth-century work *Xiaoting xulu* by Zhao Lian (1780–1833), however, on this issue Zhu and Wan Sitong were in agreement ("Mingshi gao tiao," in *Xiaoting xulu*, j. 5, p. 437). Zhu appears to have viewed it as a professional obligation to refute the popular legends that had grown up around the Jianwen emperor: "The *Veritable Records* may be flawed in the views they present of events, but the people and dates they record are verifiable and accurate, and later people did not have difficulty forming opinions on them. As for *Xunguo* and other accounts, they often include ghosts and other fantastic events that distort the truth with falsity. There are few that do not promote delusion. You should ferret out their errors" ("Shiguan shang zongcai de su shu," in Zhu Yizun, *Pushuting ji*, j. 32, pp. 5a–5b).

17. Curiously, Wei Su addressed in his own writings precisely those problems of which the novel makes him a representative. He decries the gap between officialdom and the clerks who work in local administration and sug-

gests that officials engage in accounting and other menial duties to alleviate some of the worst offenses perpetrated by clerks. See John Dardess, *Confucianism and Autocracy*, p. 67.

18. He Zehan, *Rulin waishi renwu benshi kaolue*, p. 113.

19. The capture of Wang Hui as he attempts to flee by boat cleverly evokes Wang Yangming's capture of the prince on Boyang Lake. Wang Hui's last official post, that of the governor of southern Jiangxi, is moreover the one held by Wang Yangming when the rebellion broke out.

20. Editors of the Ming History Board writing on the rebellion were somewhat skeptical of its chances for success. But in the unsettled conditions prevailing at court, victory was not inconceivable. See James Geiss, "The Cheng-te Reign," pp. 423–36.

21. See Qian Mu, *Zhongguo jinsanbai nian xueshu shi*, p. 233.

22. See Wang Yuan, "Yu Li Zhongfu xiansheng shu," in *Juyetang wenji*, j. 7, pp. 8b–11a; also Li Fu, "Fu Jidongdao Chen Fushi shu," in *Mutang xiansheng biegao*, j. 35, pp. 5b–10b. Wu Jingzi's friend Cheng Jinfang also praises Wang Yangming's influence in similar terms: "Although Wang's doctrines are close to Chan [Buddhism], his followers spoke of practical benefits and were fond of meritorious deeds. Their filial piety and loyalty are recorded in the histories. Can the followers of Cheng and Zhu say that there were no inferior people among their many thousands?" Cheng goes on to deplore the sort of learning that has come to replace Wang's teachings in the local schools, that is, of *bagu* and examination preparation (Cheng Jinfang, "Zhengxue lun 6," in *Mianxingtang ji*, j. 1, pp. 15b–16b).

23. See Geiss, "The Cheng-te Reign," p. 236.

24. According to Hung-lam Chu, during the sixteenth century Wang Yangming was in fact admired as a model of "official success." "It seems that most of Wang Yang-ming's 'followers' were at that time [1572] more interested in making him a symbol than in seriously pursuing his teaching or emulating his deeds. Wang Yang-ming's importance, ironic as it might seem to us, was then primarily perceived in terms of the success of his official career rather than in terms of the import of his philosophy" (Chu Hung-lam, "The Debate over the Recognition of Wang Yang-ming," p. 70).

25. See Brook, *Praying for Power*, p. 313 ff.

26. See Xie Zhen's biography in *Ming shi* (j. 287).

27. Zong Chen was actually considered to be one of the "Four Masters" with whom Wang Shizhen was associated during his first period of residence in Peking. Among Zong's writings, there is even a letter to Xie Zhen that alludes to literary gatherings at the Prince's palace. See Zong Chen, *Zong Zixiang ji*, j. 15, p. 14b.

28. The eighteenth-century poet and historian Zhao Yi discusses mid-Ming literati mores in his *Ershier shi zhaji* under the heading "Reckless practices of literati of the mid-Ming":

> This type of flaunting of talent and arrogance toward the world, an untrammeled freedom from convention [such as that of Tang Yin] was suffi-

cient to bring about harm. Namely, wherever these men's fame had spread, men came to flatter and please them. Not only high officials and important men bent over backward to please them, even princes of the blood felt honored by association with them, and worried only that they might fall out of favor. From this we can see that once the world has been at peace for generations, and material goods are in abundance, literati and scholars can revel in the pleasures of wine and song. This was a time of great things. (Zhao Yi, *Ershier shi zhaji*, no. 514, pp. 783–84)

29. The Jiajing emperor's lengthy struggle to have his own father posthumously elevated to imperial status (known as the "debate over the major rites," *dali zhi yi*) was widely blamed by later historians for literati disaffection with government service. In the words of Wan Sitong, the rites controversy "was not the precipitating factor in the fall of the Jiajing court, but of the entire Ming period" (quoted in Yang Xiangkui, *Qingru xuean xinbian*, p. 183). The novel's juxtaposition of Zhuang Shaoguang's visit to court with the rise of interest in ritual reverberates with the historical implications of this period.

30. Frederic Wakeman discusses the highly negative assessment of late Ming cultural elites that prevailed at court and elsewhere in the mid-to-late seventeenth century: "Moralistic officials like Yang Yongjian [castigated] the ethical laxity that had by now, even in Shunzhi's mind, become linked with Ming holdovers, Jiangnan literary coteries, social decadence, and a decline in classical scholarship" (*Great Enterprise*, p. 1005).

31. See Yu Huai, *Banqiao zaji*, p. 21. According to the early Qing gazetteer *Fenglu xiaozhi*, however, many members of the Xu family were cultivated writers and poets. In contrast to Xu Qingjun, his contemporary Xu Hongji

was highly intelligent, and collected many works of poetry and calligraphy. He was similar to the men of the Jin and Tang dynasties. During the Chongzhen era there was a drought in the Nanjing area, and he did much to alleviate the famine through good administration and was promoted to the rank of Grand Tutor. When in 1644 he heard of the fall of the capital [to the rebel Li Zicheng], he died of grief. (*Fenglu xiaozhi*, j. 2, p. 11b)

And the early Kangxi era Nanjing prefectural gazetteer similarly lauds Xu Hongji's intelligence and generosity:

Once a drunken young scholar rushed into his pavilion demanding more drink and cursing the host. He suddenly threw up and fell to the ground unconscious. The master [Xu] called a halt to the drinking games and told his servants to stay with the man until he awoke, giving him tea to drink, water to wash, and food to eat. When the young man awoke, he asked why he was there, and Xu's servants told him the reason. Ashamed, the man covered his face and left. These actions of Master Xu can be praised for handling the circumstances most appropriately. (*Jiangning fuzhi*, j. 33, p. 64b)

32. Kong Shangren, *Taohua shan*, p. 3.

33. Another intriguing coincidence is the similarity of Chen Munan's name to Chen Jinnan (also known as Chen Yonghua), Zheng Chenggong's captain, and leader of the resistance movement in Taiwan during the early Kangxi period. See Xiao Yishan, *Qingdai tongshi*, vol. 2, pp. 892–932.
34. Brook, *Praying for Power*, p. 316.
35. Sheldon Hsiao-peng Lu, *From Historicity to Fictionality*, p. 91.

Chapter 6

1. Shuen-fu Lin, "Ritual and Narrative Structure in *Ju-lin Wai-shih*," pp. 244–65.
2. Since Hu Shih first argued that *Rulin waishi* is a product of Yan-Li thought, a number of scholars have attempted to discern specific allusions to Yan Yuan or Li Gong, particularly in the use of ritual. In the words of a recent article, "If we make a simple analysis, and cut away the branches and leaves, leaving only the trunk, then *Rulin waishi* certainly can be said to use the viewpoint of the Yan-Li school to dissect society and to express its ideals" (Dong Guoyan, "*Rulin waishi* zhuti xinshuo," p. 81). Chi Hengshan's advocacy of "rites, music, military, and agriculture," and Xiao Yunxian's pacification at Qingfeng cheng, certainly sound reminiscent of Yan Yuan's doctrines. (For the most detailed discussion of this issue to date, see Chen Meilin, *Wu Jingzi pingzhuan*, pp. 386–403.) While the case for some allusions to such intellectual currents seems strong, the novel's representation of them is far more complex than these critics have suggested.
3. The fact that the temple erected for the purpose of enacting the ritual is named after Taibo has been seen as significant by a number of commentators both traditional and contemporary. Chi Hengshan justifies honoring Taibo as the "first sage of Nanjing," and Wu Jingzi's contemporaries seem to have celebrated him in part for his role in civilizing the Jiangnan region at the dawn of its incorporation into the Chinese cultural sphere (see Wang Zhong, *Shuxue ji*, buyi, pp. 29b–30b). Taibo was praised by Confucius for his "yielding" of the reins of government and subsequent eremitic life in the wilds of Wu (*Analects* 8.1: "He yielded the nation three times, yet the people had no way to praise him"). He can thus be seen as the embodiment of ritual propriety (*li* was often glossed as *rang*, or "yielding"). Yet Confucius himself was given a role in the Taibo legend, praised for having preserved his memory among the people of China proper (which was still in the north). The honoring of this particular figure appears to signal a concern with the relation between fame and moral worth. For a recent discussion of some of the issues of the Taibo legend and their relation to literati self-consciousness, see Kitamura, "Go Taibaku jōkoku no shisō shi," pp. 23–41. Kitamura argues that for writers of the Han and later, Taibo symbolized the idea that true virtue must remain hidden; to emerge from obscurity inevitably brings about its corruption.
4. The concepts of ritual, culture, writing, and pattern were inextricably linked in numerous early texts. Thus in the *Book of Rites* (*Li ji*), it is said that "music comes from within; rites are formed without. Since music comes from

within, it belongs to genuine affections; since rites are formed without, they have patterning (*wen*)" (quoted in Owen, *Readings*, p. 55). In the section devoted to rites in *Shiji*, it is stated that "all rites begin in detaching, are brought to completion in patterning (*wen*), and conclude in joy. Hence in its most perfect state, it exhausts both emotion and patterning; inferior to this is when emotion and pattern alternate in predominating; below this, it brings emotion back to the undifferentiated state of cosmic unity (*taiyi*)" (pp. 1193, 1195).

5. Chow, *Rise of Confucian Ritualism*, p. 91 ff.

6. Angela Zito, "Silk and Skin: Significant Boundaries," p. 113.

7. Zhuang's model Cheng Tingzuo is in many ways representative of the eighteenth-century preoccupation with ritual. He stressed that while ritual and music possessed both "form" (literally "numbers," *shu*) and "meaning/intent" (*yi*), the beauty of the former could inspire people to comprehend the latter. Far from remaining merely the vehicle for abstraction or contemplation, ritual provided a means of channeling innate abilities into useful functions:

> Rites and music are things born not of human invention but from heaven. Small children know how to sing. Once they have grown a bit they can dance. They do not require teachers to learn these. The five senses and hundred bones can function from birth. If they are directed into ritual then the body achieves its functions. Through drums, the lute, the zither, archery, and riding, the hands fulfill their function. Nowadays the teaching of ritual and music have been lost, and hence people's innate tendencies are stifled and cannot be fulfilled. [Moreover, many today feel that as long as the intent is understood, the fact that forms have been lost need not be of great concern.] But this is not the way of teaching and studying. ("Liyue lun shang," in Cheng Tingzuo, *Qingxi wenji*, j. 3, pp. 1a–3b)

8. As Ogawa Tamaki has noted, *Rulin waishi* employs allusions to *Shuihu zhuan* at several critical points, such as its invocation of the falling stars from the prologue of the latter work to conclude Wang Mian's biography (Ogawa, *Chūgoku shōsetsu shi no kenkyū*, p. 105 ff.). The Taibo ritual does not seem to contain any direct references to chapter 71 of *Shuihu*, but the order of the ritual presents parallels to the careful delineation of the hierarchy of the outlaws at Liangshan. For *Rulin waishi*'s debt to earlier fiction, see David Rolston, "Theory and Practice," chaps. 2, 3, and 4.

9. Quan Wuyong is reputedly based on Wu's contemporary Shi Jing, who was widely condemned for his excessiveness in observing mourning rituals. See He Zehan, *Rulin waishi renwu benshi kaolue*, p. 10.

10. Dai Zhen's associate and fellow townsman Cheng Yaotian (1725–1814) also discussed the abuse of ritual:

> Why is it that the Way may not prevail in the world? It is because the intelligent go too far; they go beyond [the proper observance of] ritual. The stupid do not go far enough; they do not attain to ritual. The [intelligent] are certainly diligent in seeking to carry out the Way; but quite simply, the Way does not prevail, leading to the transgression of proper bounds and

betrayal of this Way. Hence, the Sages set their minds on the study of ritual alone; they were determined to study ritual in order that they could establish themselves, and that is all. ("Li li pian," in *Lunxue xiaoji*, pp. 6a–7a, in Cheng Yaotian, *Tongyi lu*, vol. 1)

11. The nineteenth-century commentator Huang Xiaotian claims that the elaborate forms of the Taibo ritual merely follow Zhu Xi's "Family Rituals":

A novel that includes laboriously long descriptions of ancient ritual and music is not a novel. This section [chapter 37] appears complex, but in fact is all [derived from] Zhu Xi's "Family Ritual." In my home [of Wuhu, Anhui] it is often used for funerals and festivals. From this we can see that the author cuts his clothing to fit its wearers [i.e., the many scoundrels and fools who participate in the ritual]. While without this level of detail it could not be called a great ritual, one look and we are clear of its true nature. The author took great pains to create this scene that elicits our disgust. (*Rulin waishi*, p. 347)

12. This argument is based on a line by Wu Jingzi's friend Cheng Jinfang that the novel was in "fifty juan," which some took to mean only 50 chapters rather than 55. For a summary of the debate on the authenticity of these sections, see Chen Xin and Du Weimo, "*Rulin waishi* diwushiliu hui zhenwei bian," pp. 153–64.

13. As Shuen-fu Lin puts it,

The apparent diffuseness of Part III [chapters 37–55] is not at all a decline of the author's creative energy. The narrative diffuseness is, on the contrary, *designed* to indicate the total failure of the ideal vision of a perfectly ritualized world so cherished by the central characters in the book. We might consider, therefore, the entire third part as one vast unit corresponding, if only in an antithetical way, to the sacred ceremony at T'ai-po Temple. (Lin, "Ritual and Narrative Structure," p. 262)

14. The late-eighteenth-century scholar Weng Fanggang criticizes the tendencies of the ritualists of his day to proclaim ritual as a sort of simplistic, all-embracing creed:

Ritual is action. People act through it and uphold it, with serious and upright intent. This is ritual. Hence [Confucius said that] "restrain the self and return to the ritual" is the guiding principle, and "do not look, listen, speak, or act without propriety" are its details. This is what the sage told Yan Hui to do in order to act with benevolence. . . . If one is to teach the people of the world to become familiar with the affairs of the world, how can one subsume all this into these [few simple strictures]? One must make clear its three hundred strands, to reach its three thousand nuances. . . . To summarize [ritual] in a few words only betrays incompetence. ("Yuan xue lun," in Weng Fanggang, *Fuchuzhai wenji*, j. 7, pp. 2b–4a).

15. Du Shaoqing's condemnation of concubinage and his liberal attitudes

toward marriage and a more public role for women have generally been interpreted in a positive light by both traditional commentators and modern critics alike. For example, in a recent article Han Shi sees the novel's treatment of Du's marital relations as an attempt to "rectify the sexual excesses of late Ming society, . . . and to bring to realization the aspirations of a new stratum of urban citizenry." He cites examples of famous scholars of the eighteenth and nineteenth centuries who took their wives and female relatives on public excursions, much like Du's stroll with his wife through the Yao Gardens. See Han Shi, "Pisa zai luozhao shifen de xinling zhi guang," pp. 82–84.

16. The use of a series of puns centered on the word *feng* or "wind" seems also to undercut the moral seriousness of the Yus. The narrator as well as the Yus rail against the *fengsu* (customs or social mores) of Wuhe county; the Yu brothers discuss *fengshui* (geomancy) with a number of people in Nanjing and Wuhe; and Yu Youda's partner in crime is Feng Ying (literally "wind and shadows," but figuratively speaking, false accusations). This play on words seems to undercut the Yus by figuratively linking them (through Feng Ying) to the very practices and mores they profess to despise.

17. See T'ien Ju-kang, *Male Anxiety and Female Chastity*, pp. 44–56 ff.

18. Gan Fengchi was the subject of several vitriolic denunciations by the Yongzheng emperor for alleged subversion. He has lived on in popular legend as a member of various assassination plots connected with the succession struggles at the end of the Kangxi reign and is depicted as a Ming loyalist in early-Republican-era fiction.

19. The story of Gao's examination success appears to allude to an anecdote about his model, Cheng Wen. Cheng was said to have written successful essays for his provincial examination with a bit of divine help. See He Zehan, *Rulin waishi renwu benshi kaolue*, p. 124.

20. Li Hanqiu points out that Yu manifests the virtue of "yielding," which was cited as the ruling principle of ritual propriety in canonical texts such as *Zuozhuan, Liji*, and the *Analects*. During an incident of cheating, Yu refuses to accept thanks from a licentiate whom he protected from discovery and expulsion. Li sees this incident as an allusion to the Han figure Chunyu Gong, whom Wu Jingzi praises in his *fu* poem, *Yijiafu*. See Li Hanqiu, "*Rulin waishi* yu chuantong wenhua," pp. 118–20.

21. The words of Wolfgang Iser on literature's relation to thought seem relevant here:

> The field of action in a literary work tends to be on or just beyond the fringes of the particular thought system prevalent at the time. Literature endeavors to counter the problems produced by the system, and so the literary historian should be able not only to gauge which system was in force at the time of the work's creation but also to reconstruct the weaknesses and the historical, human impact of that system and its claims to universality. Through it, we can reconstruct whatever was concealed or ignored by the philosophy or ideology of the day, precisely because these neutralized or negated aspects of reality form the focal point of the literary work. At the

same time, the text must also implicitly contain the basic framework of the system, as this is what causes the problems that literature is to react to. (*The Act of Reading*, p. 74)

22. Chow, *Rise of Confucian Ritualism*, pp. 150–57.

23. Yuan Mei, *Xiaocang shanfang wenji*, j. 1, pp. 1165–67. Yuan also alludes elsewhere to the fragmentation of literati into professions of "scholarship" and "belles lettres," a statement that has been taken by some to refer directly to *Rulin waishi*. But Chen Guang has demonstrated the fallacious nature of this theory (see Chen Guang, "Ping 'You *Rulin waishi* yinqi de yichang fengbo,'" pp. 96–104).

Part III

1. In his discussion of novels of erudition, Lu Xun includes at least two distinct types of novels under the rubric of *yi xiaoshuo xian caixue zhe* (Lu Xun, *Zhongguo xiaoshuo shilue*, pp. 254–68). First, those written in a vernacular medium but displaying an immense body of knowledge on scholarly subjects; and second, novels written in a highly stylized classical medium such as parallel prose that give little if any attention to scholarly matters per se. It is the former that I treat in this discussion.

2. The term "scholar-novelists" was coined by C. T. Hsia to refer to the authors of *Yesou puyan*, *Jinghua yuan*, and the other novels of erudition identified by Lu Xun. See Hsia, "The Scholar-Novelist and Chinese Culture," p. 266 ff.

3. The current consensus seems to be that Xia Jingqu lived from 1702 to 1783, which makes him almost an exact contemporary of Wu Jingzi. Although there is no evidence that the two ever met, it is not inconceivable that they had certain acquaintances in common. One likely candidate is Jin Zhaoyan of Quanjiao Prefecture, Wu's home. Jin spent his younger years studying Neo-Confucian doctrines under Yang Mingshi, a well-known official and native of Jiangyin (see "Yang Mengyu shigao xu," in Jin Zhaoyan, *Zongting guwen chao*, j. 5, pp. 3a–3b). Xia was also a native of Jiangyin and was recommended by Yang Mingshi to participate in the compilation of a work on the Manchu banners (see Sun Kaidi, *Cangzhou houji*, p. 241). Xia moreover competed in the same imperial examination of 1736 to which Wu was also recommended but did not join.

Chapter 7

1. See *Analects* 17.1, 18.7; Yang Bojun, ed., *Lunyu yizhu*, pp. 180, 195.

2. Andrew Plaks has identified the ideal of the recognition and appreciation of talents as a "basic topos of the Chinese literary tradition," prominent in both classical narrative works as well as in later fiction such as *Sanguo yanyi*, *Shuihu zhuan*, and *Honglou meng*. See his "Towards a Critical Theory," p. 346.

3. See *Xunzi*, chap. 28, "Youzuo," in *Xunzi guyi*, p. 453.

4. See "Ou hui," in Wang Chong, *Lun heng*, p. 35.

5. Thomas A. Metzger, *Escape from Predicament*, p. 154.

6. Beginning in the early Qing period, the "pedantic scholar" of high ideals but little practical knowledge became a familiar character in numerous works of fiction and drama. Such characters appear to give voice to the widening gaps between scholarly knowledge and the realm of action.

7. All references to Xia Jingqu's *Yesou puyan* are to the edition published by Wenhua tushu gongsi (Taipei, 1982).

8. Luan Xing summarizes the reaction of Qing readers as one of "disgust for its bizarre, pedantic, ribald, and unrealistic passages" ("Xin jiaoben *Yesou puyan* xu," p. 102). Interestingly, however, Luan notes that while little read, the work nonetheless gave rise to several anecdotes collected in local gazetteers and *biji*, relating the author's purported attempt to present it to the Qianlong emperor during one of his trips to the south.

9. Lu Xun, *Zhongguo xiaoshuo shilue*, p. 246; Zhao Jingshen, *Xia Jinggu xiansheng nianpu*, p. 23ff. For biographical information on the author, Xia Jingqu, see also Sun Kaidi, "Xia Erming yu *Yesou puyan*," in *Cangzhou houji*, pp. 238–47).

10. Lu Xun, *Zhongguo xiaoshuo shilue*, p. 258. There are a number of superficial similarities between *Yesou puyan* and the widely popular though somewhat atypical romance *Haoqiu zhuan*. The hero of the latter work is like Wen Suchen a literatus of martial abilities (surnamed Tie, or iron), who proves his worth on the battlefield rather than in literary examinations. And his beloved is surnamed Shui, that is, the same as Wen's mother, Mme Shui.

11. According to Keith McMahon, "The fullest model of a successful man in Qing fiction is still that of the potent polygamist, who in terms of Ming-Qing literary history amounts to an idealistic reparation of the dissipated Ximen Qing." *Yesou puyan* creates perhaps the least lascivious version of this type in Wen Suchen, the "chaste polygamist" (*Misers, Shrews, and Polygamists*, pp. 11, 75).

12. The problem with the examination system is that it is often unreliable in recognizing men of talent, especially when government is in the hands of corrupt elements. Thus while Wen's friends eventually all do well in the examinations, so too do a number of uncouth and undeserving young fops. "When corruption is possible, one's essays are useless!" Wen laments on seeing a list of successful candidates (Xia Jingqu, *Yesou puyan*, chap. 52, p. 452). When Wen's eldest son Wen Long passes first in the metropolitan examinations, it is discovered that his essay is an exact copy of the one his father wrote at his first and only attempt at gaining an examination degree, proving that success is "only a matter of timing" (chap. 123, p. 1073). And in any event, examinations detract from more important concerns: "How could I ever be willing to abandon worthy actions that are within my power to accomplish, in order to pursue an unnecessary, empty examination degree?" (chap. 23, p. 217).

13. As Wen's mother Mme Shui explains, "In times of peace civil arts are valued, while in times of unrest martial skills find appreciation" (Xia Jingqu, *Yesou puyan*, chap. 60, p. 520). Since the world of the novel is perched precariously between order and disorder, both are important. But as was discussed in Chapter 6, many Qing writers of the seventeenth and eighteenth centuries

deplored the literati's lack of interest in obtaining martial skills. Perhaps the most noteworthy of these was Wang Yuan, an associate of Li Gong and admirer of Yan Yuan. See his "Yu Wang Libu shu," in Wang Yuan, *Juyetang wenji*, j. 6, pp. 6b–7b.

14. McMahon places Mme Shui in the literary tradition of the shrew, a ubiquitous character type in Ming and Qing fiction. She is an example of a shrew who "takes the form of wise mother instead of jealous wife" (*Misers, Shrews, and Polygamists*, p. 81).

15. Mme Shui appears in many respects to be the literary descendant of the *nü zhong yingxiong* or "hero among women" of late-Ming and Qing fiction, who in the words of Judith Zeitlin, "exhibits a degree of personal integrity and morality considered highly untypical of her sex" (*Historian of the Strange*, p. 130). Such women often assumed male guise in order to carry out acts of heroism or self-sacrifice, through which they gained qualities identified with the stronger sex. But as the novel's allusions to the romance tradition suggest, Mme Shui pointedly remains within the confines of her domestic boundaries. And while encouraging the young women who venture out into the male world to do good deeds while there, she uses her powers of moral suasion to return them to feminine roles at the earliest opportunity.

16. This particularly Neo-Confucian emphasis on the ordering of the household as a prerequisite to political reform is not unique to *Yesou puyan*, but as Andrew Plaks and others have argued, informs the structure of the Ming novel *Jin Ping Mei* (*Ssu ta ch'i-shu*, p. 103ff.). But Mme Shui does not act simply as Wen Suchen's surrogate during his absences from home; she is given complete authority for all aspects of domestic life.

17. This portrayal of heterodoxy could be seen as a partial rebuttal, as well as an elaboration, of the more benign views of the playwright and poet Jiang Shiquan, a slightly younger contemporary of Xia Jingqu. In the words of Alexander Woodside, Jiang

> argued in a celebrated essay on Buddhism and Taoism that the complete extirpation of these two religions had always been quite within the powers of the Chinese state. So far they had not been extirpated. Three factors, Chiang thought, accounted for their survival: the mischievously abstruse scholasticism of Chinese intellectuals, which had concealed the principles of the Confucian sages; the inadequacy of Chinese economic and educational institutions; and the paradoxical fact that such "heterodox" religions had shepherded some of the masses away from heterodoxy, or at least from an indulgence in banditry, and had thus given minor aid to the state's functions of "nourishing" and "teaching" its people. ("State, Scholars, and Orthodoxy," p. 163)

Along with this tolerance, however, Jiang also castigates the pernicious effects of these doctrines, namely, that they had been used to delude the masses: "Some devious scholars have elaborated the truths of Confucius and Mencius into Buddhist gathas, obscuring the direct and straightforward truths of the sages behind complex and abstruse words, thereby altering their appearance. This leads average people to be frightened into believing that Buddhist and Taoist teachings are superior to those of Confucius and Mencius. How foolish this is." Moreover, Jiang insists that the solution to these delusions is to impress upon the masses that Confucian doctrines also embrace realms such as the afterlife: "[When Buddhists or Taoists die], if luminous they become simply another intelligent and just god. The Confucians who have died and become gods are too numerous too count. Why do we need Buddhism and Taoism?" (Jiang makes a similar point in an essay on the Taoist doctrine of immortality) (Jiang Shiquan, *Zhongyatang wenji*, j. 1, p. 3a).

18. The culmination of this sexual frenzy comes when Wen is called to the palace to save the imperial consorts from an attack by small dragons that crawl into their sexual parts, a situation that has resulted from the palace's reckless faith in numerous Buddhist and Taoist priests. Wen counteracts them by writing his name across the bosoms of the palace ladies; and the rebellion instigated by these charlatans is finally quelled when the usurper the Prince of Jing is killed through sexual techniques (Xia Jingqu, *Yesou puyan*, chap. 108, p. 933 ff.).

19. Keith McMahon has argued that *Yesou puyan* presents a Confucian sexuality expressing "male energy" that was in many respects a departure from the eroticism of late-Ming and Qing fiction. See McMahon, "A Case for Confucian Sexuality."

20. This concern with the ordering of the family conforms to the program of "cultivation of the self, ordering of the family, and pacification of the world" enumerated in the Neo-Confucian canonical text *The Great Learning*. While other fiction of the Ming and Qing periods, most notably the romance tradition, also blends concern for family and state together along similar lines, *Yesou puyan* is unprecedented in its depiction of female domesticity as the linchpin of this entire process.

21. Hou Jian has analyzed the descriptions of sexual perversity in the novel, arguing that they express a "perverse" mentality. See Hou Jian, "*Yesou puyan* de biantai xinli," pp. 8–23. In a discussion of sexual deviancy in the novel, McMahon underscores the "cold" judgment that is exercised by its heroes toward its many grotesqueries: "The author's final construct is of the woman thus divided into lascivious spectacle versus paradise of retreat" (*Misers, and Shrews, and Polygamists*, p. 164).

22. The term *shuixing* or "watery nature" referred to female inconstancy.

23. *Lao Tzu: Tao Te Ching*, pp. 64, 140.

24. According to Pei-yi Wu, water imagery was particularly significant in a number of autobiographical writings recounting spiritual maturation or experiences: "In China the challenge of sailing over a body of water, especially amidst a tempest, seems to have a greater allegorical meaning than other trials. ... [P]assage over stormy waters would evoke primordial fears and demand appropriate responses" (*The Confucian's Progress*, p. 123).

25. The women Xu Qianqian (whose beloved is also of the Shui clan) and

Mrs. Shi, Wen's sister-in-law, are described as having fallen into the "watery realm" of prostitution. In Shi's case, she does so literally after nearly drowning in the waters of the Qiantangjiang and is rescued only to be sold to a Yangzhou brothel. Later as both are transported up the Grand Canal to be presented as palace women in the capital, water imagery continues to predominate (Xia Jingqu, *Yesou puyan*, chaps. 33–34, pp. 301–10).

26. Wen is particularly fearful of journeys into the open ocean, where he must travel on occasion to visit the rebellious forces on the "twenty-four islands." While he rushes over land at a moment's notice to save friends in danger (for example in chapter 30 when Wen leaves Jiangxi for the north without even bothering to pack clothing or money for the trip), he is hesitant to board a ship even for a noble cause: "The sea, unlike terra firma, is not my strong suit!" he complains (Xia Jingqu, *Yesou puyan*, chap. 47, p. 415).

27. While on the doctrinal level Wen champions *yang*, in his employment of Five Phases symbology he relies most frequently on the trigram *kan* (two *yin* surrounding one *yang*), in doing battle with his enemies. The virtue of this trigram lies in its qualities of concealment and quietude: "Fire [of the belligerent heterodox forces] is defeated by water, and metal by two waters, so how can fire or arrows harm us?" (Xia Jingqu, *Yesou puyan*, chap. 44, p. 395).

28. Later it is said that the dragon is actually the spirit of Jin's grandfather (Xia Jingqu, *Yesou puyan*, chap. 25, p. 222).

29. The difficulties dragons pose to females are graphically illustrated in chapter 108, where the imperial palace is invaded by a swarm of little dragons that attack the sexual parts of the palace women. For an enlightening analysis of the iconographic significance of the dragon in Chinese art and literature, see François Julien, *La Propension des choses*, pp. 141–51. Julien emphasizes the dual nature of the dragon: "Le dragon est à la fois yin au sein du yang et yang au sein du yin; son corps se métamorphose constamment sans jamais s'épuiser: on ne saurait imaginer de plus belle incarnation de l'alternance comme moteur de la continuité" (p. 143).

30. Torrential rains and flooding are an agent of divine retribution against the human corruption of Mingshuizhen (literally, "Town of Clear Waters"), the locus of the greater part of the action in the novel *Xingshi yinyuan zhuan*. This town is ironically described as a place favored by the sweet springs beneath a temple to the dragon king. Such special aqueous conditions have created an atmosphere in which learning flourishes, where everyone can "*zhi hu zhe ye*" (utter a few classical phrases), and which produces "extraordinary men" (*jieren*). Its moral climate has deteriorated, however, and divine authorities inundate its inhabitants with a flood that supposedly washes away its unsavory elements. See Xi Zhou Sheng, *Xingshi yinyuan zhuan*, chap. 29, pp. 419–32.

31. Bodies of water can also provide refuges of comfort and relaxation. Wen and his wives discover a watery world through a cave near their home, whose beauty and bathing pleasures and pleasant year-round climate make it an ideal retreat for the family, a "felicitous piece of heaven on earth." It also provides protection from dangers by virtue of its inaccessibility and is praised

as a place where "the soft can conquer the strong." Wen names it "Butan dong," the "Cave without covetousness" (Xia Jingqu, *Yesou puyan*, chap. 63, p. 549ff.).

32. Wen's eldest son Wen Long (or "dragon," named for this since he was born under the astrological sign of water) is given place of honor, and most extensive coverage, among Wen's progeny. He takes first place in the palace examinations at the age of eight and rises to the rank of provincial governor of Jiangxi in his tenth year. The son of Wen's principal wife, née Tian, he is practically adopted by his mother-in-law Wei Luanchui, who accompanies him to his official post in Jiangxi, her native province. When he becomes dangerously ill after falling into a pool of water, Wei revives him by letting him suckle at her breast (even though he is already a high official by this point). In his official duties Long comes to rely on a mysterious adviser, who helps him to turn his administration into the most effective in the history of the dynasty. Together their deeds reassert the worth of classically trained literati over other elements of the official world that have usurped their prerogatives, such as the clerks (*li*). This adviser (*muke*) ultimately turns out to be the woman Wei Jiao (also a "dragon"), who discards her male attire to wed Wen Long as his concubine (chapters 127–29). Other sons are more dependent on their natal mothers, mimicking Wen's absolute obedience to Mme Shui.

33. As Wen's father-in-law Magistrate Ren puts it after reading Wen's poem "Thinking of Mother While Aboard a Boat," "When a person does not meet with appreciation of his contemporaries, then whether sage or fool, the end is the same" (Xia Jingqu, *Yesou puyan*, chap. 21, p. 193). Elsewhere this is phrased often as "meeting with someone who recognizes [one's worth]" (*yu shizhe*).

34. Wen Suchen's treatment of his servants, in particular the boys Xi Nang and Jin Nang, is notable for his concern for their welfare (he sets out on a lengthy journey to find the former after losing him on the West Lake) and recognition of the contributions they can make toward their great enterprise against heterodoxy. As Wen prepares to wed his three concubines in chapters 58–60, Xi Nang also finds himself with two brides and exhibits similarly exemplary conduct in bringing these relationships to an honorable conclusion. Mme Shui praises him for his "magnanimity" (*yiqi*):

> Even among the literati who proclaim the Way and discourse on government administration, how many change their course with the wind, or throw rocks upon those in trouble? Truly it is as the ancients said: "Between the exalted and the humble, friendship may appear; but in a life and death situation, we can see the extent of a friendship." . . . Though of low status, Xi Nang can act like a true man [*junzi*]. (Xia Jingqu, *Yesou puyan*, chap. 59, p. 508)

35. The term *siyi*, or Four Arts, normally refers to the elegant pursuits of the *qin* (lute), *go*, calligraphy, and painting, that is, the avocations of the literati.

The arts advocated by Wen Suchen suggest more practically minded concerns similar to those of Yan Yuan's.

36. The emphasis on *qing*, or emotion, as a basis on which ethical relationships are built can be traced back to Xunzi. But *qing* in the context of theatrical entertainment suggests the late Ming aesthetics of Tang Xianzu, Feng Menglong, and other playwrights who championed its importance in drama. Feng Menglong's views on the subject can be found in his preface to *Qingshi* (pp. 1–2).

37. Alexander Woodside points out that the anti-heterodox views of many Qing writers seem to have arisen as much from low-ranking, poverty-stricken members of the intelligentsia as from the more privileged and presumably culturally sophisticated:

> Poor scholars, far from being heterodox themselves, might demand the repression of heterodox behavior as a convenient way of safely flaying the unlettered rich, and as a way also of regaining the dignity that their poverty had cost them. People whom Ch'ien-lung called "poor Confucians," of whom there were now an enormous number, might logically be the ones most interested in unimpeachably "orthodox" institutions such as the egalitarian well-field system. Ch'iu Chia-sui . . . saw Ch'ing history as a dramatic struggle between "us Confucians" and a single offensive bloc of Buddhists, Taoists, and "rich people" who had stirred up "stupid people" by jointly usurping the beautiful clothes and sophisticated music, which, in all propriety, should have been monopolized by scholars. ("State, Scholars, and Orthodoxy," pp. 175–76)

Xia Jingqu certainly seems to fit into such a category of low-ranking literati (he did not even achieve the first rank of licentiate in the examinations); and this ideological purism is indeed matched by a corresponding concern to bring recognition first and foremost to the unrecognized literati of the land.

38. See also Xia Jingqu, *Yesou puyan*, chap. 77, p. 660, on Pao Fen: "People are attracted to anomalies [*guai*]."

39. Liu Xuangu is distinguished for her mathematical abilities and spends her spare moments doing calculations. A number of the ploys used to attempt to lure her into her seducer's arms appeal to various superstitious beliefs, such as the divination technique known as "Nine light and nine dark." But in each case she recognizes the implausibility of the arguments and fails to be taken in.

40. The issue of desire and its place in human life is discussed on numerous occasions. Indeed, one of the central issues for the novel's characters, both male and female, is the question of how to achieve the ideal of chastity, that is, to bring desire into conformity with the rules of propriety. For example, when Wen first learns of Shui Lianggong's love for the prostitute Xu Qianqian, he opposes it as a dangerous liaison. But Xu's poetry convinces him of her commitment to chastity (Xia Jingqu, *Yesou puyan*, chap. 48, p. 429).

41. The most blatantly pedantic character in the novel is actually the Taoist

Hu Taixuan. Hu (a fox spirit that has assumed human form) gives a lengthy sermon on Taoist doctrines in a garbled form of classical Chinese (Xia Jingqu, *Yesou puyan*, chap. 49, pp. 433–40).

42. The popularity of stories of ghosts, fox spirits, and other supernatural phenomena reached new heights during the mid-to-late eighteenth century with the publication of *Liaozhai zhiyi, Zibuyu* by Yuan Mei and *Yuewei caotang biji* by Ji Yun, as well as numerous less well known collections. According to Leo Tak-hong Chan this reflected a serious debate in intellectual circles over the existence of ghosts, the participants of which included such eminent scholars as Hong Liangji and Qian Daxin, the painter Luo Ping, noted for his renditions of ghosts, as well as the writers of the latter two collections. Chan argues that for Ji Yun "the purpose of his collection was to bolster belief" in supernatural phenomena ("The *Yuewei caotang biji* and the Late Eighteenth-Century Elite Discourse on the Supernatural," p. 43). "Ji Yun and the raconteurs [of his stories] became engaged in what can be termed 'zhiguai hermeneutics,' taking the 'strange' events as signs to be decoded in accordance with beliefs about an unseen, second order of reality" (p. 49). The arguments in *Yesou puyan* made in favor of the existence of the supernatural appear to echo Ji Yun and others whom Chan identifies as sympathetic toward such beliefs.

43. This passage closely follows Zhu Xi's discussion of ghosts and spirits, which he explained in terms of the doctrine of *qi*. As Yung Sik Kim describes his doctrines on the subject, Zhu sought to bring occult and superstitious practices in to the realm of the rational *qi*. See Kim, "*Kuei-shen* in Terms of *Ch'i*," pp. 149–64. The real question for literati was perhaps less the recognition of the existence of deities worshiped by local populations than the acceptance of these popular deities as equals to those in the officially recognized pantheon. As Romeyn Taylor points out, "The disdain of the Confucian ceremonialists for the popular religion was apparent in such issues as 'idolatry' in popular practice and belief, the popular disposition to dispense with analytical distinctions among celestial, terrestrial, and human spirits, and its lumping of all gods under the category of human spirits" ("Official and Popular Religion and Political Organization of Chinese Society in the Ming, p. 156). What Wen Suchen appears to be advocating for the spirits, then, is the equivalent of his activities in the temporal realm: the recognition of powers and abilities beyond the narrowly circumscribed domain of the state-sponsored cults.

44. Richard Smith argues that diviners "helped bridge the gap between commoners and the élite in Ch'ing dynasty China. By summoning up visions of orthodox heroes and urging clients to embrace conventional values, fortune-tellers reinforced the dominant literati culture. For this reason, among others, they periodically received commendation by local officials for their skill as prognosticators" ("Divination in Ch'ing Dynasty China," p. 166). There is no question that Wen's assumption of such status diminishes his social standing, however; he is often turned away from official yamen, for example, which forbid "doctors, astrologers, and prognosticators" from entry (Xia Jingqu, *Yesou puyan*, chap. 51, p. 451).

45. The willingness to tolerate and even give credence to popular deities while at the same time demonstrating their temporal origins can also be found in the writings of Shen Dacheng, a contemporary of Xia Jingqu and acquaintance of Wu Jingzi. In discussing the origins of the deity Wenchang, Shen states that

> I have seen the work "An offering to the Zitong Spirit" by Sun Qiao of the Tang, in which he speaks of powers of flying through the heavens and giving rise to wind and rain. But no mention is made of prayers of examination success and official position [which Wenchang was said to have charge of]. ... Nevertheless, in ancient times gods were propitiated for many different things. Hence farmers gave offerings to the stars, and silk cocoon [cultivators] to heavenly horses. Nowadays literati give offerings to Wenchang, so he should be called the God of Wenchang. In this way the name will be fitting and offerings proper. ("Wenchang hui xu," in Shen Dacheng, *Xuefuzhai wenji*, j. 8, p. 1b)

46. There are numerous examples of discourses that attempt to correct or rationalize popular beliefs and superstitions. In a rather scientific vein, Wen points out the fallacy of using the word "Heavenly River" (the Milky Way) to describe the stars (Xia Jingqu, *Yesou puyan*, chap. 78, p. 661). He is also rather disconcerted by the news that a popular legend has already grown up around him that he is an incarnation of the Buddhist god Erlang (chap. 46, p. 409).

47. The uncanny presents perhaps the greatest challenge simply because it is not directly accessible to observation. Some, such as those associated with Buddhist and Taoist beliefs, are clearly baseless superstitions that should be repudiated. But other incidences of inexplicable phenomena must be investigated to determine their meaning. Wen himself is often confused by the contradictory signs and portents presented to him in dreams. Moreover, seemingly insignificant remarks and encounters often turn out to bear surprising relevance to future events. Essentially, the message seems to be that an open but cautious attitude represents the best way to approach supernatural phenomena.

48. Another example of this emphasis on directly perceivable, concrete knowledge is a discussion of Neo-Confucian doctrines by Mme Shui's maids (Xia Jingqu, *Yesou puyan*, chap. 62, p. 538).

Chapter 8

1. All citations to *Jinghua yuan* by Li Ruzhen are to the 1954 edition published by Zhonghua shuju (Beijing) and subsequently reprinted by Dingwen shuju (Taipei, 1981).

2. On the blending of Taoist and Confucian elements in the novel, see Chen Wenxin, "*Jinghua yuan* yu rudao wenhua," pp. 197–209.

3. Hu Shih, "*Jinghua yuan* de yinlun," in *Hu Shi wencun*, vol. 2, pp. 400–433. For more recent assessments, see Ropp, *Dissent*, pp. 116, 147 ff; Hsia, "Scholar-Novelist," pp. 286–94; Frederick Brandauer, "Women in the *Ching-hua yuan*,"

pp. 647–60; Bao Jialin, "Li Ruzhen de nannü pingdeng sixiang," pp. 620–29; and Qingyun Wu, *Female Rule in Chinese and English Literary Utopias*, chap. 4.

4. Ono Kazuko argues that the women of *Jinghua yuan* serve as vehicles for the democratization of knowledge and learning ("*Kyōka en no sekai*," pp. 40–55).

5. The scholar-beauty romance *Nü kaike zhuan* (An account of an examination for women") of the Kangxi period (Wang Xiaohai postulates its date of publication as 1703–4; see his "Nü kaike zhuan chengsu shijian ji banben zixing kaolue," pp. 183–90) foreshadows the examinations in *Jinghua yuan* in a number of ways. Like the later novel, *Nü kaike zhuan* also presents a fanciful examination for women (in this case, the prostitutes of Suzhou) that mimics and satirizes aspects of normative civil examinations such as cheating, the arrogance of successful candidates and shame of failed ones, and vacuity of examination learning. But in spite of the prominence of this event in the novel's title this examination serves primarily as a prelude to the main plot, namely the love affairs between several scholars and beauties. Moreover, unlike most examples of the generally chaste fiction of this genre it is rich in salacious passages and bawdy humor; of most relevance here is its description of uniquely feminine methods of concealing cheat sheets by its "candidates."

6. This divergence between male and female attitudes toward Wu Zetian's usurpation contrasts markedly with the vernacular novel *Lü mudan* (The green peony), which was published roughly two decades before *Jinghua yuan* (the earliest extant edition is dated 1800). This slightly earlier work is also set during Wu Zetian's reign, and its plot shares many elements with Li Ruzhen's work, including the prominence of talented young girls, a special female examination, and the banding together of Tang loyalists to fight for the restoration. But the women of *Lü mudan*, many of whom are warriors of great martial prowess, are directly involved in the opposition to Wu Zetian's rule and fully share the political ideals of their male brethren. Indeed, it seems quite possible that Li Ruzhen may have used this rather conventional "knight-errant" novel as a source or even a blueprint for his work, "transposing" the former, so to speak, into the medium of the scholarly novel.

7. The intellectualized gender reversal of *Jinghua yuan* brings to full fruition the aspects of *Yesou puyan* discussed earlier. In spite of the scholarly interests of its female characters, *Yesou puyan* has its women take up male interests and vocations largely for moral reasons. Moreover, in many romances, female chastity figures as an important motif, a concern that is rarely even mentioned in *Jinghua yuan*. As T'ien Ju-k'ang has argued, the obsession with female chastity of the Ming and Qing periods seems to correlate with the frustration of failed literati: "Recurring disappointment because of repeated failure in the examinations engendered a personal wrath in Chinese scholars which in turn then created a desire to identify with the weaker sex in order to gratify, either consciously or subconsciously, an unwarranted sense of moral superiority" (*Male Anxiety and Female Chastity*, p. 89). Judith Zeitlin's analysis of gender reversal in late Ming and early Qing fiction seems to corroborate this, for she

finds many of its women to be concerned primarily with the moral dimensions of masculine gender roles (*Historian of the Strange*, p. 127 ff.).

8. Wu Zetian is inspired to hold the examinations purportedly after being moved by the poetic talents exhibited by her female subjects (specifically, the acrostic poetry of Su Ruolan's *Xuanji tu* [chap. 42, pp. 290–306]). This is an intriguing twist to the historical Empress Wu, who is credited with being the first ruler to use imperially sponsored national examinations as an important method to recruit officials. In the words of E. A. Kracke,

> The first significant increase [in successful candidates] came abruptly with the rise to power of the ambitious Wu Tse-t'ien. Her sharp eye discerned in the technique of examinations, it seems, a tool for her projected usurpation of power. It might serve to tap the heretofore neglected source of trained men in the Southeast and help to dislodge from power the tightly knit clique from the capital region, which was devoted to the interest of the reigning dynasty. ... She thus, perhaps unintentionally, established the quantitative importance of examinations for recruitment. At the same time, by the favored treatment of the graduates, she enhanced the prestige of the new method as the accepted channel to power. The process of opening opportunities to wider groups had begun. ("Religion, Family, and Individual in the Chinese Examination System," p. 253)

The eighteenth-century historian Zhao Yi praises her ability to accept criticism and to promote men of integrity and ability—in other words to effectively utilize human talent drawn from a wide social and geographical sphere. It is appropriate that this proponent of civil examinations be cast as an advocate of casting the net of government service ever wider, to include women as well as men (*Ershier shi zhaji*, pp. 415–17). For a discussion of Wu Zetian's portrayal in the novel, see Li Qilin, "Lun *Jing hua yuan*," pp. 279–90.

9. Hsia, "Scholar-Novelist," p. 273 ff.

10. Gender reversal is, as already mentioned above, a common motif of late Ming and Qing fiction. Although as Zeitlin suggests male attributes are associated predominantly with moral qualities, *Jinghua yuan*'s transposition of such motifs into a more intellectual setting is prefigured by some of the works of *caizi jiaren* or scholar beauty romances of the early-to-mid Qing period. On this see Keith McMahon, "The Classic 'Beauty-Scholar' Romances and the Superiority of Talented Women," pp. 227–52. *Jinghua yuan* is largely unprecedented, however, in the structural complexity of its gender reversal. Moreover, while scholar-beauty romances "are often built around the conceit of cross-dressing" (McMahon, p. 243), aside from the episode at Nüerguo, and among a few martially adept women, the girls of *Jinghua yuan* do not assume male attributes other than literary and scholarly knowledge.

11. Licentiates were required to undergo examinations on a yearly basis, or whenever educational intendants visited their localities. See Shang Yanliu, *Qingdai keju kaoshi shulu*, pp. 18–19; also see Wang Dezhao, *Qingdai keju zhidu shulu*, pp. 21–22, 35 ff.

12. Its descriptions of examination fervor in *Jinghua yuan*, chapters 63–67, echo those of *Rulin waishi*, in particular the famous episode in chapters 3–4 describing Fan Jin's temporary insanity after learning of his successful passing of the *juren* examination.

13. Much is made of various wordplays of "sour" (*suan*) throughout the novel. In addition to its identification with pedantic knowledge and examination study, it is also frequently invoked to describe unpleasant experiences during the girls' examinations and later merrymaking: namely, "soreness," as when they must stand too long (*zhan suan*), "sadness," as when the girls grow teary-eyed (*yan suan*) at the mention of misfortune.

14. For a view of the contrasts between the women of *Jinghua yuan* and *Honglou meng*, see Mao Zhongxian, "Jinghua yuan dui Honglou meng nü xing wenti de fansi," pp. 56–59. Mao argues that in contrast to the helpless females of its predecessor, *Jinghua yuan* creates an image of "strong" women who "can struggle tenaciously in adversity, helping themselves and others through determined study" (p. 57).

15. Bian Bi's condition is called *jingfeng* (literally "frightened by the wind"). In the allegorical tale with which the novel begins, flowers are also vulnerable to the wind spirit, who later engages in a heated argument with the girls over her power over them (*Jinghua yuan*, chap. 88, pp. 661–67). It seems that the vulnerability of youth—both male and female—to the elements, particularly wind, serves as another reminder of the contingency of life. In a discussion of the concept of wind in traditional Chinese medicine, Shigehisa Kuriyama summarizes its function as a means to "probe the ever-present edge of chaos. This was the fascination of winds: they embodied contingency and chance, the obstinate halo of uncertainty that made all science only approximate. Evil winds arose unexpectedly, spontaneously, irregularly; they made abrupt, harsh shifts" ("The Imagination of Winds and the Development of the Chinese Conception of the Body," p. 37).

16. Ono Kazuko sees the novel as reflecting a sea change in scholarly trends of the Jiaqing era, when evidential studies turned from a "search for the past" to the "search for accuracy." See Ono, "Kyōka en no sekai," p. 54.

17. This initial controversy is echoed during the final drinking game of the banquet, the rules of which require rhyming and alliteration according to the metrical system of the *qieyun* (laid down by Shen Yue of the sixth century A.D.) and the subject of discussion at Heichiguo. Several of the girls make mistakes, generally because they follow the simplified modern pronunciations or do not follow Shen's scheme. After listening to a list of some particularly confusing examples of rhyming categories, one girl attempts to shrug off the rules of the game: "During a single lifetime he [Shen Yue] served emperors of the Song, Qi, and Liang dynasties. We can imagine what he thought of the word 'fidelity,' so why should we bother with the rest?" (*Jinghua yuan*, chap. 85, p. 638). And a particularly inept girl resorts to cursing Shen as the "old man of Huzhou" (chap. 93, p. 718). Like Duo Jiugong, these girls resort to moral sanctimoniousness when their verbal skills fail them.

18. This divergence between philosophers/statesmen and scholars is discussed in dispassionate terms by Zhang Xuecheng in his essay "Bo yue shang." Zhang notes that scholars often cite a remark by Su Shi to the effect that both can attain understanding as well as wide learning (*boshan*); but, Zhang adds, such learning is invariably shallow. Though fine for those who seek only an official career and social utility, those pursuing serious scholarship must devote themselves to in-depth study of textual minutiae ("Bo yue shang," in *Wenshi tongyi*, j. 2, p. 157).

19. Although the *Analects* first gives voice to this doctrine (13.3 and elsewhere), among classical philosophers Xunzi articulated the rectification of names in greatest detail. In his degenerate era, Xunzi complains that "men are careless in abiding by established names, strange words come into use, names and realities become confused, and the distinction between right and wrong has become unclear" (*Xunzi guyi*, pp. 615–16; Burton Watson, trans., *Hsun Tzu*, p. 141). Rectification requires returning to the original simplicity of names and simultaneously eliminating the plethora of complex and conflicting names that have proliferated due to the work of fools and petty men (*Xunzi guyi*, p. 618; Watson, pp. 143–45).

20. As commentators and critics have widely noted, *Jinghua yuan* is highly innovative in its use of legends taken from *Shanhai jing* and other sources, weaving stories out of fragmentary names and cryptic descriptions. In the view of Sun Jiaxun, this creativity is almost completely unprecedented in earlier works of fiction such as *Shuihu zhuan* or *Xiyou ji*. See Sun Jiaxun, *Jinghua yuan gongan bianyi*, p. 130; also see Shao Shiquan, "Lun *Jinghua yuan* dui Zhongguo gudian xiaoshuo meixue biaozhun de xin tuozhan," pp. 119–24.

21. Such interest in this work was undoubtedly influenced by the renascence of historical geography during the eighteenth century. Moreover, Dai Zhen's philological studies of *Shuijingzhu* (The annotated classic of waterways) created a major scholarly controversy during the mid-to-late Qianlong period. See Hu Shih, "A Note on Ch'üan Tsu-wang, Chao I-ch'ing, and Tai Chen," pp. 970–82.

22. See Bi Yuan, *Shanhai jing jiaozhu*, p. 3.

23. What perhaps interested scholars most, however, was what they felt to be the surprisingly uncorrupted state of the text's orthography. It had, Sun Xingyuan asserts, escaped transcription into a standardized orthography during the Warring States period and thus preserved the most ancient forms of many characters. See Sun's preface in Bi Yuan, *Shanhai jing jiaozhu*, pp. 2a–3a.

24. The Fairy of the Hundred Fruits appears at the banquet to protect the girls against the female spirits Chang'e and Fengyi, who are referred to here as "Yuedan" (Woman of the Moon) and "Fengkuang" (Wind Idiot). Both of these words also mean "criticism" and "satire," that is, words that can harm or destroy one's good name (*Jinghua yuan*, chap. 87, p. 660).

25. The problem of fame and its place in Confucian discourse seems to have received renewed attention in the late Qianlong and Jiaqing eras. While

286 / *Notes to Page 197*

Song and Ming Neo-Confucians tended to disparage the pursuit of fame as a distraction from true moral seriousness, Qing figures (such as Zhao Yi, quoted in Chapter 2) sought to reassert its importance, frequently quoting the passage "The gentleman hates not leaving behind a name when he is gone" (*Analects* 15.20). But in Li Ruzhen's time some came to question this enthusiasm. In his essay "Bian ming" Jiao Xun makes the following argument against the use of fame as an inducement for motivating literati to abide by moral standards:

> The recluse Gu Yanwu said that a corrupt social climate should be rectified by fame [*ming*]. In the past I thought this to be true, but later grew doubtful. Name [*ming*] is tied to content [*shi*], and corresponds to something by resemblance. Mr. Gu would have us use name to save the mores of the day. But I do not know if by "to save" he meant to award fame based upon content, or to give reward based on fame. Fame is forgotten by gentlemen and petty men alike. The gentleman says "I will act to the best of my ability, and that is all." The petty man says "I will seek [fulfillment of] my desires and that is all." But to fulfill desires a person need not be motivated by name. Since fame does not motivate, one tempts people with rewards. Those who live up to their fame are given office, while those who don't are rejected. In this way are people motivated by fame. But by doing so, it is hard to know if they truly live up to their reputation. Moreover, tempting people with profit is not any more difficult than tempting them with fame. And while it is easy to understand how mores are corrupted by profit, it is difficult to determine how they are corrupted by fame. Men turn to where fame is. To exhaust their thoughts and talents in affairs that are reprehensible and shameless is easy. To do so in the pursuit of fame, one praises and boasts, chases after vacuity and engages in sham. Seeking appearances, they fish for praise by fawning upon others, but this compromise of principles grows ever more serious, resulting in the ruin of public mores. . . . Hence I say that to save the mores of our times, this should be done by content [and not name]. (*Diaogulou ji*, j. 8, pp. 109–11)

Jiao implies that the complexity and vagaries of name make it ultimately more dangerous than a simpler and more straightforward system of rewards and punishments, a judgment with which Dai Zhen's contemporary Cheng Yaotian (in his essay "Shu ming") is essentially in agreement. Moreover, as the slightly earlier Qian Daxin and Zhang Xuecheng both warned, the pursuit of fame induces strife, competition, and the development of new heterodoxies. See Qian Daxin, "Ming jian," in *Qian Yantang wenji*, j. 17, p. 1a, and Zhang Xuecheng, "Yu Chen Jianting lunxue," in *Zhangshi yishu*, vol. 1, j. 9, pp. 332–33.

26. These four vices are often invoked in Ming and Qing vernacular fiction, most prominently by *Jin ping mei cihua*, as the sources of human calamity.

27. Wu Zetian's image in both the historical record as well as the popular imagination was one of excessive cruelty and sexual license. Zhao Yi attributes the problems of the Tang dynasty in general, both Wu Zetian's usurpation as well as its later problems, to sexual profligacy (*Ershier shi zhaji*, pp. 411–15).

28. In her contribution to the drinking game, Tang Xiaoshan cites a line from the Taoist Ge Hong, "To say that the Yellow Emperor and Lao Tzu are mistaken, is this not a pity?" To which another girl adds the commentary, "Don't even speak about becoming an immortal or comprehending the Tao. It would be enough if people can just take the pursuit of fame and fortune less seriously." Moreover, Tang says that a joke made just a few pages earlier about a "Zen koan" (*chanji*) led her to think of this. The joke pokes fun at the tendency of Zen Buddhist masters to use logical conundrums without expecting people to take them literally (*Jinghua yuan*, chap. 93, p. 713).

29. As noted in Chapter 3, Li Ruzhen's teacher Ling Tingkan stressed the formal aspects of ritual and phonological studies as antidotes to the vacuity of Confucian learning:

> Rituals are concrete manifestations of righteousness. If one accords with righteousness, then this is ritual. Even the ancient kings could not have acted merely from righteousness alone. ... Hence, in ritual not only the main principles and methods all arise from the heavenly mandate and people's laws; even a single tiny vessel or fleeting gesture has its own deep meaning informing its use. ... Hence, one must first learn about the instruments, measurements, gestures, and movements before one can understand that ritual originates in human nature. This is what is called extending knowledge. ("Fuli zhong," in Ling Tinkan, *Ling Cizhong xiansheng wenji*, j. 4, pp. 4b–9a)

30. See Charles Hammond, "The Interpretation of Thunder," pp. 487–504. Hammond argues that even the most rationalistic of Neo-Confucian philosophers failed to refute, and usually approved of, the popular belief that thunder served as an agent of Heaven's wrath: "Even when they tried to proceed cognitively, they were unable to escape the morass of popular attitudes. Such attitudes constituted a paradigm that encouraged even the educated to see thunder as a tangible physical object and tempted many of them to believe that it struck the evil as punishment ... orthodox Confucian thought merely veneered over enduring popular ideas" (p. 499). Like the argument over Wang Chong's ideas, this discussion of thunder by the girls attempts to seek an acceptable resolution of the apparent contradiction between the irrationality and randomness of nature with the moral foundations of human society.

Conclusion

1. Chow, Rise of Confucian Ritualism, p. 157.
2. In this regard, it is instructive to recall the example of *Rulin waishi*'s treatment of philosophical and literary figures and events of Ming history. The first inkling of a rejection of philistine careerism in favor of an eremitic cultivation of arts and letters (chapter 8) is marked by Wang Yangming's suppression of the Prince Ning Rebellion. As we recall, government service and its denial are juxtaposed with a discussion of Wang Yangming's brilliance as a military tactician, a discussion that passes over in silence any mention of philosophical

matters. Another textual transition from a group of men bent on examinations to the scholarly idealists of Nanjing (chapters 29–30) refers to the Seven Masters of the Jiajing period, namely, the cultural luminaries of that era. Here again such allusions stress not cultural attainments per se, but instead the depraved lifestyle of such circles. In both of these cases, the novel can be seen to implicitly downplay the ideological or cultural ramifications of its trajectory of social change—ramifications that were widely invoked by Qing scholars such as Gu Yanwu—in favor of an oscillation between the more pedestrian avenue of examination taking and its various alternatives.

3. Wu, *Female Rule*, chap. 4.
4. McMahon, *Shrews, Misers, and Polygamists*, p. 11.
5. As Andrew Plaks points out, "A certain disproportionate emphasis on 'words' over 'events' runs through much of the tradition, from the earliest treatments of mythical lore (in which the narrative function rarely goes beyond the ritualized ordering of the specific figures), to the full-length novels of the Ming and Ch'ing periods, with their endless pages of banquets and chitchat." Plaks attributes this to the lack of the European "reification of the event as a narrative unit" in the Chinese tradition. Plaks, "Towards a Critical Theory," p. 315.
6. Frederick Keener, *The Chain of Becoming*, pp. 85, 25.
7. Nakano Miyoko, *Akuma no inai bungaku: Chūgoku no shōsetsu to kaiga*, p. 6.
8. Robert Hegel ascribes the tendency of fiction writers to give their works spatial and temporal specificity to "the training literati novelists had in reading and writing history" (*Novel in Seventeenth-Century China*, p. 230).
9. Ellen Widmer, *The Margins of Utopia*, p. 47.
10. Hegel, *Novel in Seventeenth-Century China*, p. 220.
11. Hanan, *Invention*, pp. 149, 141.
12. See Wang Liqi, *Yuan Ming Qing*, esp. pp. 226–45.
13. One exception to the decline in the status of fiction in general was the renascence of the classical tale during the late seventeenth and eighteenth centuries. Its recondite language and allusiveness were consonant with the growing classicism of the mid-Qing. Already in the sixteenth century the influential figure Wang Shizhen (1525–90) and other writers had compiled numerous collections of anecdotes (biji) culled from various sources and modeled on the chuanqi of the Tang and Song. But a principal stimulus to this development was Pu Songling's *Liaozhai zhiyi*, which by the early Qianlong period was widely admired and imitated. Of particular note is the fact that two of the best known and most influential men of letters and scholarship—Yuan Mei and Ji Yun—each wrote and published collections of tales. As discussed in Chapter 8, their works became part of a wide-ranging debate over the existence of supernatural phenomena during the late eighteenth and early nineteenth centuries.
14. Lu Xun also identifies *Yanshan waishi* and *Yinshi* as "novels of erudition." Nonetheless both of these latter works are written in highly abstract

classical language and represent primarily stylistic rather than substantive attempts to incorporate erudition into fiction.

15. *Lüye xianzong* was first printed in a truncated 80-chapter version, and this version dominated until very recently, when a 100-chapter manuscript was finally published for the first time.

16. All citations to *Xingshi yinyuan zhuan* are to the Shanghai guji chubanshe (Shanghai, 1981) edition.

17. All citations to *Lüye xianzong* are to the Wenhua tushu gongsi (Taipei, 1984) edition.

18. Cao Xueqin, *Honglou meng*, chap. 36, pp. 435–36; David Hawkes, trans., *The Story of the Stone*, by Cao Xueqin, vol. 2, p. 206.

19. Jia She's speech to Jia Huan, although hardly presented in a favorable light, is perhaps representative of higher-ranking bannermen's attitudes toward examinations and learning. See Cao, *Honglou meng*, chap. 75, p. 975; Hawkes, *The Story of the Stone*, vol. 3, p. 329.

20. Angela Zito, "Silk and Skin: Significant Boundaries," in Angela Zito and Tani Barlow, eds., *Body, Subject, and Power in China*, pp. 122, 113.

21. Richard Vinograd, *Boundaries of the Self*, pp. 73, 69.

22. Zito, "Silk and Skin," p. 103.

23. For political apathy in Qianlong's reign, see Frederick Mote, "The Intellectual Climate in Eighteenth-Century China," pp. 17–55.

24. See Du Weiyun's discussion of political apathy and its relationship to intellectual change in Du Weiyun, "Qing Qian-Jia shiqi liuxing yu zhishi fenzi jian de yintui sixiang," pp. 63–72.

25. Hsia, "Scholar-Novelist," p. 270.

Bibliography

Abe Yasuki 阿部泰記. "*Jurin gaishi*—sono dokushojin jūshi no tachiba" 儒林外史―その読書人重視の立場. In *Otaru shōkadaijinbun kenkyū* 小樽商科大人文研究 1 (1979): 1–14.
Aoki Masaru 青木正児. *Shindai bungaku hyōronshi* 清代文学評論史. Tokyo: Iwanami shoten, 1950.
Baishi huibian 稗史彙編. Compiled by Wang Qi 王圻, 1596. Chinese Academy of Sciences, Beijing.
Bakhtin, Mikhail. *Problems of Dostoyevsky's Poetics*. Translated by Caryl Emerson. Minneapolis: University of Minnesota Press, 1984.
Bao Jialin 鮑家麟. "Li Ruzhen de nannü pingdeng sixiang" 李汝貞的男女平等思想. *Shihuo* 12 (1972): 620–29.
Bi Yuan 畢沅. *Shanhai jing jiaozhu* 山海經校注. Shanghai: Dushu shi 讀書室, 1924.
Billeter, Jean-François. "Contribution à une sociologie historique du mandarinat." *Actes de la recherche en sciences sociales* 15 (1977): 1–15.
Bol, Peter. *"This Culture of Ours": Intellectual Transitions in T'ang and Sung China*. Stanford, Calif.: Stanford University Press, 1992.
Brandauer, Frederick. "Women in the *Ching-hua yuan*: Emancipation Toward a Confucian Ideal." *Journal of Asian Studies* 36.4 (1977): 647–60.
Brokaw, Cynthia. "Tai Chen and Learning in the Confucian Tradition." In Elman and Woodside, *Education and Society in Late Imperial China*, pp. 257–91.
Brook, Timothy. *Praying for Power: Buddhism and the Formation of Gentry Society in Late-Ming China*. Cambridge, Mass.: Harvard University Press, 1993.
Bush, Susan. *The Chinese Literati on Painting*. Cambridge, Mass.: Harvard University Press, 1971.
Cao Xueqin 曹雪芹. *Honglou meng* 紅樓夢. Beijing: Renmin wenxue chubanshe, 1973.
Chan, Leo Tak-hong. "The *Yuewei caotang biji* and the Late Eighteenth-Century Elite Discourse on the Supernatural." *Harvard Journal of Asiatic Studies* 53.1 (1993): 25–62.
Chan, Wing-tsit. "Chu Hsi and Yuan Neo-Confucianism." In Hok-lam Chan

and William T. de Bary, eds., *Yuan Thought: Chinese Thought and Religion Under the Mongols*. New York: Columbia University Press, 1982, pp. 197–231.

———. "The *Hsing-li ching-i* and the Ch'eng-Chu School." In de Bary, *Unfolding of Neo-Confucianism*, pp. 543–79.

———, ed. *Chu Hsi and Neo-Confucianism*. Honolulu: University of Hawaii Press, 1986.

Chang, Chung-li. *The Chinese Gentry: Studies on Their Role in Nineteenth-Century Chinese Society*. Seattle: University of Washington Press, 1955.

Chen Guang 晨光. "Ping 'You *Rulin waishi* yinqi de yichang fengbo yu Meng Xingren, Meng Fanjing xiansheng shangque" 評由儒林外史引起的一場風波--與孟醒仁、孟凡經先生商榷. *Ming Qing xiaoshuo yanjiu* 15 (1990.1): 96–104.

Chen Jiru 陳繼儒. *Yanqi youshi* 岩棲幽事. In *Xu Shuofu* 續說郛 juan 27. Taipei: Xinxing shuju, 1964.

Chen Meilin 陳美林. "Shilun Wu Jingzi dui keju zhidu de pipan ji qi dui zhishi fenzi chulu de tanxun" 試論吳敬梓對科舉制度的批判及其對知識分子出路的探尋. *Ming Qing xiaoshuo yanjiu* 17 (1991.4): 80–94.

———. *Wu Jingzi pingzhuan* 吳敬梓評傳. Nanjing: Nanjing daxue chubanshe, 1992.

———. *Wu Jingzi yanjiu* 吳敬梓研究. Shanghai: Shanghai guji chubanshe, 1984.

Chen Que 陳確. *Chen Que ji* 陳確集. Beijing: Zhonghua shuju, 1979.

Chen Wenxin 陳文新. "*Jinghua yuan* yu rudao wenhua" 鏡花緣與儒道文化. *Ming Qing xiaoshuo yanjiu* 7 (1988): 197–209.

Chen Xin 陳新 and Du Weimo 杜維沫. "*Rulin waishi* diwushiliu hui zhenwei bian" 儒林外史第五十六回眞僞辨. In *Rulin waishi yanjiu lunwen ji*, pp. 153–64.

Chen Xuewen 陳學文. "Mingdai zhongye yilai qinong qiru congshang fengqi he zhongshang sichao de chuxian" 明代中葉以來棄農棄儒從商風氣和重商思潮的出現. *Jiuzhou xuekan* 3.4 (1990): 21–30.

Chen Yi (Guyu) 陳毅 (古漁), comp. *Suozhi ji* 所知集. Mianyunge 眠雲閣, Qianlong era. Chinese Academy of Sciences, Beijing.

Chen Zuwu 陳祖武. *Qingchu xueshu xibianlu* 清初學術析辨錄. Beijing: Zhongguo shehui kexue chubanshe, 1992.

Chen Zuolin 陳作霖. *Fenglu xiaozhi* 鳳麓小志. In *Jinling suozhi wuzhong* 金陵瑣志五種. Nanjing, 1900.

Cheng Jinfang 程晉芳. *Mianxingtang ji* 勉行堂集. 1820.

Cheng Tingzuo 程廷祚. *Qingxi wenji* 青溪文集. Beiping: Beijing daxue chubanshe, 1936.

———. *Wanshu dingyi* 晚書訂疑. Sanyu shuwu 三餘書屋, n.d. Faculty of Literature, Kyoto University.

Cheng Yaotian 程瑤田. *Tongyilu* 通藝錄. Yangzhou: Jiangsu Guangling guji keyinshe, 1991.

Chiu, Han-sheng. "Zhu Xi's Doctrine of Principle." In Wing-tsit Chan, *Chu Hsi and Neo-Confucianism*, pp. 116–35.

Chow, Kai-wing. "Discourse, Examinations, and Local Elites: The Invention of the T'ung-ch'eng School in Ch'ing China." In Elman and Woodside, *Education and Society in Late Imperial China*, pp. 183–219.
———. "Purist Hermeneutics and Ritualist Ethics in Mid-Ch'ing Confucianism." In Smith and Kwok, *Cosmology, Ontology, and Human Efficacy*, pp. 179–204.
———. *The Rise of Confucian Ritualism in Late Imperial China: Ethics, Classics, and Lineage Discourse*. Stanford, Calif.: Stanford University Press, 1994.
Chu, Hong-lam. "The Debate over the Recognition of Wang Yang-ming." *Harvard Journal of Asiatic Studies* 48.1 (1988): 47–70.
Chunqiu Zuozhuan zhu 春秋左傳注. Taipei: Yuanliu chubanshe, 1982.
Dai Mingshi 戴名世. *Nanshan ji* 南山集. Beijing: Zhonghua shuju, 1986.
Dai Wang 戴望. *Yanshi xueji* 顏氏學記. Beijing: Zhonghua shuju, 1958.
Dai Zhen 戴震. *Dai Zhen wenji* 戴震文集. Beijing: Zhonghua shuju, 1980.
———. *Mengzi ziyi shuzheng* 孟子字義疏正. Beijing: Zhonghua shuju, 1961.
Dardess, John. *Confucianism and Autocracy: Professional Elites in the Founding of the Ming Dynasty*. Berkeley: University of California Press, 1983.
de Bary, William Theodore. *Neo-Confucian Orthodoxy and the Learning of the Mind and Heart*. New York: Columbia University Press, 1981.
———, trans. *Waiting for the Dawn: A Plan for the Prince*. New York: Columbia University Press, 1993.
———, ed. *Self and Society in Ming Thought*. New York: Columbia University Press, 1970.
———, ed. *The Unfolding of Neo-Confucianism*. New York: Columbia University Press, 1975.
de Bary, William Theodore, and John W. Chafee, eds. *Neo-Confucian Education: The Formative Stage*. Berkeley: University of California Press, 1989.
Ding Fubao 丁福保, ed. *Qing shihua* 清詩話. Beijing: Zhonghua shuju, 1963.
Dong Guoyan 董國炎. "*Rulin waishi* zhuti xinshuo" 儒林外史主題新說. *Shanxi daxue xuebao* (1989.3): 77–81.
Du Weiyun 杜維運. "Qing Qian-Jia shiqi liuxing yu zhishi fenzi jian de yintui sixiang" 清乾嘉時期流行於知識分子間的隱退思想. *Guoli zhengzhi daxue lishi xuebao* 7 (1990): 63–72.
Ebrey, Patricia. *Confucianism and Family Ritual in Imperial China: A Social History of Writing About Rites*. Princeton, N.J.: Princeton University Press, 1990.
Elman, Benjamin. *Classicism, Politics, and Kinship: The Ch'ang-chou School of New Text Confucianism in Late Imperial China*. Berkeley: University of California Press, 1990.
———. *From Philosophy to Philology: Intellectual and Social Aspects of Change in Late Imperial China*. Cambridge, Mass.: Harvard University Press, 1984.
———. "Philosophy (*I-li*) versus Philology (*K'ao-cheng*)—The *jen-hsin tao-hsin* Debate." *T'oung Pao* 69.4–5 (1983): 175–222.
Elman, Benjamin, and Alexander Woodside, eds. *Education and Society in Late Imperial China, 1600–1900*. Berkeley: University of California Press, 1993.

Fan Ning 范寧. "*Rulin waishi* de lunli sixiang" 儒林外史的倫理思想. In *Rulin waishi yanjiu lunwen ji*, pp. 109–16.
Fang Bao 方苞. *Fang Bao ji* 方苞集. Shanghai: Shanghai guji chubanshe, 1983.
Fang Yizhi 方以智. *Dongxi jun* 東西均. Beijing: Zhonghua shuju, 1962.
———. *Jigutang wenji* 稽古堂文集. In *Tongcheng Fangshi qidai yishu* 桐城方氏七代遺書, vol. 7, 1888. Harvard-Yenching Institute Library.
Feng Menglong 馮夢龍. *Qingshi leilue* 情史類略. Changsha: Yuelu shushe, 1984.
Frye, Northrop. *Anatomy of Criticism*. Princeton, N.J.: Princeton University Press, 1957.
Fung, Yu-lan. *A History of Chinese Philosophy*. Vol. 2. Translated by Derke Bodde. Princeton, N.J.: Princeton University Press, 1953.
Gao Mingge 高明閣. "Lun *Rulin waishi* dui yuanxing de shequ" 論儒林外史對原形的攝取. *Shehui kexue jikan* (1980.2): 97–104.
Gao Yuhou 皋于厚. "*Rulin waishi* 'zhenru' xingxiang xinyi" 儒林外史眞儒形象新議. *Ming Qing xiaoshuo yanjiu* 27 (1993.3): 119–27.
Geiss, James. "The Cheng-te Reign." In F. W. Mote and Denis Twitchett, eds., *The Cambridge History of China*, vol. 7 (Ming), pp. 403–39. Cambridge: Cambridge University Press, 1988.
Graham, A. C. *Two Chinese Philosophers*. London: George Allen, 1958.
Guisso, R. W. L. *Wu Tse-t'ien and the Politics of Legitimation in T'ang China*. Pullman: Western Washington University Press, 1978.
Guo Shaoyu 郭紹虞. *Zhaoyushi gudian wenxue lunji* 照隅室古典文學論集. 2 vols. Shanghai: Shanghai guji chubanshe, 1985.
———. *Zhongguo wenxue piping shi* 中國文學批評史. Taipei: Youshi, 1976.
Guy, R. Kent. "The Development of the Evidential Research Movement: Ku Yen-wu and the Ssu-k'u ch'uan-shu." *Tsing-hua Journal of Chinese Studies* 16 (1984): 110–35.
———. *The Emperor's Four Treasuries: Scholars and the State in the Late Ch'ien-lung Era*. Cambridge, Mass.: Harvard University Press, 1987.
———. "Fang Pao and the *Ch'in-ting ssu-shu wen*." In Elman and Woodside, *Education and Society in Late Imperial China*, pp. 150–82.
Hammond, Charles. "The Interpretation of Thunder." *Journal of Asian Studies* 53.2 (1994): 487–504.
Han Shi 韓石. "Pisa zai luozhao shifen de xinling zhi guang—lun *Rulin waishi* zhong de shenghuo lixiang ji qi shidai hesheng" 披灑在落照時分的心靈之光--論儒林外史中的生活理想及其時代和聲. *Ming Qing xiaoshuo yanjiu* 17 (1991.2): 74–88.
Hanan, Patrick. *The Invention of Li Yu*. Cambridge, Mass.: Harvard University Press, 1988.
Hashimoto Takakatsu 橋本高勝. "*Mōshi jigi soshō* nitsuite—ningenteki shizen no kaishaku to sōsaku" 孟子字義疏正について――人間的自然の發展と搜索. In *Chūgoku tetsugaku no hatten to mosaku* 中国哲学の発展と模索, pp. 768–800. Tokyo: Chikuma shobō, 1976.

Hawkes, David, and John Minford, trans. *The Story of the Stone*. 5 vols. New York: Penguin, 1973–86.
He Guanbiao 何冠彪. *Mingmo Qingchu xueshu sixiang yanjiu* 明末清初學術思想研究. Taipei: Xuesheng shuju, 1991.
He Zehan 何澤翰. *Rulin waishi renwu benshi kaolue* 儒林外史人物本事考略. Second edition. Shanghai: Shanghai guji chubanshe, 1985.
Hegel, Robert. *The Novel in Seventeenth-Century China*. New York: Columbia University Press, 1981.
Henderson, John. *The Development and Decline of Chinese Cosmology*. New York: Columbia University Press, 1984.
Highet, Gilbert. *The Anatomy of Satire*. Princeton, N.J.: Princeton University Press, 1962.
Ho, Ping-ti. *The Ladder of Success in Imperial China: Aspects of Social Mobility, 1368–1911*. New York: Columbia University Press, 1962.
Hou Jian 侯健. "*Yesou puyan* de biantai xinli" 野叟曝言的變態心理. *Zhongwai wenxue* 2.10 (1974): 8–23.
Hsia, C. T. *The Classic Chinese Novel: A Critical Introduction*. New York: Columbia University Press, 1968.
———. "The Scholar-Novelist and Chinese Culture: A Reappraisal of *Ching hua yuan*. In Plaks, *Chinese Narrative*, pp. 266–305.
Hsu, Ginger Cheng-chi. "Merchant Patronage of Eighteenth Century Yangzhou Painting." In Chu-tsing Li, ed., *Artists and Patrons*, pp. 215–21.
Hu Bangwei 胡邦煒 and Wu Hong 吳紅. *Zhongguo gudian xiaoshuo yishu de sikao* 中國古典小說藝術的思考. Chongqing: Chongqing chubanshe, 1986.
Hu Shih 胡適. *Hu Shi wencun* 胡適文存. Taipei: Commercial Press, 1952–57.
———. "A Note on Ch'üan Tsu-wang, Chao I-ch'ing, and Tai Chen." In Hummel, *Eminent Chinese of the Ch'ing Period*, pp. 970–82.
———. "Yan-Li xuepai de Cheng Tingzuo" 顏李學派的程廷祚. In Cheng Tingzuo, *Qingxi wenji*, pp. 1a–16b.
Huang, Martin. *Literati and Self-Re/Presentation: Autobiographical Sensibility in the Eighteenth-Century Chinese Novel*. Stanford, Calif.: Stanford University Press, 1995.
Huang Xiaotian 黃小田. Commentary. *Rulin waishi* 儒林外史. Heifei: Huangshan shushe, 1986.
Huang Zongxi 黃宗羲. *Mingru xuean* 明儒學案. Taipei: Shijie shuju, 1984.
———. *Mingyi daifang lu* 明夷待訪錄. Taipei: Shijie shuju, 1966.
———. *Nanlei wending qianji* 南雷文定前集. Taipei: Taiwan Zhonghua shuju, 1965.
———. *Song Yuan xuean* 宋元學案. Taipei: Zhongzheng shuju, 1963.
Hummel, Arthur, ed. *Eminent Chinese of the Ch'ing Period*. Taipei: Chengwen Publishing, 1970.
Inada Takashi 稲田孝. "*Jurin gaishi* ni okeru kōteiteki jinbutsu ni tsuite" 儒林外史における肯定的人物について. *Tōkyō gakugei daigaku kenkyū hōkoku* 東京学芸大学研究報告 13 (1962): 454–69.
Iser, Wolfgang. *The Act of Reading—A Theory of Aesthetic Response*. Baltimore, Md.: Johns Hopkins University Press, 1978.

Jameson, Frederic. *The Political Unconscious: Narrative as a Socially Symbolic Act.* Ithaca, N.Y.: Cornell University Press, 1981.
Jami, Catherine. "Learning Mathematical Sciences during the Early to Mid-Ch'ing." In Elman and Woodside, *Education and Society in Late Imperial China*, pp. 223–56.
Ji Yun 紀昀. *Ji Xiaolan shiwen ji* 紀曉嵐詩文集. Shanghai: Dongfang wenxueshe, 1935.
Jiangning fuzhi 江甯府志. 1668. Peking University Library.
Jiangyin xianzhi 江陰縣志 (Ming edition). *Tianyi ge cangshu Mingdai fangzhi xuankan* (vol. 5) 天一閣藏書明代方志選刊. Shanghai: Shanghai guji shudian, 1981.
Jiang Fan 江藩. *Hanxue shicheng ji* 漢學師承記. Beijing: Zhonghua shuju, 1985.
Jiang Shiquan 蔣士銓. *Zhongyatang wenji* 忠雅堂文集. Shanghai: Shanghai guji chubanshe, 1993.
Jiao Xun 焦循. *Diaogulou ji* 雕菰樓集. Taipei: Taiwan Shangwu yinshuguan, 1966.
Jin ping mei cihua 金瓶梅詞話. Hongkong: Sanlian shudian, 1986.
Jin Zhaoyan 金兆燕. *Zongting guwen chao* 棕亭古文鈔. 1836. Faculty of Letters, Kyoto University.
Julien, François. *La Propension des choses.* Paris: Editions du Seuil, 1992.
Kahn, Harold L. *Monarch in the Emperor's Eyes: Image and Reality in the Ch'ien-lung Reign.* Cambridge, Mass.: Harvard University Press, 1971.
Kao, Hsin-sheng. *Li Ju-chen.* Boston: Twayne Publishers, 1981.
Keener, Frederick. *The Chain of Becoming: The Philosophical Tale, the Novel, and a Neglected Realism of the Enlightenment. Swift, Montesquieu, Voltaire, Johnson, and Austen.* New York: Columbia University Press, 1983.
Kim, Yung Sik. "*Kuei-shen* in Terms of *Ch'i*: Chu Hsi's Discussion of *Kuei-shen*." *Tsing-hua Journal of Chinese Studies* 17.2 (1983): 149–64.
Kitamura Yoshikazu 北村吉和. "Go Taibaku jōkoku no shisō shi—inpeisetsu o megutte" 呉泰伯讓国の思想史ーー隱蔽説をめぐって. *Chūgoku—shakai to bunka* 2 (1987): 223–41.
Kong Shangren 孔尚任. *Taohua shan* 桃花扇. Taipei: Guangwen shuju, 1972.
Kracke, E. A. "Religion, Family, and Individual in the Chinese Examination System." In John K. Fairbank, ed., *Chinese Thought and Institutions*, pp. 251–68. Chicago: University of Chicago Press, 1957.
Kuriyama, Shigehisa. "The Imagination of Winds and the Development of the Chinese Conception of the Body." In Zito and Barlow, *Body, Subject, and Power in China*, pp. 23–41.
Lao Tzu: Tao Te Ching [*Daode jing*]. Translated by D. C. Lau. Harmondsworth, UK: Penguin, 1963.
Li Baichuan 李百川. *Lü ye xianzong* 綠野仙蹤. Taipei: Wenhua tushu gongsi, 1982.
Li, Chu-tsing, ed. *Artists and Patrons: Some Social and Economic Aspects of Chinese Painting.* Seattle: University of Washington Press, 1989.
Li Dou 李斗. *Yangzhou huafang lu* 揚州畫舫錄. Beijing: Zhonghua shuju, 1984.

Li E 厲鶚. *Fanxie shantang ji* 樊榭山堂集. Guoxue jiben congshu, vol. 225. Taipei: Taiwan Shangwu yinshuguan, 1968.
Li Fu 李紱. *Mutang xiansheng biegao* 穆堂先生別稿. Fengguotang 奉國堂, 1747.
Li Gong 李塨. *Shugu houji* 恕谷後集. In *Yan-Li yishu*. Taipei: Guangwen shuju, 1965.
———. *Zhou Yi zhuan zhu* 周易傳注. Siku quanshu zhenben, series 5. Taipei: Taiwan Shangwu yinshuguan, 1974.
Li Guangdi 李光地, ed. *Zhuzi lizuan* 朱子禮纂. Preface dated 1733. Faculty of Letters, Kyoto University.
Li Hanqiu 李漢秋. "*Rulin waishi* yu chuantong wenhua" 儒林外史與傳統文化. *Wenxue yichan* (1991.5): 118–20.
———, ed. *Rulin waishi huijiao huiping ben* 儒林外史會校會評本. Shanghai: Shanghai guji chubanshe, 1985.
———, ed. *Rulin waishi yanjiu ziliao* 儒林外史研究資料. Shanghai: Shanghai guji chubanshe, 1984.
Li Qilin 李奇林. "Lun *Jinghua yuan* de Wu Zetian xingxiang" 論鏡花緣的武則天形象. *Ming Qing xiaoshuo yanjiu* 17 (1990.3/4): 279–90.
Li Ruzhen 李汝貞. *Jinghua yuan* 鏡花緣. Taipei: Dingwen shuju, 1981.
Li Tiangang 李天剛. "*Mengzi ziyi shuzheng* yu *Tianzhu shiyi*" 孟子字義疏正與天主實義. In Wang Yuanhua, ed., *Xueshu jilin* 學術集林, vol. 2, pp. 200–222. Shanghai: Shanghai Yuandong chubanshe, 1994.
Li, Wai-yee. *Enchantment and Disenchantment: Love and Illusion in Chinese Literature*. Princeton, N.J.: Princeton University Press, 1993.
Liang, Ch'i-ch'ao. *Intellectual Trends of the Ch'ing Period*. Translated by Immanuel Hsu. Cambridge, Mass.: Harvard University Press, 1955.
Lidai huajia shiwen ji 歷代畫家詩文集. Taipei: Xuesheng shuju, 1985.
Lin, Shuen-fu. "Ritual and Narrative Structure in *Ju-lin Wai-shih*." In Plaks, *Chinese Narrative*, pp. 244–65.
Ling Tingkan 凌廷堪. *Ling Cizhong xiansheng wenji* 凌次仲先生文集. In *Anhui congshu* 安徽叢書, series 4. N.p., 1935.
Liu Dakui 劉大櫆. *Liu Haifeng xiansheng wenji* 劉海峰先生文集. Hangzhou, 1874.
———. *Lunwen ouji* 論文偶記. In Wu Hongyi and Ye Qingbing, *Qingdai wenxue piping ziliao huibian*, vol. 8, pp. 431–34.
Liu Ji 劉基. *Chengyibo wenji* 誠意伯文集. In *Yingyin wenyuange siku quanshu*, vol. 1225. Taipei: Taiwan shangwu yinshuguan, 1983.
Liu, Kwang-ching, ed. *Orthodoxy in Late Imperial China*. Berkeley: University of California Press, 1990.
Liu Xizai 劉熙載. *Yigai* 藝概. Taipei: Taiwan Shangwu yinshuguan, 1972.
Lu Qian 盧前. *Baguwen xiaoshi* 八股文小史. Shanghai: Shangwu yinshuguan, 1937.
Lu Qingbin (Andrew Lo) 盧慶濱. "Baguwen yu Jin Shengtan zhi xiaoshuo xiqu piping" 八股文與金聖嘆之小說戲曲批評. Unpublished manuscript, 1987.
Lu, Sheldon Hsiao-peng. *From Historicity to Fictionality: The Chinese Poetics of Narrative*. Stanford, Calif.: Stanford University Press, 1994.

Lu Xun 魯迅. *Zhongguo xiaoshuo shilue* 中國小說史略. Taipei: n.d.
Lü Liuliang 呂留良. *Lü Wancun xiansheng wenji* 呂晚村先生文集 . Taipei: Zhongding wenhua chuban gongsi, 1967.
———. *Sishu jiangyi* 四書講義. Taipei: Guangwen shuju, 1978.
Lü mudan 綠牡丹. Hangzhou: Zhejiang guji chubanshe, 1985.
Lü Zuqian 呂祖謙. *Jinsi lu* 近思錄. Taipei: Zixue jicheng, 1976.
Luan Xing 欒興. "Xin jiaoben *Yesou puyan* xu" 新校本野叟曝言序. *Zhongzhou xuekan* 6 (1990): 101–4.
Lukacs, Georg. *The Historical Novel*. Translated by Hannah Mitchell and Stanley Mitchell. Atlantic Highlands, N.J.: Humanities Press, 1978.
Mann, Susan. *Local Merchants and the Chinese Bureaucracy, 1750–1950*. Stanford, Calif.: Stanford University Press, 1987.
Mao Zhongxian 毛忠賢. "*Jinghua yuan* dui *Honglou meng* nüxing wenti de fansi" 鏡花緣對紅樓夢女性問題的反思. *Wenshi zhishi* (1989.11): 56–59.
Matsumura Kō 松村昂. "Ō Men den kō—Mindai shikan no bungaku" 王冕伝考 ——明代史官の文学. *Nagoya daigaku kyōyōbu kiyō* 名古屋大学教養部紀要 21 (1977): 160–95.
McMahon, Keith. "A Case for Confucian Sexuality: The Eighteenth-Century Novel *Yesou puyan*." *Late Imperial China* 14.2 (1989): 3–34.
———. *Causality and Containment in Seventeenth-Century Chinese Fiction*. Leiden: E. J. Brill, 1988.
———. "The Classic 'Beauty-Scholar' Romances and the Superiority of Talented Women." In Zito and Barlow, *Body, Subject, and Power in China*, pp. 227–52.
———. *Misers, Shrews, and Polygamists: Sexuality and Male-Female Relations in Eighteenth-Century Chinese Fiction*. Durham, N.C.: Duke University Press, 1995.
Mencius. Translated by D. C. Lau. Harmondsworth, UK: Penguin, 1970.
Metzger, Thomas A. *Escape from Predicament: Neo-Confucianism and China's Evolving Political Culture*. New York: Columbia University Press, 1977.
Ming shi 明史. Shanghai: Shanghai renmin chubanshe, 1985–91.
Mizoguchi Yūzō 溝口雄三. "Lun Mingmo Qingchu shiqi zai sixiang shang de lishi yiyi" 論明末清初時期在思想上的歷史意義. *Shixue pinglun* 12 (1986): 99–140.
———. *Zen kindai shisō no kussetsu to tenkai* 前近代思想の屈折と展開. Tokyo: Tokyo University Press, 1980.
Mote, Frederick. "The Intellectual Climate in Eighteenth-Century China: Glimpses of Beijing, Suzhou, and Yangzhou in the Qianlong Period." *Phoebus* 6.1 (1988): 17–55.
Murase Yūya 村瀬裕也. *Tai Shin no tetsugaku: Yuibutsuron to dōtokuteki kachi* 戴震の哲学：唯物論と道徳的価値. Tokyo: Nitchū shuppansha, 1984.
Nakano Miyoko 中野美代子. *Akuma no inai bungaku: Chūgoku no shōsetsu to kaiga* 悪魔のいない文学：中国の小説と絵画. Tokyo: Asahi sensho, 1977.
Naquin, Susan, and Evelyn Rawski. *Chinese Society in the Eighteenth Century*. New Haven, Conn.: Yale University Press, 1987.
Nivison, David. *The Life and Thought of Chang Hsueh-ch'eng*. Stanford, Calif.: Stanford University Press, 1966.

Nü kaike zhuan 女開科傳. Shenyang: Chunfeng Wenyi chubanshe, 1983.
Ogawa Tamaki 小川環樹. *Chūgoku shōsetsu shi no kenkyū* 中国小説史の研究. Tokyo: Iwanami shoten, 1968.
Ono Kazuko 小野和子. "*Kyōka en* no sekai: Shinchō kōshōgakusha no yutopia zō" 鏡花緣の世界：清朝考証学者のユートピア象. *Shisō* 721 (1984.7): 40–55.
Ōtani Toshio 大谷敏男. "Yōshū-Chōshū gakujutsu kō-sono shakaiteki kanren." 揚州常州学術考ーーその社会的関連. In Ono Kazuko, ed., *Min Shin jidai no seiji to shakai* 明清時代の政治と社会. Kyoto: Kyōto daigaku Zinbun kagaku kenkyūzyo, 1983.
Ouyang Jian 歐陽健, ed. *Zhongguo tongsu xiaoshuo zongmu tiyao* 中國通俗小說綜目題要. Beijing: Wenlian chubanshe, 1990.
Owen, Stephen. *Readings in Chinese Literary Thought*. Cambridge, Mass.: Harvard University Press, 1992.
———. *Remembrances: Experience of the Past in Chinese Literature*. Cambridge, Mass.: Harvard University Press, 1986.
Ōzuka, Hidetaka 大塚秀高. *Zōho Chūgoku tsūzoku shōsetsu shomoku* 増補中国通俗小説書目. Tokyo: Kyūko shoin, 1987.
Paulson, Ronald. *The Fictions of Satire*. Baltimore, Md.: Johns Hopkins University Press, 1967.
Peterson, Willard J. *Bitter Gourd: Fang I-chih and the Impetus for Intellectual Change*. New Haven, Conn.: Yale University Press, 1979.
Ping Buqing 平步青. *Xiawai junxie* 霞外攟屑. Beijing: Zhonghua shuju, 1986.
Plaks, Andrew. "Conceptual Models in Chinese Narrative Theory." *Journal of Chinese Philosophy* 4 (1977): 25–49.
———. *Ssu ta ch'i-shu: Four Masterworks of the Ming Novel*. Princeton, N.J.: Princeton University Press, 1987.
———. "Towards a Critical Theory of Chinese Narrative." In Plaks, *Chinese Narrative*, pp. 309–52.
———, ed. *Chinese Narrative: Critical and Theoretical Essays*. Princeton, N.J.: Princeton University Press, 1977.
Pohl, Karl-Heinz. *Cheng Pan-ch'iao: Poet, Painter, and Calligrapher*. Nettetal, Germany: Steyler-Verlag, 1990.
Qian Daxin 錢大昕. *Qian Yantang wenji* 潛研堂文集. Shanghai: Shanghai guji chubanshe, 1989.
———. *Shijiazhai yangxin lu* 十駕齋養新錄. In *Guoxue jiben congshu*. Taipei: Taiwan Shangwu yinshuguan, 1957.
Qian Mu 錢穆. *Zhongguo jinsanbai nian xueshu shi* 中國近三百年學術史. Taipei: Shangwu yinshuguan, 1957.
Qian Zhonglian 錢仲聯. *Mengtiaoan Qingdai wenxue lunji* 夢苕庵清代文學論集. Jinan: Qilu shushe, 1983.
Qin Chuan 秦川. "*Rulin waishi* dui bagu qushi zhidu de pipan" 儒林外史對八股取士制度的批判. *Chongqing Shifan xuebao* 重慶師範學報 2 (1992): 72–76.
Qiu Chun 邱椿. "Yan Yuan de jiaoyu sixiang" 顏元的教育思想. *Beijing shifan daxue xuebao* 4 (1958.1): 160–93.

Ricoeur, Paul. *Time and Narrative*. Chicago: University of Chicago Press, 1983.
Roddy, Stephen. "*Rulin waishi* and the Representation of the Literati in Qing Fiction." Ph.D. diss., Princeton University, 1990.
Rolston, David. "Theory and Practice: Fiction, Fiction Criticism, and the Writing of the *Ju-lin wai-shih*." Ph.D. diss., University of Chicago, 1988.
Rong Zhaozu 容肇祖. *Lü Liuliang ji qi sixiang* 呂留良及其思想. Hongkong: Chongwen shulin, 1974.
Ropp, Paul. *Dissent in Early Modern China: Ju-lin wai-shih and Ch'ing Social Criticism*. Ann Arbor: University of Michigan Press, 1981.
Rulin waishi yanjiu lunwen ji 儒林外史研究論文集. Anhui sheng jinian Wu Jingzi shengdan erbai bashi zhounian weiyuanhui 安徽省紀念吳敬梓生誕二百八十周年委員會. Hefei: Anhui renmin chubanshe, 1982.
Saussy, Haun. *The Problem of a Chinese Aesthetic*. Stanford, Calif.: Stanford University Press, 1993.
Seidel, Michael. *The Satiric Dispensation—Rabelais to Sterne*. Princeton, N.J.: Princeton University Press, 1979.
Shang Yanliu 商衍鎏. *Qingdai keju kaoshi shulu* 清代科舉考試述錄. Beijing: Sanlian, 1958.
Shao Shiquan 邵士權. "Lun *Jinghua yuan* dui Zhongguo gudian xiaoshuo meixue biaozhun de xin tuozhan" 論鏡花緣對中國古典小說美學標準的新拓展. *Renwen zazhi* (1991.3):119–24.
Shen Dacheng 沈大成. *Xuefuzhai wenji* 學復齋文集. Qianlong era edition. Peking University Library.
Shen Tong 沈彤. *Guotang ji* 果堂集. In *Yingyin wenyuan ge siku quanshu*, vol. 1328. Taipei: Taiwan Shangwu yinshuguan, 1983.
Shen Xiankai 沈賢凱. *Zheng Banqiao yanjiu* 鄭板橋研究. Taipei: Xinwenfeng, 1988.
Shimada Kenji 島田虔次. *Chūgoku ni okeru kindai shii no zasetsu* 中国に於ける近代思惟の挫折. Tokyo: Chikuma shobō, 1949.
Slupski, Zbigniew. "Three Levels of Composition of the *Rulin waishi*." *Harvard Journal of Asiatic Studies* 49.1 (1989): 5–53.
Smith, Richard J. "Divination in Ch'ing Dynasty China." In Smith and Kwok, *Cosmology, Ontology, and Human Efficacy*, pp. 141–78.
Smith, Richard J., and D. W. Y. Kwok, eds. *Cosmology, Ontology, and Human Efficacy: Essays in Chinese Thought*. Honolulu: University of Hawaii Press, 1993.
Soothill, W. E. *A Dictionary of Chinese Buddhist Terms*. Reprint. Taipei: Chengwen Publishing, 1969.
Sudō Yoichi 須藤洋一. "Tai Meisei—kōshi no mujun to sono tenkai" 戴名世一一公私の矛盾とその展開. *Nihon Chūgoku gakkai hō* 28 (1976): 200–214.
Sun Jiaxun 孫佳迅. *Jinghua yuan gongan bianyi* 鏡花緣公案辨疑. Jinan: Qi Lu shushe, 1984.
Sun Kaidi 孫楷第. *Cangzhou houji* 滄州後集. Beijing: Zhonghua shuju, 1985.
Tang Xianzu 湯顯祖. *Mudan ting* 牡丹亭. Beijing: Renmin wenxue chubanshe, 1978.
Tao Qian 陶潛. *Tao Yuanming shiwen huiping* 陶淵明詩文匯評. Taipei: Taiwan Zhonghua shuju, 1970.

Taylor, Rodney L. *The Religious Dimensions of Confucianism*. Albany: State University of New York Press, 1990.
Taylor, Romeyn. "Official and Popular Religion and Political Organization of Chinese Society in the Ming." In Kwang-ch'ing Liu, ed., *Orthodoxy in Late Imperial China*, pp. 126–57.
T'ien Ju-k'ang. *Male Anxiety and Female Chastity: A Comparative Study of Chinese Ethical Values in Ming-Ch'ing Times*. T'oung Pao Monograph no. 14. Leiden: E. J. Brill, 1988.
Vinograd, Richard. *Boundaries of the Self: Chinese Portraits, 1600–1900*. Cambridge: Cambridge University Press, 1992.
Wakeman, Frederic. *The Great Enterprise: The Manchu Reconstruction of Imperial Order in Seventeenth-Century China*. Berkeley: University of California Press, 1985.
Wang Chong 王充. *Lun Heng* 論衡. Taipei: Shijie shuju, 1974.
Wang Dexiu 王德羞. "Yinggai yong xin de guannian he biaozhun pingjia *Rulin waishi*" 應該用新的觀念和標準評價儒林外史. *Ming Qing xiaoshuo yanjiu* 13 (1989): 100–9.
Wang Dezhao 王德昭. *Qingdai keju zhidu yanjiu* 清代科舉制度研究. Hongkong: Chinese University of Hongkong Press, 1982.
Wang Fuzhi 王夫之. *Sijie* 四解. Taipei: Shijie shuju, 1966.
Wang Liqi 王利器, ed. *Lidai xiaohua ji* 歷代笑話集. Shanghai: Shanghai gudian chubanshe, 1956.
———, ed. *Yuan Ming Qing sandai jinhui xiaoshuo xiqu shiliao* 元明清三代禁毀小說戲曲史料. Expanded edition. Shanghai: Shanghai guji chubanshe,1981.
Wang Qiongling 王瓊玲. *Yesou puyan yanjiu* 野叟曝言研究. Taipei: Xuehai chubanshe, 1988.
Wang Quanli 王全力. "Changshi yu qishi: lun *Lüye xianzong*" 嘗試與啓示:論綠野仙蹤. *Ming Qing xiaoshuo yanjiu* 21 (1991.4): 161–72.
Wang Xiaohai 汪孝海. "*Nü kaike zhuan* chengshu shijian ji banben zixing kaolue" 女開科傳成書時間及版本梓行考略. *Ming Qing xiaoshuo yanjiu* 21 (1991.3): 183–90.
Wang Yingzhi 王英志. *Qingren shilun yanjiu* 清人詩論研究. Nanjing: Jiangsu guji chubanshe, 1986.
Wang Yuan 王源. *Juyetang wenji* 居業堂文集. Taipei: Wenyi, 1966.
Wang Zhong 汪中. *Shuxue ji* 述學集. Taipei: Shijie shuju, 1962.
Watson, Burton, trans. *Hsün Tzu: Basic Writings*. New York: Columbia University Press, 1963.
Wei Xi 魏禧. *Wei Shuzi wenchao* 魏叔子文鈔. Shanghai: Zhonghua shuju, 1936.
Weinstein, Vicki. "Eccentricity in Yang-chow, 1710–1765: Eccentricity or the Literati Tradition?" Ph.D. diss., Cornell University, 1973.
Weng Fanggang 翁方綱. *Fuchuzhai wenji* 復初齋文集. In *JindaiZhongguo shiliao cong kan* 近代中國史料叢刊, vol. 421. Taipei: Wenhai chubanshe, 1969.
White, Hayden. *Tropics of Discourse: Essays in Cultural Criticism*. Baltimore, Md.: Johns Hopkins University Press, 1978.

Widmer, Ellen. *The Margins of Utopia: Shui-hu hou-chuan and the Literature of Ming Loyalism.* Cambridge, Mass.: Harvard University Press, 1987.
Wilhelm, Richard. "Imperial Confucianism." In Marius Jansen, ed., *China and Japan in Transition,* pp. 243–67. Princeton, N.J.: Princeton University Press, 1967.
Wilson, Thomas A. *Genealogy of the Way: The Construction and Uses of the Confucian Tradition in Late Imperial China.* Stanford, Calif.: Stanford University Press, 1995.
Wong, Timothy. *Wu Ching-tzu.* Boston: Twayne Publishers, 1978.
Woodside, Alexander. "The Divorce Between the Political Center and Educational Creativity in Late Imperial China." In Elman and Woodside, *Education and Society in Late Imperial China,* pp. 458–92.
———. "State, Scholars, and Orthodoxy: The Ch'ing Academies, 1736–1839." In Kwang-ch'ing Liu, *Orthodoxy in Late Imperial China,* pp. 158–84.
Wou, King-tseu, trans. *Chronique indiscrète des mandarins.* Paris: Gallimard, 1976.
Wu De-an 吳德安. "*Rulin waishi* de jiegou" 儒林外史的結構. *Mingbao* 22 (1988.4): 95–103.
Wu Hongyi 吳宏一 and Ye Qingbing 葉慶炳, eds., *Qingdai wenxue piping ziliao huibian* 清代文學批評資料彙編. Taipei: Lianjing chubanshe, 1982.
Wu Jingzi 吳敬梓. *Wenmu shanfang ji* 文木山房集. Shanghai, 1932.
———. *Rulin waishi.* (See under Li Hanqiu)
Wu Lang 吳 娘. *Shanting ji* 衫亭集. Hand-copied manuscript. Literature Section, Chinese Academy of Social Sciences, Beijing.
Wu, Pei-yi. *The Confucian's Progress: Autobiographical Writings in Traditional China.* Princeton, N.J.: Princeton University Press, 1990.
Wu Peiyuan 吳培源. *Huixin caotang ji* 會心草堂集. 1741 edition. Literature section, Chinese Academy of Social Sciences, Beijing.
Wu, Qingyun. *Female Rule in Chinese and English Literary Utopias.* Syracuse, N.Y.: Syracuse University Press, 1995.
Wu Xiaoru 吳小如. *Gudian xiaoshuo man'gao* 古典小說漫稿. Shanghai: Shanghai gudian wenxue chubanshe, 1982.
Wu Zuxiang 吳組緗. "Guanyu Wu Jingzi de minzu sixiang wenti" 關于吳敬梓的民族思想問題. In *Rulin waishi yanjiu lunwen ji,* pp. 1–4.
Xi Zhou Sheng 西周生. *Xingshi yinyuan zhuan* 醒世姻緣傳. Shanghai: Shanghai guji chubanshe, 1981.
Xia Jingqu 夏敬渠. *Yesou puyan* 野叟曝言. Taipei: Wenhua tushu gongsi, 1982.
Xiao Shafu 蕭箑父 and Li Jinquan 李錦全. *Zhongguo zhexue shi* 中國哲學史. Beijing: Renmin wenxue chubanshe, 1983.
Xiao Yishan 蕭一山. *Qingdai tongshi* 清代通史. Taipei: Wenhai shuju, 1965.
Xu Huijun 徐慧君. *Zhongguo xiaoshuo shi* 中國小說史. Xining: Guangxi jiaoyu chubanshe, 1991.
Xue Yongnian 薛永年. "Yangzhou baguai dui zhengtong yishu de shuli" 揚州八怪對正統藝術的抒理. *Jiuzhou xuekan* 6.1 (1993): 121–30.
Xunzi guyi 荀子詁譯. Edited by Yang Liuqiao 楊柳橋. Jinan: Qilu shushe, 1985.
Yamanoi Yū 山井湧. *Min Shin shisō no kenkyū* 明清思想の研究. Tokyo: Tokyo University Press, 1980.

Yan Changming 嚴長明. *Yan Dongyou shiji* 嚴冬有詩集. In *Ziyuan quanshu* 自園全書, vols. 129–31. Changsha: Ye Dehui 葉德輝, 1911.
Yan Yu 嚴羽. *Canglang shihua* 滄浪詩話. Beijing: Renmin wenxue chubanshe, 1961.
Yan Yuan 顏元 and Li Gong 李塨. *Yan-Li congshu* 顏李叢書. Taipei: Guangwen shuju, 1965.
———. *Yan-Li yishu* 顏李遺書. Taipei:Taiwan shangwu yinshuguan, 1970.
Yang Bojun 楊伯峻, ed. *Lunyu yizhu* 論語譯注. Beijing: Zhonghua shuju, 1980.
Yang, Hsien-i, and Gladys Yang, trans. *The Scholars*. Beijing: Foreign Languages Press, 1957.
Yang Xiangkui 楊向奎. *Qingru xuean xinbian* 清儒學案新編. Vol. 1. Jinan: Qilu shushe, 1985.
Yang Xin 楊新. *Yangzhou baguai* 揚州八怪. Beijing: Wenwu chubanshe, 1982.
Yangzhou baguai shiwen ji 揚州八怪詩文集. Nanjing: Jiangsu yishu chubanshe, 1985.
Yao Nai 姚鼐. *Xibao xuan quanji* 惜抱軒全集. Hongkong: Guangzhi shuju, n.d.
Ye Xie 葉燮. *Siqi suoyu* 巳畦瑣語. In *Zhaodai congshu* 昭代叢書, vol. 62. Shikaitang 世楷堂, 1876.
———. *Yuan shi* 原詩. In Ding Fubao, *Qing shihua*, pp. 561–612.
Yu Huai 余懷. *Banqiao zaji* 板橋雜記. Dalian: Dalian tushu gongying she, 1934.
Yu Jianhua 俞建華. *Zhongguo hualun leibian* 中國畫論類編. Hongkong: Zhonghua shuju, 1973.
Yu Ying-shih 余英時. *Lishi yu sixiang* 歷史與思想. Lianjing chubanshe, 1976.
———. "Some Preliminary Observations on the Rise of Ch'ing Confucian Intellectualism." *Ch'ing-hua Journal of Chinese Studies* 4 (1976): 105–36.
———. *Zhongguo sixiang chuantong de xiandai quanshi* 中國思想傳統的現代詮釋. Taipei: Lianjing chubanshe, 1987.
Yuan Hongdao 袁宏道. *Yuan Hongdao ji jianjiao* 袁宏道集箋校. Shanghai: Shanghai guji chubanshe, 1981.
Yuan Mei 袁枚. *Suiyuan shihua* 隨園詩話. Beijing: Renmin wenxue chubanshe, 1982.
———. *Xiaocang shanfang wenji* 小倉山房文集. Shanghai: Shanghai guji chubanshe, 1988.
———. *Xu Shipin* 續詩品. In *Shipin jijie/Xu shipin zhu* 詩品集解。續詩品註. In Guo Shaoyu, ed., *Zhongguo gudian wenxue lilun piping zhuanzhu xuanji* 中國古典文學理論批評專著選輯. Beijing: Renmin wenxue chubanshe, 1981.
Yue Hengjun 樂蘅軍. *Zhongguo gudian xiaoshuo sanlun* 中國古典小說散論. Taipei: Youshi wenhua shiye gongsi, 1980.
Yun Jing 惲敬. *Dayun shanfang quanji* 大雲山房全集. Taipei: Taiwan Zhonghua shuju, 1966.
Yun Shouping 惲壽平. *Ouxiangguan ji* 藕香館集. Taipei: Xuehai chubanshe, 1972.
Zang Maoxun 臧懋循. *Yuan qu xuan* 元曲選. Taipei: Zhengwen shuju, 1971.
Zeitlin, Judith. *Historian of the Strange: Pu Songling and the Chinese Classical Tale*. Stanford, Calif.: Stanford University Press, 1993.

Zhang Shunshui 張舜水. *Qingdai Yangzhou xueji* 清代揚州學記. Beijing: Zhonghua shuju, 1962.

———. *Qingren wenji bielu* 清人文集別錄. Beijing: Zhonghua shuju, 1980.

Zhang Xuecheng 張學誠. *Wenshi tongyi* 文史通義. Beijing: Zhonghua shuju, 1985.

———. *Zhangshi yishu* 章氏遺書. Shanghai: Shangwu yinshuguan, 1936.

Zhao Jingshen 趙景深. *Xia Jingqu xiansheng nianpu* 夏敬渠先生年譜. Taipei: Taiwan Shangwu yinshuguan, 1979.

Zhao Lian 昭槤. *Xiaoting xulu* 嘯亭續錄. Beijing: Zhonghua shuju, 1980.

Zhao Yi 趙翼. *Ershier shi zhaji* 二十二史札記. Beijing: Zhonghua shuju, 1984.

Zheng Taixie 鄭台燮. "Gan Gen no reiron" 顏元の礼論. *Tōyōshi gakuhō* 35 (1987): 755–73.

Zheng Xie 鄭燮. *Banqiao ji* 板橋集. Taipei: Guangwen shuju, 1975.

Zhu Xi 朱熹. *Daxue zhangju* 大學章句. Taipei: Guoxue jicheng, n.d.

———. *Shi jizhuan* 詩集傳. Beijing: Zhonghua shuju, 1978.

Zhu Yixuan 朱一玄, Xiao Zeyun 蕭澤雲, and Liu Jiandai 劉建代, eds. *Gudian xiaoshuo xiju shumu* 古典小說戲劇書目. Changchun: Jilin wenshe, 1991.

Zhu Yizun 朱彝尊. *Pushuting ji* 曝書亭集. Taipei: Shijie shuju, 1964.

Zito, Angela. "Silk and Skin: Significant Boundaries." In Zito and Barlow, *Body, Subject, and Power in China*, pp. 102–29.

Zito, Angela, and Tani Barlow, eds. *Body, Subject, and Power in China*. Chicago: University of Chicago Press, 1994.

Zong Chen 宗臣. *Zong Zixiang ji* 宗子相集. In *Yingyin wenyuange siku quanshu*, vol. 1287. Taipei: Taiwan Shangwu yinshuguan, 1983.

Character List

bagu wen 八股文
Baqi tongzhi 八旗通志
Baiguo xianren 百果仙人
baishi 稗史
ben 本
bi 蔽
biji 筆記
Bingfa 兵法
boshan 博贍
boshi 博士
boxue hongci 博學鴻詞
buren zhi xin 不忍之心
buyu 不遇
cai (talent) 才
cai (wealth; covetousness) 財
cai feng 采風
cainü ke 才女科
caiqi 財氣
caizi jiaren 才子佳人
chandiao 蟾吊
chanji 禪機
chang 長
Changzhou 常州
chengyi 誠意
Chouren zhuan 疇人傳
churen toudi 出人頭地
chuanqi 傳奇
ci 刺
dai shengren shuohua 代聖人說話
dao 道
daoyi 道藝

dao yu yi he 道與藝合
dexing zhi 德性之知
di yi yi zhi wu 第一義之悟
dushuren 讀書人
duilian 對聯
fa 法
feng 風
fengshui 風水
fengsu 風俗
fu 賦
fuhui 附會
gewu 格物
gewu zhizhi 格物致知
gongming 功名
gongming fugui 功名富貴
guai 怪
gudan 孤淡
Guanchang xianxing ji 官場現形記
guantong 貫通
Guang "Fangyan" 廣方言
gui 詭
guo 果
Haizhou 海州
Hanxue shangdui 漢學商兌
haojie 豪傑
haoju 豪舉
haoranjin 浩然巾
hen you tiaoli 很有條理
hongqi baojie 紅旗報捷
ji 技
jici 譏刺

jishi xingle 及時行樂
jia 甲
Jiangyin 江陰
jiangxue 講學
jiao 教
jiaofu 轎夫
jiaolong 蛟龍
jieren 傑人
Jiezi yuan 芥子園
jinshen 縉紳
jinshi 進士
jing 敬
jingfeng 驚風
jinghua shuiyue 鏡花水月
jingshen 精審
jingshi 經世
juren 舉人
juru 巨儒
jushu 拘束
jue 覺
junzi 君子
kaiwu chengwu 開物承務
kaozheng 考證
Ke bao yu jun 克報于君
kongshu 空疏
kuo er chong zhi 擴而充之
li (profit) 利
li (principle; reason) 理
li (ritual; propriety) 禮
lirang 禮讓
liyue bingnong 禮樂兵農
lianzong 聯宗
liangfa aoyi 良法奧義
longxue 龍穴
luo 倮
madiao 馬吊
ming 名
mingdan 名單
mingjue 明覺
mingwu dushu 名物度數
mogu hua 沒骨畫
moshi 末事
mu 穆
muke 幕客
muliao 幕僚

najian 納監
Nanke yi meng 南柯一夢
Nü yue ji ming 女曰雞鳴
nü zhong yingxiong 女中英雄
pi 癖
Pinhua baojian 品花寶鑑
pomo 潑墨
qi (unconventional) 奇
qi (spirit; vigor; material ether) 氣
Qihong ting 泣紅亭
qizhi zhi xing 氣質之性
qianze xiaoshuo 譴責小說
Qieyun 切韻
qin 琴
Qin Han 秦漢
qing 情
qingke 清客
qingzhu 情主
qiongli 窮理
Quanjiao 全椒
rang 讓
rechang 熱腸
renxia 任俠
ru 儒
rulin 儒林
rulin zhuan 儒林傳
shanren 山人
Shang shu 尚書
shenming 神明
Shennong bencao 神農本草
shenqi 神氣
shenshi 紳士
shi (literati) 士
shi (to serve) 仕
shi (content) 實
shi (historical forces) 勢
shidaifu 士大夫
shi er you 仕而優
shiqi 士氣
shiren zhi mianmu 詩人之面目
Shiwen shuo 時文說
shiyun 時運
shu (dredging, clearing) 疏
shu (form, numbers) 數
shuanglu 雙陸

shui 水
shuixing 水性
Siku quanshu 四庫全書
siyi 四藝
su 俗
suan 酸
suosui 瑣碎
Taibo 泰伯
taiyi 太一
tiandi pan 天地盤
tongsheng 童生
tongyao 童謠
touxu 頭緒
wanwu sangzhi 玩物喪志
wei jing ren shuo guo 未經人說過
wen 文
wenjian zhi zhi 聞見之知
wenren langzi 文人浪子
wenshi 文士
wenzi yu 文字獄
wu (military; martial) 武
wu (error) 誤
wudao 無道
wuse yingxiong 物色英雄
wu xing 五行
xi 習
Xianglie niangniang 香烈娘娘
xiao ji 小技
xieqi xinzhi 血氣心知
xiezi 楔子
xing (nature) 性
xing (stimulus) 興
ya 雅
yan suan 眼酸
yanwai zhi yi 言外之意
yang 陽
yangqi 陽氣
ye 野
yeshi 野史
yi (duty; righteousness; significance) 義
yi (mind, intent; ideas) 意
yi (art) 藝
yi hua wei le 以畫為樂
yijian 臆見

Yijing 易經
yili 義理
yi li sha ren 以理殺人
yimin 逸民
yiqi 義氣
yi wen wei xi 以文為戲
yi xiaoshuo xian caixue zhe 以小說見才學者
yin (licentious) 淫
yin (female principle; passivity) 陰
yinjie 音節
yinxiu 隱秀
youxue 游學
yu 遇
yulu 語錄
yuru 迂儒
yu shizhe 遇識者
yuan 緣
zalan 雜覽
zhanghui xiaoshuo 章回小說
zhen 真
zhenru 真儒
zheng 政
zhengming 正名
zhengqiang 爭強
zhengtong 正統
zhi 質
zhiguai 志怪
zhi hu zhe ye 之乎者也
zhijue 知覺
zhiyan 知言
zhi zhi 致知
zhi zhishan 致至善
zhongjie 中節
Zhong Kui zhuan 鍾馗傳
zhongxin 忠信
Zhou li 周禮
zhushuzhe liu 著述者流
zigui 子規
zishi 自適
zixu wuyou 子虛無有
zizhuzhen 自誅陣
Zong Ji 宗姬
zongzi 宗子

Index

In this index an "f" after a number indicates a separate reference on the next page, and an "ff" indicates separate references on the next two pages. A continuous discussion over two or more pages is indicated by a span of page numbers, e.g., "57–59." *Passim* is used for a cluster of references in close but not consecutive sequence.

Actors, 73, 133f
Alchemy (Taoist), 155
Amateur ideal (in painting), 46
Analects (*Lunyu*), 68, 149, 205, 285
Ancient-style prose (*guwen*), 41f
Arts, *see Yi*
Astronomy, 19, 81
Autobiography (in poetry), 40f

Bada Shanren, 46
Bagu (examination essay), 49, 51–58, 220, 254; in *Rulin waishi*, 92–93, 96–102, 136
Baqi tongzhi, 77
Baishi, 110, 264
Bakhtin, Mikhail, 256
Bannermen, 77, 223, 225
Ben (moral root), 65f
Bi Yuan, 191, 229
Bol, Peter, 21, 242
Book of Changes (*Yijing*), 61, 72, 92–93
Boxue hongci examination, 144
Brokaw, Cynthia J., 242ff, 255
Brook, Timothy, 127

Buddhism, 74, 127f, 275f, 287; in fiction, 152–61 *passim*, 171
Bush, Susan, 247

Caizi jiaren romances, 152f
Canglang shihua, 41, 246
Cao Xueqin, 77
Celibacy, 155
Chan, Leo Tak-hong, 280
Chan, Wing-tsit, 75
Changzhou Prefecture, 75ff
Chastity, 153, 166
Chen Jiru, 34, 45
Chen Meilin, 238f, 253
Chen Que, 241
Chen Yi (Guyu), 260
Chen Zuwu, 248
Cheng Jinfang, 73, 77, 257f, 267
Cheng Tingzuo, 28, 63, 70–73, 143, 208, 257f, 262, 270
Cheng Yaotian, 15, 74, 270f
Cheng Yi, 68
Cheng-Zhu (Song Neo-Confucian) orthodoxy, 6, 13–23, 31ff, 58–62 *passim*, 64–77 *passim*,

310 / Index

80ff, 152, 161ff, 166, 181, 189, 204, 210ff
Chouren zhuan, 204, 255
Chow, Kai-wing, 15, 64, 74, 131, 144, 240, 252
Chu, Hung-lam, 267
Chunqiu (Spring and autumn annals), 102
Ci songs, 56
Classic of Poetry (Shijing), 11–14, 89–91
Classical exegesis, 15, 27, 44, 72, 80, 212
Cognition, 28, 68, 71
Commiserating heart (*buren zhi xin*), 71
Concubinage, 172, 182
Correlative mode, 19

Dai Mingshi, 56–57
Dai shengren shuohua (to speak for the sages), 100
Dai Zhen, 18, 54, 59f, 69, 70, 72, 78–81, 141; and *Mengzi ziyi shuzheng*, 27–34
Dao yu yi he (The way and literary art merge together), 43
Daoxue, 22
Dardess, John, 15
Daxue, see Great Learning
De Bary, William Theodore, 21, 240
Desire, 71
Dialects, 78
Dilettantism, 34
Divination, 167, 204
Dong Qichang, 45ff
Donglin partisans, 75, 127
Dragons, 92, 158f, 277
Du Fu, 41, 50

Ebrey, Patricia, 251
Education, 68, 71, 172, 179
Elegance (in painting), 46f
Elman, Benjamin, 12, 15, 64, 75
Elvin, Mark, 226
Encounter, *see Yu*

Enlightenment, 37–47 *passim*, 175
Epistemology, 28
Epistemological doubt, 18ff, 33, 38f, 60
Evidential studies, see *Kaozheng*
Examination essay, see *Bagu*
Examination system, 5, 53f, 75f, 274, 283; in fiction, 92–94, 97, 99, 116, 136, 153, 174–85 *passim*, 194, 220ff

Factional disputes, 144
Fame (*ming*), 53, 190, 193–202 *passim*, 285f
Fang Bao, 54, 76, 248f, 256
Fang Xiaoru, 96, 260f, 266
Fang Yizhi, 23ff, 241
Feminine intuition, 168
Fengshui (geomancy), 108, 272
Five Phases (*wu xing*), 150, 155, 277
Foot-binding, 172, 176
Four Arts, 154, 161, 278f
Four Books, 52, 54
Four virtues (four beginnings), 28f
Fuhui (baseless accretions), 164f, 215
Fujian, 126
Fushe (Restoration Society), 52

Games, 193, 196
Gan Fengchi, 127, 141
Gao Bin, 210
Gao Fenghan, 103
Gao Qi, 118, 120
Gender reversal, 154, 157, 162, 171–79, 181–90, 195–99
Geography, 72, 76, 191
Geomancy, see *Fengshui*
Go, 56, 178f, 203, 253
Great Learning, 18
Gu Yanwu, 51, 52, 73
Guan Shiming, 57
Guanchang xianxing ji, 229
Guang Fangyan, 78
Gui Youguang, 261f
Guy, R. Kent, 78f
Guo Shaoyu, 34f, 39

Hammond, Charles, 287
Han Learning, 27, 64, 74, 79–82, 201f
Hanan, Patrick, 217, 245
Hangzhou, 94f, 158
Hanxue shangdui, 201
Hashimoto Takakatsu, 28
He Zehan, 109, 118
Heavenly principle (*tianli*), 71f
Hegel, Robert, 217, 239, 288
Henderson, John, 19, 242
Highet, Gilbert, 88
Ho, Ping-ti, 238
Hong Bang, 27
Honglou meng, 183f, 217ff, 222–25
Hou Wailu, 28
Hsia, C. T., 174, 214
Hsu, Ginger Cheng-chi, 248
Hu Shih, 27, 63f, 70, 172
Huang Xiaotian, 271
Huang Zongxi, 51, 116–18
Hui Dong, 70, 252
Huineng, 47
Huizhou Prefecture, 44f, 74, 81, 139ff

Imitation (in poetry), 38, 40f
Individuality (in poetry), 38f
Inspiration (literary), 37
Intellectuality, 5–6, 20–23, 28–34 *passim*, 38ff, 55, 67–72, 168ff
Intelligence, 68, 70
Integrity of the will (*chengyi*), 67
Intention (moral), 32, 71
Intuitive knowledge, 29f, 60, 67, 169
Iser, Wolfgang, 272f

Jami, Catherine, 76
Ji Yun, 57f, 74, 280
Jiajing period, 123f, 201, 268
Jiang Shiquan, 260, 275f
Jiang Yong, 27, 74
Jiang Yu, 73
Jiangnan, 16f, 64, 73
Jiangyin Prefecture, 75, 210
Jiao Xun, 11–14, 22, 55f, 81, 286
Jin He, 109

Jin Nong, 103
Jing (reverence), 67
Jinshi, 94, 119
Jin Zhaoyan, 73, 253, 257ff, 262f
Jin Zhi, 156, 158–59
Jinghua yuan, 148, 171–206, 212–15; and gender reversal, 171–79, 181–90, 195–99; and the examination system, 174–85 *passim*, 200; and philology, 180, 182, 185–90, 201f; and games, 183f, 196, 202–6
Julien, François, 277
Junzi (gentleman), 5, 29, 180

Kao, Hsin-sheng, 82
Kangxi emperor, 77
Kangxi period, 81
Kaozheng (philology or evidential studies), 4, 11–16, 27f, 33, 58–60, 75f, 78–83 *passim*, 90, 131, 162, 185–89, 201, 207, 212f
Keener, Frederick, 215
Kitamura Yoshikazu, 269
Knight-errant (*renxia*), 153
Kracke, E. A., 283
Kuriyama, Shigehisa, 284

Laozi (Daode jing), 157, 163
Legitimation (in historiography), 128
Li (immanent principle), 18–20, 65–66
Li (ritual propriety), 28, 162, 180, 287; and Yan Yuan, 65ff, 69, 72; in *Rulin waishi*, 85f, 91f, 130–41, 143f
Li Bai, 41, 50
Li Dou, 253
Li E, 259f
Li Fu, 77, 210f
Li Gong, 63, 66–70, 72, 143, 251f
Li Guangdi, 252
Li Panlong, 123f
Li Ruzhen, 8, 77f, 83, 171, 201, 205, 212
Li Tiangang, 255
Li Yu, 217
Li Zhi, 22, 127
Licentiousness (in *Shijing*), 89f

Liji, 71f, 89
Lin, Shuen-fu, 131, 271
Ling Tingkan, 18, 78–83, 204, 287
Literary Inquisition (*wenzi yu*), 111
Literati, 4, 237; reformulation of identity, 14–22 *passim*, 33, 48, 50f, 67ff; of the Ming period, 16, 113–28 *passim*; as Confucian scholars (*ru*), 32, 60ff, 88–93, 95, 223; and painting, 45–51; representations in fiction, 87–108 *passim*, 145, 153, 160, 162–70, 173–86 *passim*, 196–200, 218–24
Liu Dakui, 42, 54f, 259
Liu Ji, 117, 265f
Liu Zhu, 63
Liu Zongyuan, 42
Liyue bingnong (ritual, music, military, and agriculture), 92
Lü Liuliang, 52–54, 99
Lü mudan (The Green Peony), 218, 282
Lü Qian, 57
Lu, Sheldon Hsiao-p'eng, 128
Lu Xiangshan, 77
Lu Xun, 2, 152
Luan Xing, 274
Lüye xianzong, 219, 221f
Lun heng, see Wang Chong

Martial values, 65, 104–6, 121, 126, 153, 184f, 274f
Mathematics, 19, 63, 69, 72, 76, 81, 202-05
Matsumura Kō, 265
McMahon, Keith, 214, 274, 276
Medicine, 1, 76
Mei Wending, 69, 76
Mencius, 28ff, 52, 55, 68, 71, 149f, 189, 205
Meng Haoran, 50
Mengzi ziyi shuzheng, see Dai Zhen
Merchants, 81, 104, 138
Metzger, Thomas, 150
Miao tribes, 105
Military campaigns, 105f

Military skills, 65, 169
Ming History (Mingshi), 111
Ming History Board, 111, 117
Ming literary theory, 38f, 244f
Ming literature, 32, 34ff, 123f
Ming loyalism, 111, 126f, 217, 264f
Misogyny, 157
Moral (ethical) knowledge, 5f, 13f, 20ff, 32, 69
Moshi (inessential), 64f
Muliao, 17
Murase, Yuya, 27

Nakano Miyoko, 216
Nanjing, 7, 63, 70, 77, 87, 92, 96, 109, 122f, 126, 130
Neo-Confucianism, see Cheng-Zhu orthodoxy
Ning, Prince, 118–21
Nivison, David, 249f
North China, 64
Nü kaike zhuan, 282

Ogawa Tamaki, 270
Ono Kazuko, 284
Opera, see Theater
Ortai, 144
Ouyang Jian, 234
Owen, Stephen, 245f

Painters, 45–51, 102f, 115
Pan Lei, 76
Paulson, Ronald, 256
Philology, see Kaozheng
Philosophical tale, 215f
Phonology, 186–89, 193
Physical desires, 29
Pinhua baojian, 229
Plaks, Andrew, 87, 239, 273
Play, 202-06
Plum blossoms, 115, 126
Praxis (*xi*), 65
Professional painters, 46
Professional scholars, 96
Professional writers, 35

Profit (*li*), 53
Prognostication, 167, 204
Psychology, 215
Puns, 195, 205f

Qi (material ether), 18, 166
Qian Daxin, 244, 260
Qian Mu, 29f
Qian Qianyi, 36
Qian-Jia (Qianlong and Jiaqing) periods, 4, 216, 226
Qianlong emperor (Gaozong), 144
Qianze xiaoshuo (novels of chastisement), 147, 229
Qieyun, 186, 284
Qing (emotions), 162, 279
Qingke (literary guest), 34f
Qizhi zhi xing (physical nature), 30, 68
Quan Zuwang, 111

Rationality, 28, 30, 38
Recluse (*yimin*), 113
Rectification of names (*zhengming*), 190
Ressentiment, 77
Rhythm (in prose), 42
Ricci, Matteo, 255
Ritual propriety, *see Li*
Ropp, Paul, 238
Ru (Confucian), *see under* Literati
Ruan Yuan, 204, 255, 266
Rulin, 85, 88, 109
Rulin waishi, 1ff, 6f, 63, 70, 72f, 85f, 207–10; and literati vocations, 87–107; use of Ming historical frame, 109–29; representations of ritual propriety, 130–44
Rulin zhuan, 85

Sagehood, 14, 21f, 195
Salt merchants, 100ff, 137f, 263
Satire, 2, 88, 135, 143, 147, 256
Scattered ink (*pomo*), 47
Scholar-beauty romance, *see Caizi jiaren*

Scholarly novels, 147f, 214ff, 218
Science, 69, 73, 76
Seidel, Michael, 256
Self-cultivation, 6, 13f, 21, 30, 45, 79, 131
Selfish desires, 72
Sexual desire, 158f, 163, 172, 197f, 272, 276f, 286
Sexual perversion, 155
Shanhai jing, 191f, 206
Shanren, 123
Shang Yanliu, 57
Shen Dacheng, 281
Shen Deqian, 37
Shen Tong, 15, 76
Shi Tao, 46, 48
Shijing, *see Classic of Poetry*
Shuihu zhuan, 87, 116, 132, 217
Shun (legendary ruler), 50
Siku quanshu, 8, 74, 144
Six Arts, 24, 65, 69
Skepticism (Confucian), 166ff
Skill (*ji*), 37
Slupski, Zbigniew, 265
Smith, Richard, 280
Smogolenski, Nicolas, 255
Social justice, 29, 31
Song Learning, 27, 74, 75, 79f, 82, 189. *See also* Cheng-Zhu orthodoxy
Song Lian, 113–8
Spontaneity (literary), 38
Statecraft (*jingshi*), 75
Sun Jiagan, 210
Sun Xingyan, 191
Supernatural fiction, 280f
Supernatural phenomena, 166f
Suzhou, 75, 81

Taibo, 130, 134f, 180, 269
Taiwan, 126
Tang Shunzhi, 75
Taohua shan (*The Peach Blossom Fan*), 126
Tao Yuanming, 1, 163

Taoism, 74, 154, 157f, 163f, 171, 178, 199f, 219, 224, 275f, 287
Taylor, Rodney, 240
Technical expertise, 75
Theater, 73, 162
T'ien, Ju-k'ang, 282
Tongcheng School, 42f, 75
Topical references (in fiction), 109
Triad Society, 126

Unifying thread, 21

Vinograd, Richard, 227
Vulgar (in painting), 46f

Waishi, 109f
Wakeman, Frederic, Jr., 241, 268
Wan Sida, 117
Wan Sitong, 117
Wanli period, 124–27
Wang Chong, 150f, 195
Wang Liqi, 218
Wang Mian, 98, 102f, 113–18
Wang Shizhen, 123f
Wang Wei, 48, 50, 208
Wang Xishan, 76
Wang Yangming, 22, 28, 62, 66, 77, 119–22 *passim*, 165, 267
Wang Yuan, 274f
Wang Yuanqi, 47
Wang Zhong, 18, 269
Water (as narrative motif), 157–60, 177, 276ff
Way (*dao*), 14, 22f, 32, 35, 50, 58, 60ff, 67, 79
Wei Su, 118
Wei Xi, 19f
Weinstein, Vicki, 49
Wen (culture/writing), 34, 131, 135, 226ff
Weng Fanggang, 144, 271
Western science, 81f, 205
Widmer, Ellen, 217
Widow suicide, 140f
Will to omniscience, 21

Woodside, Alexander, 16, 253f, 275f, 279
Woxian caotang commentary (of *Rulin waishi*), 136, 227
Wu (error), 67
Wu Guodui, 63
Wu Jingzi, 6, 63f, 209, 219; and *Rulin waishi*, 109f, 143ff, 209f, 227
Wu Lang, 63, 253
Wu Pei-yi, 276
Wu Peiyuan, 263
Wu Qing, 260
Wu, Qingyun, 214
Wu Taibo, *see* Taibo
Wu Zetian, 171–75, 177, 179, 184f, 194, 197f, 283

Xia Jingqu, 74–77; and *Yesou puyan*, 74, 152f, 210f
Xie Zhen, 123f
Xing (moral nature), 29
Xingshi yinyuan zhuan, 219ff, 224, 277
Xu Qingjun, 126, 268
Xu Xian, 113, 116
Xue Xue, 259f
Xunzi (Hsun-tzu), 67, 71, 150, 285

Yan Ruoju, 73
Yan Xishan, 69
Yan Yu, *see Canglang shihua*
Yan Yuan, 24, 28, 63–70, 72f, 143, 250
Yan-Li philosophy, *see* Yan Yuan
Yang Mingshi, 75f, 210
Yang Xin, 46f
Yangzhou, 7, 81f, 102
Yangzhou eccentric painters, 46, 103
Yangzhou scholarship, 78
Yao (legendary ruler), 50
Yao Nai, 37, 42f, 54f
Yeshi, 110f, 264
Yesou puyan, 148f, 151–70, 173, 210ff; women in, 153–60
Ye Xie, 37; and *Yuan shi*, 37–41
Yi (ideas/mind), 48
Yi (Arts), 23ff, 37, 44f, 56

Yili (philosophy, meaning), 12, 33, 189f
Yijian (preconceived ideas, prejudice), 31, 48
Yijing, see Book of Changes
Yinjian (Mirror of pronunciation), 78
Yin-yang cosmology, 156–59, 166
Yongle usurpation, 95–96, 120, 264
Yongzheng emperor, 52
Yu (encounter), 149ff, 160, 172
Yu (legendary sage), 72, 170, 250
Yu Jianhua, 49
Yu Ying-shih, 5f, 27, 33, 238
Yuan (fate), 194, 200
Yuan Hongdao, 244f
Yuan Mei, 35f, 43f, 145, 259ff, 280
Yuan shi ("On the Origin of Poetry"), 37–41
Yuan shi ("On the Origin of the Literati"), 145
Yulu (recorded sayings), 34, 244
Yun Jing, 242
Yun Shouping, 50
Yuru (pedantic scholar), 92, 141, 169

Zeitlin, Judith, 257
Zhang Boxing, 76
Zhang Tingyu, 144
Zhang Wenhu, 100, 124
Zhang Xuecheng, 17, 41f, 58–62, 86, 144, 246f, 261f, 285
Zhang Zai, 66
Zhao Jingshen, 152
Zhao Lian, 266
Zhao Mengfu, 48, 208
Zhao, Prince of, 123f
Zhao Yi, 41, 267f, 283
Zheng Chenggong (Coxinga), 126
Zheng Xie, 46–51, 103, 253
Zhengde period, 122
Zhong Kui zhuan, 216
Zhou administration, 61f
Zhou li, 115f
Zhu Xi, 6, 11–14, 22, 30, 52ff, 66, 77, 89ff, 189, 251, 257, 271, 280
Zhu Yizun, 36, 113–8, 266
Zhu Yun, 74
Zhu Yuanzhang, 116ff
Zhuang Cunyu, 76
Zhuangzi, 163
Zito, Angela, 131, 226f
Zong Chen, 123f, 267

Library of Congress Cataloging-in-Publication Data

Roddy, Stephen
    Literati identity and its fictional representations in late imperial China / Stephen Roddy.
        p.   cm.
    Includes bibliographical references and index.
    ISBN 0-8047-3131-4 (cloth : alk. paper)
    1. Chinese fiction—Ch'ing dynasty, 1644–1912—History and criticism.   2. Wu, Ching-tzu, 1701–1754. Ju lin wai shih.   3. Hsia, Ching-chü. Yeh sou p'u yen.   4. Li, Ju-chen, ca. 1763–ca. 1830. Ching hua yüan.   5. Scholars in literature.   I. Wu, Ching-tzu, 1701–1754. Ju lin wai shih.   II. Hsia, Ching-chü. Yeh sou p'u yen.   III. Li, Ju-chen, ca. 1763–ca. 1830. Ching hua yüan.   IV. Title.

PL2437.R64   1998
895.1'34809—dc21   97-40032
                                                                                                                        CIP

This book is printed on acid-free, recycled paper.

Original printing 1998
Last figure below indicates year of this printing:
07   06   05   04   03   02   01   00   99   98